FISMA Compliance Handbook

FISMA Compliance Handbook
Second Edition

Laura P. Taylor

Patricia Moulder, Technical Editor

AMSTERDAM • BOSTON • HEIDELBERG • LONDON
NEW YORK • OXFORD • PARIS • SAN DIEGO
SAN FRANCISCO • SINGAPORE • SYDNEY • TOKYO

Syngress is an Imprint of Elsevier

Acquiring Editor: *Chris Katsaropoulos*
Development Editor: *Benjamin Rearick*
Project Manager: *Malathi Samayan*
Designer: *Matthew Limbert*

Syngress is an imprint of Elsevier
225 Wyman Street, Waltham, MA 02451, USA

First edition 2007

Library of Congress Cataloging-in-Publication Data
Taylor, Laura P.
  FISMA compliance handbook / Laura P. Taylor. – Second edition.
    pages cm
  Includes bibliographical references and index.
  ISBN 978-0-12-405871-2 (paperback : alkaline paper)
1. United States. Federal Information Security Management Act of 2002. 2. Electronic government information–Security measures–United States. 3. Computer security–Law and legislation–United States. 4. Data protection–Law and legislation–United States. I. Title.
  KF4850.A3282002A2 2013
  342.73'0662–dc23

                                                                                    2013025238

British Library Cataloguing-in-Publication Data
A catalogue record for this book is available from the British Library.

For information on all Syngress publications, visit our website at store.elsevier.com/Syngress

ISBN: 978-0-12-405871-2

Contents

Dedication

In Memory of Shaam

Author Acknowledgments

This book is a better book due to the support of many individuals. Ben Rearick, my project manager, was instrumental in keeping the momentum of the book going forward by keeping me on schedule. Thank you to Chris Katsaropoulos, the editor of Elsevier, for giving me the opportunity to update the first edition. Technical Editor, Patricia Moulder, read through the drafts and offered excellent suggestions for polishing up the rough edges. The entire Elsevier team is a world-class publishing organization, and others at Elsevier who helped with various ad hoc matters include Steve Elliott, Stephen Fiedler, Malathi Samayan, and Amy Pedersen. Jim Meyer of Coordinated Response was kind enough to help write many of the abstracts for the online version (and on short notice) when I needed an extra helping hand. Thank you to my colleague Francis Benjamin for helping to review some of the final proofs.

Without the first edition of this book, there would be no second edition. Editors Gary Byrne and Matt Shepherd made much appreciated contributions to the first edition. Stephen Northcutt of SANS was instrumental in helping get the first edition of this book off the ground. Thank you to Chris Williams and Andrew Williams who gave me the opportunity to write the first edition of this book for Syngress. The first edition of this book started out originally as an O'Reilly book, and therefore, I'd also like to thank my former editors at O'Reilly Media, Allison Randal and Tatiana Apandi Diaz, who helped me refine some of the earlier drafts of this book. Thank you also to Nathan Torkington of O'Reilly who was one of the early believers in this book. If Bobby Porter (FISMA Center Advisory Board) had not cajoled me into taking on a FISMA project shortly after FISMA was passed, the first edition would have never been written. Richard Bejtlich provided insightful critique on the first edition which was taken into consideration during the writing of the second edition.

Various members of the FISMA Center Advisory Board offered recommendations on some of the tools discussed in Chapter 20: Seth Friedman, Glenn Jacobsen, and Kevin Sanchez-Cherry. Glenn was also a contributing author to the first edition. Anton Chuvakin offered a few tips for this chapter as well.

Certain individuals that I've worked with, known, and exchanged ideas with over the years have provided me with various insights and perspectives on FISMA (or other information security topics) which likely enabled me to make this book more intelligible. Alphabetically by last name, I'd like to thank Dawn Adams, Janet Bauer, Bo Berlas, Bruce Brody, David Caplan, Anthony Cornish, Jaren Dougherty, Pranjali Desai, Ralph Echemendia, David Felton, Thomas Galligan, Kurt Garbars, Justin Matteo, Jim Molini, Bob Morningstar, Pete Nicoletti, Ron Ross, Rachael

Sokolowski, Verdis Spearman, Angela Vessels, Dan Waddell, and Randy Williams. A special thank you to Alan Paller who tries to keep the rest of us honest by focusing on which security controls give you the most bang for your buck.

Thank you to Wanda Headley, Library Manager at the Natural Hazards Center at the University of Colorado, Boulder, for help with research on natural hazards. Additionally, Eileen McVey, at the National Oceanic and Atmospheric Administration (NOAA) Central Library, helped with information on natural hazard probabilities.

Various members of the FedRAMP team created the diagrams found in Chapter 23. Figure 23.6 was created by Matt Goodrich. Bill Burns, Matt Goodrich, James Ruffin, Monette Respress, Nadine Haddad, and Jacqueline Smith all worked on Figure 23.5. Figures 23.1 and 23.2 were created by an anonymous early FedRAMP visionary.

Thank you to Jennifer Leggio of Sourcefire for contributing to Chapter 16.

Thank you to my good friend Brien Posey for review comments on an early draft. There's not likely another information technology author as widely published as Brien and his opinion always counts for a lot.

Thank you to my Mother (who is not easily impressed) for challenging me to demonstrate favorable outcomes to all endeavors. Dad (R.I.P.), a little more forgiving, was happy with the first edition, even though he could not have cared less about FISMA.

Last, but always at the forefront of my thoughts, I am most grateful to my college-aged son, Sam Taylor, for keeping the humor flowing during the writing of the last few chapters, providing a welcome relief from the stress of deadlines.

Laura Taylor
Columbia, MD
August 2013

About the Author

Laura Taylor is an information security and IT consultant with over 30 years of experience. She currently holds an executive level position with an information security consulting firm and serves as the Technical Development Lead of FedRAMP. Ms. Taylor's security and privacy expertise spans program management, strategic solutions, compliance laws, security assessments and audits, cloud computing, and policies and standards development.

Ms. Taylor serves as the Chair of the FISMA Center Advisory Board and founded the Certified FISMA Compliance Practitioner (CFCP) qualification program. Earlier in her career, Ms. Taylor was CIO of a defense contractor, Director of Information Security of a web hosting company, Director of Security Research for an industry analyst firm, Director of Security Compliance of a defense contractor, ZDNet columnist, and held various engineering positions at BBN, Interleaf, MITRE, and Sun Microsystems.

Ms. Taylor's security research has been used by various federal agencies including the FBI, FDIC, and the White House. Her columns and the first edition of this book are used by various college curriculums at both the graduate and undergraduate level.

Foreword

When I was the Chief Information Security Officer at the Department of Veterans Affairs, and then later as the CISO at the Department of Energy, I didn't like FISMA at all. For a few of my like-minded colleagues and me, it was a distraction that diverted precious resources away from implementing real security programs, all for the sake of paperwork checklists. Even worse, it was born out of a Congress that could no longer batter Executive Branch agencies over Y2K challenges, and needed another vehicle by which to hold grandiloquent hearings and generate histrionic headlines. Thus came the flawed Y2K-like system-by-system, site-by-site approach that was born as GISRA in 2001 and became FISMA a year later.

The more that agencies parsed the legislation, the more the challenges worsened. General counsels argued that Congress denuded the agency CIO of any authority or clout when it chose to use the word "ensure" rather than "enforce," as in "the CIO shall ensure compliance with the act." Inspectors general were given no guidance on how to assess an agency's progress against FISMA mandates, and therefore no two agencies were reported on consistently. OMB made matters much worse, if that was even possible, when its implementation guidance over-emphasized scorecards and grades that could be gamed in many agencies. Thus was born a culture of faking compliance while agency security became a sieve. CISO hires came to be based on the ability to get a higher compliance grade, and not on any ability to properly manage risk in an enterprise.

A federal CISO greets each day with an anticipatory wince, because he or she is responsible for protecting critical information resources from those who wish to do them harm. Thanks to the politicians on Capitol Hill and bureaucrats in OMB, our defenses were largely unattended for most of a decade.

What Laura Taylor accomplishes in this book is nothing short of amazing. She makes FISMA a means to an end, and not the end itself. She darts through the legislative inadequacies and volumes of NIST standards and special publications with remarkable clarity. She elevates FISMA from the paperwork compliance drill to an actual value-added process by which to manage the risk in a large federal enterprise. In a clear and consistent style, Ms. Taylor lays out the roadmap by which agencies can advance from the useless paperwork compliance exercises of the recent past to the more proactive continuous monitoring processes of the present and future.

Armed with the knowledge that this book imparts, the federal CISO can now manage risk across a large enterprise while at the same time achieving compliance. Security is no longer subordinate or secondary to compliance; it is the partner of compliance. With a concise and readable style, and a base of knowledge that is second to none, Ms. Taylor covers the entire cyber battlespace from A to Z. Her attention to detail and her relentless focus on the right outcome at every stage of the process is a rare and refreshing approach to an immensely complex topic.

Ms. Taylor's work is uniquely insightful and significantly helpful. A federal CISO and his or her staff will now have the choice of reading and interpreting mountains of information from NIST, OMB and GAO. Or, they can simply read this book and have it all condensed for them into a single and highly useful guide. If I had this book in my hands when I was a federal CISO, I would have been grateful.

Most readers of this book, from the information system security officer (ISSO) to the CISO or CIO, are charged with protecting our nation's most sensitive information and systems from those who wish to do us harm. For over a decade, that charge was often papered over so that compliance could be claimed in the absence of actual risk management. Thanks to Laura Taylor, you can now have effective risk management and compliance at the same time.

Bruce A. Brody, CISSP, CAP, CISM, CFCP, ISSPCS
Former Chief Information Security Officer
U.S. Department of Veterans Affairs and
U.S. Department of Energy

FISMA Compliance Overview

1

The law cannot be enforced when everyone is an offender.
—Chinese Proverb

TOPICS IN THIS CHAPTER

- Terminology
- Processes and paperwork
- Templates streamline the process
- Oversight and governance
- Supporting government security regulations

INTRODUCTION

The Federal Information Security Management Act (FISMA) is the most important cyber security law affecting U.S. federal agencies. No other cyber security law creates as much oversight, audit, and scrutiny as FISMA—at least as far as federal departments and agencies are concerned.

FISMA, also known as Title III of the E-Government Act (Public Law 107-347), requires that all systems and applications that reside on U.S. government networks undergo a formal security assessment before being put into production. System authorization is the ultimate output of a FISMA compliance project, and a system or application cannot be authorized unless it meets specific security control requirements. However, keep in mind that no system can be completely secure—unless it is powered off and locked in a vault. Of course, then it is not very usable. Determining the security controls for the system is a balancing act between making the system usable and making the system secure. These two endeavors are often at odds with each other. In order to find the balance, security experts analyze the probability and impact of vulnerabilities being exploited (or not) and then make risk-based decisions based on the analysis. Clearly, the goal of FISMA is to force federal agencies to put into production secure systems and applications and then to analyze risk periodically, all for the purpose of making risk-based decisions.

Before FISMA came along, implementing security controls on U.S. government networks was optional. Some agencies did a good job and others didn't. Today,

1

implementing security controls, looking for vulnerabilities, and performing security assessments are no longer an option. All federal agencies and departments work on FISMA compliance projects for all of their systems as a routine part of their information security agenda.

New applications and systems require a security assessment and authorization before they can be put into production, and existing applications and systems require a new assessment and authorization every 3 years. Systems that have already been authorized to operate must be reassessed every 3 years.

An additional requirement of FISMA is that federal departments and agencies develop and implement an agency-wide Information Security Program. The agency Information Security Program should be described in a document known as an Information Security Program Plan. I'll talk more about what goes into an *Information Security Program Plan* in Chapter 5.

Though U.S. federal departments and agencies have no choice but to comply with FISMA, private sector organizations can optionally take advantage of FISMA compliance methodologies to help mitigate risks on their own information systems and networks. About 90% of the nation's critical infrastructure is on private networks that are not part of any U.S. federal department or agency. The nation's critical infrastructure includes those information technology systems that run electrical systems, chemical systems, nuclear power plants, transportation systems, telecommunication systems, banking and financial systems, and agricultural, food and water supply systems—to name only a few. The FISMA compliance methodologies described in this book can be adopted and used by not just federal agencies but by the private sector as well. Though federal departments and agencies seem to get repeated criticisms belittling their security initiatives, it's my experience and belief that the criticisms are somewhat exaggerated and that their security conscientiousness far exceeds that of private industry. Any enterprise organization can adopt the FISMA compliance methodologies explained in this book. A special license is not required, and no special tools are required to make use of the model—it is simply a way of doing things related to information security.

The FISMA compliance process culminates with a very comprehensive and standardized security assessment. Essentially, the security assessment is an audit. Having worked in both private industry and on government networks, my experience shows that contrary to what you read in the news, most private and public companies do not put nearly as much time, effort, and resources into implementing security controls as government agencies do. Except for security incidents involving personally identifiable information, there are few federal laws that require companies to disclose security incidents. The percentage of those security incidents that are disclosed is very small. Many organizations purposefully do not report incidents to avoid bad press.

To demonstrate FISMA compliance, descriptions of security control implementations, policies, procedures, and risks are explained formally in a collection of documents known as a Security Package. The Security Package includes details of a review and analysis of all the hardware and software components of the system, as well as the data center, or location where the system resides. In some cases, a system may span multiple geographic locations and may consists of numerous connections from one or multiple data centers to other data centers that are either part of the system or are owned by other entities. A system's Security Package demonstrates that due-diligence in mitigating risks and maintaining appropriate security controls has occurred.

TERMINOLOGY

Since the first edition of this book, FISMA terminology has changed somewhat. Originally, the process by which agencies complied with FISMA was known as Certification and Accreditation (C&A). Those terms were originally coined by someone at the National Security Agency and were gradually adopted by the Department of Defense, the National Institute of Standards and Technology (NIST), and all the civilian federal agencies. A Security Package was originally referred to as a C&A Package. In the first edition of this book, I said that the term "Certification" can be confusing because the system does not really get "Certified" by anyone for anything. I also said that a more apropos name might have been a "Security Package." As luck would have it, in the newly revised version of NIST 800-37 (Revision 1) [1], the terms Certification and Accreditation were dropped and NIST changed the terminology of the suite of security documents from a C&A Package to a Security Package.

The original version of NIST 800-37 was titled *Guide for the Certification and Accreditation of Federal Information Systems*. Revision 1 of Special Publication 800-37 is titled *Guide for Applying the Risk Management Framework to Federal Information Systems*. However, old traditions die hard and government agencies are slow to change. Therefore, many federal departments and agencies still use the terms "Certification" and "Accreditation" or "C&A" when referring to their FISMA compliance process. If you're going to be working on FISMA compliance, it will help you to understand the meaning of these original terms, even if they have fallen out of fashion. As of this writing, many federal agencies still use these terms, even though current standards have abandoned them.

The original version of NIST Special Publication 800-37 [2] defined Certification as:

> *A comprehensive assessment of the management, operational, and technical security controls in an information system, made in support of security accreditation, to determine the extent to which the controls are implemented correctly, operating as intended, and producing the desired outcome with respect to meeting the security requirements for the system.*

Experts among us don't always agree on the definition of a particular term and government agencies are no different. In June 2006, the Committee on National Security Systems, Chaired by the Department of Defense, defined Certification in the National Information Assurance Glossary [3], as:

A comprehensive evaluation of the technical and nontechnical security safeguards of an IS to support the accreditation establishes the extent to which a particular design and implementation meets a set of specified security requirements.

The definitions are similar enough and if you're going to be working in this industry, you'll hear both terms sooner or later. From a legal standpoint, the term Certification means attesting to the truth about something. You may at some point in your life need to sign a document that says something like "I certify that this, that, and the other thing are true." You could be held liable for any falsifications made if you certify something. The idea behind certifying a set of information security documents means that you're attesting to the truth about the fact that they are accurate.

Accreditation refers to the positive evaluation made on the *Certification and Accreditation Package* by an evaluation team. The original version of NIST Special Publication 800-37 referred to accreditation as:

The official management decision given by a senior agency official to authorize operation of an information system and to explicitly accept the risk to agency operations (including mission functions, image, or reputation), agency assets, or individuals, based on the implementation of an agreed-upon set of security controls.

And the National Information Assurance Glossary referred to accreditation as a:

Formal declaration by a Designated Accrediting Authority (DAA) that an IS is approved to operation at an acceptable level of risk, based on the implementation of an approved set of technical, managerial, and procedural safeguards.

An accreditation is a statement about a decision. As far as FISMA goes, before a system is deemed FISMA compliant, a decision is made by an oversight team after reviewing a suite of documents containing information about the system and its risk exposure. The oversight team may be referred to by different names in different agencies. You should think of the oversight team as specialized information security auditors and these days, they are most commonly referred to as independent assessors. Since the most current version of NIST Special Publication 800-37 refers to these folks as independent assessors, that is the term that I will be using in this book.

Each agency has their own independent assessors to evaluate the various Security Packages within their own agency. The independent assessors review the system's security controls, interview the system owner and team members, and create a Security Assessment Report that describes the vulnerabilities, threats, and risks. The AO then makes a risk-based decision on whether to issue an Authority to Operate (ATO).

Once a Security Package has been evaluated, the independent assessors then provide recommendations to the Authorizing Official (AO) based on their findings. The Senior Agency Information Security Officer (SAISO)[1] then makes a decision on

---

[1] SAISOs are sometimes referred to as Chief Information Security Officers (CISO).

whether to issue an Authority to Operate (ATO) for the system. A positive authorization indicates that a senior agency official has formally made the decision that the documented risks to the agency, assets, and individuals are acceptable. Senior agency officials employ large teams of information assurance oversight staff that go over the Security Packages with fine-toothed combs. Authorization does not come lightly and occurs only after each Security Package has undergone a scrupulous review. By authorizing an information system, the senior agency official agrees to take responsibility for the accuracy of the information in the Security Package and consents to be held accountable for any security incidents that may arise related to the system.

Much of the terminology that federal agencies use in their FISMA compliance programs comes from the Office of Management and Budget (OMB) Circular A-130, Appendix III (listed in Appendix B). The OMB was created in 1970 and essentially replaced the Bureau of Budget and is part of the Executive Office of the President of the United States. Aside from assisting the president with the budget, the OMB's mission is also to create and oversee information and regulatory policies. The fact that the OMB plays a significant regulatory role in FISMA compliance shows just how important information security has become to our national infrastructure. It also means that FISMA compliance initiatives will have a budget and are clearly a priority to the Executive Office of the President of the United States—and that's a good thing.

PROCESSES AND PAPERWORK

Federal agencies typically use a standardized process for FISMA compliance. Each agency decides what their standardized security process consists of and documents it. The different U.S. federal departments and agencies develop their own unique standardized process based on standards and guidance from one of the following organizations:

- the National Institute of Standards (NIST)
- the National Security Agency (NSA)
- the Committee on National Security Systems (CNSS)
- the Department of Defense (DoD).

Federal agencies create multiple documents related to the security of the system to serve as evidence of compliance. This book will help you learn how to develop the various documents and artifacts required for FISMA compliance. The amount of security documentation that you will find in one Security Package is extensive, and these tomes of documents needed to prove compliance with FISMA have received much criticism from some industry experts. Unfortunately, today, showing evidence of compliance on paper is really the only way that compliance can be verified.

While some aspects of compliance can be automated, today there are no solutions available to fully automate the continuous monitoring of an entire system. The futuristic goal of automated compliance aside, many security experts fail to realize the value that the Security Package offers aside from compliance. Most large complex engineering feats require that the details of the design and operations are written down and there are many reasons for doing so. First, complex systems need to be managed and it's hard to know what you're managing if you don't have reference documents that spell out the details. No one would ever expect anyone to be able to manage all of the intricacies of the Hoover Dam without all of the requisite operation documents. Boeing would never deliver an F-15E Strike Eagle to the U.S. Air Force without any reference documents on how to perform maintenance. How would you feel if our nuclear power plants were being operated without any manuals? Even if a Chief Information Security Officer (CISO) is briefed on how a system and network is architected, it is not possible for any CISO to simply hear all the details once and then remember them.

We write things down when there is too much information to remember. In the 1800s, a German psychologist, Herman Ebbinghaus, performed some important studies on the limitations of human memory. In the 1870s, Ebbinghaus researched the retention of learning and developed a curve of forgetting. He proved empirically that only one-third of an audience remembers a delivered message after 1 hour. After 2 days, the retention goes down to 28%. If any of us tried to memorize all of the intricacies of an enterprise information system, we would fail miserably. For that reason, the thousands of details about how enterprise information systems are built and configured need to be written down. People who manage complex systems perform better when they have reference documents. Trying to manage complex enterprise systems and networks without reference documents is a roadmap to failure. People involved in FISMA compliance projects should understand that developing the suite of documents that are required for the Security Package is not just a compliance exercise. The Security Package documents should be considered living documents and that CISOs (also referred to as SAISOs) count on using these documents to help manage the security of the system it describes.

TEMPLATES STREAMLINE THE PROCESS

To create some order out of the paper work challenge, most agencies now have templates that they use for all the different types of documents that go into the Security Package. Templates ensure that all the different types of documents that go into the Security Packages have the same look and feel. Using templates is a way of standardizing the documentation to create recurring best practices to enable efficiencies. A good template helps to ensure that all key information is included in the document. Well-written templates also assist oversight teams in finding the information that they are looking for because they will know exactly in which section of the document to expect it.

The amount of information that is required in any one Security Package is so great that if each Security Package had a different format, it would be nearly impossible for assessors to evaluate the package. When independent assessors evaluate a Security Package, they want to know where to look to find key information and they don't want to have to hunt for it. I have seen Security Packages receive negative findings not because the right information wasn't in the Security Package, but because the right information was not where it was supposed to be.

In spite of the criticisms of the voluminous documentation required for FISMA, it would be a mistake to get rid of it all.

FISMA OVERSIGHT AND GOVERNANCE

A goal for any agency is to make sure that all Security Packages are properly evaluated and that all production systems have ATOs. Each agency is audited annually by an Inspector General (IG) and most agencies have a dedicated Office of Inspector General (OIG). Inspectors come on site annually and review agency Information Security Programs and the various systems that come under the purview of the program. They look to see if all systems have ATOs, and they also look to see if vulnerabilities that were previously reported are being mitigated. You can go to any agency Web site and find out various information about the Office of Inspector General by putting "OIG" into the search box on the agency home page. Here are some agency OIG sites that you can browse through:

U.S. Treasury Office of Inspector General
http://www.treasury.gov/about/organizational-structure/ig/Pages/default.aspx

U.S. Department of Justice Office of Inspector General
http://www.justice.gov/oig/

U.S. Department of Agriculture Office of Inspector General
http://www.usda.gov/oig/

Inspector Generals ensure that compliance takes place and they produce compliance reports on FISMA for each agency every year. Here are some FISMA compliance reports produced by Inspector Generals that you can take a look at:

U.S. General Services Administration FY 2012 FISMA Audit
http://www.gsaig.gov/?LinkServID=51BAE9CB-F490-F070-
EA662E16B12CB00A&showMeta=0

U.S. Department of Veteran's Affairs FY 2012 FISMA Audit
http://www.va.gov/oig/pubs/VAOIG-11-00320-138.pdf

U.S. Department of Transportation FY 2012 FISMA Audit
http://www.oig.dot.gov/sites/dot/files/FISMA%2011-14-2011.pdf

The Department of Homeland Security (DHS) keeps track of FISMA metrics for all U.S. federal departments and agencies. They track whether or not agencies are improving their cyber security posture and decreasing vulnerabilities or not and then they report the statistics to Congress. Agency CIOs, CISOs, and SAISOs naturally want the reports on their agency to be favorable.

Additionally, the U.S. Government Accountability Office also reports on FISMA periodically to Congress. The GAO reports reflect how effective agency security practices are and how effective agencies are at implementing security controls. A current GAO report on FISMA that you can browse through is located here: http://www.gao.gov/assets/590/585570.pdf.

SUPPORTING GOVERNMENT SECURITY REGULATIONS

Though FISMA is the overriding law that necessitates the need for system risk assessment, there are other laws, regulations, and national policies that provide secondary authority. The secondary laws, regulations, and policies that support FISMA initiatives include:

- The Clinger-Cohen Act of 1996[2]
- Homeland Security Presidential Directive (HSPD-7)
- The Government Management Reform Act (GMRA) of 1994
- The Government Performance and Results Act (GPRA) of 1993
- Critical Infrastructure Protection Act of 2001
- Homeland Security Act of 2002 (Public Law 107-296)
- Homeland Security Presidential Directive 12
- OMB Circular A-123, Management Accountability and Control
- OMB Circular A-130, Management of Federal Information Resources
- Executive Order 13130 of July 14, 1999—National Infrastructure Assurance Council
- The Computer Security Act of 1987
- The Computer Fraud and Abuse Act of 1986
- The Computer Abuse Amendments Act of 1990
- Executive Order 12958 of April 17, 1995, Classified National Security Information
- The E-Government Act of 2002
- The Privacy Act of 1974
- Executive Order 10865 of February 20, 1960—Safeguarding Classified Information Within Industry

---

[2]Clinger-Cohen Act was formerly known as the Information Technology Management Reform Act.

SUMMARY

In the first edition of this book, I forecasted that in the future, the importance of FISMA would increase—and that has turned out to be true. Inspectors come down tougher on agencies that don't comply with the law. Congress has introduced bills to amend, modify, and change FISMA more times than I can count. Many lawmakers in Congress seem determined to get their name on a cyber security law. However, none of the bills introduced to change FISMA have ever been passed. As of this writing, there is no such thing as "FISMA 2.0" even though you may see references to that in trade rags. The original text of the FISMA law has never been changed. It still exists in its original incantation.

The current trend is that security incidents continue to wreak havoc on federal information systems and private sector information systems. Breaches in security on both government information systems and those maintained by the private sector create millions of dollars in losses and also threaten the national security of our country, and everyone in it. In 2011, 107,655 security incidents were reported to US-CERT and within those incidents, 43,889 occurred at U.S. federal agencies [4]. Threats are becoming more sophisticated and terrorists continue to use high technology to threaten not just data and our infrastructure, but worse yet, human lives. With security incidents at federal agencies on the rise, securing government systems becomes more important every day.

References

[1] Joint Task Force Transformation Initiative, Special Publication 800-37, Revision 1. Guide for applying the risk management framework to federal information systems. National Institute of Standards and Technology; February 2010.

[2] Ron Ross, Marianne Swanson, Gary Stoneburner, Stuart Katzke, Arnold Johnson. NIST Special Publication 800-37. Guide for the security certification and accreditation of federal information systems. National Institute of Standards and Technology; May 2004.

[3] National Information Assurance Glossary. CNSS Instruction No. 4009, http://www.cnss.gov/Assets/pdf/cnssi_4009.pdf; Revised June 2006.

[4] Fiscal Year 2011. Report to Congress on the implementation of the Federal Information Security Management Act of 2002; March 7, 2012.

FISMA Trickles into the Private Sector

2

I'll lie here in the gutter, and you'll trickle down on me, right?
—Bill Murray on Saturday Night Live

TOPICS IN THIS CHAPTER

- Introduction and authorities
- Inspector General reports
- What should NGOs do regarding FISMA?
- FISMA compliance tools

INTRODUCTION AND AUTHORITIES

It has been over 10 years since FISMA was first passed. In the beginning, it was all federal agencies could do to put compliance processes in place internally. However, to be sure, Congress always intended for private companies who have contracts with the government to comply with FISMA. The word "contractor" is used nine times in the text of FISMA.

Section 3543 says:

> *The Director shall oversee agency information security policies and practices, including requiring agencies, consistent with the standards promulgated under such section 11331 and the requirements of this subchapter, to identify and provide information security protections commensurate with the risk and magnitude of the—harm resulting from the unauthorized access, use, disclosure, disruption, modification, or destruction of...information systems used or operated by an agency or by a contractor of an agency or other organization on behalf of an agency.*

A little bit further in the text of FISMA, Section 3544(a)(1)(A)(ii) of FISMA describes federal agency security responsibilities as including "information systems used or operated by an agency or by a contractor of an agency or other organization on behalf of an agency."

In the early years, agencies were somewhat lax on enforcing FISMA compliance with their managed service providers. However, that phenomenon has changed. Government contract officers are now educated in what sort of contract clauses to insert into contracts with service providers. The U.S. Department of Health and

Human Services requires the following contract clause to be added to contracts with service providers:

> *Contracting Officers are responsible for ensuring that all information technology acquisitions comply with the Federal Information Security Management Act (FISMA), the HHS-OCIO Information Systems Security and Privacy Policy, and FISMA-related FAR and HHSAR requirements.*[1]

The General Services Administration (GSA) published a document titled *Security Language for IT Acquisition Efforts CIO-IT Security-09-48* that specifically states:

> *Because FISMA applies to both information and information systems used by the agency, contractors, and other organizations and sources, it has somewhat broader applicability than prior security law.*

OMB published a memorandum (M-09-29) on August 20, 2009 that identified five primary categories of contractors as they relate to securing systems and information: (1) service providers; (2) contractor support; (3) Government Owned, Contractor Operated facilities (GOCO); (4) laboratories and research centers; and (5) management and operating contracts. This same OMB memo also stipulates that grantees, State and local Governments, industry partners, and providers of software subscription services must comply with FISMA.

I've spoken to information technology staff from hospitals, nonprofit corporations, medical schools, biomedical research companies, and nuclear power plants who are all working on FISMA compliance projects. A gentleman from a privately owned power company once told me that his company did not have to comply with FISMA due to any contracts, but they were simply choosing to comply with FISMA because they needed an audit methodology and they couldn't find any standards better than the NIST standards. In the early years, FISMA by choice was unheard of.

INSPECTOR GENERAL REPORTS

There are many reasons why government contractors and managed service providers should start looking twice at FISMA (if they haven't already). Like any organization, federal agencies undergo a learning curve when new laws, regulations, and policies are passed. The government practices on itself first. In the beginning, right after FISMA was passed, federal agencies were not so sure themselves how to comply with FISMA.

An IT Director from a government contracting research firm told me, "The government did not previously enforce my company to comply with FISMA, so why should we believe that they're going to come around now and enforce

---

[1]Subpart 339, Acquisition of Information Technology, http://www.hhs.gov/policies/hhsar/subpart339.html.

compliance?" Such a good question! Most business processes undergo a maturity life cycle, and FISMA is no different.

In the early years, federal agencies were barely complying with FISMA internally, and it was very easy for Inspector Generals to come up with numerous findings on audit reports internally at agencies, without having to go the extra mile and start looking at contractor systems. An Inspector General is an auditor, and it's their job to find findings. They find what they can find in the time that they have slated for a particular audit. If Inspector Generals can fill reams of pages of FISMA findings without having to look outside the agency, there is not as much motivation to look externally. Auditors typically go for the low-hanging fruit first. As FISMA has matured internally at agencies, it has become harder to find findings. Auditors need to look elsewhere. Contractors that are storing or transmitting government data are ripe for audit findings. As these contractors start feeling the heat, and realize that they could lose government contracts, or are unable to bid on new contracts, they become easy converts.

OMB issues compliance areas and requirements that they would like Inspector Generals to report on. For government Fiscal Year (FY) 2012, one of those compliance areas was contractor systems. The Department of Homeland Security (DHS) collects FISMA outcomes from federal agencies and rolls it up into an annual report known as the Federal Information Security Management Act Reporting Metrics report. DHS also publishes a guide for Inspector Generals on what to look for when performing FISMA reviews. The FY 2013 guide says:

Inspector General Federal Information Security Management Act Reporting Metrics can be found at the following URL: http://www.dhs.gov/sites/default/files/publications/FY13%20IG%20metrics.pdf.pdf. In the FY 2013 guide, DHS stipulated eight areas that they wanted Inspector Generals to report on with regard to contractor systems. The DHS FY 2013 report gave reasons for the inquiry into contractor systems as:

> *These questions are being asked because in the past some Federal Agencies tended to assume that they were not responsible for managing the risk of contractor systems. Are these contractor-operated systems being managed to ensure that they have adequate security, and can the organization make an informed decision about whether or not to accept any residual risk?*

The specific instructions to Inspector Generals are listed in the DHS guide as follows:

> *Has the organization established a program to oversee systems operated on its behalf by contractors or other entities, including organization systems and services residing in the cloud external to the organization? Besides the improvement opportunities that may have been identified by the OIG, does the program include the following attributes?*
>
> - *Documented policies and procedures for information security oversight of systems operated on the organization's behalf by contractors or other entities, including organization systems and services residing in a public cloud.*

- *The organization obtains sufficient assurance that security controls of such systems and services are effectively implemented and comply with Federal and organization guidelines (NIST SP 800-53: CA-2).*
- *A complete inventory of systems operated on the organization's behalf by contractors or other entities, including organization systems and services residing in a public cloud.*
- *The inventory identifies interfaces between these systems and organization-operated systems (NIST SP 800-53: PM-5).*
- *The organization requires appropriate agreements (e.g., MOUs, Interconnection Security Agreements, contracts, etc.) for interfaces between these systems and those that it owns and operates.*
- *The inventory of contractor systems is updated at least annually.*
- *Systems that are owned or operated by contractors or entities, including organization systems and services residing in a public cloud, are compliant with FISMA requirements, OMB policy, and applicable NIST guidelines.*

Many agencies have seen Inspector Generals cite findings related to lax oversight of contractor and managed service provider systems. In November 2012, the Social Security Administration's Office of Inspector General (OIG) issued a report titled *The Social Security Administration's Compliance with the Federal Information Security Management Act of 2002 for Fiscal Year 2012.* In that report, the OIG states:

> *SSA did not maintain a complete inventory of all contractor systems and services and did not ensure all contractor systems and services met Federal security requirements. Specifically, we identified seven systems and services that met the FISMA criteria for contractor systems but either were not included in the Agency's systems inventory or were not identified as a contractor system or service, as required by FISMA guidance. Further, some of SSA's contracts did not include Federal security requirements, as required by FISMA guidance.*

Of course, Inspector Generals find good news to report as well. In March of 2011, Inspector Generals from the U.S. Securities and Exchange Commission reported:

> *The SEC has a contractor oversight program and has documented policies and procedures utilizing adequate security controls in accordance with the NIST and OMB guidance.*[2]

WHAT SHOULD NGOS DO REGARDING FISMA?

If you work for a Nongovernmental Organization (NGO), how do you know if you need to comply with FISMA or not? Quite simply, if your organization is storing or transmitting government owned data, it is supposed to comply with FISMA. Some

---

[2]http://www.sec-oig.gov/Reports/AuditsInspections/2011/489.pdf.

NGOs may report that there is nothing in their government contracts that stipulate that they need to comply with FISMA. If and when that occurs, that is an oversight on the part of the contracting officer. It is usually just a matter of time before this oversight gets noticed. A new contracting officer might come along who is well versed in FISMA, an Inspector General might make the discovery, or a Program Manager might notice. Contracting officers can request contract modifications at any point in time. Therefore, if you are an NGO, and you are storing and transmitting government data, whether anyone from the government has advised you of this or not, you should be complying with FISMA. NGOs storing or transmitting government data that have not been notified that they need to comply with FISMA should take notice and start preparing today.

FISMA COMPLIANCE TOOLS

FISMA compliance has created a new market for security compliance tools. As federal departments and agencies try to buff up their internal security processes, interest in understanding how to automate these processes and track them online has started to increase. Tools that claim to decrease the amount of time that it takes to put together required FISMA compliance documents have become more popular. However, these compliance tools have not really automated the compliance process. They are survey-driven tools that generally use an online content management system of sorts to collect information that you could alternatively put in a document. These survey-based content management compliance tools don't really make it any easier to comply with FISMA—they simply organize FISMA compliance information in an online repository where it can be more easily shared. It's often the case that these tools take quite a bit of time to set up and configure.

FISMA compliance tools don't do the work for you. But they can make it easier for agencies to manage FISMA compliance projects on an enterprise level. These tools organize your compliance documents and send alerts when artifacts are past due. Many of these tools enable agencies to authorize different staff members to respond to different security controls in parallel.

Compliance management tools should not be confused with automated continuous monitoring tools, which, today, are still evolving.

SUMMARY

It's only natural that FISMA has evolved to a new level of maturity. In the course of this evolution, federal departments and agencies have improved their security controls, and there are often less audit findings in any given agency than there were 10 years ago. Inspectors are looking for new territory to uncover findings, and contractor entities are the next in step for close scrutiny. Companies that store and transmit government data can get ahead of the curve by performing a gap analysis, and figuring out which security controls are in place, and which ones are missing. NGOs should not wait for government inspectors to call on them. By starting to put in place security controls and compliance artifacts today, NGOs will not have to fear the loss of contracts in the future.

FISMA Compliance Methodologies

3

It is common sense to take a method and try it. If it fails, admit it frankly and try another.
—Franklin Delano Roosevelt, Oglethorpe University, Atlanta, Georgia, May 22, 1932

TOPICS IN THIS CHAPTER

- The NIST Risk Management Framework (RMF)
- Defense Information Assurance C&A Process (DIACAP)
- Department of Defense (DoD) Risk Management Framework (RMF)
- DCID 6/3 and ICD 503
- The common denominator of all methodologies
- FISMA compliance for private enterprises
- Legacy methodologies

INTRODUCTION

There are five methodologies that agencies use as a basis to carry out FISMA compliance. The five methodologies are all slightly different, though the concepts among them are largely the same. Here's the list:

- NIST Risk Management Framework
- DIACAP
- DoD RMF
- DCID 6/3 ⇒ ICD 503
- FedRAMP

There are some legacy methodologies, none of which are used anymore, though you may come across them in reference materials and those are DITSCAP, NIACAP, JAFAN 6/3, and NISCAP. You'll notice that we are starting to get heavy on acronyms. Some of the acronyms used in FISMA compliance are so well known that many people don't remember what the acronyms stand for anymore. Before I dive into the differences between these methodologies, I'm listing the acronyms and complete name in Table 3.1 for reference. If you're new to FISMA, don't let acronyms scare you off—they're benign.

I won't be discussing much about the legacy methodologies, though I'll briefly touch on them near the end of this chapter for historical purposes. Some online job

Table 3.1 Acronyms for FISMA Compliance Methodologies

Acronym	Name	Era
NIST	National Institute of Standards & Technology Risk Management Framework	Up to date, in use today
DIACAP	Defense Information Assurance C&A Process	Up to date, soon to be phased out
DoD RMF	Department of Defense Risk Management Framework	Soon to replace DIACAP
DCID 6/3	Director of Central Intelligence Directive 6/3	Remnants still around
ICD 503	Intelligence Community Directive 503	Up to date, in use today
FedRAMP	Federal Risk and Authorization Management Program	Up to date, in use today
DITSCAP	Defense Information Technology	Legacy, not in use
NIACAP	National Information Assurance C&A Process	Legacy, not in use
NISCAP	NSA Information Systems C&A Process	Legacy, not in use
JAFAN 6/3	Joint Air Force Army Navy 6/3	Legacy, not in use

bulletin boards still reference the legacy methodologies, most likely because whoever wrote the job description doesn't realize that these methodologies are no longer in use. Similarly, some current government solicitations still reference these older methodologies—likely because the government contracting officer does not realize that these legacy methodologies are no longer in use. Many government RFPs are built from templates that don't often get updated. For those reasons, these legacy methodologies are worth a mention in case you're ever steered into a discussion or proposal where these terms come up.

Although all federal agencies base their FISMA compliance program on one of the current methodologies, each agency's program is at the same time unique to that particular agency. No two compliance programs are exactly alike, with the exception of FedRAMP. Chapter 23 is dedicated to FedRAMP, so I won't be discussing it much prior to that chapter.

THE NIST RISK MANAGEMENT FRAMEWORK (RMF)

The NIST Risk Management Framework (RMF) was designed for unclassified information. Unclassified information used to be referred to as Sensitive But Unclassified (SBU), however, that terminology has been replaced with Controlled Unclassified Information (CUI). The framework for the NIST RMF methodology is described in a publication known as *NIST Special Publication 800-37, Revision 1, Guide for Applying the Risk Management Framework*. A copy of it is available online at http://www.csrc.nist.gov/publications/nistpubs/800-37-rev1/sp800-37-rev1-final.pdf.

The NIST standards and methodology are updated more frequently than any of the others. Additionally, the NIST high-level methodology document, SP 800-37 includes a vast amount of supporting documents that complement the foundational guidelines. Prior to updating their guidelines, NIST goes to a lot of trouble to solicit review and comments from both public and private industries, which greatly enhance the quality of their publications. They receive thousands of comments and painstakingly comb through each one of them—intellectual crowdsourcing at its best.

The NIST guidance is well written and easy to follow. SP 800-37, Revision 1 provides a framework—following it won't answer all your compliance questions as it leaves some room for interpretation to allow flexibility. Agencies and bureaus embracing the NIST RMF typically use NIST Special Publication 800-37, Revision 1 as a guide to develop their own internal process and handbook customized for their own unique requirements. In essence, NIST Special Publication 800-37, Revision 1 is a call to action and provides to agencies a "to do" list for information security program plans, information security control selection and implementation, policies, procedures, training, and security business processes that need to be put into place.

The NIST RMF process takes you through all the different steps of the security life cycle and this is discussed at a more in-depth level in Chapter 4. The different deliverables that are discussed in this book are consistent with the deliverables noted in the NIST RMF. I'll be talking more about the NIST RMF in Chapter 4.

DEFENSE INFORMATION ASSURANCE C&A PROCESS (DIACAP)

The Defense Information Assurance C&A Process (DIACAP) is the primary compliance methodology in place at U.S. Department of Defense agencies. DIACAP has been used by the Department of Defense since November 28, 2007. The overarching reference architecture for the DIACAP can be found in a document known as DoD Instruction 8510.01. That document can be found at the following URL: http://www.js.pentagon.mil/whs/directives/corres/pdf/851001p.pdf. DoD Instruction 8510.01 is comparable to the NIST SP 800-37, Revision 1—it provides the framework for the DoD C&A program. The baseline security controls that DIACAP uses can be found in DoDI 8500.2—an interesting read, even if you don't work for the Department of Defense. DoDI 8500.2 makes reference to various other security standards such as the Common Criteria Evaluation and Validation Scheme (CCEVS), NIST Federal Information Processing Standards (FIPS), and NIST FIPS 140-2. You can find 8500.2 at the following URL: http://www.dtic.mil/whs/directives/corres/pdf/850002p.pdf. The DIACAP life cycle is illustrated in Figure 3.1.

A unique element of DIACAP is that it focuses on the Global Information Grid (GIG). The GIG is a complex interconnection of systems, networks, and communication devices that operate with multilevel security using components that have well-defined mission assurance categories. Consisting of satellite systems, terrestrial systems, voice systems, and data systems, the GIG is an extremely complex and

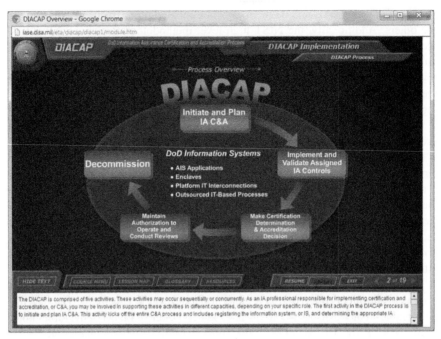

FIGURE 3.1

Free DoD DIACAP training course. (For color version of this figure, the reader is referred to the online version of this chapter.)

Table 3.2 GIG Networks		
Acronym	**Name**	**Security Classification**
NIPRNet	Non-Classified Internet Router Network	Nonclassified
SIPRNet	Secret Internet Router Network	Secret
NSANet	National Security Agency Network	Top secret/SCI
JWICS	Joint Worldwide Intelligence Communications System	Top secret

evolving network of communication systems. The GIG is made up of four different networks that are integrated together in various capacities. The four networks are known as NIPRNet, SIPRNet, NSANet, and JWICS. The four GIG network acronyms and the network security classifications are listed in Table 3.2.

SIPRNet's primary purpose is to transmit military orders. JWICS primary purpose is to transmit intelligence information to the military. NIPRNet is used primarily for nonclassified combat support, and there is an air gap between NIPRNet and SIPRNet. NSANet is used by the National Security Agency/Central Security Service for signals intelligence, communications monitoring, cryptology, and research.

The Department of Defense offers a free online DIACAP training course that will help you better understand the DIACAP principles. You can access the course here: http://iase.disa.mil/eta/diacap/index.htm.

DEPARTMENT OF DEFENSE (DoD) RISK MANAGEMENT FRAMEWORK (RMF)

In the near future, the Department of Defense will be phasing out the DIACAP and replacing it with a new methodology known as the Department of Defense (DoD) Risk Management Framework (RMF). The DoD RMF is closely aligned with the NIST RMF and makes use of NIST security control baseline controls with additional controls added from *Security Categorization and Control Selection for National Security Systems* (CNSSI) 1253, published March 15, 2012. CNSSI 1253 is available at the following URL: http://www.cnss.gov/Assets/pdf/Final_CNSSI_1253.pdf. CNSSI 1253 prescribes minimum standards that national security systems must use, based on the definition of National Security System (NSS) as described in FISMA section 3542 as

> *...any information system (including any telecommunications system) used or operated by an agency or by a contractor of an agency, or other organization on behalf of an agency—"(i) the function, operation, or use of which—"(I) involves intelligence activities;"(II) involves cryptologic activities related to national security; "(III) involves command and control of military forces; "(IV) involves equipment that is an integral part of a weapon or weapons system; or "(V) subject to subparagraph (B), is critical to the direct fulfillment of military or intelligence missions....*

CNSSI was developed by the Joint Task Force Transformation Initiative Working Group and the Committee on National Security Systems (CNSS) working with representatives from the civil, defense, and intelligence communities. National Security Systems are systems that contain National Security Information (NSI). Classified NSI includes information determined to be either "Top Secret," "Secret," or "Confidential" under Executive order 12958,[1] which was released by the White House office of the Press Secretary in April 1995.

National security systems are those systems related to intelligence activities, equipment that is an integral part of a weapons system, command and control of military forces, cryptologic activities related to national security, or equipment that is critical to the direct fulfillment of military of intelligence missions. NIST clarified the definition of National Security Systems in August 2003 when it released, NIST SP 800-59, *Guideline for Identifying an Information System as a National Security System*. More information on the DIACAP to DoD RMF transition can be found on the URL for the Joint Task Transformation Initiative

---

[1]http://www.fas.org/sgp/clinton/eo12958.html.

Working Group here http://www.csrc.nist.gov/groups/SMA/ispab/documents/minutes/2012-10/ispab_oct2012_dcussatt_dod-rmf-transition-brief.pdf.

ICD 503 AND DCID 6/3

Intelligence agencies that come under the purview of the Office of the Director of National Intelligence use ICD 503 and DCID 6/3 for FISMA compliance. DCID 6/3 is the older of the two, and the goal is to phase it out. Old systems are still following DCID 6/3 until they are up for reaccreditation. ICD 503 was signed and went into effect on September 15, 2008.

DCID stands for Director of Central Intelligence Directive and 6/3 refers to the process described in Section 6, part 3 of the compendious Director of Central Intelligence Directives.[2] The DCID 6/3 requires that systems be characterized by Protection Levels (PL), and DCID 6/3 defines five different protection levels. DCID 6/3 deals only with classified information, and its PL model was designed to ensure that only properly cleared people had access to classified information. The DCID Standards Manual defines the DCID 6/3 certification and accreditation process. DCID 6/3 makes use of the DCID 6/3 Policy Manual.

ICD 503 is more closely related to the NIST RMF than DCID 6/3. It refers to CNSS and NIST guidance and minimizes the amount of IC-specific guidance. An illustration of how ICD 503 incorporates CNSS and NIST documents is depicted in Figure 3.2. ICD 503 addresses policies for:

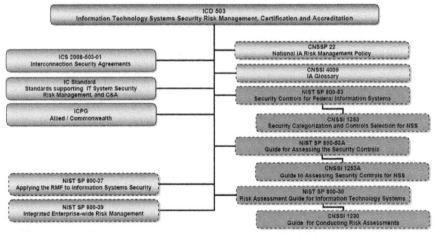

FIGURE 3.2

ICD 503 incorporation of other standards. (For color version of this figure, the reader is referred to the online version of this chapter.)

Source: National Industrial Security Program Policy Advisory Committee (NISPPAC).

---

[2]http://www.fas.org/irp/offdocs/dcid.htm.

- Risk Management
- Accreditation
- Certification
- Reciprocity
- Interconnections
- Governance and Dispute Resolution

A key element of ICD 503 is that ICD 503 established joint Department of Defense and Director of National Intelligence (DNI) reciprocity objectives.

Many of the requirements for IC certification and accreditation are based on physical security, as classified information must always be physically secured. Aside from physical security, the IC puts a lot of emphasis on encryption. The emphasis in these two areas is what really sets the DCID 6/3 and ICD 503 apart other methodologies.

THE COMMON DENOMINATOR OF FISMA COMPLIANCE METHODOLOGIES

The common denominator of all the FISMA compliance methodologies, and this book, is that they are all based on three attributes: Confidentiality, Integrity, and Availability of information and information systems. All the methodologies include definitions for categorizing Confidentiality, Integrity, and Availability qualitatively. In all of the methodologies, information technology assets and controls must be categorized qualitatively by sensitivity related to Confidentiality, Integrity, and Availability.

Confidentiality of information is assurance that the information will not be disclosed to unauthorized persons or systems. Integrity of information is assurance that the information will not be altered from its original and intended form. Availability ensures that the information will be available as planned. Though Availability might seem so obvious at first that it is not worth mentioning, the reason it is important is because it forces the information owner to make provisions for contingencies and outages. Because Availability is important, FISMA compliance requires that contingency plans are developed and tested.

All the compliance methodologies call for accountability. Security accountability of IT systems means that activities can be traced back to a person or a process and that system users will be held accountable for their actions. One of the reasons that roles and responsibilities are clearly defined in every Security Package is to make it clear who is responsible for what. The different compliance methodologies described in this chapter are very similar in numerous ways. If you read all the guidance documentation for each, you might come to the conclusion that the different methodologies are essentially the same thing written from different perspectives.

For the most part, the recommendations in this book will apply to all methodologies unless I point it out otherwise. The guidance I will refer to most often will be the NIST RMF since it is more up to date than the guidance for the other methodologies. NIST guidance is also publicly available for anyone to review, and in that sense, it is the most open source of the compliance methodologies. It is not my intent to republish any of the methodologies.

Something to remember is that every agency, bureau, and department in the government that has built a robust and thorough security assessment and authorization process has their own unique requirements built into it.

FISMA COMPLIANCE FOR PRIVATE ENTERPRISES

The security assessment and authorization methodologies discussed in this book are well entrenched in U.S. federal agencies. However, there is nothing that says that these methodologies and practices cannot be adopted and used by private businesses, publicly traded corporations, and nonprofit organizations. As discussed in Chapter 2, in order to obtain new contracts under government task orders, government contractors must now sign agreements that stipulate that they are in compliance with FISMA. However, any organization can make use of these methodologies, whether they have government contracts or not.

As a result of Executive Order 13636,[3] a group of experts is working on transforming much of NIST's guidance used for information security management of critical infrastructure which is primarily owned by the private sector. The group is known as the Integrated Task Force (ITF), and it is facilitated by the Department of Homeland Security. The ITF is composed of eight working groups with eight different focus areas:

Stakeholder Engagement
Cyber-Dependent Critical Infrastructure
Planning and Evaluation
Situational Awareness and Information Exchange
Incentives
Framework Collaboration with NIST
Assessments: Privacy, Civil Rights, and Civil Liberties
Research and development

Any organization that processes sensitive information should have a methodology for assessing and authorizing the security of their systems whether they are subject to regulatory laws or not. One of the goals of Executive Order 13636 is to create incentives for private sector companies to be more proactive about cyber security.

---

[3]http://www.whitehouse.gov/the-press-office/2013/02/12/executive-order-improving-critical-infrastructure-cybersecurity.

LEGACY METHODOLOGIES

In your travails, you may come across references to various government legacy security assessment and authorization methodologies. These methodologies are no longer used. I've included information about them below for your reference in the event that you come across references to them.

NIACAP (National Information Assurance Certification and Accreditation Process)

Formerly, National Security Systems used the NIACAP which was based on *National Security Telecommunications and Information System Security Instructions,*[4] otherwise known as *NSTISSI No. 1000*. The NIACAP C&A model was developed by the CNSS, and its intent was to be used as guidance for the C&A of national security systems. NIACAP guidelines were described in a document known as *NSTISSI No. 1000*, which is still available at http://www.cnss.gov/Assets/pdf/nstissi_1000.pdf.

DITSCAP (Defense Information Technology Certification and Accreditation Process)

DITSCAP was developed and published by the Defense Information Systems Agency (DISA), and it was applied to the acquisition, operation, and on-going support of any Department of Defense system that collects, stores, transmits, or processes unclassified or classified information. At one time, it was mandatory for use by all defense agencies. The DITSCAP guidance was described in a document known as DoDI 5200.40 and is still available for review at http://csrc.nist.gov/groups/SMA/fasp/documents/c&a/DLABSP/i520040p.pdf.

DISTCAP used an infrastructure-centric approach and stressed that DoD systems were network-centric and interconnected. All the directives were named with numbers and begin with the numbers 5200. One of the most important DoD directives with which DITSCAP required was DoDD 5200.28. The subject of 5200.28 is *Security Requirements for Automated Information Systems (AIS)*. 5200.28 is still available at http://www.csrc.nist.gov/groups/SMA/fasp/documents/c&a/DLABSP/i520040p.pdf. 5200.28 is a 32-page document that named numerous other directives that must be followed. 5200.18 was released in 1988 and is no longer in effect today. The DITSCAP model in particular emphasized accountability perhaps more so than the other methodologies.

JAFAN 6/3

JAFAN 6/3 was published on October 15, 2004 as a methodology to use for Department of Defense Special Access Programs (SAP). JAFAN 6/3 used a notion of protection levels and defined requirements for five protection levels using many of the processes and definitions found in traditional C&A techniques.

---

[4]http://www.cnss.gov/Assets/pdf/nstissi_1000.pdf.

SUMMARY

FISMA compliance processes formally evaluate the security of an information system, determine the risk of operating the information system, and lead to a decision to either accept or not accept that risk.

There are various different methodologies in use today for performing FISMA compliance: NIST RMF, DIACAP, DCID 6/3, ICD 503, and FedRAMP. These different methodologies were developed for different audiences within the federal community: civilian federal departments and agencies with unclassified information, national security and defense agency information systems, information systems operated by the intelligence community, and cloud computing system. Despite the different nuances in these methodologies, they all have the goal of accomplishing the task of assessing and authorizing information systems from a cyber security standpoint.

The NIST model is very current, and NIST solicits and receives feedback from a much larger community of experts. Of all four methodologies, the NIST model is more "open source" than the others—if you can call a methodology open source.

The important thing is to make sure that whatever terminology is being used is well defined, understood by all, and consistent throughout all the other agency documents. Keep in mind that the goal of creating a FISMA compliance process is to create a well-defined repeatable process.

Notes

[1] National Information Assurance Certification and Accreditation Process (NIACAP). NSTISSI No. 1000. National Security Telecommunications and Information Systems Security Committee, http://www.cnss.gov/Assets/pdf/nstissi_1000.pdf; April 2000.

[2] Ron Ross. Joint task force, guide for applying the risk management framework to federal information systems. NIST special publication 800-37, Revision 1. National Institute of Standards and Technology, http://www.csrc.nist.gov/publications/nistpubs/800-37-rev1/sp800-37-rev1-final.pdf; February 2010.

[3] National Industrial Security Program Policy Advisory Committee (NISPPAC), meeting minutes. In: 34th meeting at the National Archives Building, 700 Pennsylvania Avenue, NW, Washington, DC; October 8, 2009.

[4] Executive Order 13636. The white house office of the press secretary, http://www.whitehouse.gov/the-press-office/2013/02/12/executive-order-improving-critical-infrastructure-cybersecurity; February 12, 2013.

[5] Department of Defense Information Technology Security Certification and Accreditation Process (DITSCAP) application manual. DoD 8510.1-M. United States Department of Defense, http://www.dtic.mil/whs/directives/corres/pdf/851001p.pdf; July 31, 2000.

Understanding the FISMA Compliance Process

4

You say it as you understand it.
—**Johann Friedrich von Schiller, famous German dramatist and poet**

TOPICS IN THIS CHAPTER

- Recognizing the need for FISMA compliance
- Roles and responsibilities
- Stepping through the process
- FISMA project management

INTRODUCTION

The FISMA compliance process begins when an information system owner recognizes that an application, system, group of systems, or site requires authorization. The systems owner might be an IT operations director, an IT operations manager, a security officer, or an application development manager. When the need for FISMA compliance is recognized, it is time to put in motion a plan to carry out and oversee the compliance process.

RECOGNIZING THE NEED FOR FISMA COMPLIANCE

All general support systems and major applications are required by FISMA and the Office of Management and Budget (OMB) *Circular A-130, Appendix III* (see Appendix B) to be fully certified and accredited before they are put into production. Production systems and major applications are required to be reaccredited every 3 years. Going forward, we will refer to systems that require FISMA compliance (e.g., general support systems and major applications) simply as information systems.

One of the primary objectives of FISMA compliance is to force the authorizing official to understand the risks an information system poses to agency operations. Only after understanding the risks can an authorizing official ensure that the information system has received adequate attention to mitigate unacceptable risks. Evaluating risk and documenting the results are something that should be incorporated throughout a system or application's system development life cycle. NIST has defined the system development life cycle to consist of five phases:

1. System initiation
2. Development and acquisition
3. Implementation
4. Operation and maintenance
5. Disposal

The Risk Management Framework (RMF) provides a disciplined and structured process that integrates information security and risk management activities into the system development life cycle.[1]

FISMA mandates that new systems and applications need to be fully assessed and authorized before they can be put into production. The best time to begin working on the compliance of new systems and applications is while they are still in development. It is easiest to design security into a system that has not yet been built. When new information systems are being proposed and designed, part of the development should include discussions on "What do we need to do to ensure that this information system will incorporate all required baseline security controls?" After a new application is built and ready to be implemented, is not the best time to figure out if it will withstand a comprehensive security assessment.

Legacy systems that are already in their operational phase are harder to authorize because it is altogether possible that they were put into production with little to no security taken into consideration. In putting together the Security Package for a legacy system, it may be discovered that adequate security controls have not been put into place. If it becomes clear that adequate security controls have not been put into place, the FISMA compliance project leader may decide to temporarily put on hold the development of the Security Package while adequate security controls are developed and implemented. It makes little sense to spend the resources to develop a Security Package that ends up with a recommendation that an information system not be authorized. Coming to an understanding that an information system has not been properly prepared for authorization is precisely one reason why security assessments are performed—it is a process that enables authorizing officials to discover the security truths about their infrastructure so that informed decisions can be made.

ROLES AND RESPONSIBILITIES

Section 3544 of FISMA assigns roles and responsibilities to agency information technology staff. A FISMA compliance project involves a lot of different people all working together on different tasks. There are the folks who develop the compliance program, the team that prepares the documents that describe the information system, the independent assessors that evaluate the system prior to authorization, and the federal inspectors who audit the agency to make sure that they are performing security assessments and authorizations according to federal standards.

---

[1]NIST SP 800-37, Revision 1.

Chief Information Officer

The agency Chief Information Officer (CIO) is the most obvious person held accountable for a successful information security program and the FISMA compliance program. It is the CIO's responsibility to make sure that an information security program, including a compliance program, exists and is implemented. However, most agency CIOs don't play a hands-on role in developing these programs. Usually, the CIO will designate the development of these programs to the Senior Agency Information Security Officer. Delegating the program development does not mean that the CIO does not need to understand the process. If the CIO does not understand all the elements of a successful FISMA compliance program, there is little chance that the CIO will be able to hold the Senior Agency Information Security Officer responsible for developing a complete program. Without understanding the particulars of what a program should include, the CIO will not know if the Senior Agency Information Security Officer has left anything out.

A piece of FISMA compliance that cannot be overlooked is the need for the CIO to develop a budget for compliance. FISMA compliance is very time intensive, and a typical compliance project takes on average 6 months to do a thorough job, replete with all the required information. The CIO works together with the authorizing official to ensure that there is enough of a budget to staff the resources necessary to put together the certification program. If CIOs do not budget for FISMA compliance, the compliance activities may not get done. The CIO enables compliance to take place by fully understanding the federal budgetary process as documented in a publication put out by the White House known as *Circular No. A-11 Part 7 Planning, Budgeting, Acquisition, and Management of Capital Assets*. This publication can be found at the following URL: http://www.whitehouse.gov/sites/default/files/omb/assets/a11_current_year/s300.pdf.

A-11 Part 7 references other budgetary guidelines that the CIO should also become familiar with, including one known as OMB Exhibit 300. Guidance on OMB Exhibit 300 is currently available at http://www.whitehouse.gov/sites/default/files/omb/assets/egov_docs/fy13_guidance_for_exhibit_300_a-b_20110715.pdf. In Section 300.2 of this document, it specifically states:

> *Security: For IT investments, agencies should maintain up-to-date tracking of systems in the FISMA inventory to the appropriate IT investment. Costs for security will be collected in both the Exhibit 53A and 53B.*

The Clinger-Cohen Act, passed in 1996, created new responsibilities for agency CIOs. The act stated that CIOs need to establish policies and procedures for assessments and performance measurements "in the case of investments made by the agency in information systems."

Authorizing official

The authorizing official is a generic term for a senior management official within an agency who authorizes operations of an information system, declaring that the risks associated with it are acceptable. It is unlikely that any person would hold the title of "authorizing official"; hence, I am not punctuating it here with capital letters. There may be multiple authorizing officials within each agency, all responsible for their own designated areas. In many agencies, the authorizing official is referred to as the Designated Accrediting Authority (DAA). NIST SP 800-37, Revision 1, Section 2, specifically says:

> *The authorizing official explicitly understands and accepts the risk to organiza-tional operations and assets, individuals, other organizations, and the Nation based on the implementation of a defined set of security controls and the current security state of the information system.*

The authorizing official usually has budgetary responsibilities for ensuring that a certain amount of resources are set aside for overseeing the FISMA compliance process. Usually, the agency CIO reports to the authorizing official. However, in large agencies, where some bureau CIOs report to the agency CIO, it can be the case that a CIO is the authorizing official. In other cases, the authorizing official may be the commissioner or an assistant commissioner. If the authorizing official and CIO are two different people, they must work together to make sure that an adequate budget has been set aside for FISMA compliance.

The authorizing official should, according to the National Institute of Standards, Special Publication 800-37, Revision 1 (February 2010), be an employee of the U.S. government and cannot be a contractor or a consultant. However, the authorizing official may designate a representative to carry out the various tasks related to FISMA compliance, and the designated representative can be a contractor or a consultant. However, the final security authorization decision and its accompanying authorization decision letter must be owned and signed by a U.S. government employee—the authorizing official.

Senior Information Security Officer

The Senior Information Security Officer (SISO)[2] is the person that CIO holds accountable to oversee all of the agency's information security initiatives. The SISO is akin to a Chief Information Security Officer in private industry, and many agencies are now using the term CISO in lieu of SISO. Many agencies still refer to the more old school term Senior Agency Information Security Officer (SAISO) as the person that holds this position.

The SISO works with the agency authorizing officials to ensure that they are in agreement with the security requirements of the information system as well as the key documents contained in the Security Package such as the risk assessments and the Security Plan. In working together, the SISO and the authorizing officials should be sure to take into consideration the mission and business requirements of the agency.

---

[2]http://nvlpubs.nist.gov/nistpubs/SpecialPublications/NIST.SP.800-53r4.pdf.

The SISO provides management oversight to the FISMA compliance process, ensuring that the process is well thought out, and includes all the necessary documentation and guidance.

The SISO is also responsible for developing the internal compliance process, and all the documentation that describes this process—including instructional handbooks, wikis, internal intranets with agency information security policies, and templates. The SISO appoints the independent assessment team and holds them accountable for performing their duties. It is very important for the SISO to choose their independent assessors carefully because they will come to rely on their recommendations.

The SISO may wish to review all the Security Packages that are processed within the agency; however, as a practical matter, this may be next to impossible to do this. In most agencies, there are far too many Security Packages for one individual to review and validate all of them. Due to this very reason, the SISO employs independent assessment teams to read packages, perform evaluations, write recommendations, and produce a document called a *Security Assessment Report*. The Security Assessment Report is basically an evaluation summary and should justify and support the recommendation on whether or not to authorize the system. The Security Assessment Report should have all the information that the SISO needs to justify the signing of an authorization letter. (Going forward, I will be using the acronym "CISO" to refer to this position since that is the direction that agencies are trending towards.)

Senior Agency Privacy Official

Each agency is supposed to have a Senior Agency Privacy Official. For a large agency, a Senior Agency Privacy Official might be a full-time job. However, for a small agency, it's possible that the responsibilities of this official may be performed by the CIO, the CIO's staff, or the SISO. The person in this role could hold the title of Chief Privacy Officer—he or she does not necessarily have to be called the Senior Agency Privacy Official. What's most important is that someone is designated to perform the duties of safeguarding confidential and private information.

Independent assessor team

Independent assessors review the Security Packages and make recommendations as to whether the system warrants a positive authorization or not. Essentially, the independent assessor team acts as an auditor. They comb through the unwieldy Security Packages looking for missing information and information that doesn't make sense. The assessors also perform testing of the security controls including scanning, penetration testing, and manual testing. See Chapter 18 for more information on testing security controls.

An assessor's goal is to determine if the system is in compliance with the agency's documented processes, security policies, and the agency's information security baseline security requirements. In some agencies, there are so many packages to evaluate that an agency may employ multiple assessment teams. The team may have a departmental name such as Mission Assurance, Information Assurance, or Compliance. The organizational name is for the most part irrelevant as it could be different from agency to agency.

After reviewing the Security Packages and performing testing, the independent assessment team makes recommendations to the SISO and authorizing official on whether or not a package should be authorized or not. The independent assessment team develops a document known as the Security Assessment Report which justifies the recommendation. I will talk more about the *Security Assessment Report* in Chapter 21.

When agencies employ teams of independent assessors, they usually split up the different tasks that need to be accomplished in order to expedite the process. For example, certain staff members might evaluate packages for the General Support Systems, other staff members might evaluate packages for Major Applications, another person might create and update templates, and another person might update the handbook.

In order to demonstrate objectivity, it is often the case that the evaluation team consists of outside consultants. FISMA, §3454 states:

> *Each year each agency shall have performed an independent evaluation of the information security program and practices of that agency to determine the effectiveness of such program and practices.*

If an agency decides to use its own staff, it should be sure that there is a clear separation of duties between the evaluators and the officers that are presenting the systems for evaluation.

System owner

The system owner is the person responsible for administering the systems that the application runs on. A system owner can be one lone systems administrator, or a systems department. In a large distributed application, it is possible that the different systems that are a piece of the application infrastructure have different system owners. When a large distributed application has different system owners, sometimes the different system owners can be different geographic locations or different buildings.

All Security Packages, whether it is a package for a Major Application, or the General Support Services infrastructure that the application runs on, should specify who the system owner is. The system owners are the folks who provide the systems support. The system owner should be indicated in the Asset Inventory. The contact information for the system owners should be indicated in the System Security Plan and Information System Contingency Plan.

Information owner

The information owner is the person who owns the data. It's possible that the system owner and information owner are one in the same person (in cloud computing, that is usually not the case). There is more discussion on cloud computing in Chapter 23.

If the information owner is different from the system owner, the system owner maintains and safeguards the data for the information owner.

The information owner holds the system owner responsible for safeguarding the confidentiality, integrity, and availability of the data. If the system owner and information owners are not one in the same people, this should be noted in the Security Package.

Information System Security Officer

The Information System Security Officer (ISSO) is responsible for ensuring that the appropriate security posture of the information system is maintained. The ISSO has detailed knowledge of the system and maintains the day-to-day security operations, ensuring that the information systems configuration is in compliance with the agency's information security policy.

The system's Security Package documents are prepared either by the ISSO or for the ISSO by staff or contractors. Typically, ISSOs have a large plate of responsibilities and they may need to augment their staff with contractors to prepare a Security Package expeditiously. It is not uncommon for one ISSO to be responsible for the preparation of many systems and many Security Packages. Since one package could easily take a year for a well-versed security expert to prepare, it is considered standard and acceptable for ISSOs to hire consultants from outside the agency to prepare the package documents. It also improves the objectivity of the Security Package to have it prepared by third-party individuals that are not part of the agency's own staff.

Once a Security Package is complete, the ISSO presents it to an independent assessment team who then proceeds to validate the findings. The independent assessors typically perform their work on behalf of the SISO. If there are security findings that need to be resolved in any way, it is up to the ISSO to ensure that risks are mitigated and new safeguards are implemented as necessary.

Document preparation team

The document preparation team, sometimes referred to as the document prep team, prepare the Security Packages documents for evaluation. In many cases, the document prep team are outside consultants—they certainly don't have to be, but my experience has shown that agencies often contract this work to outside consultants. The document prep team can also be a mixed team of outside consultants and internal agency staff which is possibly the best arrangement since you then have a mix of people who are familiar with the system, and experts who will look at all the controls from a fresh perspective.

The document prep team works under the direction of the Information System Security Officer. When it comes to putting together the Security Package, it is the document prep team that performs the bulk of the work. The document prep team needs to have an expert background in information security with the breadth of understanding the various facets of security architecture, and how to safeguard confidentiality, integrity, and availability. Understanding security policies and FISMA is of course a given expectation of the document prep team.

Agency inspectors

To prepare for visits from the Government Accountability Office (GAO), all agencies, and some bureaus, have their own inspectors that come on site to agency offices to periodically assess if proper FISMA compliance is taking place. In most cases, the agency inspectors are not required to give much advanced notification and their visits can take place without warning. The agency inspectors come from the agency Office of Inspector General (OIG). Many agency OIG offices have their own Web sites, and you can read more about the different responsibilities of the OIG there. A short list of OIG Web sites you can take a look at is listed in Table 4.1.

The goal of the agency OIG is to review agency FISMA processes and report findings to the agency. OIG reports are public information and are available for review by Congress. The OIG offices have their own investigation and review process, and different OIG offices may perform their audits using different techniques. OIG offices that are more vigilant in their audit and review process are more likely to prevent the agency from being cited as deficient in GAO reports.

GAO inspectors

Oversight auditors from the GAO visit federal agencies on an annual basis and review Security Packages to make sure that they have been properly assessed and authorized. The GAO also reviews the agency's FISMA compliance program in its entirety to determine if it is acceptable. If the GAO discovers that Security Packages were inappropriately assessed or authorized, or if the agency's compliance process is deficient in any way, the GAO inspectors will document the findings in GAO reports.

Levels of audit

Taking into consideration the independent assessors, the OIG inspectors, and the GAO inspectors, you can see that the FISMA process undergoes rigorous levels of audit (see Figure 4.1). Usually, there are no less than three levels of audit. Some

Table 4.1 Agency OIG Web Sites	
Agency Name	**Agency OIG Web Site**
Environmental Protection Agency	http://www.epa.gov/oigearth/
Federal Communications Commission	http://www.fcc.gov/oig/
Department of Agriculture	http://www.usda.gov/oig/
Department of Health and Human Services	http://www.oig.hhs.gov/
Social Security Administration	http://www.ssa.gov/oig/
United States Postal Service	http://www.uspsoig.gov/

GAO Inspectors

OIG Inspectors

Authorizing Official

Security Assessment Team

Security Package

FIGURE 4.1

FISMA levels of oversight for reviewing the Security Package.

agencies may even have an additional level of audit. After the evaluation team reviews the Security Package, it is possible that another internal compliance organization may review the Security Package again to see if the assessment team did their job correctly. The original evaluation team and an ancillary compliance team may not in fact agree on whether a Security Package should be accredited, and often the two internal audit organizations will have to have numerous discussions among themselves to come to an agreement on the final Authorization recommendation.

Having so many levels of audit can in fact seem like overkill; however, the agencies that seem to indulge in these audit redundancies, and separation of duties, often fare the best in their annual reports to Congress.

STEPPING THROUGH THE PROCESS

There are six phases to the FISMA compliance process as recommended by NIST in *SP 800-37, Revision 1, Guide for Applying the Risk Management Framework to Federal Information Systems*. To get from one phase to another, a lot of stuff happens along the way. This book explains how to develop the deliverables required to get from one step to the next. Next is an overview of the general requirements for each of the six steps (Figure 4.2).

Step 1: Categorize

Step 1 requires that you categorize the sensitivity of the data that will reside on your system. It is during this step that you determine the impact that would occur if the confidentiality, integrity, or availability were breached. There is more detailed information on this step in the next chapter.

Step 2: Select

NIST Special Publication 800-53, Revision 4 provides Security control selection guidance for nonnational security systems. (CNSS Instruction 1253 provides similar guidance for National Security Systems.)

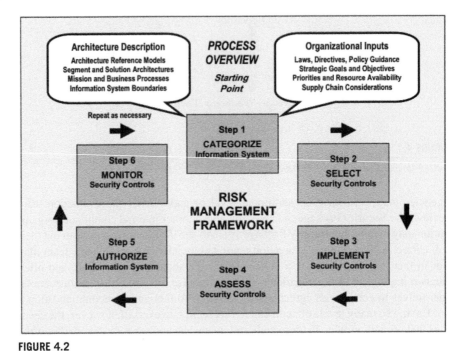

FIGURE 4.2

The NIST Risk Management Framework.[1]

Step 3: Implement

After the baseline security controls have been selected, they must then be implemented. If this is a brand new system, hopefully the security controls were taken into consideration all along the way, making this task very manageable. If the system has already been built, it is sometimes more challenging to implement the security controls, so allow a bit more time if that is the case.

Step 4: Assess

The assessment phase begins when the Security Package has been completed. The evaluation team reads through the Security Package in its entirety, and validates if the information presented in it are accurate, and if all the required information is present. A Security Package can easily be in excess of 500 pages. Approximately 4-6 weeks should be allotted for the authorization phase. Most evaluation teams will have checklists of particular criteria and items they expect to find in the Security Package before they actually begin the evaluation.

Step 5: Authorize

If a Security Package passes muster with the security assessors, a recommendation will be made that the package be authorized. The authorizing official will review the recommendation, and as long as it appears justified, will sign a formal letter of Authorization. The authorization letter will also need to be signed by the ISSO, the information owner, and then will be sent to the CIO. The CIO is supposed to acknowledge receipt of the letter by signing it.

Step 6: Monitor

Once an information system has been authorized, it should be continuously monitored. Some agencies may require a document dedicated to continuous monitoring, for example, a Continuous Monitoring Plan. Security controls should be monitored and any changes made to them should be documented. If firewall policies are changed, the changes and reasons for the changes should be documented. If intrusion detection configuration changes are made, they should be fully described and the reasons for the changes should be documented. If configuration changes are made, configuration guides should be updated and all changes should be recorded through the configuration management process.

It is often the case that not nearly enough time is put into Continuous Monitoring. After an authorization has been made, most ISSOs and information system owners tend to breathe a sigh of relief and seem to like to put the entire compliance process behind them. Putting together a Security Package and obtaining an authorization is a daunting task and doing more of it, after the job is done, is not usually high on anyone's agenda after the fact. However, keeping the documents up to date will make any future recertifications much easier. Unless the information system is decommissioned, it in fact will need to be assessed again and reauthorized in 3 years. OMB Circular A-130 specifically says:

> *Review the security controls in each system when significant modifications are made to the system, but at least every three years. §3(a)(3)*
>
> . . .
>
> *Ensure that a management official authorizes in writing use of the application by confirming that its security plan as implemented adequately secures the application. Results of the most recent review or audit of controls shall be a factor in management authorizations. The application must be authorized prior to operating and re-authorized at least every three years thereafter. Management authorization implies accepting the risk of each system used by the application. §(3)(b)(4)*

The documents that are a part of the Security Package are considered live documents and can be updated at any time. It is best to update the documents as soon as changes are made to the information systems since that is when the new information is most fresh in everyone's mind. Updating documentation never seems to be high on the list of important tasks to complete, and for that reason, I recommend that updating Security Package documents be built into the change management process.

FISMA PROJECT MANAGEMENT

The initiation phase of the system development is usually informally managed by the information system owner and the ISSO. While all information system owners should be aware of the fact that FISMA requires new information systems to be positively authorized, this may not be at the forefront of their mind. Therefore, it is altogether likely that the ISSO may bring the need for a security assessment and authorization to the attention of the information system owner. Whether the need for an assessment and authorization is initiated by the information system owner, or the ISSO, some sort of acknowledgment between these two individuals that an assessment and authorization needs to take place should occur. The acknowledgment does not have to be formal, or even written. A simple hallway conversation can suffice as long as both parties come to agree that it's time to get the compliance project started.

During the initiation phase in the system development life cycle, the information system owner and the ISSO should agree on what resources to use as far as the document prep team goes. Decisions need to be made on whether to hire outside contractors or use in-house staff. FISMA compliance projects tend to usually be a much bigger job than most people realize. If the system owner or ISSO has any doubts about what it will take to prepare the system for a security assessment and authorization, I cannot emphasize enough the value in using outside consultants. Preparing a system for a FISMA compliance security assessment and authorization is not a small side project that you can do on top of your other responsibilities. It would be unreasonable for an ISSO or system owner to expect that a system administrator perform this on top of their other duties. Putting together a Security Package is a full-time job and usually the results will be insufficient if the federal agency tries to double up its existing information technology staff to perform compliance duties in conjunction with other responsibilities.

In outsourcing the preparation of a Security Package to outside consultants, it is important for the ISSO to ensure that he or she is hiring capable individuals with the appropriate expertise. The ISSO should ask numerous questions to a potential contracting company and its staff before enlisting the Contractor Officer or Contracting Officer Representative (COTR) to close an agreement. Questions that may assist an ISSO in determining the capabilities of potential consultants might be:

- For what other agencies have you performed FISMA compliance/C&A activities?
- Do you have a track record in obtaining positive authorizations?
- Which FISMA compliance documents are experienced in preparing?
- Will you be able to make numerous trips on site to meet with our staff?
- Can you provide resumes for the available consultants?
- Do you have a description of your FISMA compliance preparation services?
- How long do you anticipate a FISMA compliance project to take?
- Can you provide past performance references from other agencies?

Due to federal acquisition regulations, it may very well be these questions would need to be placed into a Request for Proposal (RFP). Not all FISMA consulting services are the same. One clear indication that a contracting company does not fully understand FISMA compliance is if they list only a few of the required document types in their FISMA compliance service description. Some companies claim to understand FISMA compliance, but, for example, will list that their compliance service consists of a System Security Plan and a vulnerability assessment (which of course is only part of the picture). You really want to hire consultants that understand the whole picture and can develop all the documents required for compliance.

Before preparing a Security Package, the ISSO should have some understanding of whether or not the proposed Security Package will result in a positive authorization. If the ISSO knows up front that proper security controls have not been put into place, that security is improperly configured, and that security policies have not been adhered to, even if these items have not been cited previously, it is better to fix these problems before beginning a new security assessment. This does not mean that compliance is optional. What I am suggesting is that if you know of weaknesses that require correction, start correcting them immediately. Don't wait for the 3-year reauthorization date to come along before making the necessary corrections.

If the proposed security assessment and authorization is for a brand new information system, no prior Security Package will exist, and therefore, it will take longer to prepare the system for the assessment. For a system that is not brand new such as an older information system, a prior Security Package should exist and be available for review. The prior package can be updated which usually doesn't take as long as writing an entire new package from scratch. New authorizations are required every 3 years. An assessment and authorization for an information system that previously has been authorized is referred to as a "reauthorization." Reauthorizations require the same suite of documents that new Security Packages require. When working on a reauthorization, the prior Security Package should be reviewed thoroughly to ensure that all risks previously cited in the prior Security Assessment Report have been mitigated.

The ISSO's document prep team will need to come on site to the agency's office to be available to interview the information system's development and management team. It is critical for the team to learn as much about the information system as possible and ask as many questions as necessary. The information system owner should advise his or her development staff to accommodate the document prep team and provide them with as much information as possible about the design and configuration of the system slated for assessment and authorization. It will work to the system owner's advantage if they advise their developers and system integrators up front as to why the document prep team will be asking questions. When staff start working on compliance projects, and their responses to inquiries are, "I'm not authorized to give you this information," that will only slow the project down. Roadblocks such as this can be avoided by clear communications from the system owner and ISSO up front.

Once the ISSO's prep team is assembled, scheduling a kick-off meeting for the ISSO's document prep team and the independent security assessment team always seems to help these projects work a bit more smoothly. It's a good idea for the document prep team to establish a positive relationship with the security assessment team. At the kick-off meeting, both teams should agree on what templates, and what versions of the templates, should be used. I have seen document prep teams work diligently on preparing documents for review by the security assessment team, only to learn at the last minute that they used the wrong templates. A key date that both teams should agree on is the date on which the ISSO turns over the documents to the security assessment team. This date can sometimes be the most contentious part of the project since both teams want to maximize the amount of time that they have to do their jobs. The document prep team wants more time to prepare the documents and, typically, jockeys for a date on the calendar that is further out (closer to the authorization date) and the assessment team usually pines for a date farther back in time from the assessment date. It's not a good idea to just see when the security assessment team asks for the documents. The assessment team has the upper hand, and if no date has been agreed on in advance, they might surprise the ISSO and document prep team by saying, "We'll need your Security Package in three days." Such unwanted surprises can all be avoided by establishing positive communications up front and agreement on the document handover date up front.

A FISMA document prep team may consist of anywhere from a few people up to a dozen or so depending on the complexity of the information system slated for assessment and authorization. An average document prep team is more typically around four to six full-time staff. What should determine the number of individuals on the document prep team is the scope of the project and time frame of the project. As you increase the scope, and decrease the timeframe, the need for a bigger document prep team increases. Most teams require at least 3-4 months minimum to assemble an adequate Security Package. With fewer people on the project, you need to allow for more time. It would not be out of the question, however, for a FISMA compliance review team to take 6 months to prepare a Security Package for a large and complex infrastructure.

SUMMARY

As prescribed by NIST, the FISMA compliance process consists of six phases. Throughout all six phases, there are several roles participating in the process, and each role is responsible for the execution of specific tasks. As a FISMA compliance professional, you are responsible for the execution of your tasks, but in order to accomplish them, you'll need to work with other staff that will be critical to your success. It is important to understand the overall process, and how all the pieces described in this chapter fit together in order to manage a FISMA compliance project. Additional information about FISMA roles and responsibilities can be found in Appendix D of SP 800-37, Revision 1.

Establishing a FISMA Compliance Program

5

A bad beginning makes a bad ending.
—Euripides

TOPICS IN THIS CHAPTER

- Compliance handbook development
- Create a standardized security assessment process
- Provide package delivery instructions
- Authority and endorsement
- Improve your compliance program each year
- Problems of not having a compliance program

INTRODUCTION

FISMA requires that federal agencies have an overarching Information Security Program. System security assessment and authorization are just a piece of the greater Information Security Program, albeit a big piece. The Information Security Program includes the whole ball of wax—security policies, procedures, requirements, guidelines, and all the documentation that goes with it. The compliance piece of the program is a well-thought-out process, with documentation to support it, that explains how security assessment and authorization will be done within the agency.

If your agency already has an Information Security Program in place, now it might be a good time to start thinking about how you can improve your program. Once an Information Security Program has been developed, an astute agency will find the need to update and revise the program each year. The more your program is used, the better it will become.

There are no federal restrictions on which people within the agency can participate in developing the compliance program. The agency itself, however, may set their own policies on who is responsible for the development of the compliance program. As developing the program is a big job, whoever manages the project to develop the program should reign in participants throughout the agency to help build and document the program.

COMPLIANCE HANDBOOK DEVELOPMENT

In developing the program, it's a good idea to develop a compliance handbook that instructs your agency or bureau on how to prepare security documents and work through the security assessment and authorization process. The idea is to standardize the development of all Security Packages that are submitted for evaluation, and then to assess and evaluate each system according to the same standards, requirements, and principles. Without a handbook and a specified process, the Security Packages will have a different look and feel. If 50 different Security Packages all have the right information in it, but in different formats, it is going to be very difficult for the assessment team to find the information. If the Security Packages have different types of information in them, it is going to be very hard for assessors to review the packages according to the same standards.

Writing the handbook is a big job. A good handbook is likely to be several hundred pages long. The handbook has to include very specific information on what your agency evaluators need to see in every Security Package. It should instruct the folks preparing the Security Packages on what documents they will be required to submit and what should be included in each document. Agencies may decide to call the handbook by some other name, perhaps *Agency Compliance Manual* or *Security Package Guidelines*. The name is somewhat irrelevant. The point is to create a repeatable process regardless of what it is called.

What to include in your handbook

Each agency's handbook will be somewhat different and take on slightly different organizational formats, which is perfectly acceptable. However, it is highly advisable that all handbooks include sections in the following areas:

- Background, purpose, scope
- Regulatory citations (FISMA; FIPS 199; OMB Circular A-130. Appendix III)
- Reference to associated internal security policies
- System life-cycle information
- An overview of the process
- Roles and responsibilities
- Definitions of key terms
- Information on the requirements for Security Package documents
- Requirements for secure configurations
- How to define security requirements when building a new system
- How to understand authorization boundaries
- Threat and risk assessment guidelines
- Security controls
- Required security tests
- Security assessment checklists
- Plan of action and milestones

- Acronyms
- Glossary
- References and related publications

Who should write the handbook?

There are no restrictions on who can write a *Security Assessment & Authorization Handbook*. An agency can use its own staff or outside consultants. However, the development of the handbook should probably be done under the authority of the department that will oversee the program. It makes sense that the agency authorizing official should designate the appropriate staff to write the handbook since he or she will need to live by its guidelines and authorize packages according to its stipulations. There is nothing that says the authorizing official cannot author the handbook themselves. However, given the daily day-to-day responsibilities of most authorizing officials, the time it takes to develop the handbook may require that it be done by an appointed staff or outside consultants.

CREATE A STANDARDIZED SECURITY ASSESSMENT PROCESS

The evaluation of a Security Package should be standardized. Before going through the Security Package, the security assessment team should know up front exactly what it is that they are looking for. Without a standardized methodology for evaluating Security Packages, it's possible that each system will be evaluated differently.

Security Packages consist of a set of documents that all go together and complement one another. A Security Package is voluminous, and without standardization, it takes an inordinate amount of time to evaluate it to make sure all the right information is included. Therefore, agencies should have templates for all the documents that they require in their Security Packages. Agencies without templates should work on creating them. If an agency does not have the resources in-house to develop these templates, they should consider outsourcing this initiative to outside consultants.

The best way to create a standard process is to create templates for each required security document. The template should be developed using the word processing application that is the standard within the agency. All of the relevant sections that the assessment team will be looking for within each document should be included. Text that will remain constant for a particular document type also should be included. An efficient and effective compliance program will have templates for the following types of compliance documents:

- FIPS 199 Sensitivity Level Recommendation
- Hardware and Software Inventory
- eAuthentication
- Security Awareness and Training Plan
- Rules of Behavior

- Incident Response Plan
- Business Impact Assessment
- Information System Contingency Plan
- Configuration Management Plan
- System Security Plan
- Security Assessment Plan
- Security Assessment Report
- Plan of Action & Milestones

The latter chapters in this book will help you understand what should be included in each of these types of documents. Some agencies will also require a Privacy Impact Assessment and a Business Risk Assessment, and possibly other types of documents as required by their Information Security Program and policies.

Templates should include guidelines for what type of content should be included and also should have built-in formatting. The templates should be as complete as possible, and any text that should remain consistent and exactly the same in like document types should be included. Though it may seem redundant to have the exact same verbatim text at the beginning of, say, each Security Assessment Report, each document needs to be able to stand-alone and makes sense if it is pulled out of the Security Package for review. Having similar wording in like documents also shows that the packages were developed consistently using the same methodology and criteria.

With established templates in hand, it makes it much easier for the different team players to understand what it is that they need to document. Even seasoned security experts appreciate document templates. Finding the right information to include in the documents can by itself be extremely difficult without first having to figure out what it is that you are supposed to find—which is why the templates are so very important. It's often the case that a large complex application is distributed and managed throughout multiple departments or divisions and it can take a long time to figure out not just what questions to ask, but who the right people are that will know the answers.

PROVIDE PACKAGE DELIVERY INSTRUCTIONS

Your program should include information on how specifically the ISSO should submit the final Security Package to the evaluation team. The security assessment team needs to understand whether to expect the package by e-mail, CD, and flash drive or to look on a protected network share. Some agencies use Web-based compliance tools and like to have their documents uploaded to a portal. It's a good idea for agencies to require that both hardcopy and softcopy documents be submitted to the evaluation team. Hardcopy documents should be bound together. I recommend using a three-ring binder because it is easy to update a piece of the package and insert it easily after removing the outdated pages.

Most of these documents will contain sensitive information, and for that reason, they should not be e-mailed to anyone over the Internet unless they are protected by strong encryption—either by file encryption or through a Virtual Private Network (VPN).

> For more information on VPNs, see *NIST SP 800-77 Guide to IPSec VPNs* at the following URL: http://www.csrc.nist.gov/publications/nistpubs/800-77/sp800-77.pdf and *NIST SP 800-113 Guide to SSL VPNs* at the following URL: http://www.csrc.nist.gov/publications/nistpubs/800-113/SP800-113.pdf.

Before e-mailing Security Package documents out of the agency over any external public networks, you should really check the security policies of your particular agency to find out what the requirements are for protecting sensitive information. If outside consultants are being used to prepare a Security Package, it may very well be that the only safe way to exchange documents with them is for them to come on site. Some agencies do not like to use VPN clients for outside contractors. Though it may seem trailing edge, sometimes exchanging documents in person using a USB flash drive is the easiest way to exchange documents. If you do use a USB flash drive, make sure that the files are encrypted and that the agency allows the use of flash drives. Some agencies allow the use of flash drives, but it has to be an agency supplied secure flash drive.

AUTHORITY AND ENDORSEMENT

It is important that a security program be developed and endorsed at a high level within the agency. The purpose of the program will be completely defeated if individual departments each try to create their own unique program. The idea is to create a standard, and a standard means one process. The program should be spearheaded by the CISO or authorizing official. That doesn't mean that the technical staff within various departments can't contribute to the program's development. Some of the best ideas often come from the technical staff that takes the most interest in a project. It's also always worth it to have as many seasoned experts review the program documents before the final edition is approved. The completed program should be endorsed by the CIO and authorizing official.

IMPROVE YOUR COMPLIANCE PROGRAM EACH YEAR

Once an Information Security Program, a compliance handbook, and templates are established, they should be improved upon and refined as necessary. However, updating them every single year may be counterproductive. You want the people within the organization to gain familiarity with the handbook and process. If you change the handbook, process, and templates every year, they will not become familiar. Therefore, once you have a handbook and process in place that has been reviewed, edited, and published, it is best not to rewrite the handbook more often than every 2 years. Of course if there are egregious errors or new government regulations that need to be added, it is important to make those revisions as they come up.

Developing a handbook and templates takes a long time. Once an agency has invested the time to develop these materials, they should hold training courses to train the agency's ISSOs on how to make the best use of them. Once ISSOs have been duly informed and trained, they can clearly be held accountable for their role in developing proper Security Packages according to the agency requirements.

PROBLEMS OF NOT HAVING A COMPLIANCE PROGRAM

If your agency does not have a standardized compliance program, you can expect the security assessment and authorization process to become extremely confusing and overly complicated. Without standardization, it's possible that each type of document written will include entirely different types of information from one package to the next. The document prep team will not know what should be included in each document and package, and it will become challenging for security assessors to evaluate different packages consistently within the agency.

Missing information

Without compliance instructions and standards, different Security Packages will include different types of information. For example, one Security Package might have an Information System Contingency Plan (ISCP) and others might not. One Security Package might include a network topology map, and others might not. When it comes time to evaluate the entire Security Package, it is hard to fail a package for not having an ISCP if no policy or organizational process ever required that an ISCP exist to begin with. It is very hard to hold the information system owners and the ISSOs accountable for putting together adequate Security Packages if your agency has not yet defined what constitutes an adequate Security Package.

Organizational challenges

Though specifying the right information to include in a Security Package is of primary importance, the format of the package should not be overlooked. A Security Package can be 500 pages long. Unless each one is organized the same way, it will be very cumbersome for the assessors to wade through the voluminous information and check to see if all the right material has been included. It's best to make things easiest for the assessors. Assessors who can't make heads or tails out of the information presented to them, and can't find key pieces of information, are going to be reluctant to recommend that a package be authorized.

Inconsistencies in the assessment process

You want each Security Package to be assessed and evaluated the same way. One agency may have many government contractors from different organizations assessing systems. Without any sort of standard for Security Package content or format, you are leaving the entire evaluation up to the subjective opinion of one (or a small group) of people. Different assessors may put emphasis on different areas. If each package has the same organizational format, it improves the chances that different assessors will evaluate the packages, and the systems, using the same process because they will look for and expect the same type of information. Using a standardized format levels the playing field from system to system ensuring that all systems are evaluated the same way.

Unknown security architecture and configuration

Without a Security Package, it may be the case that the security architecture and configuration of your information infrastructure are not known. By working through the compliance process, you will become aware of whether this is the case or not. If the security architecture is well documented, compliance serves as an opportunity to make sure the architecture diagrams and network maps are correct. If systems are not well documented, or not documented at all, you'll need to do a fair amount of research before you can come up with an accurate network diagram. The same holds true for the security configuration. All software requires configurations. When operating systems and applications are installed, even if they are installed securely, are the security settings documented? If the security settings are not documented, they are basically unknown. Even expert and seasoned systems administrators cannot usually remember every little thing they have done to a system when configuring it because today's operating systems and applications are so feature rich. That is why security architecture and configuration documentation are critical. The compliance process is designed to find the unknowns of the security architecture and configuration settings and then resolve the unknowns by creating the necessary documentation along the way.

Unknown risks

Federal laws aside, the primary reason for understanding the security posture of your information systems is to identify risks, understand them, and take mitigating actions. With compliance left undefined, you are leaving the risks that you want your agency to look for open to speculation. Maybe the agency ISSOs will identify all the key risks, but maybe they won't. One ISSO may put emphasis on disaster recovery planning, and another might put emphasis on configuration settings. It is unlikely that they all will put the same emphasis on all aspects of information security. When it comes to identifying risks, there are numerous items to take into consideration. There are business risks, system risks, training risks, policy risks, inventory risks, and so on. A well-defined compliance program ensures that all the relevant types of risks are taken into consideration.

SUMMARY

There is no complex task that can be effectively accomplished using a repeatable process without having adequate documentation in place. Therefore, the first step in implementing a compliance program in is developing a compliance handbook. Templates for each required document should be developed to standardize the format and to reduce the time required to populate them with meaningful information. Once these items are in place, Security Packages can effectively and efficiently generated. The compliance program should also include mechanisms by which the process itself can be evaluated and improved. Cars are not manufactured the same way today as they were 20 years ago due to process improvements. In any discipline, process improvements are discovered and incorporated into new and better processes, and FISMA compliance programs are no exception to this. If an organization's compliance program is constantly evolving and improving, then by extension, the organization's security posture will evolve and improve over time as well.

Getting Started on Your FISMA Project

He who has begun, is half done.
—Horace

TOPICS IN THIS CHAPTER

- Initiate your project
- Analyze your research
- Develop the documents
- Verify your information
- Retain your ethics

INTRODUCTION

Before you'll be able to start putting together a Security Package, you'll need to acquire as much information as possible about the systems or applications you'll be reporting on. You need to be a good detective, and not lose faith when the details appear unclear. The more information you gather, the clearer the details will become. You are about to put together an information technology jigsaw puzzle.

INITIATE YOUR PROJECT

When you begin your compliance project, don't expect that everyone who has played a role in developing and administering the application or system you are reporting on to start volunteering information for you to use. You will need to take the initiative to go out and collect as much information and supporting documentation as you can, and conduct interviews with the appropriate staff. If you are a consultant, first you will need to figure out who the appropriate staff are that you need to talk to. You are going to have to ask a lot of questions. The sponsoring manager that signed you up for completing the compliance project is the best person to start this. The sponsoring manager may be the system owner, the ISSO, the contract officer, or an application development manager.

Put together a contact list

You first need to figure out who will have the knowledge of all the security particularities of the information system. You should start by identifying the people involved. The sponsoring manager should be able to answer a lot of your questions. Some of the questions you will need to ask, in order to find out who the appropriate people are who understand the security of the information system(s) requiring accreditation, are along these lines:

- Was the application developed in-house or purchased from a vendor?
- If the application was purchased from a vendor, was any customization done to it?
- Who did the customization?
- If the application was developed in-house, who designed it?
- Are there design specifications and documents? Who has them?
- Is the application hosted on-site or at a remote site?
- If the application is hosted remotely, who is responsible for its operations?

These questions are the "Who?" questions. From the answers to your questions, you should be able to start putting together a contact list of the people who have been a part of the design and implementation of the information system. Include their phone numbers and e-mail addresses because you'll need to contact them often.

Some federal agencies are quite large, and due to the size of the operations, sometimes impersonal. When you contact the various people on your contact list, you'll need to explain to them who you are and why you are contacting them. Don't expect them to know that a FISMA compliance project is underway or even to know what FISMA is all about. If you contact them and suggest that you need to meet with them to discuss a FISMA compliance project, be prepared to tell them what FISMA means as there is a good chance they may not have a clue as to what you are talking about.

Finding out all the information you will need to create a Security Package is much like going on a treasure hunt. If you are an outside consultant, at the start of the project, it is altogether possible that no one except the sponsoring manager will know why you are on-site at the agency. It's very unlikely that someone will come up to you and say, "I hear that you are on-site to put together a Security Package for our information system. Here are all the security policies, design documents, and the security configuration of the system that you will need." In large federal agencies, my experience has been that no one readily and quickly volunteers information about system security.

Hold a Kick-off Meeting

Once you have found out who the key players are (the people that have been part of designing, developing, coding, and implementing the information system), you should schedule a Kick-off Meeting and invite them all. Do your best to form good relationships with these folks because you will become reliant on them for information. During the Kick-off Meeting, introduce them to the compliance team and explain to them briefly what FISMA is all about. During this first meeting, you should tell them that you will need as much documentation as you can get on the particular information system that is slated for authorization (or reauthorization). Ask them if they can e-mail you documentation as soon as possible; otherwise, they may take weeks to get it to you. You will need information on the design, development, implementation, configuration, network topology, and testing of the information system. You'll want to review all this documentation to find the right pieces of information to put into the Security Package.

Obtain any existing agency guidelines

It is key to find out if the agency you are working for has a *FISMA Compliance Program Handbook* or some other set of guidelines for FISMA compliance. If a handbook exists, you should follow all the guidelines written in it when preparing your Security Package—even if they are poor guidelines. If the evaluation team does its job properly, they will be evaluating the Security Package for how well it follows the agency *FISMA Compliance Program Handbook* and requirements.

If a handbook exists and you think parts of it are so wrong that you shouldn't follow it, you need to take this up with the ISSO and package evaluation team before making any decisions. When you are preparing a Security Package is not necessarily the best time to try to get the agency to change their regulations and policies. If you think that some of the guidelines are incorrect, before you go ahead and decide to go your own way and create a more "correct" Security Package, bring the issues to the attention of the ISSO and offer justification as to why you would like to proceed differently. Some agencies will fail your Security Package if you don't follow their handbook—even if the handbook is wrong.

All agencies should have a handbook (or some sort of guidelines) and templates to standardize the FISMA compliance process. However, some agencies are less prepared than others, and if you embark on a FISMA project, and find out that no handbook or templates exist, you'll have to do without. You can still put together a solid Security Package without a handbook or templates, and if you do a good job, perhaps you will be enlisted as a future contributor to develop the much-needed handbook and templates. If a compliance handbook is not present, then see if the parent agency has one. For example, a bureau or agency department may not have their own handbook, but the parent agency might. If no compliance handbook at all exists, figure out which methodology your agency should be using (NIST, DIACAP, ICD 503, etc.) and look to that for guidance.

ANALYZE YOUR RESEARCH

Once you have received the various documents from the information system developers and administrators, you'll need to analyze these documents to see if they include the kind of information that you'll need to include in the Security Package.

It is likely that much of the information you need for the Security Package will not be included in the various documents you receive. If the information system(s) that are up for assessment and authorization have been previously authorized, then a prior Security Package should exist. You should make it a point to review the prior Security Package, and use any information from it that is still relevant. If anything appears incorrect in the prior Security Package, you should correct it, even if it was not cited for deficiencies in the prior assessment.

Put together a list of questions regarding the kinds of things you still need to find out from the information system developers and administrators, and schedule meetings with the folks that you think can best answer your questions. Keep meeting with the team and contacting them on the phone and by e-mail until all your questions are answered. It often takes several rounds of inquiries before you receive all the appropriate information.

DEVELOP THE DOCUMENTS

Although there are likely no regulations that require you to put together the Security Package documents in any particular order, I happen to think that the order in which you put the documents together is important. For example, if you put together the *Hardware and Software Inventory* up front, it will help you in writing the descriptive text about the authorization boundaries that are required in the Security Plan. In the subsequent chapters of this book, I present the various Security Package documents in the order that I have found works well for cohesiveness in understanding the information system. In some cases, it may make sense for you to change the order of these documents when putting together your Security Package. The main point to take away is that if a document contains information that is dependent on a prior document, develop the prior document first. It will be hard to know how to rate the impact of an disruption in the *Business Impact Assessment* if you don't yet know what the assets are—that is, if the *Hardware and Software Inventory* has not yet been completed.

It's okay to be redundant

Many of the documents in the Security Package include information that is redundant from one document to the next. The reason for this is because each document needs to be able to stand on its own. It is possible that the staff who has access to the *Information System Contingency Plan* will not have access to the *System Security Plan*. Access to security documents is typically provided on a need-to-know only basis. Some of the information that you find for some of the earlier documents can and should be used in subsequent documents. You want to give the impression that all the documents are consistent with each other and support each other. Though in many forms of writing being redundant is not desirable, in crafting Security Packages, it is necessary. One of the things that the evaluators look for are inconsistencies between the various Security Package documents. Any inconsistencies usually raise a flag and call for closer inspection.

Different agencies have different requirements

Not all agencies require the exact same documents. FISMA allows for flexibility, and one agency may require certain documents that other agencies don't require. Though it could be argued that this is inequitable, FISMA was designed to allow each agency to determine its own needs within the boundaries of the stipulation. The Security Package documents that I will be discussing in this book are among the most frequently required FISMA compliance documents. However, there may be others that some agencies require that are not discussed in this book. If your agency requires documents not discussed in this book that are part of the stated FISMA compliance program, that doesn't mean that your agency is administering their FISMA compliance program the wrong way. However, to be sure, agencies should be able to justify to the Inspector Generals, and to the GAO, which documents they require and why.

Include multiple applications and components in one package

It is acceptable to include multiple applications and components in one Security Package. You should define the authorization boundaries of your Security Package as widely as you possibly can. Determining the boundaries is sometimes the trickiest part of putting together a Security Package. You need to understand where the boundary starts and stops. In general, you should define a boundary that is large and logical. For example, if you are assessing and authorizing general support systems, you may want to define your boundary by network domains. If you are reporting on major applications, you will need to include all the pieces of the infrastructure that the application touches. For example, an IBM mainframe that hosts multiple logical partitions at different physical locations should all be internal to the same authorization boundary.

Usually applications are managed by a different organization than the underlying general support systems. Operating systems and networks typically have different information system owners than the applications. FISMA compliance is about holding information system owners accountable, and therefore, the boundaries need to lie within the jurisdiction over which the information system owner has control. If you are reporting on an application that is dependent on general support systems that the application gets installed on top of, then this should be clearly stated in the Security Package. An underlying general support system usually has a different Security Package than the applications that are installed on top of it. When your Security Package and the security of your systems are in part dependent on other systems, that needs to be specifically stated. You can reference other Security Packages and other systems that are not within your authorization boundaries in your documentation. It would be perfectly plausible to insert a statement such as:

> *The major applications described in this Security Package are dependent on the underlying general support systems that have been previously assessed and authorized in the* Agency ABC System Security Package, V2.0, July 14, 2013.

You should list the formal Security Package name of any other packages that you reference. If you don't know the package name, try to find it out. It's even better to obtain a copy of it if you can. In some cases, it may be against the security policies of the agency to share such information between one information owner and another. However at the very least, an outside information owner should be able to share with you the official document name and publication date of the related Security Package.

VERIFY YOUR INFORMATION

Once you have completed a document, before submitting it to the ISSO, send it out first to the information system developers and administrators that are most familiar with the information system that you are reporting on. Ask them to review it and inform you of any factual errors. Network diagrams should always be reviewed for accuracy. If something doesn't make sense, it's probably either not well documented or plain wrong. Your FISMA compliance project is a time of ensuring that all known information about the system is accurate.

In reviewing design documents that you receive, do not just assume that information contained in them is how the application or information system was actually developed. Designs go awry and management changes their minds about requirements halfway into a project. Just because an information system was supposed to turn out one way, doesn't mean it didn't turn out a different way. You need to take everything you read with a grain of salt, and ask questions about things that don't make sense.

RETAIN YOUR ETHICS

In most agencies, the information system owner is heavily focused on simply obtaining a positive Authority to Operate (ATO) for the information system. They don't necessarily want to know how you will go about making this happen as long as you get it done. Even though you should do everything possible to make that happen, by all means do not compromise your ethics.

Retain Your Ethics

Never compromise your ethics. Under no circumstances should you invent security controls that do not exist, or write in a document that risks have been mitigated if they really haven't. If the information owner or ISSO pressures you to document items that are obviously not true, you should refrain from doing so and report the problem to your management. If in the course of preparing the compliance documents you find that certain security controls that should have been implemented were not, report that to the ISSO and recommend that they get implemented as soon as possible. As long as they are implemented before the Security Package is submitted, your documentation will not be incorrect. If you feel that there is absolutely no way the information systems will obtain a positive Authority to Operate, discuss this with the ISSO. It is not your job as a compliance document preparer to resolve security problems that should have been put in place previously. The information system owner and ISSO are likely both aware that security controls are mandated by law and need to be in place. If they are responsible individuals with ethics of their own, they will not expect you to resolve agency security problems that you have no control over.

If it appears to you that a positive Authority to Operate cannot be obtained, there are really two options:

- Stop the compliance process and put in place the necessary security controls
- Continue with the compliance process, documenting accurately the existing security controls, and hope the evaluator will grant the business owner an *Interim Authority to Operate (IATO)*.

An IATO is basically like a consolation authorization, and in most cases, IATOs expire after 6 months. An IATO means that you have convinced the evaluators that the information owner is at least putting forth a good faith effort in trying to implement proper security controls. And for that reason, the authorizing official may give you extra time to come into compliance. An IATO usually will include a list of security controls that will need to be in place when the IATO expires. At that time, if the requirements of the IATO have been met, the system usually will receive an Authority to Operation (ATO), but if not, the systems can be shut down. Without an authorization in hand, the agency Inspector General (or the GAO) can come in and shut your systems down. However, although oversight officials could require the systems to be shut down, for practical purposes, in real life this rarely happens. Certainly an IATO is better than no authorization at all. Something to keep in mind however is that OMB does not recognize IATOs. Therefore, when it comes time for annual FISMA reporting, IATOs are not considered.

SUMMARY

Developing a Security Package is a big endeavor. One of the biggest problems that I have noticed is that often business owners and ISSOs do not start the compliance process soon enough and do not allocate enough resources to get the job done. An average time to get through the process is about 180 business days. The first Security Package you develop for your information system will be the most challenging. After that, unless a significant architectural or configuration change occurs, continuous monitoring and updating of the package are easy enough and should not require as many resources the second or third time around.

Preparing the Hardware and Software Inventory

The prudent heir takes careful inventory of his legacies and gives a faithful accounting to those whom he owes an obligation of trust.
—**John F. Kennedy**

TOPICS IN THIS CHAPTER

- Determining the accreditation boundaries
- Collecting the inventory information
- Structure of inventory information
- Delivery of inventory document

INTRODUCTION

OMB Circular A-130 and 44 U.S.C. 3511 requires all U.S. federal agencies to maintain hardware and software inventories of their systems. The very direct wording from A-130 §9(a)5 states:

> *Maintain an inventory of the agencies' major information systems, holdings and information products, as required by 44 U.S.C. 3511.*

The inventory should include all hardware and software components of the system. You'll also need this *hardware and software inventory* when you develop your *Business Impact Assessment*. Hardware and software should be thought of as assets. All key assets that make up the information system should be reported.

DETERMINING THE SYSTEM BOUNDARIES

One of the biggest challenges in putting together a hardware and software inventory is figuring out which servers, devices, and software components belong in the inventory. Usually, a server has multiple components. All servers have operating systems, and on the top of the operating system, there might be a database, some developer toolkits, and a Web server.

Determining what components should be part of your inventory will assist you in describing the system boundaries when you write your *System Security Plan* (see Chapter 16). It may be that the staff that developed the system you're reporting on never formally acknowledged or described the boundaries. However, you can still come up with clear boundaries based on certain guidelines. As a general rule, the hardware and software components of the information system that you are reporting on should:

- Have the same general information security sensitivity requirements
- Be managed by the same information system owner
- Have a consistent function or mission
- Have consistent operational characteristics (router access control lists, network zones, security zones, firewall policies, etc.)

In federal agencies, it is usually the case that enterprise applications are reported on in one Security Package, and the underlying general support systems (GSSs) are reported on in a different Security Package. Usually, the reason for this is because there are different system owners. The management of the hardware is performed by the GSS owner. If an application system owner is running an enterprise application on the top of the GSS, the application system owner doesn't really own the hardware. However, since the application could not run without the hardware, the application owner should include the hardware in their system inventory, making note that the hardware is managed by the GSS owner and that more information about the GSS can be found in the *GSS System Security Plan*. In this sort of circumstance, it makes the most sense for the application owner to obtain the hardware information from the GSS owner.

If you are the GSS owner, you do not need to list the applications that reside on your system in your inventory unless the applications are actually owned and managed by you. Applications that might typically be part of the GSS are things like IP address management tools or event log management tools.

When putting together your hardware inventory, you should include the following information:

- Vendor (Dell, IBM, Hewlett Packard, etc.)
- Model (for hardware)
- Physical location including address, building number, room number
- All storage devices
- Backup devices and tape robots
- Associated IP address(es) and hostnames

Most security programs do not require you to list the amount of RAM and disk space, so it is safe to leave that information out unless agency security policies and standards specifically require that you list such things. There are likely various physical systems that safeguard the information system (e.g., fire suppression systems and temperature alarm systems), but you do not need to list these items in the asset inventory because you'll be listing them in the System Security Plan when you describe the physical and environmental controls.

When putting together your software inventory, you should include the following information:

- Operating system name and version
- Patch level and version
- IP host addresses
- Application names and version
- Database names and version
- Middleware
- Backup software and version
- Software license keys

When trying to figure who the system owner is, the best rule of thumb to use is to ask the question, "Who has the authority to control this component?" If no one in your group has the authority to make changes to the component, it doesn't belong to you.

A complicating factor is that you might have an outside service provider that is providing a key service for your system. For example, perhaps your system uses an outside service provider to perform the backups. The system owner who contracted with the third-party organization is on the hook to make sure that the third-party organization complies with FISMA. Since that outside service provider is performing a service directly for the system owner, the system owner should include information about the backup hardware and software in the system inventory, even if the backup hardware and software is owned by the outside service provider. Incidentally, it is the responsibility of the system owner to make sure that any outside service provider follows federal policies and requirements.

COLLECTING THE INVENTORY INFORMATION

There is no requirement for how you collect the inventory information. If your information system consists of a large enterprise application, it surely makes things easier if the inventory information is collected through an automated process such as an asset inventory tool. However, even if the agency or bureau you are working with has access to an automated asset inventory, the information contained in the inventory still will not necessarily tell you which of the assets are part of the information system that belong in your Security Package.

Usually, there is no fast and easy way to collect asset inventory information. You will have to have discussions with the in-house subject matter experts, developers, and management team to come to an understanding of which components should be included. It is more than likely that much of the collection will have to be done manually by asking various people to look up IP addresses, find out the patch levels, find out the version number, look on the back of systems to find the serial numbers, and so on. You may need to ask support staff who are in entirely different departments, organizational groups, or locations to help you obtain this information. Don't expect that they will know anything about your FISMA compliance project. You will have to explain to them why you are collecting the information. Due to security concerns, support staff likely will require various types of authorization before they can give you the information you are looking for.

Be prepared for a lot of red tape and responses such as "I can't give this information to you. You will have to have your supervisor request it and then the request will have to be approved by my supervisor." Due to the long chain of authorizations that may be required to assist you, collecting the asset inventory information usually takes longer than you might expect.

STRUCTURE OF INVENTORY INFORMATION

I strongly recommend that you document the hardware and software inventory into a well-organized table or spreadsheet. You can use this same tabular format later to put together your Business Impact Assessment. (I'll be discussing the *Business Impact Assessment* in Chapter 13.) The function of the asset should be listed somewhere in the inventory table. Aside from listing the information in a table, you will want to put a short description of the information system at the beginning of the inventory document. The information system description should be consistent with the description that will be used later in the System Security Plan. The hardware and software inventory can be included as part of the System Security Plan, or it can be developed as a separate document entirely.

You should include the following information in your system inventory:

- Cover page with data classification, warnings, date of publication, and version
- Table of contents
- Record of changes
- An overview section that describes the purpose of the document
- A brief description of the information system
- A brief description of the agency security program requirements for assets
- Names of related documents
- Asset inventory tables

Table 7.1 shows a sample hardware and software inventory table. Large distributed applications may have several pages of system components listed. If you are including an entire network domain of general support systems in one Security Package, that may also require a lengthy asset inventory table.

DELIVERY OF INVENTORY DOCUMENT

If your inventory document contains IP addresses, you will want to be sure not to e-mail it to anyone over the Internet. If you are an outside consultant and are working from your company office, you may have to go on-site to deliver the inventory document or else e-mail it through secure channels such as a VPN or file encryption. Alternatively, it is usually considered acceptable to deliver documents by CD and courier. However, in case there are any security policies associated with the file delivery, you should consult with the security policies of the agency you are working for.

Table 7.1 Hardware and Software Inventory

Description	Function	Hardware or Software	Hostname	IP Address	Vendor	Model or Version
Server	Hardware platform	Hardware	NY01	64.82.2.39	Dell	PowerEdge SC410
Operating system	Operations of server	Software	NY01	64.82.2.39	Microsoft	Windows Server 2012
Database	Customer records	Software	NY01	64.82.2.39	Oracle	Oracle DB 11G Enterprise
Server	Hardware platform	Hardware	NY02	64.82.2.40	Oracle	SPARC T4-1
Operating system	Operations of server	Software	NY02	64.82.2.40	Oracle	Solaris 11
Database	Payroll records	Software	NY02	64.82.2.40	Microsoft	SQL Server 2012

SUMMARY

Collecting hardware and software inventory information is the first big step in developing a Security Package. This inventory will define the authorization boundary as well as the scope (and the cost) of your project, so it is important to develop a complete and accurate inventory. To develop the inventory, you will need to work with many of the people in charge of day-to-day operations of the organization's information systems. These people are not always focused on information security issues, and they are just as busy as you are. You need to keep in mind that you should make collecting inventory information as simple and efficient as possible for people assisting you. It's important to develop and maintain a positive relationship with them. Without timely and accurate assistance from other departments, your FISMA compliance project can suffer the negative impacts of delays and inaccuracy.

Categorizing Data Sensitivity

The guardians of government data face a difficult task. If they classify too much information, counterintelligence experts say, no one will take the designation seriously. But if too many files are unclassified, the nation's enemies could collect enough here and there to discover some crucial technological and military secrets.
—*New York Times*, **November 16, 1986**

TOPICS IN THIS CHAPTER

- Heed this warning before you start
- Confidentiality, Integrity, and Availability
- Template for FIPS 199 Profile
- The explanatory memo
- National Security Systems

INTRODUCTION

The way that the government protects data is by implementing security controls. How do you know what security controls should be implemented for your system? How much security is enough? It's difficult to answer those questions without knowing more about the system's data and just how sensitive it is. You wouldn't want to implement all the security controls you can think of for data that are not that sensitive. And you wouldn't want to leave out important security controls for data that are highly sensitive.

The different FISMA compliance methodologies have slightly different ways of determining data sensitivity; however, the concepts behind these different methodologies all have a common denominator: Confidentiality, Integrity, and Availability.

All Security Packages get assessed and authorized at a particular sensitivity level. The data owner (supported by the ISSO and the document prep team) should determine the sensitivity level and justify this level in a document known as the FIPS 199 Profile. Unless the agency is a noncivilian agency that has decided to use some other methodology for determining the sensitivity level, the best guidance that exists for determining the sensitivity level is a document known as Federal

Information Process Standard 199 (FIPS 199). FIPS 199 is found in Appendix C of this book.

The information owner is supposed to decide at what level to assess and authorize the information system and then obtain buy-in on that level from the authorizing official. The ISSO and document prep team should assist the information system owner in determining the proper level at which to assess and authorize the system.

Determining the sensitivity level of the Security Package is often a misunderstood part of FISMA compliance. I have seen some agencies wait to perform this step until the entire Security Package has already been developed, which is the wrong way to go about this.

HEED THIS WARNING BEFORE YOU START

The biggest mistake you can make in categorizing the Confidentiality, Integrity, and Availability of your data is to overclassify it. Agencies do this all the time thinking that by overclassifying the data, the information system owners are protecting themselves. I have seen ISSOs that use the thought process, "I don't want the fingers pointing at me if there is a system break-in, therefore, let's categorize this data as highly sensitive. Then, if the system gets broken into, we can say 'I told ya so'" which is the worst of all methods you can use to categorize data sensitivity. Categorizing data to a higher sensitivity level does not increase the security of the data unless more security controls are put in place. It is the controls that you apply to the data that increase their security and preserve Confidentiality, Integrity, and Availability.

Most information system owners and systems administrators seem to think that their data's importance is greater than it actually is. Upon first consideration, most people will assume that their information is mission critical. It seems that if information system owners claim that their data are mission critical, they feel that they are covering themselves in the event that something goes awry—they told everyone that it was mission critical, so if an incident occurs, it is not their fault. However, overstatement of data classification could actually lead to unforeseen investigations and disciplinary action for the information system owner—if a security incident really were to occur. For example, if data should be protected at the highest Confidentiality, Integrity, and Availability rankings, then that means that the most stringent security controls should be applied to it. If a security incident occurs for data that were characterized by the highest Confidentiality, Integrity, and Availability ratings and it is discovered that the security controls that were put in place were minimal, there could be egregious consequences in an investigation or audit. Auditors may wonder why more stringent security controls were not applied, or they may wonder why the data were characterized to be of such high sensitivity if in fact they are actually not very sensitive.

Furthermore, FISMA compliance is an expensive process, and the expense goes up as the sensitivity level goes up. If you don't need to categorize your system as a High system, then don't. Stating that a system is a High sensitivity system will not make it more secure. Performing an assessment for a High sensitivity system will cost more, and take longer, than a Moderate sensitivity level system. System owners are more apt to get audit findings on systems categorized as High sensitivity because there are far more controls that auditors will be expecting, and if they don't find these controls implemented, it will not bode well for the system owner in the final *Security Assessment Report*.

You want the sensitivity level to be just right—not too high and not too low.

Independent assessors will evaluate your package at whatever level you submit it for. They do not tell you what level to select. However, if you select the wrong level and your documentation is not consistent with the level selected, assessors may have challenging questions you'll have to answer, which could become problematic for authorization.

Underclassifying data should also be avoided. Data that are not used to make critical decisions and would have little impact if it were unavailable for a period of time should not require expensive and elaborate security controls. When filling out Exhibit 300 forms, agencies have to justify their information technology spending. Independent assessors typically are not concerned with OMB Exhibit 300 budget audits; however, Inspector Generals may ask to see Security Package documents in order to understand if large expenditures of monies on elaborate security implementations were indeed necessary. OMB Exhibit 300 audits are performed to verify if government funds for information technology were appropriately spent. For example, an Inspector General report from the Social Security Administration (September 2008) stated:

> *Our review found weaknesses in how security costs were allocated to individual projects. OMB requires that agencies identify project-specific IT security costs and integrate these costs into the overall costs of investment.*[1]

Traditionally, information security and capital planning were thought of as two disparate activities, but FISMA changed that. For information on how to integrate information security into the capital planning process, including Exhibits 300, a good reference to use is NIST *Special Publication 800-65, Integrating IT Security into the Capital Planning and Investment Control Process*, January 2005, which can be downloaded from the following URL: http://www.csrc.nist.gov/publications/nistpubs/800-65/SP-800-65-Final.pdf.

Inconsistencies in your data classification and your security controls raise the brows of independent assessors and inspector generals. For example, an auditor may wonder if your data have such low requirements for Confidentiality and Availability, why have you implemented such grandiose encryption and PKI controls? Or if your data have such high requirements for Availability, why haven't you implemented highly available, fault-tolerant RAID systems? If your data have

---

[1]http://oig.ssa.gov/sites/default/files/audit/full/pdf/A-14-08-18018.pdf.

low Confidentiality, Availability, and Integrity requirements, why did independent assessors perform such a comprehensive, exhaustive, and expensive network vulnerability scan and penetration test? You need to be able to justify everything to an auditor and the best way to do that is to make sure that your decisions and statements are consistent with the government-recommended processes for security sensitivity categorization. In the NIST RMF, categorizing the sensitivity of the information system is Step 1 (see Chapter 4).

CONFIDENTIALITY, INTEGRITY, AND AVAILABILITY

Preserving the Confidentiality, Integrity, and Availability of your information systems is one of the key objectives of FISMA. FIPS 199 helps you understand how to categorize the Confidentiality, Integrity, and Availability of your information systems so you can take that information and determine a sensitivity level.

Another document that can help you understand how to properly categorize Confidentiality, Integrity, and Availability is the NIST *Special Publication 800-60, Revision 1, Volumes 1 and 2: Guide for Mapping Types of Information Systems to Security Categories*, August 2008. You can download both of these documents from the main NIST Special Publications page here: http://www.csrc. nist.gov/publications/PubsSPs.html.

SP 800-60, Volume II, describes many different information types and presents recommendations (Low, Moderate, High) for each of their Confidentiality, Integrity, and Availability sensitivities. The different information types listed are spread over 15 Operational Areas and include both Services Delivery Support Information and Government Resource Management Information. To categorize the sensitivity of an unclassified system, first select the appropriate information types from SP 800-60, Volume II. (The different information types presented in this document all come from the *Federal Enterprise Architecture Consolidated Reference Model*, Version 2.3.) You may need to browse through the document reading descriptions of the different information types, until you find the one that is closest to the data on your system. When looking though SP 800-60, Volume II, you'll see that once you find the information type that pertains to your system, a qualitative rating for Confidentiality, Integrity, and Availability is noted along with rationale for the rating (Figure 8.1).

FIPS 199 summarizes the characterization of Confidentiality, Integrity, and Availability according to adverse impact in the event of a security incident. Low, Moderate, or High adverse impacts are described by FIPS 199 as indicated in Table 8.1. The levels of impact described in Table 8.1 are consistent with the data classification levels for Confidentiality, Integrity, and Availability that we have already discussed.

What is important in following these guidelines is being able to justify the rationale behind selecting the category of Low, Moderate, or High for your information

NIST Special Publication 800-60 Volume II
Revision 1

NIST
**National Institute of
Standards and Technology**
U.S. Department of Commerce

Volume II: Appendices to
Guide for Mapping Types of
Information and Information
Systems to Security Categories

Kevin Stine
Rich Kissel
William C. Barker
Annabelle Lee
Jim Fahlsing

INFORMATION SECURITY

Computer Security Division
Information Technology Laboratory
National Institute of Standards and Technology
Gaithersburg, MD 20899-8930

August 2008

U.S. DEPARTMENT OF COMMERCE
Carlos M. Gutierrez, Secretary

**NATIONAL INSTITUTE OF STANDARDS AND
TECHNOLOGY**
James M. Turner, Deputy Director

FIGURE 8.1

NIST SP 800-60, Volume II, Revision 1.

system. Questions that you will want to ask the in-house subject matter experts to help you determine the Confidentiality, Integrity, and Availability impact levels are:

- Does the information system perform operations that put human lives at stake?
- Are the data read-only data?

Table 8.1 Summary of FIPS 199 Levels of Impact

Level of Impact	Description from FIPS 199
Low	The potential impact is low if the loss of Confidentiality, Integrity, or Availability could be expected to have a limited adverse effect on organizational operations, organizational assets, or individuals
Moderate	The potential impact is moderate if the loss of Confidentiality, Integrity, or Availability could be expected to have a serious adverse effect on organizational operations, organizational assets, or individuals
High	The potential impact is high if the loss of Confidentiality, Integrity, or Availability could be expected to have a severe or catastrophic adverse effect on organizational operations, organizational assets, or individuals

- Does the data include executable programs?
- Who are the stakeholders of the data?
- If the data disappeared completely and forever, what would be the impact?
- If the data disappeared for 1 hour, what would be the impact?
- If the data disappeared for 1 day, what would be the impact?
- Does the information system connect to any other systems or networks?

The impact levels noted in SP 800-60, Revision 1, Volume II, are considered "Provisional" Impact Levels. Agencies are allowed to change the Provisional Impact Level as long as it can justify the change. SP 800-60, Revision 1, Volume II, includes recommendations on what circumstances may warrant changing the impact level to something different than the given Provisional Impact Level.

Confidentiality

According to FIPS 199, Confidentiality is a legal term defined as:

> ... preserving authorized restrictions on access and disclosure, including means for protecting personal privacy and proprietary information...

Legal terms aside, Confidentiality means that people who are not supposed to see sensitive data don't end up seeing it. Confidentiality can be breached in numerous ways, including shoulder surfing, capturing network packets with a protocol analyzer (sometimes referred to as "sniffing"), capturing keystrokes with a keystroke logger, social engineering, or dumpster diving. Confidentiality can also be breached completely accidentally, for example, if systems administrators accidentally configure an application such that people who are not supposed to see the data have login access to it.

Confidentiality typically is preserved through use of the following techniques:

- Encryption
- Role-based access control (RBAC)

- Rule-based access controls
- Classifying data appropriately
- Proper configuration management
- Training users and systems administrators

Determining the Confidentiality level

In determining the proper level at which to categorize your information system, you need to determine what impact a breach of Confidentiality of the data would have on your organization. If the impact of disclosure would be of little consequence, the rating of Low should be selected. If the impact of disclosure to the wrong individuals would be disastrous, the rating of High should be selected. If the impact of adverse disclosure would be somewhere between Low and High, the rating of Moderate should be selected.

For example, data that are to be made publicly available on the Web would have a Low Confidentiality rating. Data that should be viewed by only a very small group of people, where disclosure to the unauthorized viewers would have critical consequences, would require a High degree of Confidentiality. Data that should be viewed by an intermediate amount of users, that would have a moderate adverse effect if it were disclosed to the wrong individuals, would have a Moderate Confidentiality rating.

When considering impact of disclosure, it helps if your organization has a data classification scheme. If it does, you can create numerical weights based on the data classification scheme that are somewhat more specific than the assignments of High, Moderate, or Low.

Integrity

Like Confidentiality, Integrity is also a legal term defined by FIPS 199 and reads as follows:

> *... means guarding against improper information modification or destruction, and includes ensuring information nonrepudiation and authenticity...*

Preserving the Integrity of the data ensures that the information is reliable and has not been altered either by unauthorized users or processes gone awry. After all, if data are not accurate, they are of little use and in fact can be detrimental if they are being used to make decisions where lives are at stake. Attackers may attempt to purposely alter data, but systems administration errors and sloppy programming can also create data that contain the wrong information. If input variables in programs are not checked for memory bounds, buffer overflows can occur, which have the potential to alter good data. Integrity often is preserved through the same techniques you use to preserve Confidentiality. However, additional techniques that help ensure that Integrity of data is left intact are

- Perimeter network protection mechanisms
- Host-based intrusion prevention systems

- Network-based intrusion detection systems
- Protection against viruses and other malware
- Physical security of the information systems
- Adherence to secure coding principles
- Backups and off-site storage
- Contingency management planning

Determining the Integrity level

Similar to determining the Confidentiality level, when you determine the Integrity level, you need to determine what impact a loss of data Integrity would have on your organization. If the impact of disclosure would be of little consequence, select the Low rating. If the impact of disclosure to the wrong individuals would be disastrous, select the High rating. If the impact of adverse disclosure would be somewhere between Low and High, you should select Moderate.

Remember, loss of Integrity means that the data have been modified through unauthorized channels, either on purpose or by accident. If it is a company calendaring application that has its Integrity breached, this will not be anywhere near the same consequences as a system that puts human lives at stake. A breach of Integrity on a system that provides services for a manned space flight could have life or death consequences.

Availability

FIPS 199 stipulates the legal definition of Availability to be:

> ... means ensuring timely and reliable access to and use of information.

Not all data have the same requirements for Availability. Data that have an impact on human lives need to have their Availability ensured at higher levels than data that are intended for trivial purposes (e.g., the cafeteria lunch menu). Data that have high Availability requirements need more elaborate safeguards and controls to ensure that Availability is not compromised. Data that have low Availability requirements may have few availability safeguards or controls.

Availability typically is preserved through use of the following techniques:

- Load balancers
- Hot failover systems
- Denial-of-service appliance
- Accessible system backups
- Uninterruptable power supply
- Generators
- Dual-homed routers and switches
- Dual Internet service connections/providers

Determining the Availability level

In determining Availability, you need to understand how urgent it is (or not) that the data exist in their everyday state. What would happen if the data were to become unavailable for a period of time? Would the unavailability of the data prevent critical decisions from being made? Would human lives be at stake? Would anyone even notice or care? Some information security experts claim that risks to Availability should be concerned only with security, and not performance. However, security vulnerabilities often are exploited through attacks on performance, and therefore, taking performance into consideration is important. If a denial-of-service attack prevents data from becoming available due to degradation in system performance, it would be prudent to consider the performance impact caused by the attack on security.

Categorizing multiple data sets

If your goal is to authorize multiple applications together, or applications for multiple lines of business or multiple Operational Areas, you will need to do some additional work to figure out your Confidentiality, Integrity, and Availability scores. However, as long as the system owner is the same, it is much more efficient to assess and authorize multiple applications together and multiple lines of business together than to develop two entirely separate Security Packages.

First, you figure out the Confidentiality, Integrity, and Availability qualitative ratings individually for each application, line of business, or Operational Area. Once you have done that, you put the final scores for each of the individual areas into a summary table. The different individual areas may have different scores for Confidentiality, Integrity, and Availability. However, your Security Package needs to be geared toward one level. To obtain the final Confidentiality, Integrity, and Availability rating, you will want to select the highest rating in all categories and use that one. For example, if you have three lines of business and they have Confidentiality ratings of High, Moderate, and Low, you will select High for your final Confidentiality rating. Table 8.2 shows a sample table of multiple Confidentiality, Integrity, and Availability data sets.

Figuring out Confidentiality, Integrity, and Availability using the approach I have just described is the ideal way to figure Confidentiality, Integrity, and Availability scores if you have multiple information types on the same system. Don't create three different Security Packages for the same server. Due to the large amount of time and resources it takes to assess and authorize a system, it is usually best to take into consideration all the information for one server or storage device in the same package.

Once the information types have been categorized, system owners are required to select the high water mark of the different data categorizations to determine the system categorization. The Security Profile is said to be the final Confidentiality, Integrity, and Availability rating and can be displayed in tabular format as depicted in Table 8.3.

Table 8.2 Sensitivity Level of Multiple Data Sets

Information Type	Confidentiality	Integrity	Availability	Page # of NIST SP 800-60, Volume II, Revision 1
Energy supply	Low	Moderate	Moderate	133
Higher education	Low	Low	Low	160
Legal prosecution and litigation	Low	Moderate	Low	195
Sensitivity level of system		Moderate		–

Table 8.3 Example of Security Profile

Information Type	Security Categorization
Confidentiality	Moderate
Integrity	Low
Availability	Moderate
System categorization	Moderate

TEMPLATE FOR FIPS 199 PROFILE

Below you will find a structure and framework that you can use as a template for authoring a *FIPS 199 Profile* document. You may need to modify certain sections of this to meet the unique requirements of your department or agency.

> **Memorandum**
> <Date>
> To: <Name of Authorizing Official, Title of Authorizing Official>
> From: <Name of System Owner, Title of System Owner>
> Re: FIPS 199 Profile for <Information System Name>

Federal policy mandates that every federal information system be assigned a sensitivity level based on three aspects of its operations: Confidentiality, Integrity, and Availability. Each of these three aspects is to be categorized as being of Low, Moderate, or High sensitivity. The documents that provide guidance for this categorization are the following.

- The Federal Information Processing Publications Standard (FIPS) 199, *Standards for Security Categorization of Federal Information and Information Systems,* February 2004,[2] mandates the determination of the Security Profile for each Federal Information System.
- The National Institute of Standards and Technology (NIST) *Special Publication (SP) 800-60, Revision 1, Guide for Mapping Types of Information Systems to Security Categories, Volumes I and II*, assists in the application of FIPS 199 by providing guidance based on the degree of impact resulting from the loss or misuse of an IS or its data.

The *<agency name> FISMA Compliance Program Handbook, <publication date>* requires that each <agency name> information system be categorized with a sensitivity level. The process for determining the sensitivity level is described on pages <page numbers> of the *Handbook.*

<Agency name> has tasked <name of organization authoring this document> to apply this guidance to <name of information system> to make recommendations for its FIPS 199 Profile and to document the analysis and rationale for the recommendations they make.

<Name of organization authoring this document> conducted interviews with <information system name> management and subject matter experts (SME) during <time period of interviews>. Specifically, <name of organization or people completing this document> met with <person1> on <date> and with <person2> and <person3> on <date>. All results stated in this memorandum are the result of these interviews.

Based upon information presented by the <information system name> management and SMEs, and using the earlier guidance, <name of organization authoring this document> recommends that the FIPS 199 Profile for the <name of information system> be established as:

• Confidentiality	<Low, Moderate, High, or Not Applicable>
• Integrity	<Low, Moderate, High, or Not Applicable>
• Availability	<Low, Moderate, High, or Not Applicable>
• Overall system	<Low, Moderate, High, or Not Applicable>

Based upon its assessment of the characteristics of the <name of information system> and using the earlier guidance, <name of organization authoring this document> recommends that the <name of information system> be certified and accredited at Level <number>.

FIPS 199, *Standards for Security Categorization of Federal Information and Information Systems,* February 2004, requires that a new federal information system be categorized in three aspects of its operations: Confidentiality, Integrity, and Availability. Each aspect is to be categorized as having Low, Moderate, or High

---

[2]http://www.csrc.nist.gov/publications/fips/fips199/FIPS-PUB-199-final.pdf

sensitivity. These three determinations are referred to collectively as the information system's sensitivity level.

NIST SP 800-60, Revision 1, *Guide for Mapping Types of Information Systems to Security Categories, Volumes I and II*, assists in the application of FIPS 199 by providing guidance based on the degree of impact that would result from the loss or misuse of an information system or its data.

<Name of organization authoring this document> conducted interviews with <information system name> representatives <names of subject matter experts> on <date range>. These interviews established that, of the <number> Information Types that were identified, only <number> are applicable to <name of information system>: <names of Information Types>.

Subject Matter Expert (SME), <name of person>, notes that < list any rationale, observations, or conclusions drawn>. As a result, <name of organization authoring this document> recommends that the Information Type <name of Information Type> for Operational Area <name of Operational Area> be included in all systems analyses. In the case of <name of information system>, this recommendation applies to <Confidentiality, Integrity, Availability> and not to <Confidentiality, Integrity, Availability>. <Brief description on why the recommendation is applicable to as described to Confidentiality, Integrity, and Availability.>

The Confidentiality, Integrity, and Availability summary analysis of the multiple data sets taken into consideration in this Security Package is presented in Table 8.4.

Based upon this analysis and using the earlier guidance, <name of organization authoring this document> recommends that the final Security Profile for the <name of information system> be established as:

Table 8.4 Data Sets and Security Profile Recommendations Applicable to <name of information system>

Operational Area	Business Line	Information Type	Confidentiality	Integrity	Availability
<name>	<name>	<type>	<High, Moderate, Low, N/A>	<High, Moderate, Low, N/A>	<High, Moderate, Low, N/A>
<name>	<name>	<type>	<High, Moderate, Low, N/A>	<High, Moderate, Low, N/A>	<High, Moderate, Low, N/A>
<name>	<name>	<type>	<High, Moderate, Low, N/A>	<High, Moderate, Low, N/A>	<High, Moderate, Low, N/A>
Highest rating			<High, Moderate, Low, N/A>	<High, Moderate, Low, N/A>	<High, Moderate, Low, N/A>

N/A, not applicable.

- Confidentiality   <Low, Moderate, High, or Not Applicable>
- Integrity   <Low, Moderate, High, or Not Applicable>
- Availability   <Low, Moderate, High, or Not Applicable>
- Overall system   <Low, Moderate, High, or Not Applicable>

THE EXPLANATORY MEMO

In many federal departments and agencies, once a security categorization with a sensitivity profile has been developed, the information owner is required to submit an explanatory memo to the authorizing official that summarizes and supports the recommended sensitivity level. The purpose of this memo is to get buy-in from the authorizing official before further work on the system takes place. The ISSO typically prepares this memo for the system owner who then signs it and submits it to the authorizing official. The authoring official should acknowledge the letter with a signature and then return it to the information system owner. If the authorizing official will not accept the recommended sensitivity level, then the security categorization will need to be revised until it has been found to be acceptable. Although the memo does not have to be in any particular format, I have provided a template to help you understand what to include.

Template for explanatory memo

Memorandum
<Date>
To: <Name of Authorizing Official, Title of Authorizing Official>
From: <Name of System Owner, Title of System Owner>
Re: FIPS 199 Profile for <Information System Name>

This memorandum is to advise you on the security categorization of <name of information system> and to obtain your approval on the appropriate sensitivity level. The <*agency name*> *FISMA Compliance Program Handbook*, <*publication date*>, requires that each <agency name> Information System (IS) must be assigned a sensitivity level. The sensitivity level, in turn, is determined by assessing the Confidentiality, Integrity, and Availability characteristics of the IS to determine the magnitude of harm to the agency that can be expected to result from the consequences of unauthorized disclosure of information, unauthorized modification of information, unauthorized destruction of information, or loss of information or information system availability.

This process is described in detail on page <page number> of the *Handbook*.

An assessment was conducted by <name of organization or department> to determine a recommended sensitivity level for <name of information system>. Based upon the assessment of <name of information system>, the recommended sensitivity level for <name of information system> is <Low, Moderate, or High>.

In conducting this assessment, Federal Information Processing Standards Publication 199, *Standards for Security Categorization of Federal Information and Information Systems*, and National Institute of Standards and Technology (NIST) *Special Publication 800-60, Revision 1, Volumes 1 and 2: Guide for Mapping Types of Information Systems to Security Categories*, August 2008, have been taken into consideration. With this in mind, I am recommending that < name of information system > be assessed and authorized for operation at a < Low, Moderate, or High > sensitivity level.

APPROVED:_____ DATE: _____
< name of information owner >, < title of information owner >
< bureau, agency, or department name >

DISAPPROVED: _____ DATE: _____
Attachment < attach FIPS 199 document >

NATIONAL SECURITY SYSTEMS

The system categorization process for National Security Systems is similar to the NIST RMF methodology. The concepts of the two methodologies are essentially the same. For details on the particulars of the system categorization process for National Security Systems, you should refer to CNSSI No. 1253, March 15, 2012, Security Categorization and Control Selection For National Security Systems, Version 2.0 found at the following URL: http://www.cnss.gov/Assets/pdf/Final_CNSSI_1253.pdf (Figure 8.2).

SUMMARY

Determining the sensitivity level for the system can be the step that is most often performed incorrectly. System owners frequently overclassify the sensitivity of their system. Implementing unnecessary security controls and performing a more exhaustive assessment on a system that does not warrant it are a waste of time and money. Incorrect system sensitivity categorization could negatively affect an Inspector General review of an OMB Exhibit 300 review.

It is the ISSO's job to make sure that the system sensitivity level is properly determined. The ISSO and document prep team must have a solid understanding of the Confidentiality, Integrity, and Availability security objectives: to be able to evaluate the sensitivity of each with regard to a particular system and to elicit accurate and thorough information from the system owner on which this evaluation will be based.

Once the information has been gathered to make the determination about the correct sensitivity level, it must then be codified in a formal document that will be included in the final Security Package. An example of a FIPS 199 Profile memo

FIGURE 8.2

CNNSI No.1253. (For color version of this figure, the reader is referred to the online version of this chapter.)

has been provided, but if a template is already in use at your agency, that is the one you should use. The system owner should use an explanatory memo to get final signed approval of the sensitivity level that has been determined for the information system. Once the sensitivity level has been determined, there will be a clear picture of the level of effort required throughout the rest of the security control implementation and assessment tasks.

Addressing Security Awareness and Training

The ultimate value of life depends upon awareness and the power of contemplation rather than upon mere survival.
—Aristotle

TOPICS IN THIS CHAPTER

- Introduction and authorities
- Purpose of security awareness and training
- The Security Awareness and Training Plan
- Specialized security training
- Security awareness
- Security awareness and training checklist
- The awareness and training message
- Security awareness course evaluation

INTRODUCTION AND AUTHORITIES

Probably one of the most oft-overlooked pieces of a security program, security awareness and training is paramount to improving your agency's security posture. All systems slated for government authorization require that its users undergo annual security and privacy training. Therefore, each Security Package for a system undergoing assessment and authorization has to include a *Security Awareness and Training Plan*. The word "training" is used four times in FISMA, and §3544(b)(4) of FISMA specifically states that one of the agency responsibilities is to provide:

> *Security awareness training to inform personnel, including contractors and other users of information systems that support the operations and assets of the agency, of—(A) information security risks associated with their activities; and (B) their responsibilities in complying with agency policies and procedures designed to reduce these risks.*

Additionally, OMB Circular A-130 Revised refers to training requirements in numerous areas and §7 states:

> *Users of Federal information resources must have skills, knowledge, and training to manage information resources....*

§8 of OMB Circular A-130 Revised states:

> *Agencies will provide training and guidance as appropriate to all agency officials and employees and contractors regarding their Federal records management responsibilities.*

And §9 of OMB Circular A-130 Revised states:

> *Establish personnel security policies and develop training programs for Federal personnel associated with the design, operation, or maintenance of information systems.*

PURPOSE OF SECURITY AWARENESS AND TRAINING

Security training should be mandatory for all users including contractors. By making security training mandatory, users get the message that your agency is serious about security. If you advise your users of your expectations in regard to security, you can much more easily hold them accountable. Many users simply don't understand how rampant security threats are. A security awareness and training program forces users to become aware of these threats. By participating in security awareness and training, users come to realize that your agency cares about security. Even knowledge-able users need reminders about how to keep the systems secure. Employees leave the organization and new ones come along. It's possible that new employees may not have an understanding of the various bad actors that threaten information systems.

Security awareness and training are two different things. Security awareness refers to the marketing and promotion of security inside your agency. Security awareness programs put in place signs, booklets, posters, and e-mail reminders. Awareness programs serve as constant reminders that your agency or organization takes information security seriously and are motivational by nature.

Security training refers to actual security coursework. The course can take place in a classroom or via an online training program. Most users enjoy having the opportunity to learn new things. By assisting users in increasing their actual knowledge of security, they will naturally use this knowledge to help protect the enterprise infrastructure. Your best security stewards are really your employees. Your employees use and administer the systems that need to be secured. They understand how the systems are used, how they operate, and know them more intimately than anyone else. Your employees (and contractors) have invested a lot of time in your organization and likely care about doing the right thing. By training employees and contractors, you empower them to assist you in security compliance.

Since there are practical limitations to the amount of employee time you can take up, your information security and training program need to be keenly focused. The focus of your security awareness and training program should be to protect the confidentiality, integrity, and availability of your organization's information. Many

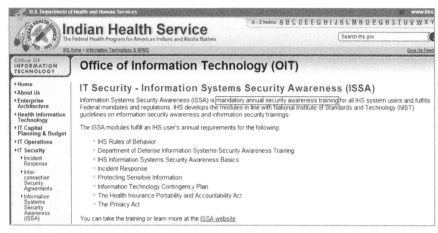

FIGURE 9.1

Example of mandatory security awareness training. (For color version of this figure, the reader is referred to the online version of this chapter.)

federal and DoD organization now make it mandatory to complete security awareness training before being granted access to the system. The training must be updated yearly or access is revoked. Most agencies make this requirement a policy. An example of such an agency policy from the Indian Health Service is depicted in Figure 9.1.

ELEMENTS OF THE SECURITY AWARENESS AND TRAINING PLAN

The *Security Awareness and Training Plan* should include accurate information about training that has taken place in the past and must also include information about any training that will take place in the future. A *Security Awareness and Training Plan* is simply a documented description of the security awareness and training program. A goal of the plan is to create a written record of all training classes and the users that participated in them. All training records should be securely archived either on paper or online.

In October 2003, the National Institute of Standards published [1] recommendations for security awareness and training programs. The document, *Building an Information Technology Security Awareness and Training Program Special Publication 800-50*, describes four critical elements that all security awareness and training programs should include:

1. Design and planning of the awareness and training program
2. Development of the awareness and training materials
3. Implementation of the awareness and training program
4. Measuring the effectiveness of your program and updating it

Your *Security Awareness and Training Plan* should discuss how your program addresses each of these four elements. As far as design and planning go, someone needs to own this responsibility. Who is that person and what are their qualifications? Security awareness and training can be designed and planned at an overall organizational level or on a system level. Most agencies these days are trending toward making this responsibility an overall agency responsibility so that it is centrally managed. However, there are no stipulations about whether this should take place on a system or agency level.

The training course itself should be firmly rooted in the agency information security program and policies. The training class can be developed in-house or can be contracted out. The *Security Awareness and Training Plan* should state who developed the course material and what their credentials are. One of the goals of security training is to modify user behavior. There are certain security safeguards that cannot be controlled by technology and can only be controlled by users doing the right thing. Influencing user behavior should be emphasized throughout the course.

In implementing the program, you'll need to decide whether the training should take place in person or online. Regardless of which way the course is implemented, you'll need to keep records on who has taken the course. If the course is given in person, you need to take attendance by having employees sign a sign-in sheet. The paper sign-in sheet records need to be securely archived because an auditor could ask to see it in the future. If the course is given online, your agency will need to plan a method for tracking which employees have taken the class and which ones haven't.

With widespread use of intranets, most agencies will find it easy to distribute a basic security training course electronically. A good online training course will quiz the user at the end of the course and offer the user feedback on missed questions. Some agencies require users to retake the course if they do not achieve a certain threshold of correct answers. You'll want an online course to track the users who have logged on and completed it. Users should be given a deadline to complete the course by a certain date or have their access removed.

For online training, most agencies advise employees of how to access the course and then mandate that it be taken by some certain date in the future. Most courses are announced 45 days in advance of the deadline. Online courses typically take between 1 and 2 hours for most employees to finish.

Note

To assist you in writing your plan, NIST SP 800-50 has a template for a *Security Awareness and Training Plan* in Appendix C. You can find NIST SP 800-50 at the following URL: http://www.csrc.nist.gov/publications/nistpubs/800-50/NIST-SP800-50.pdf.

SPECIALIZED SECURITY TRAINING

In implementing a training program, you need to take into consideration your employee's roles and responsibilities. There should be an overall basic training course that all employees participate in, and there should be specialized security training for the personnel that have actual security responsibilities. The following types of individuals should participate in at least one or more advanced security training courses per year:

- Information System Security Officers
- Network engineers
- Security engineers
- System administrators
- Developers writing code
- Chief Information Security Officers
- Mission assurance staff

To find out how well the training program works, it is a good idea to present the employees with a quiz at the beginning and end of each course. If the class is a good one, at the end of each course their score on the quiz should be much higher than it was before they took the course. You should also ask the employees to fill out an evaluation of the course after it is over. You'll want to try to find out if your employees felt the training material was appropriate and if they thought the instructor understood the material and was able to present it in a manner that was understandable.

SECURITY AWARENESS

Reminders work and that's what security awareness is about. However, security awareness requires some management. For the system that is undergoing assessment and authorization, the ISSO needs to ensure that awareness materials are made available. The awareness material may be e-mail reminders, pamphlets, or even tchotchkes. Security awareness materials should be attention getting. They need to be prominently displayed in highly trafficked areas such as near elevators. People notice awareness materials more easily if they are colorful and pleasing to look at. If an auditor walked through the user community offices, security awareness materials should be in plain sight. Typically security awareness is focused on one issue or a subset of issues. An example of an agency security awareness pamphlet can be found here: http://www.ihs.gov/ISSA/security_pamphlet_slick.pdf.

THE AWARENESS AND TRAINING MESSAGE

Since information security is a very broad topic, you will clearly not be able to train your employees in all aspects of it. Except for your actual information security engineers and staff, most of your end users have much work to do, and most of it is likely unrelated to security. Therefore, you need to selectively pick and choose the security topics you want your users to learn about. You will want to hone in on security topics that will have the greatest impact on improving the security posture of your organization. Make your employees aware of the greatest threats and how to avoid them.

Items that I recommend that you include in your security awareness and training program are the following:

- Review your agency's most important security policies.
- Explain what is meant by confidentiality, integrity, and availability.
- Explain the dangers of social engineering and instruct your users how you would like them to handle suspicious phone calls.
- Explain the concept of threats—both active and passive threats.
- Explain what vulnerabilities and safeguards are.
- Explain what spear-phishing is and how to identify it.
- Describe to your users what constitutes a safe password. Some users may not realize how easy it is to do dictionary attacks. Good passwords also include mixed-case characters and numbers.
- Explain any requirements for encryption. Are certain files supposed to be stored only in an encrypted state?
- Advise your users how they should report suspicious activity including viruses, denial of service attacks, and possible break-ins.
- Expectations for laptop security should be discussed. Should users lock them in their desks if they leave their laptops in the office overnight? Are there any security requirements for laptops when taken on business travel?
- Expectations for mobile devices should also be specified. Are users allowed to connect them to the corporate network? What types of mobile devices are allowed? Are users allowed to use their own devices?
- Personal firewall requirements should be discussed. Are they required or optional? Which ones are supported and who do users call for assistance with them?
- Explain what malicious code is and how it can impact systems.
- Describe expectations for posting on social network sites.
- Describe the Privacy Act and the penalties for noncompliance.
- Explain what Personally Identifiable Information (PII) is and how to safeguard it.
- Describe expectations for the use of removable media (e.g., flash drives).
- Personal use of laptops and desktops should be stated. Are employees allowed to send personal e-mails from agency accounts?

Chances are your agency has unique security requirements for users. New employees are joining the agency every day. Time goes by and people forget what they learned last year. You need to enlist your users in training on a regular schedule.

Your *Security Awareness and Training Plan* is simply a document that describes how security awareness and training is developed and implemented. The fact that you are already doing excellent security awareness and training is not enough. As far as security compliance is concerned, if it is not documented, it doesn't exist. You need to indicate who is responsible for updating the plan and who is responsible for implementing security awareness and training initiatives. For example, who makes the security awareness posters? Is it done in-house or does your agency use an outside graphic design company. Who puts up the posters? Who teaches the courses and where are they held? If it sounds simple, that's because it is.

SECURITY AWARENESS AND TRAINING CHECKLIST

The following checklist will help you ensure that you have not forgotten to note anything in your plan:

- Is the frequency of the training noted?
- Is specialized training for security personnel described?
- Are training classes for basic users described?
- Are instructors for the training classes noted?
- Is it noted that security training is tracked and logged?
- Is it noted that all courses are evaluated by the users?
- Are roles and responsibilities for security awareness noted?
- Are roles and responsibilities for security training noted?
- Does the plan indicate that a record is kept of user training participation?
- Does the plan indicate that users are assessed for their security knowledge after they undergo training?

SECURITY AWARENESS COURSE EVALUATION

Here is an example of an evaluation form for a security awareness and training course.

Topic: _____   Date: _____

Name: (Optional) _____   E-mail: < email address >

Strongly Disagree	Disagree	Neutral Opinion	Agree	Strongly Agree
1	2	3	4	5

Using the scale shown, please evaluate the awareness material by circling the most appropriate response.

I recently took a course on information security topics.	1 2 3 4 5
The information presented helped me understand my responsibilities.	1 2 3 4 5
The information was clear and easy to understand.	1 2 3 4 5
The information was useful in helping to understand the issues.	1 2 3 4 5
Information was included that I was not previously knowledgeable about.	1 2 3 4 5
The information was useful to me in helping me to understand my security responsibilities.	1 2 3 4 5
I would benefit from more training similar to this.	1 2 3 4 5
The information effectively explained the topics.	1 2 3 4 5
Did you have questions about the material presented?	Yes/No
If yes, have you received a response to your question?	Yes/No

If no, please explain:

Are there any other topics on information security that you would like to see covered? Yes/No What topics?

SUMMARY

Security awareness and training are important parts of any information security program. In essence, the training and awareness program serve to facilitate and improve the security compliance process and the overall security posture of the organization. A primary goal of security training and awareness is to change user behavior. Specialized security training needs to be targeted at the variety of audiences within that overall group (such as developers, ISSOs, and the network operations support group), and feedback from the individuals undergoing training helps to refine and improve the overall program. The methods by which the awareness and training program will be executed need to be documented in the *Security Awareness and Training Plan*.

Reference

[1] Mark Wilson, Joan Hash. *NIST Special Publication 800-50, Building an Information Technology Security Awareness and Training Program*, National Institute of Standards and Technology; October 2003.

Addressing Rules of Behavior

10

Rules are made for people who aren't willing to make up their own.
—Chuck Yeager

TOPICS IN THIS CHAPTER

- Implementing Rules of Behavior
- Rules for internal and external users
- What rules to include
- Consequences of noncompliance
- Rules of behavior checklist

INTRODUCTION

Rules of Behavior describe security controls associated with user responsibilities and include expectations of behavior for the following security policies, standards, and procedures. Users must agree to abide by Rules of Behavior before they are allowed access to the system. Rules of Behavior, and your plans for implementing them, have to be clearly articulated in the Security Package.

Clearly, users need to know what these rules of the road are before they can be expected to agree to them. A signed agreement should be verified before giving the user access. All users of any information system being authorized for government use (including contractors) should agree to the rules.

Users may already have access to the agency network or have other logins to other applications. Therefore, the Rules of Behavior should be unique and specific to the information system that is being assessed and authorized. Just because a user has agreed to rules for other applications doesn't mean they have agreed to rules for that is undergoing assessment and authorization.

IMPLEMENTING RULES OF BEHAVIOR

The Rules of Behavior can be implemented either on a paper form or online. In some cases where you are giving a user access to a general support system, and they do not yet have an account of any kind, a paper form may be the only possibility. If a user already is set up on the enterprise network, and has a private key from an internal Certificate Authority, you can have the user sign rules for access to a new application with their private key. There are administrative advantages to having users sign the rules online. By signing the rules online, administrators can more easily track who has signed them. If paper forms are used, the forms need to be collected and archived in a central and secure place with limited access. The ISSO is responsible for either keeping the rules secure or designating an appropriate staff person to store and secure them.

RULES FOR INTERNAL AND EXTERNAL USERS

Rules of Behavior for internal users are rules that you want your own employees (and your own contractors) to follow. Rules of Behavior for external users are rules that you want outsiders (who are not part of your staff) to follow. External users could be customers, partners, or anyone that is not part of your organization that is accessing your system through a remote interface.

There are multiple reasons why internal and external users might be treated differently. You know much more about your internal users than your external users. You know what information security policies your internal users are required to follow. You may not know much about the security policies of external organizations. For example, for external users, you might not know what browsers are supported and required by the security policy of the external organization. For your own organization, whatever browser that has been installed on your desktop by the IT department is likely the agency-approved browser and has likely already been configured for the correct version of SSL. For external users, you likely have no idea what browser they are using and how it has been configured. Therefore, you may want to include the following rule for an external user, but not for an internal user:

> *You must ensure that Web browsers use Secure Socket Layer (SSL) version 3.0 (or higher) and Transport Layer Security (TLS) 1.0 (or higher). SSL and TLS must use a minimum of 256-bit, encryption.*

Other browser rules for external users might be:

> *You must ensure that web browsers warn about invalid site certificates. You must ensure that web browsers check for server certificate revocation. You must ensure that web browsers check for signatures on downloaded files. You must ensure that web browsers do not allow the navigation of sub-frames across different domains.*

The following rule might not be appropriate for an external user and you may want to only include this rule for internal users:

> *You must challenge unauthorized personnel in their work area.*

If the system contains Personally Identifiable Information (PII), you may want to inform external users about the violations of the Privacy Act:

Your access to systems and networks owned by <Agency Name> is governed by, and subject to, all Federal laws, including, but not limited to, the Privacy Act, 5 U.S.C. 552a, if the applicable <Company Name> system maintains individual Privacy Act information. Your access to <Agency Name> systems constitutes your consent to the retrieval and disclosure of the information within the scope of your authorized access, subject to the Privacy Act, and applicable State and Federal laws.

It's possible that you may have a special support number for external users. Therefore, you might have a rule for external users that refers the users to a customer support number such as:

If you notice any suspicious activity, please report this to the Central Customer Service Center at 202-###-####.

While most rules for internal and external users will be the same, you should customize each set of rules if there are any differences at all between the two rule sets.

WHAT RULES TO INCLUDE

Each information system requires a unique set of rules—rules that apply to one system may not apply to another. Database systems may require different rules than, say, an application meant for mobile devices. Systems that process financial transactions may require an entirely different set of rules. Rules for a desktop system and the enterprise network may be vastly different than, say, rules for an Employee Resource Processing (ERP) system.

Although some rules are redundant because they simply agree to abide by specific citations of the agency security policy, it is worth listing them to emphasize their importance and to create an accountability log in the form of a user signature. To help you understand the types of rules that should be listed, some sample rules are listed in Tables 10.1–10.4.

Rules for applications and general support systems

Different applications may require different rules. The rules in Table 10.1 can be adapted to most applications, servers, and databases. Some rules from Tables 10.2 through 10.4 may also be appropriate for applications, servers, and databases.

Additional rules for mobile devices

Many of the rules in Table 10.1 also apply to mobile devices—for example, the rules for passwords—and are not repeated in Table 10.2. Additional rules that mobile devices such as smartphones and tablets may require are listed in Table 10.2.

Table 10.1 Rules of Behavior for Applications and General Support Systems

Rules of Behavior for the Enterprise <Name> System

I agree to:

Use an eight-character password that includes mixed cases, characters, numbers, and letters;
Ensure that my web browser window is closed before navigating to other sites/domains;
Protect my user ID from unauthorized disclosure;
Refrain from sharing my password with others;
Refrain from trying to subvert the security of any application;
Refrain from trying to use any other account except my own;
Refrain from representing myself as somebody else;
Refrain from disclosing data presented by the application to unauthorized individuals;
Report any bugs to the information system owner;
Report any vulnerabilities discovered to the information system owner;
Report suspicious activity or use of agency IT resources to the ISSO;
Use the application only for its stated purpose;
Follow the stated logon and logoff procedures;
Change my password every 90 days;
Complete security awareness training and education classes as required;
Retrieve all hard-copy printouts in a timely fashion;
Abide by security awareness notices and reminders;
Abide by all agency security policies;
Safeguard resources against waste, loss, abuse, unauthorized users, and misappropriation;
Challenge unknown personnel who do not display an identification or visitor's badge.

ACCEPTANCE AND SIGNATURE

I have read the above *Rules of Behavior for* the <Name> System. By my electronic acceptance and/or signature below, I acknowledge and agree that my access to the <Name> Systems and its networks is covered by, and subject to, such Rules. Further, I acknowledge and accept that any violation by me of these Rules may subject me to civil and/or criminal actions and that <Agency Name> retains the right, at its sole discretion, to terminate, cancel or suspend my access rights to the <Agency Name> systems at any time, without notice.

_____
Print Name

_____   _____
Signature   Date

Additional rules for laptops and desktop systems

Many of the rules in Table 10.2 also apply to laptops—for example, the rules for antivirus software. Additional rules that laptops may require are listed in Table 10.3.

Table 10.2 Rules of Behavior for Mobile Devices

Rules of Behavior for Mobile Devices

I agree to:

Disable device synchronization capabilities when not needed;
Register my mobile device with the Office of Information Security;
Use the approved secure remote access VPN to connect to the corporate network;
Ensure that any sensitive information that I put on my smartphone/tablet is encrypted;
Refrain from storing Classified information on my mobile device;
Run agency-approved antivirus software on my mobile device;
Keep the antivirus signatures on my mobile device up to date;
Connect only to approved wireless networks;
Report any suspicious activity that I become aware of.

ACCEPTANCE AND SIGNATURE

I have read the above *Rules of Behavior* my mobile device. By my electronic acceptance and/or signature below, I acknowledge and agree that my use of my mobile device is covered by, and subject to, such Rules. Further, I acknowledge and accept that any violation by me of these Rules may subject me to civil and/or criminal actions and that <Agency Name> retains the right, at its sole discretion, to confiscate my mobile device at any time, without notice.

_____
Print Name
_____   _____
Signature   Date

Additional rules for Privileged Users

All the rules in Table 10.3 apply to Privileged Users; however, there are additional rules that Privileged Users should agree to, some of which are listed in Table 10.4. Rules from Table 10.1 also apply to Privileged Users and are not repeated in Table 10.4.

CONSEQUENCES OF NONCOMPLIANCE

Somewhere in the Rules of Behavior, consequences for noncompliance should be described. Possible consequences might be:

- Disciplinary action (unspecified)
- Mandatory security awareness training
- A supervisory warning

Table 10.3 Rules of Behavior for Laptops

Rules of Behavior for Laptops

I agree to:

Make sure I do not leave my laptop unattended in a public place;
Use an approved cable lock to lock my laptop to my desk;
Make sure that approved laptop recovery software is installed on my laptop;
Turn on the screen lock when I step away from my desk;
Run an agency-approved personal firewall on my laptop;
Refrain from installing unapproved hardware (e.g., Wi-Fi card) on my laptop;
Refrain from disabling mandatory antivirus software;
Connect to the agency network using the approved remote connection software and procedures;
Abide by the agency limited personal use policy;
Refrain from e-mailing information in the clear over the Internet;
Refrain from downloading freeware and shareware without authorized permission;
Refrain from using my system to access pornography;
Refrain from using my system for illegal activities;
Refrain from using my system for commercial profit-making activities;
Abide by all federal copyright laws;
Refrain from violating any software license agreements;
Report any security incidents I become aware of;
Refrain from disclosing my private keys;
Report the loss of my private key;
Protect agency resources from unauthorized disclosure, modification, and deletion.

ACCEPTANCE AND SIGNATURE

I have read the above *Rules of Behavior* my laptop. By my electronic acceptance and/or signature below, I acknowledge and agree that my use of my laptop is covered by, and subject to, such Rules. Further, I acknowledge and accept that any violation by me of these Rules may subject me to civil and/or criminal actions and that <Agency Name> retains the right, at its sole discretion, to revoke the use of my laptop at any time, without notice.

Print Name

Signature   Date

- Revocation of a security clearance
- Termination

The noncompliance consequences should be well thought out. For example, it may not be in the best interest of the agency to terminate key personnel for leaving a paper document overnight on a printer. Each case of noncompliance should be evaluated individually to determine the magnitude of the risk to the agency.

Table 10.4 Rules of Behavior for Privileged Users

Rules of Behavior for Privileged Users

I agree to:

Refrain from programming login IDs or passwords into scripts or routines;
Refrain from disclosing account or login information without proper approvals;
Refrain from disclosing the *administrator* and *root* passwords;
Disclose user passwords in accordance with the agency security policy;
Terminate user accounts according to the agency security policy;
Ensure that all system configuration changes are documented;
Submit configuration changes through the change management configuration change approval process;
Install all security patches as required;
Monitor and review firewall, intrusion detection, and system logs in a timely manner;
Configure systems to abide by the agency security policies;
Ensure that *groups* and *netgroups* are properly registered with the LDAP server;
Assist users with security help as required;
Ensure that servers log appropriate security events;
Ensure that I configure systems to be in compliance with agency security policies;
Refrain from inserting backdoors for any reason including systems administration;
Refrain from altering data except in accordance with my job responsibilities;
Refrain from disclosing the remote login procedures to unauthorized users.

ACCEPTANCE AND SIGNATURE

I have read the above *Rules of Behavior* my privileged users. By my electronic acceptance and/or signature below, I acknowledge and agree that my position of employment is covered by, and subject to, such Rules. Further, I acknowledge and accept that any violation by me of these Rules may subject me to civil and/or criminal actions and that <Agency Name> retains the right, at its sole discretion, to terminate my role as a privileged user at any time, without notice.

_____
Print Name

_____   _____
Signature   Date

RULES OF BEHAVIOR CHECKLIST

To ensure that your Rules of Behavior is deemed acceptable by auditors, use the following checklist to ensure that you have not forgotten anything:

- Have all users signed a statement agreeing that they have read and understand the Rules of Behavior?
- Are the consequences of noncompliance stated in the Rules of Behavior?
- Are signed Rules of Behavior archived?
- Does the ISSO know where to find the archived Rules of Behavior?

- Are paper-based Rules of Behavior protected from fire and flood threats?
- Are noncompliance breaches of Rules of Behavior treated as a security incident?
- If private keys are used for signing an online rules form, are the private keys properly protected?
- Are users required to report if their private keys are lost or stolen?
- Have Privileged Users been identified?
- Are the Rules of Behavior published in a place where they can be reviewed by the users after they have been previously agreed to?

SUMMARY

Rules of Behavior are important to any organization because they formally set the standards by which users are expected to conduct themselves. Typically, Rules of Behavior control actions that cannot be controlled by technological means. Rules of Behavior also set forth the consequences of noncompliance. Without outlining Rules of Behavior, it is hard to hold users accountable for their actions, and it's difficult to expect that they are employing basic principles of security while using the organization's information resources. Users need to be informed of the Rules of Behavior upfront, and they need to understand that by using the information system, they are agreeing to abide by the rules.

Developing an Incident Response Plan

11

It has long been a grave question whether any government...can be strong enough to maintain its existence in great emergencies.
—Abraham Lincoln

TOPICS IN THIS CHAPTER

- Purpose and applicability
- Policies, procedures, and guidelines
- Reporting framework
- Roles and responsibilities
- Definitions
- Incident handling
- Forensic investigations
- Incident types
- Incident Response Plan checklist
- Security Incident Reporting Form

INTRODUCTION

All IT organizations that take cyber security seriously should have an *Incident Response Plan* whether their systems are candidates for FISMA compliance or not. The goal of the Incident Response Plan is to describe the incident response process that the information security response team plans to follow if an incident were to occur.

Due to its unscheduled nature and its potential for damage, a security incident can predispose an otherwise competent staff into immediate anxiety and frustration. A well thought-out Incident Response Plan helps retain order and efficient organizational processes during a stressful situation. Every Incident Response Plan should contain certain key instructional elements and any assessment audit team may fail your Incident Response Plan if any of these elements are missing. Though your plan can include more information than the required key elements, be sure at the very minimum to include a section on each of the following:

- Purpose and applicability
- Policies, procedures, and guidelines
- Reporting framework

- Roles and responsibilities
- Definitions
- Incident handling
- Incident types
- Incident Reporting Form

If time permits, you may also want to include information on how to detect incidents and how to proceed with forensic investigations.

PURPOSE AND APPLICABILITY

Even though it may seem obvious that your document should include a stated purpose, it is important not to forget this section. If you don't say what information system(s) the Incident Response Plan is applicable to, an assessment team could come to the conclusion that an Incident Response Plan for the system that is up for audit does not exist. The name of the Incident Response Plan should be consistent with the name of all the other document plans in your Security Package, and it is a good idea to state the information system in the document title. For example, if the goal is to authorize an information system known as System ABC, make sure your Incident Response Plan is titled *Incident Response Plan for System ABC*.

POLICIES, PROCEDURES, AND GUIDELINES

In this section, you will want to cite the agency security policies, the agency standards, and the guidelines that the incident response team follows and adheres to. You should list the formal policy document names in their entirety and include information on where these documents can be found (e.g., the Web URL on the agency intranet). Do not confuse policies with incident handling procedures. Policies describe what the rules are, and the incident handling procedures describe how to follow those rules. If your agency has an agency-wide *Incident Response Manual* or handbook, you will want to list this document as reference material in this section. You should also include references to any of the following federal mandates that you follow:

- The Office of Management and Budget (OMB) Circular A-130, Appendix III, *Security of Federal Automated Information Resources*, specifies that federal agencies will "Ensure there is a capability to provide help to users when a security incident occurs in the system and to share information concerning common vulnerabilities and threats."
- Critical Infrastructure Protection (CIP): Presidential Decision Directive 63 (PDD-63) directs that each department and agency shall develop plans for protecting its own critical infrastructure. Accordingly, the <Agency Name> has

created the < Agency Name > CSIRC to provide a 24×7 single point of contact (POC) for computer security incidents detected within the < Agency Name >.

- OMB Memo M-07-16, Safeguarding Against and Responding to the Breach of Personally Identifiable Information.
- The < Agency Name > Security Manual < official document name > directs the < Agency Name > and the < Agency Name > Inspector General to establish a capability that will "serve as the first tier of incident response and the investigative and reporting body…" for the < Agency Name >.
- The CSIRC is sponsored by the < Agency Name > Deputy Commissioner for Modernization and Chief Information Officer and is designed to be proactive in preventing, detecting, and responding to computer security incidents targeting < Agency Name >'s enterprise Information Technology (IT) assets.

REPORTING FRAMEWORK

Your incident response-reporting framework establishes who should be contacted and the order in which escalation occurs. Depending on the agency requirements, it may be necessary to establish time frames for escalation. If your agency does not require specific incident escalation time frames, you can still establish these thresholds in your Incident Response Plan if your information system owner and ISSO require it. Time frames for escalation often are based on the severity of the incident and the extensiveness of the damage—the more systems that are impacted, the more resources you will likely need to resolve the incident.

Most federal agencies have a Computer Security Incident Response Center (CSIRC). The agency CSIRC provides centralized incident response services and coordinates incident response activities agency wide. In developing an Incident Response Plan for FISMA compliance, you'll need to make sure that the Incident Response Plan for each unique system is consistent with the processes already established by the respective agency CSIRC. The Incident Response Plan developed for the Security Package does not replace the process already established by the CSIRC—it augments it and embellishes it with the particulars relevant to the unique information system. Essentially, the Incident Response Plan should be an extension of the agency-wide Incident Response Plan.

Agency CSIRCs are required to report significant security incidents to the United States Computer Emergency Readiness Team (US-CERT). However, before that occurs, the incident should be reported up through the bureau, and agency CSIRC, as depicted in Figure 11.1.

It's important to describe an escalation process in your plan that is consistent with your described response framework. An incident could occur at night when some of the staff is unavailable, and sometimes people do not respond to e-mail or cell phones if it is off hours. The person who detects the incident needs to know who to report it to and how long to wait to escalate it if there is no response. Even with a quick response, security policies may require your incident response team to escalate high-impact

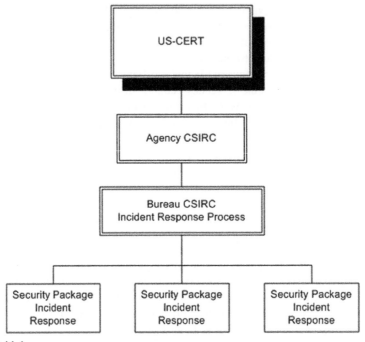

FIGURE 11.1

Incident Response Plan as an extension of agency CSIRC.

incidents up through the escalation framework according to particular time frames. If escalation time frames are required by your security policy and your security standards, be sure to include them.

ROLES AND RESPONSIBILITIES

In this section of the Incident Response Plan, you'll want to state specifically what the expected responsibilities are for the different levels of the response framework. You should include as an appendix to your Incident Response Plan, a contact list that includes every person, and each organization, that has documented responsibilities in the plan.

Agency CSIRC

Each agency CSIRC will have unique responsibilities. You should list high-level bullets of the expected responsibilities of your agency CSIRC in your Incident Response Plan. Typical CSIRC responsibilities are as follows:

- Develop and maintain the agency computer security incident response capability policy and procedures

- Maintain an incident response capability to ensure timely reporting of security incidents
- Coordinate the remediation of incidents agency wide
- Provide implementation guidance for processes and procedures
- Establish procedures to ensure timely reporting of security incidents
- Analysis of net flow data during incident investigations
- Report significant computer security incidents to US-CERT as soon as possible but no more than 1 hour after detection with a follow-up report every 4 hours thereafter until the incident is resolved
- Obtain assistance from external sources, or US-CERT, if necessary
- Report minor incidents in a monthly incident report to the agency CIO and CISO
- Report all planned penetration testing and vulnerability assessments to the CISO
- Write lessons learned and follow-up reports on agency computer security incidents
- Implement tools and processes supporting the agency computer security incident response capability and procedures to collect and safeguard evidence for use in legal or administrative functions
- Distribute advisories and vulnerability bulletins received from the CSIRC to appropriate agency CSIRC personnel and designated points of contact at their respective sites.

US-CERT monitors net flow data for all U.S. federal agencies and coordinates incident response across the government. CSIRCS and ISSOs should not hesitate to call upon US-CERT for assistance. It is better to ask for assistance, and close a security incident quickly, than to try to resolve an incident without assistance, and allow an intruder to remain on your network for a long period of time. The US-CERT Web site can be found at the following URL: http://www.us-cert.gov.

Information system owner an ISSO

System owners usually designate an ISSO to manage day-to-day cyber security responsibilities. While processing a security incident, the ISSO should keep the information system owner apprised of the status of the incident. The system Incident Response Plan should list the names and contact information for both the information system owner and the ISSO. Typical responsibilities of the ISSO include the following:

- Identify and assign a computer security incident response team (CSIRT) that interacts with the CSIRC to resolve security incidents
- Ensure that the CSIRT has implemented procedures to reduce the risk of, and minimize the damage of, a computer security incident
- Ensure that the CSIRT complies with:
    - Agency computer security incident response policies
    - Agency Security Awareness Training
    - Agency security auditing and record retention procedures
    - Agency IT standards
    - The agency security program

- OMB Circular No. A-130, Appendix III
- The Federal Information Security Management Act of 2002
- Use guidance from the National Institute of Standards and Technology, Special Publication 800-61, Revision 2, *Computer Security Incident Handling Guide*
- Ensure that the information system undergoing security assessment and authorization has a formal computer security Incident Response Plan to include the timely identification, detection, management, containment, capture, and safeguarding of evidence
- Ensure that users of the information system understand how to report suspected security incidents to the information system security incident point of contact
- Ensure that security incident information will be logged and tracked by reporting, completing, and submitting the agency *IT Security Incident Reporting Form* to the CSIRC
- Appoint a CSIRT point of contact that acts as a central coordination point for the agency CSIRC.

Incident Response Manager

The security incident point of contact (POC) for the information system is known as the Incident Response Manager. The ISSO may designate someone as the Incident Response Manager; however, the ISSO may also choose to act as the Incident Response Manager. The Incident Response Manager should coordinate notification and escalation and ensure that the incident response team is properly assembled. The Incident Response Manager typically holds the following responsibilities:

- Evaluate known threats and vulnerabilities to ascertain if additional safeguards are needed and brief the ISSO as appropriate
- Develop procedures to receive information on security incidents and common vulnerabilities from the agency CSIRC
- Determine the incident priority level of security incidents
- Determine the incident impact to the information system
- Perform appropriate and immediate investigation of every security incident, whether the event was detected by the system or reported by a user
- Establish and implement tools and processes supporting the computer security incident response capability's procedures to ensure timely reporting of security incidents
- Fill out the *Security Incident Reporting Form*
- Report security incidents in accordance with agency security policy and standards to the ISSO and agency CSIRC as appropriate
- Report minor computer security incidents in a monthly security incident report to the agency CSIRC on a regular monthly basis
- Forward reports and documents pertaining to computer security incidents such as incident summary, lessons learned, and follow-up reports, to the CSIRT upon the receipt of the information

- Appoint a backup POC to take their own place in the event of absence
- Notify the CSIRT and ISSO when the Incident Response Plan changes

DEFINITIONS

Your Incident Response Plan should include a section on definitions, and in it you should define any significant terms used in the plan. Some definitions that you'll want to include are incident, threat, exposure, vulnerability, event, and incident severities.

Incident

If your agency has its own unique definition of a security incident, you should use it. Various definitions I have seen used in reputable Incident Response Plans include:

- **Definition 1** A security incident is a violation of a security policy for a system, network, telecommunications system, or facility.
- **Definition 2** A security incident is any real or suspected adverse event in relation to the security of computers or computer networks.
- **Definition 3** A security incident is any compromised or suspected compromised system; any type of attack or preattack reconnaissance levied on or from a computer resource; or misuse of IT resources (such as chain letters, unauthorized access, and virus hoaxes), or any other anomalous activities detected.

The National Institute of Standards and Technology makes a distinction between system events and adverse events (aka security incidents). According to NIST SP 800-61, Revision 2:

> An event *is any observable occurrence in a system or network. Events include a user connecting to a file share, a server receiving a request for a web page, a user sending email, and a firewall blocking a connection attempt.* Adverse events *are events with a negative consequence, such as system crashes, packet floods, unauthorized use of system privileges, unauthorized access to sensitive data, and execution of malware that destroys data.*

In the section on "Definitions" of your plan, I suggest you make a distinction between the two. You are free to use the NIST definition if your agency has not yet standardized on events and incidents.

If your agency has a FISMA compliance handbook or guidelines, there should be a section in it on incident response. You should refer to that section when documenting your definitions and follow the recommended guidance. I usually use the rule of thumb that if the agency-wide guidance is lacking a definition or guidance, then the Incident Response Plan authors have the liberty to become creative and incorporate their own recommendations.

Impact, notification, and escalation

Although all security incidents should be taken seriously, they may not all have the same severity. Your Incident Response Plan should define how incident severities will be determined and what this means in terms of incident handling. Some of the things that you will want to take into consideration when recommending severity levels are the following items:

- Number of sites or networks affected
- Importance of systems affected
- Number of agency systems affected by this incident
- Number of other agency systems vulnerable to the same exploit
- Consistency with the latest vulnerability scan of the target system
- Known countermeasures and existence of tested vendor patches/hot-fixes
- Entry point of the incident (e.g., network, telephone line, router, application)
- Potential damage resulting from the incident
- Estimated time to close out the incident
- Resources required to handle the incident
- Business impact of system(s) involved
- Exposure to agency data
- Potential of incident to spread to multiple sites/systems.

NIST has defined severity categories and escalation thresholds in the publication, *Computer Security Incident Handling Guide*, NIST Special Publication 800-61, Revision 2, August 2012. Many agencies may elect to use the NIST guidelines verbatim from p. 2 and p. 25 of this document. I have taken the NIST guidelines and made a few modifications as depicted in Table 11.1. The time frames listed in Table 11.1 should be interpreted as the maximum amount of time allowed to pass

Table 11.1 Incident Response Escalation Time Frames

	Escalation Notification Increments		
Type of Incident	**High Sensitivity System**	**Moderate Sensitivity System**	**Low Sensitivity System**
Root or administrator compromise	15 minutes	30 minutes	1 hour
Unauthorized data modification	15 minutes	30 minutes	2 hours
Unauthorized access to sensitive data	15 minutes	1 hour	1 hour
Unauthorized access to user data	30 minutes	2 hours	4 hours
Services unavailable	30 minutes	2 hours	4 hours
Annoyance	60 minutes	As required	As required

till the next escalation action is taken, and the time frames listed in Table 11.1 are examples and are not mandatory government escalation time frames. For example, if an incident for a high-sensitivity system is reported, and there is no response after 15 minutes from the authority it was reported to, it should be escalated to an even higher authority. If the system has a lower sensitivity level, it makes sense to waiting a longer period of time before escalating the issue to a higher authority.

In your Incident Response Plan, you should create a way to categorize the severity of an incident based on the impact that the incident will have on your organization. An example is to designate the severity of security incidents as High, Medium, or Low, based on the type of system compromised, and the extent of the network penetration. In general, unauthorized access to security systems such as firewalls is more critical than unauthorized access to user workstations. Therefore, unauthorized access to firewalls may be considered High priority and unauthorized access to a user workstation may be considered Low priority. However, if the unauthorized access to user workstations is network wide, and in multiple geographic locations, this type of compromise in fact might be considered High priority. The combinations of the type of different systems that can be compromised, and the extent of the compromise, are vast. Due to all the possible combinations of compromise, it is difficult to describe the severity of impact for every situation. Deciding on the severity of impact is a qualitative decision and a judgment call at best. In general, if the impact to the business mission is Low, the severity of the impact is Low. Similarly, if the impact to the business mission is high, the severity of the impact is High. On p. 33 of NIST SP 800-61, Revision 2 there are some nice definitions of different impact categories.

Providing guidelines for escalation and response speeds up the decision-making process when administrators are challenged with an anxiety-provoking security crisis. In conjunction with the time frames, your plan should also establish what sort of action should be taken as far as notification to a higher authority goes. When does the system owner, data owners, and CIO get notified? Are they notified at the same time as the agency CSIRC? If your agency security policies do not offer guidelines on reporting, the information system ISSO will need to make the appropriate recommendations.

You need to be clear as to who is part of the CSIRT. The CSIRT should be described in your plan with key personnel identified. Security incidents are never convenient and some members of the incident response team might not be immediately available. Your Incident Response Plan should include detailed contact lists that include home phone numbers, cell phone numbers, and e-mail addresses for everyone that is part of the CSIRT. I also suggest putting in some contact information for outside consultants that specialize in incident handling in the event that you require assistance.

INCIDENT HANDLING

Incident handling refers to the operational procedures used to actually manipulate the incident and purge it from your systems. If your agency already has detailed instructions for incident handling, it is acceptable simply to republish those instructions in the respective section of your plan. If you republish agency-wide incident handling instructions, be sure to state what publication or document these instructions come from, and that your incident response team is required to follow these instructions. If agency-wide incident handling instructions do not exist, that means the Incident Response Plan author should take the time to develop these instructions.

Something that is very important to keep in mind while processing a security incident is that once a system has been compromised, you cannot trust any of the information on it. A compromised system has lost its integrity. You don't know which files have been altered, and it isn't practical to perform a file by file comparison. Systems that have been compromised will ultimately have to be rebuilt.

OMB Memo 07-16 has very specific incident handling and reporting requirements and you'll want to review these requirements while you're in the process of developing your Incident Response Plan. You can find this OMB memo at the following URL: http://www.whitehouse.gov/sites/default/files/omb/memoranda/fy2007/m07-16.pdf.

Detecting an incident

Your agency may require that you include some information on how to detect a security incident. Not all suspicious activities are incidents.

Suspicious accounts and logins are often characterized by:

- Single or multiple unsuccessful login attempts
- Unexplained or suspicious entries in system log files
- Questionable user permissions on accounts
- Multiple successful login attempts in a short amount of time on multiple systems

Suspicious activities that could indicate an incident has occurred, include:

- Unexplained modification or deletion of data
- Unauthorized creation of new user accounts
- User accounts with unauthorized increased privileges
- Accounts without passwords
- Activities that breach existing security policies
- Unexplained discovery of new files or unfamiliar filenames
- Recurring viruses that keep coming back after they have been eradicated
- Unexpected and unusual file sizes and/or timestamps
- Unauthorized or unexplained attempts to write to system files
- Unexplained attempts to make changes in system files
- Detection of unauthorized mirrored sites
- Domain Name System (DNS) cache corruption
- Documents that contain malicious code or unauthorized macros
- Unauthorized modification of Web sites
- Unauthorized Access Control Lists (ACLs) on routers
- Unauthorized ports open on firewalls

- Unauthorized source or destination addresses for authorized ports
- Connectionless Transmission Control Protocol (TCP) traffic
- Missing data, files, or applications
- Unexpected processes running
- Attempted connections to ports that are not typically used
- Activation of a system alarm or similar indication of an intrusion
- Denial of service on an otherwise available system
- Multiple users logged into a single account
- Entire system failures or restarts
- Unsatisfactory system performance (e.g., system is slow or locking up)
- Unauthorized operation of programs or processes
- Appearance of new files on the system, previously unknown to users or administrators
- Applications that do not execute properly, or as expected
- Suspiciously high network traffic
- E-mail server functionality loss or complete e-mail system failure
- Unusual network, system, or user activity occurring at "abnormal" operating hours

Containment and eradication

Upon discovery of a security incident, it is very important to prevent it from spreading to other systems and networks. You should always try to contain an incident before you try to eradicate it. Somewhere in your Incident Response Plan you should state that you have a containment strategy and describe what it is based on.

Each type of security incident may require a completely different containment strategy. Various measures that can be used to contain security incidents and eradicate the intruder include:

- Blocking all incoming network traffic on border routers
- Blocking networks and incoming traffic on firewalls
- Blocking particular services (e.g., ftp, telnet) and ports on firewalls
- Disconnecting infected systems from the network
- Shutting down the infected system
- Locking compromised accounts
- Changing passwords on compromised systems
- Isolating specific network segments

Before you power down an infected system, you should consider the fact that once a system is powered off, the live memory is no longer available for forensic investigations. There are various forensic tools that can analyze live memory and recover data that could be useful to an investigation. In the course of an investigation, a conscientious decision should be made on whether or not you want to proceed with memory forensics.

Before you attempt to remove and overwrite files associated with an incident, decisions need to be made on whether the evidence should be saved for forensic investigation. In fact, if the goal is to catch the perpetrator and turn the evidence over to a prosecuting attorney, system administrators should not even open files that they suspect have been tampered with. Once you open a file, you change the read time on the file which means that you have corrupted the evidence. The incident response team should report the facts to the agency legal counsel and take into consideration their advisement before proceeding with forensics. Usually, it is not worth the time and expense it takes to find out who the perpetrator is. However, before conceding that the intruder will not be caught, the question should at least be asked if evidence preservation is required.

During the containment and eradication process, the CSIRT will need to make various decisions on how to proceed. You may want to stipulate in your Incident Response Plan that the CSIRT will make the following determinations while processing the incident:

- Determine which systems, applications, and networks have been affected
- Determine whether to inform users that a security incident has occurred
- Determine to what extent the affected systems should remain operational
- Determine the scope, impact, and damage to the compromised systems
- Determine if the prescribed course of action will destroy the evidence
- Determine if other ISSOs should be informed of the incident

Recovery and closure

As mentioned earlier, all compromised systems need to be rebuilt. Whether they will be rebuilt on the originally compromised system or built on a new system is one of the decisions that will need to be made. Before rebuilding the system, if the decision has been made not to proceed with a forensic investigation, a regular backup should be performed. The operating system should be reinstalled, hardened, and have relevant patches installed prior to installing any applications.

When an incident is closed, both the CSIRT and CSIRC should be in agreement that the incident has been completely resolved and the affected systems have been recovered and restored. The Security Incident Reporting Form should be updated to indicate the incident has been closed.

After an incident has been closed, the CSIRT should have a meeting to discuss lessons learned. It is always worthwhile to document the lessons learned. The types of questions to be answered and documented in the lessons learned meeting include:

- Exactly what happened and at what times?
- How well did the CSIRT perform in dealing with the incident?
- Was the CSIRC responsive to the CSIRT's needs?
- Were the documented procedures followed? Were they adequate?
- What information was needed sooner?
- Were any steps or actions taken that might have inhibited the recovery?

- What would the CSIRT do differently the next time a similar incident occurs?
- What is the monetary estimate for the amount of damage the incident cost?
- How many hours did it take to resolve the incident?
- What corrective actions can prevent similar incidents in the future?
- What additional tools or resources are needed to detect, analyze, and mitigate future incidents?

Documenting lessons learned can help improve the ability to more efficiently handle security incidents in the future. It may also provide justification for the information system owner's security budget to procure new assets like intrusion detection systems and security incident management consoles.

FORENSIC INVESTIGATIONS

Not all security incidents will require forensic investigations. In the event that a forensic investigation is required, it will expedite the process if the course of action is planned out up front. Forensic investigations require that the evidence be preserved in its original state. Any modifications made to the system containing the evidence could be construed as tainting of the evidence.

The way to preserve the evidence is to perform a bitstream backup. A bitstream backup is a special kind of backup that replicates the evidence exactly without making any changes to the original data. When preserving evidence, it is important not to change the timestamps of the data that indicate the access times. You don't want to change the read access of the data because it might have been the intruder who last read the data and created the last-read access timestamp. You also want to preserve the file slack, which is the data stored in swap files or memory buffers. Therefore, if a forensic investigation is to take place, you need specific policies and procedures. If a forensic investigation should occur, you may want to stipulate that the CSIRT follows these policies:

- Only tools that create evidence-grade backups (bitstream backups) can be used to access the compromised system
- Forensic investigations must be done by staff who have prior experience or training in this competency
- A chain of custody documenting who has access to the evidence must be established
- The obtained evidence must be submitted to the agency legal team along with a report of evidence findings
- Send evidence preservation request letters to ISSOs in charge of systems that are connected to the information system being investigated
- Follow all U.S. Department of Justice search and seizure guidelines

When performing forensic analysis, you'll need to use fresh software tools that are not currently installed on the system where the incident has occurred. Any forensic tools on the breached system could have been replaced with Trojan pro-grams; therefore, you can't trust their integrity. A good example is to take into con-sideration the output of the `ps` program that you run on a UNIX system to view the process table. The `ps` program displays a list of the UNIX daemons currently running on the system. However, certain Trojan programs have been designed to display everything except the hacker backdoor daemons. What I'm suggesting is that the `ps` program itself could be a fake, put there by an intruder, so that when you use it, their evil process will not show up in the process table.

If you need to preserve the evidence and integrity of the breached system for a forensic investigation, it is best to use fresh software tools installed on an entirely different system or drive such as a portable flash drive. Though operating systems contain some built-in programs that are useful for collecting evidence, there are also some very powerful commercial off-the-shelf tools designed just for this purpose.

Some well-known commercial off-the-shelf tools have been designed specifi-cally for preserving evidence. Tools that are currently being used by various federal agencies and law enforcement include products made by some of the following vendors:

- Access Data (http://www.accessdata.com)
- Digital Intelligence, Inc. (http://www.digitalintelligence.com)
- Guidance Software (http://www.guidancesoftware.com)
- Cellebrite (http://www.celebrite.com)
- Paraben (http://www.paraben.com)

Some of the things that you'll want to look for and retain for evidence and analysis are:

- Suspicious IP addresses and their geographic locations
- Open ports that should not be open
- Open files that should not be open
- File slack, RAM slack, and drive slack
- Timestamps and dates
- Services running that should not be running
- Unauthorized port listeners
- World-writeable files with new timestamps
- Aberrant packet behavior

There are some UNIX-based forensics tools available for free on the Internet that are very good at collecting and analyzing forensic evidence. Some of these UNIX tools are already included as part of the operating system for some versions of UNIX. Popular UNIX tools for security forensics include:

- **awk** Good to use for formatting log files to look for trends
- **egrep and grep** Good to use in conjunction with **awk** to perform searches in log files to look for trends

- **find** Finds and identifies files and directories that have changed since their last timestamp
- **dd** Used for converting and copying a file to another media device
- **dig** Similar to nslookup. Performs DNS lookups
- **lastcomm** Displays process accounting records and execution times
- **lsof** Displays list of open files
- **netcat** A port listener (also used as a popular hacker backdoor)
- **netstat** Displays current network connections, interface information, routing tables, multicast memberships, and masquerade connections
- **nmap** A port scanner (good for finding which ports are open on your systems)
- **nslookup** Used to investigate hostname resolution or suspicious DNS anomalies
- **ps** Displays the current process table
- **tcpdump or winpcap** Used for packet forensics
- **traceroute** Displays routes that packets take to reach their destination

INCIDENT TYPES

If security incidents are thoughtfully categorized, it can speed up the ability to respond to incidents by establishing a uniform understanding among the incident response team. It is certainly possible for a security incident to consist of multiple types of violations. If a security incident consists of multiple violations, all violation types should be noted on the Incident Reporting Form.

Your agency CSIRC may already have the different types of security incidents categorized with identification numbers. If incident categories do not exist, or are not acceptable to the information owner or the ISSO, the FISMA compliance team may need to develop its own categories. Table 11.2 lists a sampling of security incidents. This table is by no means exhaustive, however, it is comprehensive and most

Table 11.2 Types of Security Incidents		
ID No.	**Incident Name**	**Incident Description**
1	Adverse Mission Impact	Any type of circumstance that prevents agency missions, functions, or lines of business from being achieved
2	Annoyance	Any type of circumstance that creates an unprecedented annoyance that may impact the ability to perform daily job functions (e.g., hoaxes, chain letters)
3	Buffer Overflow Attack	Any circumstance that results in massive memory flooding
4	Data Modification	Unauthorized modification of files or data

Continued

Table 11.2 Types of Security Incidents—cont'd

ID No.	Incident Name	Incident Description
5	Data Removal or Deletion	Removal of files or data where that removal has not been properly authorized
6	Denial-of-Service Attack	Any type of circumstance that degrades system performance of normal functions when overwhelmed from activity from one or more sources
7	Failed Access Attempts	Any failed attempts of unauthorized access to accounts
8	Identity Fraud	Any type of access to information technology resources where an individual (either outside the agency or within the agency) masquerades as another individual
9	Infrastructure Outage (including natural disasters)	A power loss, flood, natural disaster, or other occurrence that results in the loss of service, data, or security of the information technology infrastructure
10	Insider Threat—Misuse of Privileges	Any unauthorized use of data or systems in which the user has an authorized account
11	Insider Threat—Unauthorized Access	Any type of unauthorized use of an account outside the account's authorized levels of privilege for normal usage
12	Insider Threat—Administrator Error	An unintentional security breach that occurs due to an administrative error (e.g., incorrect configuration)
13	Installation of Unlicensed Software	Installation of software that is not approved or licensed by the agency (includes commercial software, custom code, freeware, and media)
14	IP Address Spoofing	An attack where an unauthorized user gains access to a computer or a network by making it appear that a message or packet has come from a trusted machine by "spoofing" the IP address of that machine
15	Java or ActiveX Exploitation	Any circumstance that creates exploitation of Java or Active X
16	MAC Address Spoofing	An attack where an unauthorized user gains access to a computer or a network by making it appear that a message or packet has come from a trusted machine by "spoofing" the MAC address of the trusted machine
17	Malicious Code	Indication of a computer virus, worm, or Trojan whether destructive or harmless
18	Loss or Theft	An indication that a computer, system or media has been lost or stolen

19	Man-in-the-Middle Attack	An attack where a malicious party intercepts and/or alters a legitimate communication between two friendly parties without the knowledge of the original sender or recipient
20	Network Bandwidth Attack	An unusual and unauthorized increase in network traffic (possibly induced by a user downloading excessive amounts of data or using unauthorized tools that reserve large amounts of bandwidth)
21	Other Attacks	All other circumstances in which a security incident occurs but cannot be identified by any other predefined category
22	Packet Sniffing/Network Wiretap	A circumstance where a malicious user gathers, monitors, or analyzes data communications traveling between two or more systems
23	Reconnaissance Scans	Indication of a network probe by an unauthorized user (possibly gathering information such as open ports, running services, operating systems, and configuration information)
24	Security Attack	Any circumstance where a system or network's security support infrastructure fails and the data on that system or network is left open to security attacks (e.g., failure of a host- or network-based intrusion detection system)
25	Sensitive Compromise	Any theft of sensitive resources (e.g., passwords; protected, classified, or restricted data; licensed applications or software; restricted applications, software or code)
26	Stolen or Misplaced Equipment	A circumstance that results in stolen or misplaced agency hardware, equipment, or media
27	Unauthorized Web Surfing	Web surfing by employees to untrusted and potentially dangerous or inappropriate Web sites
28	Unauthorized Access	Any type of unauthorized use of a valid account by someone who is not an employee of the agency
29	Unauthorized Access and Modification of Access Control Lists	Any circumstance where an unauthorized user changes the configurations of access control lists located on critical network infrastructure such as routers or firewalls
30	User Data Breach	Any type of circumstance that creates unauthorized loss, theft, alteration, or compromise of user data or private user information
31	Web Site Defacement	Any activity that causes, or attempts to deface, or create unauthorized modification of internal or external agency Web sites

security incidents will fit in one of these categories. Before developing your own categories of security incidents for your Incident Response Plan, you should inquire with the assessment team if this is acceptable or if you are required to use the CSIRC definitions. It is reasonable and acceptable to ask questions of the assessment team along the way when you require clarification. If you want your package to be authorized, you're usually better off following the direction of the assessment team even if you don't completely agree with it.

Regardless of how your agency categorizes incidents, if an incident is reported to US-CERT, US-CERT will categorize the incident from 0-6 as noted in Appendix J of NIST Special Publication 800-61, Revision 1. Agencies may want to keep the US-CERT incident categories in mind when developing their incident definitions and categories.

INCIDENT RESPONSE PLAN CHECKLIST

Once your Incident Response Plan is finished, use this checklist to make sure you didn't forget anything:

- Does your plan accurately describe the systems it applies to?
- Does your plan include a contact list of key personnel?
- Does your plan include information on roles and responsibilities?
- Does your plan include a diagram of the escalation framework?
- Does your plan include how to contact the agency CSIRC?
- Does your plan list the members of the CSIRT team?
- Does your plan list the members of the CSIRC team?
- Does your plan include a description of incident types?
- Does your plan include guidance on severity levels?
- Does your plan include information on agency security policies?
- Does your plan include incident handling guidelines?
- Does your plan include a section on information forensics?
- Does your plan include a Security Incident Reporting Form?

SECURITY INCIDENT REPORTING FORM

Every incident response program should have an Incident Reporting Form to standardize and track the collection of security incident information. The Incident Reporting Form that applies to the information system slated for FISMA compliance should be included at the end of your Incident Response Plan. The information contained on the Incident Reporting Form should be consistent with the information described in the Incident Response Plan. For example, if you include a section on the form that calls for a severity classification, be sure that severities are defined in the Incident Response Plan. A sample Incident Reporting Form is shown in Figure 11.2.

SECURITY INCIDENT REPORTING FORM
Incident Report Number:
Date and Time: _____
Incident Response Manager:_____   Alternate POC:_____
Name: _____
Phone: _____   Fax:_____
Incident Geographic Location:
 Building: _____Cubical/Room: _____
Incident Type, Name(s) and ID:
Incident Type Identification Numbers (from list):
 Data: ☐ Classified   ☐ Unclassified
Methods Used to Confirm Incident (check all that apply)
       ☐ IDS/IPS
       ☐ Log Files
       ☐ Sniffer/Protocol Analyzer
       ☐ Security Information Monitoring Console
       ☐ Other
System Information: (Report operating system name, version, and patch level/Service Pack)
Platform: ☐ Workstation   ☐ Server   ☐ Laptop
 Asset Identification Bar Code Number: _____
Networks and Domains Affected:
Has Personally Identifiable Information (PII) Been Compromised?

Incident Summary: (Be specific. List dates and times. Include how incident was detected and resolved and describe what forensics tools and programs were used.)

Incident Status:
Open
Closed

FIGURE 11.2

Sample Security Incident Reporting Form.

SUMMARY

An Incident Response Plan formally documents the agency's strategy for responding to security breaches. By its very nature, a security incident is a time of crisis to some degree, and during this time, more so than any other time, you need to ensure that decisions being made are levelheaded and based on sound judgments. The best way to do this is to define clear procedures and protocols for responding to the crisis before the crisis ever hits and then to train employees about these procedures and protocols. This is why the Incident Response Plan is such a vital document.

The Incident Response Plan should cover all foreseeable security events, and it should lay out the rules and triggers by which agency personnel should take action in response to the event. Although it may be impossible to predict when and where a denial-of-service attack will strike, it is somewhat easier to determine what the appropriate response should be. If this response is documented and agency employees are trained on the response, then cooler heads will prevail when and if the possibility of the attack ever becomes a reality.

ADDITIONAL RESOURCES

This section provides you with information about organizations involved with incident response. It also includes lists of books and other material related to incident response and forensics.

INCIDENT RESPONSE ORGANIZATIONS

The organizations listed in Table 11.3 offer valuable information on computer security incidents, vulnerabilities, and response activities.

BOOKS ON INCIDENT RESPONSE

The following books offer useful information on computer security incident response:

> Farmer, Dan and Wietse Venema. *Forensic Discovery*. Addison-Wesley, December 2004. ISBN: 020163497X.
> Grama, Joanna Lyn. Jones & Barlett Learning, 2011. ISBN: 978-0-7637-9185-8.
> Jones, Keith J. *Real Digital Forensics: Computer Security and Incident Response*. Addison-Wesley, September 2005. ISBN: 0321240693.
> Kruse, Warren G. and Jay G. Heiser. *Computer Forensics: Incident Response Essentials*. Addison-Wesley, September 2001. ISBN: 0201707195.
> Lucas, Julie and Brian Moeller. *The Effective Incident Response Team*. Addison-Wesley, 2004. ISBN: 0201761750.

Table 11.3 Incident Response Organizations

Organization and Web Site	Description
Common Vulnerabilities and Exposures http://www.cve.mitre.org	A list of standardized names for vulnerabilities developed by the MITRE Corporation
Forum of Incident Response and Security Teams http://www.first.org/	An organization that specializes in computer security incident response
IBM's X-FORCE Alerts and Advisories http://www.iss.net/threats/Advisories.php	Information on Internet threats and vulnerabilities operated by Internet Security Systems
SANS Incident Reading Room—Incident Handling http://www.sans.org/reading_room/whitepapers/incident/	A library of computer security white papers on incident handling
United States Computer Emergency Readiness Team http://www.us-cert.gov/	Coordinates defense and response against cyber attacks on the U.S. infrastructure
United States Department of Interior http://www.blm.gov/pgdata/etc/medialib/blm/wo/Information_Resources_Management/policy/ib_attachments/2013.Par.30902.File.dat/BLM%20Incident%20Response%20Plan.pdf	Incident Response Plan

Mandia, Kevin and Chris Prosise. *Incident Response, Investigating Computer Crime*. Osborne/McGraw Hill, 2001. ISBN: 0072131829.

Oriyano, Sean-Philip and Michael Gregg. *Hacker Techniques, Tools, and Incident Handling*. Jones & Bartlett, 2011. ISBN-13: 978-0763791834.

Northcutt, Stephen. *Computer Security Incident Handling*. SANS Institute, March 2003. ISBN: 0972427376.

Schweitzer, Douglas. *Incident Response, Computer Forensics Toolkit*. Wiley, 2003. ISBN: 0764526367.

Van Wyk, Kenneth R. and Richard Forno. *Incident Response*. O'Reilly & Associates, 2001. ISBN: 0596001304.

ARTICLES AND PAPERS ON INCIDENT RESPONSE

Various useful articles and papers on computer security incident response are listed here:

Computer Security Incident Handling Guide. NIST Special Publication 800-61, Revision 2, August 2012 (http://www.csrc.nist.gov/publications/nistpubs/800-61rev2/SP800-61rev2.pdf).

FBI Law Enforcement Bulletin. Digital Evidence, August 2011 (http://www.fbi.gov/stats-services/publications/law-enforcement-bulletin/august-2011/digital-evidence).

FCC Computer Security Incident Response Guide. United States Federal Communications Commission, December 2001 (http://www.csrc.nist.gov/groups/SMA/fasp/documents/incident_response/Incident-Response-Guide.pdf).

Handbook for Computer Security Incident Response Teams (CSIRTS). The Software Engineering Institute, April 2003 (http://www.sei.cmu.edu/library/abstracts/reports/03hb002.cfm?DCSext.abstractsource=SearchResults).

Office of Legal Education, Executive Office for United States Attorneys, Searching and Seizing Computers and Obtaining Electronic Evidence in Criminal Investigations, 2009 (http://www.justice.gov/criminal/cybercrime/docs/ssmanual2009.pdf).

Taylor, Laura. *Old-School UNIX Tools Help Track Down Hackers*. TechRepublic, June 19, 2002 (http://www.techrepublic.com/article/old-school-unix-tools-help-track-down-hackers/5030955).

Taylor, Laura. *Read Your Firewall Logs*. ZDNet, July 5, 2001 (http://www.asia.cnet.com/read-your-firewall-logs-30086707.htm).

Federal Guidelines for Searching and Seizing Computers, July 1994, (http://www.epic.org/security/computer_search_guidelines.txt).

Wotring, Brian. *Host Integrity Monitoring*. SecurityFocus, March 31, 2004 (http://www.symantec.com/connect/articles/host-integrity-monitoring-best-practices-deployment).

Conducting a Privacy Impact Assessment

12

It seems to me, Golan, that the advance of civilization is nothing but an exercise in the limiting of privacy.
—**Janov Pelorat in Isaac Asimov's** *Foundation's Edge*

TOPICS IN THIS CHAPTER

- Privacy laws, regulations, and rights
- When to conduct a PIA?
- Questions for a Privacy Impact Assessment
- Personally identifiable information
- Persistent tracking technologies
- Decommissioning of PII
- System of Record Notice
- Posting the privacy policy
- PIA checklist

INTRODUCTION

A *Privacy Impact Assessment* (PIA) is the process that one goes through to determine if personally identifiable private information is being appropriately safeguarded. Aside from financial losses and losses to life, there are also privacy considerations for information technology systems. Some federal agencies have databases with highly sensitive information such as medical records, tax records, and information about private citizens. The Privacy Act of 1974 requires each federal agency to establish:

> *... appropriate administrative, technical and physical safeguards to insure the security and confidentiality of records and to protect against any anticipated*

threats or hazards to their security or integrity which could result in substantial harm, embarrassment, inconvenience or unfairness to any individual on whom information is maintained [1].

Agencies need to establish rules of conduct for systems users as well as penalties for noncompliance. Privacy Impact Assessments of public Web sites, databases, and sensitive systems need to be conducted to ascertain if individuals' social security numbers, gender, race, date of birth, and financial status are subject to exposure. The point of a Privacy Impact Assessment is to determine if systems, and the organizations that manage them, comply with all federal laws, regulations, and security policies. Threats to privacy and mitigating factors should also be noted in a PIA. Assets that store data subject to privacy policies and laws need to be determined and understood.

PRIVACY LAWS, REGULATIONS, AND RIGHTS

The Homeland Security Act of 2002[1] requires all federal departments and agencies to appoint a Privacy Officer and further assigns certain responsibilities to the Privacy Officer. (In some agencies, the Privacy Officer is known as the Senior Agency Official for Privacy.) Conducting a Privacy Impact Assessment is one of the responsibilities. Another responsibility of the Privacy Officer is to ensure that systems of record adhere to the Privacy Act. Aside from managing the internal oversight of privacy, the senior privacy official is supposed to prepare

. . . a report to Congress on an annual basis on activities of the Department that affect privacy, including complaints of privacy violations, implementation of the Privacy Act of 1974, internal controls, and other matters.

On May 22, 2006, after it was thought that private information of 26 million US Veterans was stolen on a USB flash drive, Clay Johnson III, the Acting Director of the OMB, issued an important memorandum on privacy to heads of federal departments and agencies. In the memo, Mr. Johnson reminded heads of departments and agencies that, "The loss of personally identifiable information can result in substantial harm, embarrassment, and inconvenience to individuals and may lead to identity theft or other fraudulent use of the information. Because Federal agencies maintain significant amounts of information concerning individuals, we have a special duty to protect that information from loss and misuse."

Mr. Johnson goes on to cite an excerpt from the Privacy Act with a reminder that each federal department or agency should establish

. . . rules of conduct for persons involved in the design, development, operation, or maintenance of any system of records, or maintaining any record, and instruct each such person with respect to such rules and the requirements of [the Privacy

---

[1]http://www.dhs.gov/xlibrary/assets/hr_5005_enr.pdf.

Act], including any other rules and procedures adopted pursuant to this [Act] and the penalties for noncompliance, and

appropriate administrative, technical and physical safeguards to insure the security and confidentiality of records and to protect against any anticipated threats or hazards to their security or integrity which could result in substantial harm, embarrassment, inconvenience or unfairness to any individual on whom information is maintained. (5 U.S.C. § 552a(e)(9)-(10))

The memo further states that heads of departments and agencies should: conduct a review of privacy policies and processes, take corrective action as appropriate to ensure that the agency has adequate safeguards to prevent the intentional or negligent misuse of, or unauthorized access to, personally identifiable information. Mr. Johnson requested that heads of departments and agencies should include the results of the review with FISMA compliance reports. The memo in its entirety can be viewed at http://www.whitehouse.gov/omb/memoranda/fy2006/m-06-15.pdf.

OMB MEMORANDA WITH PRIVACY IMPLICATIONS

Various additional memoranda have been published by the White House Office of Budget and Management (OMB) that contain a wealth of information on privacy concerns and what to include in a Privacy Impact Assessment. You'll find the following five OMB Memoranda very helpful:

- *OMB Memorandum 01-05, Guidance on Inter-Agency Sharing of Personal Data–Protecting Personal Privacy* (December 20, 2000) provides a set of privacy principles in conducting interagency data sharing [2].
- *OMB Memorandum 00-13, Privacy Policies and Data Collection on Federal Web Sites* (June 22, 2000) requires that agencies comply with the Web site privacy policies that they post following the guidance of OMB Memorandum 99-18 and specifically prohibits the use of persistent "cookies" on Federal Web sites [3].
- *OMB Memorandum 99-05, Instructions on complying with President's Memorandum of May 14, 1998 "Privacy and Personal Information in Federal Records"* includes what actions agencies must take for compliance and requirements for agencies to track disclosure of private information [4].
- *OMB Memorandum 99-18, Privacy Policies on Federal Web Sites* (June 2, 1999) provides guidance and model language for Federal Web site privacy policies [5].
- *OMB Memorandum 03-22, Guidance for Implementing the Privacy Provisions of the E-Government Act of 2002* includes when to conduct a PIA, what elements to include in one, and definitions, and PIA-reporting requirements [6].

Note that it is OMB Memo 03-22 that describes when to conduct a Privacy Impact Assessment, definitions for Privacy Impact Assessments, requirements for privacy policies on government Web sites, and what to include in a Privacy Impact Assessment. This OMB memo can be found at the following URL: http://www. whitehouse.gov/omb/memoranda_m03-22#a. This OMB memo also includes a definition for a Privacy Impact Assessment as follows:

> ... an analysis of how information is handled: (i) to ensure handling conforms to applicable legal, regulatory, and policy requirements regarding privacy, (ii) to determine the risks and effects of collecting, maintaining and disseminating information in identifiable form in an electronic information system, and (iii) to examine and evaluate protections and alternative processes for handling information to mitigate potential privacy risks.

LAWS AND REGULATIONS

Aside from Federal Information Security Management Act of 2002, other laws bestow the necessity of privacy rights management as well. These laws include:

- 5 U.S.C. § 552, Freedom of Information Act (FOIA) of 1966, as Amended by Public Law No. 104-231, 110 Stat. 3048
- 5 U.S.C. § 552a, Privacy Act of 1974, as Amended
- Public Law 100-503, Computer Matching and Privacy Act of 1988
- Section 208 of the E-Government Act of 2002
- Section 5 of the Federal Trade Commission Act
- Children's Online Privacy Protection Act of 1998 (COPPA)
- OMB Circular A-130, Management of Federal Information Resources, 1996 [7]
- The Health Insurance Portability and Accountability Act of 1996 [8]
- The Homeland Security Act of 2002

With so many laws and regulations governing privacy, and because privacy information disclosures and breaches of information related to both public and private entities are making headlines, noncompliance is clearly a liability to any agency, company, or nonprofit organization.

WHEN TO CONDUCT A PIA?

According to the E-Government Act of 2002, a Privacy Impact Assessment should be conducted when an agency program is performing any of the following:

- Developing or procuring IT systems or projects that collect, maintain, or disseminate information in identifiable form from or about members of the public, or
- Initiating, consistent with the Paperwork Reduction Act, a new electronic collection of information in identifiable form for 10 or more persons

Most agencies require a Privacy Threshold Assessment to be conducted first. The outcome of the Privacy Threshold Assessment determines if a Privacy Impact Assessment is necessary. A Privacy Threshold Assessment typically four questions in it such as the below questions which come from the FedRAMP Privacy Impact Assessment template found on http://www.fedramp.gov:

(1) Does the <Information System Name> collect, maintain, or share PII in any identifiable form?
  ❑ No
  ❑ Yes

(2) Does the <Information System Name> collect, maintain, or share PII information from or about the public?
  ❑ No
  ❑ Yes

(3) Has a Privacy Impact Assessment ever been performed for the <Information System Name>?
  ❑ No
  ❑ Yes

(4) Is there a Privacy Act System of Records Notice (SORN) for this system?
  ❑ No
  ❑ Yes, the SORN identifier and name is: [   ]

If there is a Yes answer to any of the above questions, the system owner is then required to conduct a Privacy Impact Assessment.

QUESTIONS FOR A PRIVACY IMPACT ASSESSMENT

A Privacy Impact Assessment is usually designed in a survey format. It is acceptable to ask different people in the organization to answer the different questions. It is also acceptable to hold one person accountable for answering, or finding out the answers to, all of the questions. You should work with the ISSO to discuss the best approach. The best approach is the one that will help you obtain accurate answers in an acceptable amount of time. It is acceptable to conduct in-person interviews or use an e-mail or online survey. At the very minimum, a *Privacy Impact Assessment* should answer the following top 10 questions:

1. What information is collected?
2. How is the information collected?
3. Why is the information collected?
4. What is the intended use of the information?
5. Who will have access to the information?
6. With whom will the information be shared?
7. What safeguards are used to protect the PII?

8. For how long will the data be retained/stored?

9. How will the data be decommissioned and disposed of?

10. Have rules of behavior for administrators of the systems storing or transmitting PII been established?

If the answers to these questions result in new questions, the new questions should be asked. For example, if it is discovered that the privacy information will be retained for 50 years, you'll want to ask why. Use your common sense and good judgment in developing the questions and evaluating their answers. If the answers you receive don't sound reasonable, then they probably won't pass muster with the independent assessors either. It's possible that you may need to go and ask a different person the same question to see if you get the same answer. What you are looking for are facts. If you come up short no matter whom you ask, don't be afraid to simply put down "unknown" for your answer. You definitely don't want to invent answers simply because the ones you were given sound questionable.

It helps in obtaining accurate answers from the respondents if you do not convey a confrontational manner. You may need to explain to them the value of the PIA and how their responses will help agency officials put together a Privacy "To-Do" list. Expound the virtues and responsibilities of being good data stewards of confidential information. It helps put respondents at ease if they feel their time spent answering the PIA questions will serve to benefit people just like themselves—you may want to convey that to them in a conversation, or through e-mail.

On April 30, 2013, the National Institute of Standards and Technology published a new edition of Special Publication 800-53 that includes an appendix of privacy controls that federal departments and agencies should consider implementing. A more didactic description of privacy controls that should be assessed during a PIA can be found in Appendix J of this document. Special Publication 800-53 is also known as *Security and Privacy Controls for Federal Information Systems and Organizations* and it can be found at the following URL: http://nvlpubs.nist.gov/nistpubs/SpecialPublications/NIST.SP.800-53r4.pdf.

PERSONALLY IDENTIFIABLE INFORMATION (PII)

In considering what information is collected, of utmost importance should be what's known as personally identifiable information (PII). PII includes information that is associated with the identity of a person. A Privacy Impact Assessment should determine if PII is collected and should list all types of PII that are collected. Some types of PII that may be in use at your agency are:

- Name (if accompanied with another identifier)
- Home Address (if accompanied with another identifier)
- Social Security Number
- Cell Phone Number
- Passport Number
- Bank Account Information

- Driver's License Number
- State Identification Number
- Account Number
- Biometric Fingerprint
- DNA
- Photograph

Certain items in the above list are only considered to be PII if they are accompanied with another identifier, and that's because more than one person could use the listed identifier. For example, there might be thousands of people named John Williams in the United States, so it's not possible to know which John Williams we're talking about unless we add say an address to the same record.

Since PII includes data that are attributable to a person's identity, in most cases, PII would not exist if that person did not exist. Essentially, an individual owns the attributes of the PII. Therefore, it's necessary that all system owners ensure that there is a process for individuals to individuals to correct inaccurate PII regardless of how the inaccuracy occurred.

System owners should have an understanding of where PII is located on their system and should be able to map the PII to specific applications, indicating that they understand exactly what mechanisms are collecting and using PII. An example of how to do this is illustrated in Table 12.1. If you don't understand where PII is located, it's going to be a lot more challenging to safeguard it. There are various commercial PII scanners that are available to help find lost or unknown PII.

Once ISSOs, system owners, and independent assessors are certain that they have located all PII on a system, they can more easily determine if safeguards are in place

Table 12.1 PII Mapped to Applications

	Applications That Collect PII			
PII	**Tax Records**	**Payroll System**	**Building Access Card System**	**Health Records**
Social Security No.	✓	✓		✓
Bank Account No.	✓	✓		
Driver's License No.			✓	
PIN			✓	
Biometric Fingerprint			✓	
DNA				✓
Photograph			✓	

Table 12.2 Summary of Privacy Threats and Safeguards

Privacy Threat	Asset that Stores Private Information	Type of Safeguards	Description of the Privacy Controls
Physical threats from intruders trying to break into the data center	The DB-01 database in building 12, room A-2. Part of an IBM cluster	Physical protection	Physical controls of the facility include guards, locks, and surveillance cameras which prevent entry by unauthorized entities
Intentional and unintentional threats from authorized and unauthorized users	The DB-12A5 database in building 9, room A-5	Authorization and access control systems	Enforced by Authorization Manager role based access control system
Systems administration errors	All databases and servers on the .secret domain	Training and systems and database administration documentation	System admins and database admins undergo training once a year. Documentation is updated biannually
Trojans that seek to obtain and distribute PII	All databases and in the Pensacola facility	Enterprise antivirus software	Enforced by automated signature updates and regular virus scans
Loss or theft of laptop containing sensitive information	Access database on Linda Parker's laptop	Encryption	The database is encrypted using a FIPS 140-2-validated encryption product, and keys are stored securely in a locked safe in the Privacy Officer's office

to protect it. Safeguards should include both physical and logical safeguards. For reporting purposes, assets that contain PII, and their safeguards, can be neatly summarized in a table similar to Table 12.2.

PERSISTENT TRACKING TECHNOLOGIES

Since persistent tracking technologies are often the biggest violators of privacy, they deserve special mention. Persistent tracking technologies record and maintain information about Web site visits after the user leaves the Web site. The most commonly used tracking technologies are cookies and Web beacons. Cookies store information about a user's visit to a Web site on the user's hard drive. Web beacons are typically a one-by-one graphic pixel placed in e-mails or Web sites that send visitor information to another destination—perhaps a server, a database, or even directly to a person in the form of an e-mail. A Web beacon can be completely invisible since the pixel can be "clear," matching the background color of the Web site. Using Web beacons often represents dodgy motives and their use is not recommended in most cases. (Web beacons are often used to do e-mail tracking, e.g., has the receiver opened your e-mail, when did that occur, and was it forwarded anywhere?)

If any persistent tracking technologies are used, a good PIA will discover that and will describe the usage and ascertain if it is in compliance with the agency privacy policy. Agencies should, under most circumstances, not use cookies or Web beacons. OMB Memo 03-22 has specific guidance on the exceptions where cookies and/or Web beacons are allowed.

DECOMMISSIONING OF PII

With the advancements in technology occurring at such a rapid rate, it is understandable that databases get merged, systems get upgraded, old systems get decommissioned, and disks with confidential PII on them are turned off never to be used again—in theory. However, in reality, old systems sometimes end up in inadvertent places. To prevent the disclosure of confidential and private information, PII should be properly decommissioned according to the agency security and privacy policy. Depending on how sensitive the data are, old disks that contain PII may require bit wiping, a degausser, or destruction by a disk crusher.

A draft document on media sanitation known as *NIST Special Publication 800-88, Guidelines for Media Sanitation*, was published by NIST on February 3, 2006. You may find the NIST guide to be a useful resource for understanding if the appropriate measures are being undertaken when a system reaches the end of its System Development Life Cycle (SDLC). You can access Special Publication 800-88 at the following URL: http://www.csrc.nist.gov/publications/nistpubs/800-88/NISTSP800-88_with-errata.pdf.

SYSTEM OF RECORD NOTICE (SORN)

A System of Record Notice (SORN) is a required public notice for any system that stores privacy information in such way that the information is retrieved through personally identifiable information identifiers. Specifically, the Privacy Act states that a SORN is required for:

> . . . *a group of any records under the control of any agency from which information is retrieved by the name of the individual or by some identifying number, symbol, or other identifying particular assigned to the individual.*

Whereas a PIA includes only information technology records, a SORN includes both paper and electronic records. To clarify further, a SORN is not a PIA and a SORN is not required by FISMA—it is required by the Privacy Act. Today, most agencies require that somewhere within the Privacy Impact Assessment, there should be a statement as to whether the system being reviewed has a System of Record Notice (SORN) associated with it or not. If there is a SORN, the SORN will have a numeric identifier.

Unless your agency specifically states that a SORN needs to be included in your PIA, it's not necessary to include one. However, just because your PIA and Security Package may not require a SORN, that doesn't mean your agency is exempt from creating SORNs. The Privacy Act requires SORNs to be published in the Federal Register (PIAs are not published in the Federal Register). The Federal Register is part of the National Archives and Records Administration (NARA). You can view the Federal Register online at http://www.gpoaccess.gov/fr/index.html.

It is up to each agency to determine whether or not the system should have a SORN. The Department of Homeland Security publishes an excellent reference on SORNs which is available at the following URL: http://www.dhs.gov/xlibrary/assets/privacy/privacy_guidance_sorn.pdf.

POSTING THE PRIVACY POLICY

All public Web sites that collect information on citizens, veterans, staff, and military personnel require privacy policies. The privacy policy should list laws and regulations that it claims to comply with. Once a privacy policy has been established, it should be posted for the users and administrators to see. For Web sites, it should be posted right on the front page. For systems and applications that require logins, the privacy policy should be posted in the banner before a user logs in.

According to OMB Memo 03-22:

> ... agencies are required to: notify users of the authority for and purpose and use of the collection of information subject to the Privacy Act, whether providing the information is mandatory or voluntary, and the effects of not providing all or any part of the requested information.

Notifying the users whose personally identifiable information is being collected is mandatory. If a Web site is not part of the system, then the system owner will need to notify the users via some other method such as a hardcopy notice through the US Postal Service. All privacy policy postings or distributions should include information about what PII is shared with other entities and what the reason is for the sharing.

PIA CHECKLIST

Use the following checklist to help you ensure that you haven't forgotten anything in your PIA:

- Is the name(s) of the individual(s) who completed the PIA noted?
- Is the Security Package name listed on the PIA?
- Is the method of collecting the information (e.g., interviews or e-mail) noted?
- Are the privacy threats and safeguards included?

- Are privacy controls noted?
- Have risks to privacy been determined?
- Are high privacy risks mitigated?
- Do the PII data stewards have access to the privacy policy?
- Is the Privacy Policy published on all online Web sites and logon banners?
- Has personally identifiable information (PII) been identified?
- Is PII mapped to applications?
- Do procedures to correct inaccurate PII exist?
- Has the purpose of the system or application been described?
- Is there a compelling need to collect the PII?
- Is the PII consistent with the application requirements?
- Is unnecessary PII collected?
- Are system administrators aware of their privacy responsibilities?
- Is PII appropriately decommissioned?
- What happens to decommissioned PII?

SUMMARY

In this day and age, preserving privacy is a fundamental requirement for maintaining the positive reputation of an organization. There is a balance that we try to strike between sharing personal information and preserving information that is very personal and descriptive of an individual. Unfortunately, preserving privacy often languishes on the bottom of the information security to-do list. As soon as your own private information is disclosed against your wishes, privacy becomes far more important. As data stewards of other people's private information, system owners, ISSOs, and administrators are ethically obligated to act responsibly to preserve that information.

BOOKS ON PRIVACY

The following books offer useful information on information technology privacy:

Garfinkel, Simson. *Web Security Privacy and Commerce, 2nd Edition*. O'Reilly Media, 2001. ISBN: 0596000456.

Garfinkel, Simson. *Database Nation: The Death of Privacy in the 21st Century*. O'Reilly Media, 2000. ISBN: 0596001053.

Nemati, Hamid. *Privacy Solutions and Security Frameworks in Information Protection*. IGI Global, September 30, 2012. ISBN-13: 978-1-4666-2050-6.

Tynan, Dan. Computer Privacy Annoyances. O'Reilly Media, 2005. ISBN: 0596007752.

Windley, Phil. *Digital Identity*. O'Reilly Media, 2005. ISBN: 0596008783.

References

[1] The Privacy Act of 1974. United States Department of Justice, http://www.justice.gov/opcl/privstat.htm; September 26, 2003 [updated].

[2] Jacob J. Lew. Guidance on inter-agency sharing of personal data—protecting personal privacy. Memorandum for Heads of Executive Departments and Agencies. United States Office of Management and Budget, http://www.whitehouse.gov/omb/memoranda_m01-05; December 20, 2000.

[3] Jacob J. Lew. Privacy policies and data collection on federal web sites. Memorandum for Heads of Executive Departments and Agencies. United States Office of Management and Budget, http://www.whitehouse.gov/omb/memoranda_m00-13; June 22, 2000.

[4] Jacob J. Lew. Instructions on complying with President's Memorandum of May 14, 1998, 'Privacy and Personal Information in Federal Records'. Memorandum for Heads of Executive Departments and Agencies. United States Office of Management and Budget, http://www.whitehouse.gov/omb/memoranda/m99-05.html; January 7, 1999.

[5] Jacob J. Lew. Privacy policies on federal Web sites. Memorandum for Heads of Executive Departments and Agencies. United States Office of Management and Budget, http://www.whitehouse.gov/omb/memoranda_m99-18; June 2, 1999.

[6] Joshua B. Bolten. OMB guidance for implementing the privacy provisions of the E-Government act of 2002. Memorandum for Heads of Executive Departments and Agencies. United States Office of Management and Budget, http://www.whitehouse.gov/omb/memoranda/m03-22.html; September 26, 2003.

[7] Management of federal information resources. Memorandum for Heads of Executive Departments and Agencies. Circular No. A-130 Revised. United States Office of Management and Budget, http://www.whitehouse.gov/omb/circulars_a130_a130trans4; November 30, 2000.

[8] Health information privacy. United States Department of Health and Human Services. Office for Civil Rights, http://www.hhs.gov/ocr/hipaa/.

Preparing the Business Impact Analysis

13

Business? It's quite simple: it's other people's money.
—Alexandre Dumas, French dramatist

TOPICS IN THIS CHAPTER

- Terminology
- Conduct the Business Impact Analysis
- Document recovery times
- Establish relative recovery priorities
- Define escalation thresholds
- Record license keys
- BIA organization

INTRODUCTION

A *Business Impact Analysis* (BIA) articulates the component restoration priorities that an interruption in service may have on an information system, application, or network. If you have a group of systems that include Web servers, directory servers, application servers, file servers, firewalls, DNS servers, and authentication servers, and your facility suffered an unprecedented disaster, which one would you try to restore first? Do you know?

An interruption in service could be as minor as a power outage, or as catastrophic as a bomb. In either case, at that time you, the system, and network support group will have enough anxiety without having to think about which system to restore first. A BIA is all about removing some of that anxiety so that systems administration staff can just go down a list of relative priorities and get to work without having to spend time figuring out which systems should be restored first. By planning for a recovery before you need to orchestrate one, you can more efficiently manage your recovery effort. Planning for a recovery up front also more effectively provides assurances for the continuity of your agency's mission.

In a Security Package, most of the time the independent assessor expects to see the BIA as one of the appendices of the *Contingency Plan*. When I write a Contingency Plan, I often like to have the BIA in front of me as a snapshot of what's important, and therefore I find that it works best to write the BIA before writing the Contingency Plan.

FIGURE 13.1

Business Impact Analysis sequence. (For color version of this figure, the reader is referred to the online version of this chapter.)

Figure 13.1 shows where the Business Impact Analysis falls in the contingency planning development cycle.

TERMINOLOGY

When it comes to system outages, there are different ways to represent downtime. NIST SP 800-34, Revision 1, *Contingency Planning Guide for Federal Information Systems*, recognizes three key terms that help organizations plan for outages.

Maximum Tolerable Downtime (MTD) represents the total amount of time the system owner/authorizing official is willing to accept for a mission/business process outage or disruption and includes all impact considerations.

Recovery Time Objective (RTO) represents the maximum amount of time that a system resource can remain unavailable before there is an unacceptable impact on other system resources, supported mission/business processes, and the MTD.

Last, **Recovery Point Objective (RPO)** represents the point in time, prior to a disruption or system outage, to which mission/business process data can be recovered (given the most recent backup copy of the data) after an outage.

RTO must ensure that the MTD is never exceeded and is therefore a shorter period of time than the MTD. A system with a short RTO likely has in place expensive recovery solutions such as highly available servers and network devices. RPO represents how much data loss the organization can tolerate from any given outage. You'll want to come up with estimates for each of these downtime and recovery objectives in your BIA.

DOCUMENT ACTUAL RECOVERY TIMES

In Chapter 7, I discussed how to put together a *Hardware and Software Inventory*. You should have the systems you want to recover already identified by way of that inventory. Now you need to figure out how long it will take to rebuild each of those systems. In your BIA, you should document estimated actual recovery times. The estimated recovery time should be made by trained support staff that typically administer the servers and network devices and configure them on a routine basis.

You are not trying to figure out what the management team wants the recovery times to be, you are trying to figure out what the recovery times actually are. If an IT manager wants a server to be recovered within 2 hours, but a systems administrator tells you that under the best possible conditions it takes 4 hours to build the server, it makes little sense to document the recovery time as 2 hours. Go and talk to the systems administrators, the application administrators, the database administrators, and the backup support staff to find out the recovery times.

The reason that recovery times are important to know is because in the event of a disaster, management may need to make decisions based on recovery times. For example, it may be necessary to hire additional temporary staff to help with the recovery, and staffing decisions may need to be made based on recovery time information. If it takes too long to recover a particular server—so long that it impacts the business mission—management may make the decision that an already built standby system is available at all times at an alternate facility.

ESTABLISH RELATIVE RECOVERY PRIORITIES

In thinking about establishing recovery priorities, you need to take two things into consideration—the importance of the system to the mission and the dependencies of each system. If a particular application server is the most important system to the agency mission, but it won't work without a DNS server and router, in the event of a disaster it does little good to rebuild the application server and get it up and running before the DNS server is operational. Of course, it is altogether possible that both systems could be built in parallel. However, one of the reasons for establishing recovery priorities is that there may not be enough staff available to build everything in parallel.

Each of the systems named in the Hardware and Software Inventory should have a relative restoration priority of High, Moderate, or Low assigned to it. The priorities should take into consideration the risk exposure metrics you calculated in the *Business Risk Assessment*, as well as the dependencies the Hardware and Software have on other assets listed in the inventory. Keep in mind that your servers may have dependencies on other servers or systems that are not named in the Security Package you are working on. Don't include those systems (the other systems) in the BIA. The systems that you include in the BIA are the same ones you listed in the Hardware and Software Inventory.

If there are systems or applications that your systems are dependent on, but are not part of your Security Package (e.g., are not listed in the Hardware and Software Inventory), simply document a statement that describes that. You can refer to that section of the BIA in a variety of ways such as:

- External dependencies
- Dependencies on general support systems

- Dependencies on network segment 45
- Dependencies on other agencies
- Dependencies on the Information Systems department assets
- Outside dependencies

Your relative recovery priorities can be defined simply as:

High: Recover these systems and applications first
Moderate: Recover these systems and applications second
Low: Recover these systems and applications last

Every line item in your Hardware and Software Inventory should have a relative recovery priority associated with it.

Telecommunications

In the event of a disaster, in most cases the very first item that you'll want to restore is the telecommunications system. However, if the telecomm system is not part of the Security Package that you're creating, you won't need to include it. Telephones are necessary to reestablish services provided by vendors, contactors, other agencies, and employees. Today, many employees have cell phones, smart phones, or tablets, which can serve as backup devices in the event that the telecomm switch goes down. Keep in mind, though, that if you don't have someone's cell phone number on hand, you won't be able to call them. Additionally, in some facilities, cell phones don't function well due to interference from the building and lack of signal.

Infrastructure systems

After telephone services are restored, usually the most important pieces of the IT operations are the infrastructure systems, as all other systems usually depend on these systems for connectivity purposes. Infrastructure systems consist of:

- DNS servers
- Routers, switches, hubs
- Firewalls
- Gateways
- Connectivity provided by managed service providers (Internet connectivity)
- Domain controllers
- Directory servers (LDAP, or Lightweight Access Protocol, an IETF standard; Active Directory; NIS+; etc.)

It may not be necessary to include information about the infrastructure servers in your Security Package if these systems have a different system owner that includes them in an altogether different Security Package. If infrastructure systems were not listed in the Hardware and Software Inventory, you won't need to include recovery priorities for them in your BIA.

Secondary systems

Secondary systems include any of the types of systems that would not be able to function properly without the infrastructure systems. (Infrastructure systems are often referred to as *general support systems*.) A secondary system cannot function on its own. It needs the infrastructure systems for routing and connectivity purposes. Examples of possible secondary systems that may exist on your network are:

- Messaging servers
- Web servers
- Database servers
- File and print servers
- Application servers
- Mainframes

DEFINE ESCALATION THRESHOLDS

Escalation thresholds are predecided time frames for notifying the right people about an outage. You can set up your escalation thresholds to whatever you want them to be, taking into consideration the importance that the components of the system have to the business mission. Define your escalation thresholds by unique and pertinent names. You'll also want to decide who to notify when the defined escalation time frame is reached. For example:

- Level 0: Monitor the situation, take no action
- Level 1: Notify users and stakeholders
- Level 2: Notify developers, management, and CSIRC
- Level 3: Notify a higher authority (FEDCIRC, FBI, FEMA, local police)

Each level of escalation should have an associated time frame. Some organizations will want to use more granular time frames than others. If your agency has predefined escalation time frames that have been standardized across the agency, use those. If no escalation time frames have been previously defined in an agency security handbook, by policy, or by management, simply use what makes sense given the mission at hand. Possible escalation time frames you may want to consider are:

- 15 minutes
- 1 hour
- 2 hours
- 4 hours
- 8 hours
- 24 hours
- 3 + days
- Never
- Undecided

Table 13.1 Escalation Thresholds and Priorities

Server Role	Level 1	Level 2	Level 3	Priority
Application server	1 hour	4 hours	3 days	Moderate
Database server	15 minutes	8 hours	3 days	Moderate
DNS server	15 minutes	1 hour	24 hours	High
File server	1 hour	4 hours	3 days	Moderate
File server	4 hours	8 hours	Never	Low
Production Web server	1 hour	4 hours	Never	Moderate
Test Web server	8 hours	3 days	Never	Low

Generally speaking, the systems and applications that need to be installed first should have the shortest escalation thresholds. It is altogether possible that two different systems, both assigned a Level 1 priority, may have different escalation thresholds depending on their usage, mission, and the number of other systems that are dependent on it. If many systems are dependent on a key server, you'll want to decrease the time of the escalation threshold (on the key server) and increase the priority. An example of escalation thresholds and priority levels are shown in Table 13.1.

RECORD LICENSE KEYS

Almost all software products require licenses. Software license are typically long strings of numbers mixed with letters—something like:

LTP24-W9SJT-A4BMQ-CAWZ5-71XV3

Without a license key, it's likely and possible that the software won't run. Although backup media should have all your systems' and applications' license keys stored safely, there is no substitute for having a list of all the license keys documented together in one easy-to-find location. As systems are restored, there are numerous reasons why it may be quicker to copy a license key off of document than to find it on backup media. Since the BIA is a document that you would ostensibly use during a recovery endeavor, it makes sense to record the license keys in the BIA.

If you think it is a nuisance to track down all these license keys and record them, you're right, it is. Just think of how much of an anxiety-provoking-nuisance it would be in the face of a disaster. That's why you want to find out this information up front. Chances are you'll have to resort to simply talking to folks and asking around to get the right people to give you the license keys. Some may even question your motives about asking for the keys. Simply explain why you're asking for the keys, and what you plan on doing with them. You'll want to obtain license keys primarily for operating systems, databases, and applications. Any of the following types of IT support staff may be good sources of license keys:

• Systems administrators
• Database administrators

- Network administrators
- Application support staff
- The Helpdesk

You'll want to call or e-mail support staff and ask them to look on the back of CD cases to look up these keys. If support staff prefer to e-mail you the keys, be sure to advise them not to e-mail them out unprotected over the Internet. If you are working from a remote location, and there is no Virtual Private Network (VPN) between your system and the person sending you the keys, it is better to obtain the keys over the phone, by FAX, or by having them encrypt the keys using a file encryption program.

BIA ORGANIZATION

In your BIA, it makes it very easy for the assessment team if you put all the information you've accumulated on priorities, escalation time frames, and such in a summary table. You'll still want to include some explanatory text to explain how to use the table. It is okay to submit the BIA as two documents—a summary table and a separate document that provides explanatory text. In the primary BIA document that contains the explanatory text, be sure to indicate that a summary table exists as a separate file. If you don't like the idea of submitting two files, you can embed a table into the primary BIA document.

Aside from what I have already discussed in this chapter, other items that you'll want to include on your BIA summary table (or spreadsheet) are:

- Server role (Directory server, Web server, authentication server, file server, etc.)
- Hostname (the name known by the network and the DNS server)
- Manufacturer (e.g., HP, IBM, Dell, etc.)
- Model number (the number you would need to order a new replacement)
- Location (e.g., building, room, street address, data center)
- Description (e.g., Solaris 8 database server, Windows Domain Controller)
- Asset tracking number (often this is on a sticker with a bar code on it)
- Primary point of contact (e.g., the sysadmin who keeps it running and builds it)
- Secondary point of contact (e.g., who you call when the primary is out sick)
- Contact phone numbers and e-mail address for points of contact

SUMMARY

A BIA helps you prepare for an unscheduled outage. It should be submitted as an appendix to your Contingency Plan; however, I have found it works out best to write the BIA before you write your Contingency Plan. If done properly, your BIA is almost like an abbreviated Contingency Plan—a cheat sheet if you will. If you take the time to figure out the escalation thresholds, recovery times, and priorities in the BIA, you can more easily document the contingency operations process in the Contingency Plan.

Aside from recovery time frames and priorities, your BIA contains a record of essential information that you will need during recovery operations. Points of contact, license keys, make and model numbers of equipment, and so on are information that are critical to recovering your systems in a timely fashion should the need arise.

ADDITIONAL RESOURCES

Books related to business impact assessment include the following titles:
Fulmer, Kenneth L. and Philip Jan Rothstein. *Business Continuity Planning: A Step-by-Step Guide with Planning Forms on CD-ROM*. Third Edition. Rothstein Associates, October 2004. ISBN: 1931332215.
Hiles, Andrew. *BCM Framework CD-ROM for Business Continuity Management*. Rothstein Associates, September 2000. ISBN: 0964164876.
Hiles, Andrew. *Business Continuity—Best Practices*. Rothstein Associates, December 2003. ISBN: 1931332223.
Hiles, Andrew. *Enterprise Risk Assessment and Business Impact Analysis: Best Practices*. Rothstein Associates, March 2002. ISBN: 1931332126.
Wallace, Michael and Lawrence Webber. *The Disaster Recovery Handbook: A Step-by-Step Plan to Ensure Business Continuity and Protect Vital Operations, Facilities, and Assets*. AMACOM, December 2010. ISBN 978-0-814-41613-6.

Developing the Contingency Plan

14

O to be self-balanced for contingencies, to confront night, storms, hunger,
ridicule, accidents, rebuffs, as the trees animals do.
—**Walt Whitman**

TOPICS IN THIS CHAPTER

- List assumptions
- Concept of operations
- Roles and responsibilities
- Levels of disruption
- Procedures
- Line of succession
- Service-Level Agreements
- Contact lists
- Testing the Contingency Plan
- Appendices
- Contingency Plan checklist

INTRODUCTION

The *Contingency Plan* is one of the most important documents in the Security Package. Contrary to popular belief, you may need to use it someday. IT systems and networks are vulnerable to disruptions due to a variety of reasons—power outages, natural disasters, and terrorist attacks to name a few. The nature of unprecedented disruptions can create confusion and often predispose an otherwise competent IT staff toward less efficient practices. Confusion and inefficiency create risk. Contingency planning and testing enables you to eliminate some of that risk. Contingency planning should take into consideration the system sensitivity impact level that is determined during the FIPS 199 process (Chapter 8).

You'll never be able to plan for all the contingencies that may come your way. That being said, you still need to plan for some of them. How many? A Contingency Plan (sometimes referred to as an Information System Contingency Plan (ISCP) or an Information System (IS) Contingency Plan) should be described in general terms in order to cover as many adverse situations as necessary. Some of the objectives of your Contingency Plan should be to:

- Maximize the effectiveness of contingency operations through an established plan
- Provide a roadmap of actions for continuing operations
- Reduce the complexity of the recovery effort
- Minimize loss of, and damage to, assets
- Identify resources to be used in the recovery operations
- Facilitate the coordination of recovery tasks
- Establish management succession and escalation procedures
- Minimize the duration of the disruption
- Assign responsibilities to designated personnel
- Provide guidance in recovering operations
- Identify an alternate site

LIST ASSUMPTIONS

When it comes to planning for contingencies, there are various assumptions you'll need to make based on your information system and application requirements. You can't plan for every possible scenario, but you can plan for some things. Listing assumptions explains to the reader that you intend to count on certain things being a particular way if the Contingency Plan is to work as documented—it defines a starting point. Assumptions are circumstances that exist whether the Contingency Plan gets activated or not. Examples of assumptions are:

- Key staff have been correctly identified and are appropriately trained
- The Kansas City data center will be available as an alternate recovery site
- The off-site storage site where backup media is stored will be operational
- Current backups of the systems are intact and available at the off-site storage location

CONCEPT OF OPERATIONS

The concept of operations section of your Contingency Plan, sometimes referred to as the CONOPS (or ConOps), should describe in dialogue how the system components that make up your Security Package work and interoperate. Three key subsections of your CONOPS are the system description, network diagrams and maps, and data sources and destinations.

System description

Include a description of the information system and major applications to which the Contingency Plan applies. Your description should be consistent with the system description that you document in your *System Security Plan* (discussed in

Chapter 16). If there are three major applications all bundled into one Security Package, include a summary of each of them. If there are two network domains, describe their architecture and connectivity requirements.

Network diagrams and maps

Network diagrams and maps are extremely helpful in understanding how a failover scenario is supposed to work and how the network components should connect to each other. Every Contingency Plan should have at the very least one high-level network architecture map that represents each system listed in the Hardware and Software Inventory. Aside from what's listed in your Hardware and Software Inventory, you'll also want to include on your diagram some of the key infrastructure devices such as routers, firewalls, domain controllers, and directory servers.

You should include logical diagrams of how major applications, Web sites, and databases interact with each other. Such diagrams are often very useful in plotting the data source and destinations.

Data sources and destinations

Data that are stored on information systems have sources and destinations. The sources are the inputs. It is where the data come from originally. It might come from a user typing it in from his/her desktop, or it might come from another system through a secure file transfer process or a VPN. Similarly, the data have a destination. The destination is their final resting place—where they are stored.

In taking into consideration contingency planning, you need to know the source and destination for your data. In the event of a disaster, you are going to want to be able to continue to obtain data from your sources. If you can't connect to your sources, your system is not entirely operational. It's altogether possible that your source and destination system is the same system. Users might input data right into the database over the Web and the stakeholders might view it from that same database over the Web. However, it's also the case that the system described in your Security Package might have different sources and destinations.

You need to understand how the data get from the source to the destination. Is a secure file transfer tool used? Do users input the data from their desktops over the Web? Are files distributed from a central distribution server? The technology pipe that is used for getting the data from the source to the destination—the data conduit—should also be documented. (If the data conduit is an interconnection to another system that is outside the boundary of your system, this interconnection should be documented in your System Security Plan.) In order to restore your infrastructure in the event of an outage, you'll need all this information. You can document the sources and destination of your data in a table similar to the one depicted in Table 14.1.

Table 14.1 Data Sources and Destinations

Source	Data Conduit	Destination
Users located at different remote locations input data over the Web	Internet using HTTPS and SSL	SQL Database #5 on the network segment 12
IBM Mainframe #1 in Washington, DC	Connect:Direct	Oracle Database #2 in the Seattle field office
Sun Solaris System #5 in Dallas Datacenter	Cron job kicks off file transfer over Cisco IPSec VPN	Sun Solaris System #6 in the Boston datacenter
Windows Server 2003 #2 in the Vanguard Building	Secure FTP	Linux Server in the Test Lab on the 7th floor of the Jackson Building
Legacy Windows 2003 server in Detroit datacenter	Microsoft System Center 2012 Configuration Manager	Windows Server 2012 #8 in the Los Angeles data center

ROLES AND RESPONSIBILITIES

The Contingency Plan should establish roles and responsibilities designed to recover operations. Depending on the outage or disaster that has occurred, the recovery operations ostensibly could be at the original facility or at a fully operational hot site setup as an alternate facility. Because there are so many different recovery scenarios, you'll want to have the roles and responsibilities defined in general terms so that they can be applied to as many different types of situations as possible.

Depending on the size of your organization or department, some of your staff may provide support for more than one role. Typically, the roles of the recovery team are additional roles to a staff member's regular and ordinary duties. For example, the ISSO may act as the Contingency Planning Coordinator and an IT manager may act as the Information Systems Operations Coordinator. It is also conceivable that two people could act as a team in assuming the responsibilities of a particular role. For example, the Damage Assessment Coordinator has such an extensive list of duties that it might make sense to assign two people to this role. The names of the particular staff who will be assuming each role should be documented. An example of how to document these roles is depicted in Table 14.2.

Roles and the associated responsibilities of the recovery team that seem to work well for many Contingency Plans are included in the sections that follow. However, you should not limit your Contingency Plan to what is documented in these sections. Your plan may require additional or altogether different roles depending on your operations and your business mission.

Table 14.2 Recovery Roles Noted		
Name	**Regular Job Title**	**Recovery Team Role**
Barbara Williams	ISSO	Contingency Planning Coordinator
Stan Armstrong	Contracting Officer	Logistics Coordinator
Cindy Bishop	IT Manager	Information Systems Operations Coordinator
Bill Weintraub	Development Team Lead	Damage Assessment Coordinator
Amit Franghali	Security Team Lead	Security Coordinator
Godfred James	Director of Applications	Emergency Relocation Site Advisor
Terry McDuffy	Telecomm Engineer	Telecommunications Coordinator

Contingency Planning Coordinator

The Contingency Planning Coordinator has the following responsibilities:

- Establishes personnel rosters and maintains staff location information
- Evaluates supporting information for accuracy and correctness
- Ensures that supporting information is consistent with requirements
- Receives status reports from recovery staff
- Prepares and keeps current recovery team status reports
- Keeps the staff at remote locations advised of the situations
- Advises the Logistics Coordinator on new equipment that should be ordered
- Identifies and coordinates alternate processing location and requirements
- Coordinates annual testing of the Contingency Plan

Damage Assessment Coordinator

The Damage Assessment Coordinator has the following responsibilities:

- Assesses damage to the assets
- Determines the cause of the disruption
- Determines the level of the disruption
- Determines if key personnel have been lost or have perished
- Determines if there has been a violation of classified information
- Determines assets requiring replacement
- Determines if personnel are in danger
- Makes recommendations on whether or not to relocate to an alternate site
- Estimates the recovery time
- Estimates level of backup personnel required
- Contacts outside service organizations for additional support (if necessary)
- Ensures the security of the primary (original) site
- Alerts vendors of the situations and requests their assistance as necessary
- Makes recommendation on whether to relocate to alternate site

- Briefs team members on recovery duties and responsibilities
- Reports status and recommendations back to the Contingency Planning Coordinator

Emergency Relocation Site Adviser and Coordinator

The Emergency Relocation Site Adviser and Coordinator has the following responsibilities:

- Notifies team leaders of relocation arrangements and plans
- Ensures that all backup media is transported to the alternate site
- Coordinates transportation of employees to alternate site
- Ensures complete restoration of resources upon return to primary site
- Reports status and recommendations to back the Contingency Planning Coordinator

Information Systems Operations Coordinator

The Information Systems Operations Coordinator (ISOC) has the following responsibilities:

- Assists in testing of applications prior to putting into production at alternate site
- Initiates restoration of services
- Provides technical support to recovery staff as needed
- Overseas operations between primary site and alternate site
- Reports status and recommendations to back the Contingency Planning Coordinator

Logistics Coordinator

The Logistics Coordinator has the following responsibilities:

- Initiates standby procurement actions
- Coordinates the delivery of equipment, supplies, parts, and software
- Expedites the acquisition of supplies and equipment
- Maintains communications with vendors providing equipment
- Documents estimated delivery times for new equipment
- Retains copies of all Service-Level Agreements and provides them to team
- Retains any encryption keys that are escrowed
- Reports status and recommendations back to the Contingency Planning Coordinator

Security Coordinator

The Security Coordinator has the following responsibilities:

- Ensures that security safeguards are restored to primary site after reconstitution
- Ensures the security of the secondary (alternate) site

- Ensures that only approved personnel have access to alternate facility
- Maintains list of all approved personnel who have access to facilities
- Reports status and recommendations to back the Contingency Planning Coordinator
- Ensures that all encryption keys are properly restored and recovered
- Maintains a checklist of security configuration restoration activity
- Verifies that security safeguards are in place before bringing alternate site into production

Telecommunications Coordinator

The Telecommunications Coordinator has the following responsibilities:

- Initiates alternate communications arrangements
- Coordinates the need for new telecomm equipment with the Logistics Coordinator
- Expedites the acquisitions of communications facilities and services
- Supervises all telecomm installations and configurations
- Overseas access to telecomm wiring closets
- Works with ISOC to restore connectivity between systems and networks
- Oversees testing of alternate communications
- Reports status and recommendations to back the Contingency Planning Coordinator

In some cases, an organization may have a separate team whose sole responsibility is to return the primary site back to operational status. This team usually is referred to as the Reconstitution Team. While operations is ongoing at the alternate site, the Reconstitution Team works at the primary site cleaning up, repairing equipment, and preparing everything to return to normal operations so that a clean cutover back to the original site can be made.

LEVELS OF DISRUPTION

Disruptions to systems, networks, and major applications occur in varying degrees of magnitude. In order to clearly communicate the magnitude of a disruption, it helps to have disruption levels defined up front. By defining disruption levels up front, it makes it much easier for the Damage Assessment Coordinator to assess and communicate the type of disruption so that the recovery team can get prepared. The following levels of disruption serve as examples for your Contingency Plan:

- A *Limited Disruption* consists of a temporary disruption not associated with damage or loss of assets (e.g., disruption due to a power failure)
- A *Serious Disruption* consists of repairable damage to equipment or a facility that can be resolved by replacing equipment or software (e.g., a blown circuit board)

- A *Major Disruption* consists of irreparable damage to a facility, or loss of key personnel, data, or software (e.g., destruction of a computer room by water or fire)
- A *Catastrophic Disruption* consists of irreparable damage to equipment or a facility, or loss of a facility, its assets, or operations staff (e.g., disruption due to a tornado or a bomb)

You may decide to define the levels of disruption using different names. For example, a Level 1 disruption may be used *in lieu* of Limited Disruption and a Level 2 disruption may be used *in lieu* of a Serious Disruption.

PROCEDURES

Your Contingency Plan should contain detailed guidance and procedures for license key restoration and recovery operations. Imagine that a prolonged outage or a disaster has occurred. You have the backup media in your hand. Now what should you do with it? With the backup media in hand, you need to be able to recreate the entire business. Good procedures include low-level file execution instructions such as what Command Line Interface (CLI) commands to run and what Graphical User Interface (GUI) parameters to click on. The various types of procedures you should include are described in the following sections.

Backup and restoration procedures

Backup and restoration procedures for restoring systems and major applications from backup media need to be thoroughly documented. The procedures should include the name of the off-site storage facility, its address, phone number, and which employees are authorized to obtain backup media from it.

You'll want to describe the backup and restoration architecture so that the reader can understand the backup and recovery process enough to completely recreate it from your description. The restoration procedures should indicate if any particular software recovery programs (and their version number and patch level) are used to recover files. Are backups done locally on servers or are the data backed up to a Storage Area Network (SAN)? Are files restored over the network or is file restoration done locally? If backups are done over the network, is the backup server identified? Are backup agents deployed on the systems that are being backed up? All these questions should be answered.

You'll also need to document the backup rotation schedule. What file systems are backed up on what night of the week or day of the month? How often are full backups performed and how often are incremental backups performed? Include the backup schedule in a table.

When files need to be recovered, what are the commands that are used to recover these files? In restoring data, it should be very clear precisely which commands are to restore one file, a directory of files, or an entire file system. Should the administrator performing the restore launch a GUI? What should they click on? It helps to provide screenshots. If the restoration is done using a command line interface, what are the commands that need to be typed?

Procedures to access off-site storage

It's most often the case that not just anyone can walk into the off-site storage facility and obtain a copy of the backup media. Typically, the people who are allowed to access the backup media are authorized in advance. The people who are authorized to obtain the backup media may need facility access cards and a PIN to get into the off-site storage facility. Or perhaps you have an off-site storage service that delivers media. How do you contact them and who is authorized to notify them?

The names of the people who are authorized to obtain backup media should be documented. It's also a good idea to document their supervisors' names in case any one of them is out on vacation, out sick, or has perished in the disaster. At least two people should have access to the off-site storage facility and their full contact information needs to be documented.

Operating system recovery procedures

Procedures for recovering operating systems should be documented. You'll want to indicate whether systems are restored from an image file, or whether they should be rebuilt from scratch. If multiple operating systems are used (e.g., Windows and UNIX), you'll need multiple procedures. If operating system installation procedures are already documented in another document, it is sufficient to simply name the document and attach it as an appendix. When naming the document, you need to provide its official name with version and data. An example of an official document name would be:

Solaris Installation Guide for System ABC, Version 2.0, July 7, 2013

One of the things you'll want to be sure to document is what size the file systems should be partitioned to. The moment when you are trying to recover systems in a hurry is not the time to have to figure all this out. You may even want to include a screenshot of the disk partition table.

If a separate document exists on how to harden and lockdown the operating system, that document name should be recorded as well. It is not sufficient to simply say, "Lock down the operating system to secure it." All the operating system hardening procedures need to be documented. If there is a section in the installation and configuration guide on hardening and securing the operating system, that is acceptable.

You will need to be sure to include information on auditing records. Where is auditing information kept? Name the auditing files and directories including the full and absolute pathnames. You'll also want to include information on how to verify that the system is actually writing to log files once it is up and running.

Application recovery procedures

Application recovery procedures should include anything that is required to restore major applications once operating systems have been recovered. This section should include information about what services are supposed to be running and how to restore databases. Database configuration parameters should be listed. Do databases need to be synchronized with other databases? If all this information already exists in another document, it is acceptable to simply name that document using its official and formal name and then attach it as an appendix.

If this information does not already exist, you will need to take the time to gather it all and document it. You'll want to talk to the support staff, developers, and database administrators.

Connectivity recovery procedures

You need to document what sort of connectivity requirements are necessary to reconnect your systems at an alternate site in the event that moving to an alternate site becomes necessary. Do your systems and major applications require any sort of throughput? Are VPNs required? Are dedicated telephone lines to managed service providers required? Are T-1 lines required? Who are the current service providers and is their contact information documented? If systems are simply plugged into an Ethernet port and obtain their IP addresses from DHCP, that should be documented as well. If there are requirements to connect your network to any other networks, this should be indicated and should be consistent with the interconnection table listed in your System Security Plan.

Part of the connectivity recovery procedures should include documenting the particulars of important infrastructure files such as DNS zone maps, messaging server configuration files, routing tables, and firewall rulesets. Document what ports and services should be open and closed on the firewalls. If routers are included in your Hardware and Software Inventory, then you should either document the router Access Control Lists (ACLs) or be able to point to some other document that stipulates what these ACLs are.

Key recovery procedures

A list of what encryption keys will need to be recovered should be documented. For example, your systems and major applications may use encryption keys for any of the following reasons:

- Hash functions in authentication mechanisms
- Digital signatures
- File encryption applications
- Disk encryption applications
- Public Key Infrastructure (PKI) applications
- Encryption keys for VPNs
- Wireless encryption keys

You should describe what keys are needed and what they are used for. You should also document where the keys are kept and who has access to them. If the keys are on the backup tapes, you can simply say that. However, sometimes keys are stored by the systems administrators on separate media. Keys may even be kept on pieces of paper locked in a safe.

If your infrastructure doesn't use encryption keys for any reason, simply say so. It's better to include a section on key recovery, and then in the section, say "not applicable," than to not talk about this in your plan, which may leave the restoration team wondering whether there are keys or not.

Power recovery procedures

In the event of an electrical failure, it is possible to run your infrastructure on an uninterruptable power supply (UPS) for a short length of time. If your current operation is reliant on a UPS for any length of time, this should be described. The type of UPS (make and model number) should be described, and how long your systems can expect to continue to run off of UPS power should also be noted. At what point do generators turn on? Where are the generators and who is the company on contract to service them? How long can the generators run before a fuel provider needs to refill them?

Do you know the power requirements for your systems? What are the amps and voltage requirements? In order to provide for protection with a UPS, you need to understand the associated amps and voltage requirements. Your Contingency Plan should also make note of when the last time the UPS was tested—provide the date.

Recovering and assisting personnel

Don't forget about the people. Although most of this book describes how to plan for information technology scenarios, it goes without saying that people are more important than computers. You should include a section on recovering and assisting personnel. This section should include information on how to contact local fire, ambulance, and paramedic services. If a particular staff member is certified in CPR or first aid, this should be noted as well.

Notification and activation

It's important to define under what conditions the Contingency Plan will be activated and how the recovery team and general support staff will be notified. For example, it might be the case that the Contingency Plan should be activated only for either a major or a catastrophic disruption. Or, there could be a specific time frame associated with the activation criteria. For example, it could be that the Contingency Plan is activated if major applications are unavailable for more than 48 hours. Whatever the criteria is for activating the Contingency Plan, it should be spelled out and agreed upon ahead of time. The business owner, in discussions with support staff and the

ISSO, should make a decision ahead of time under what conditions the Contingency Plan should be activated. Examples of activation criteria are:

- The plan is activated if high priority systems (from BIA) are not recovered within 3 hours
- The plan is activated if water starts to come through the ceiling
- The plan is activated at the CIO's request
- The plan is activated if the military installation comes under hostile attack
- The plan is activated if all the high priority systems fail at the same time
- The plan is activated if the building is bombed
- The plan is activated if cyber attacks result in complete corruption of data
- The plan is activated if a denial of service attack continues for more than 7 days
- The plan is activated if snow threatens to cause the roof to cave in
- The plan is activated if all climate control systems fail for more than 48 hours
- The plan is activated if health records cannot be accessed for more than 3 days
- The plan is activated if a Category 4 or 5 hurricane is scheduled to hit the location within the next 48 hours

Upon determination that the plan will be activated, your document should specify how support staff and the recovery team will be notified. Will people be called on mobile phones? Will text messages be sent out? If e-mail, landline telephone, and mobile phones are all considered acceptable methods of contacting staff, the section on "Notification and activation" should specifically say this. In some environments, where classified information is at stake, the method of notification can be especially important.

LINE OF SUCCESSION

A management line of succession should be stipulated in the event that key personnel are lost in a disaster or cannot be located. Some of these people might very well have roles on the recovery team. For example, a line of succession might look like the one shown in Figure 14.1.

SERVICE-LEVEL AGREEMENTS

Are there Service-Level Agreements (or Memorandums of Understanding) that pertain to the information systems and applications in your Security Package? If there are, you should include such agreements as an appendix to your Contingency Plan. If your department or agency uses a managed service provider, where can contracts be found so that they can be reviewed to verify services are properly restored? Any agreements or contracts that stipulate what type of service you should

Agency CIO
↓
Business Owner
↓
Deputy Business Owner
↓
Functional Manager
↓
ISSO
↓
Security Team Lead

FIGURE 14.1

A management line of succession. The line of succession should include names and a primary and alternate phone number for each person listed.

expect from another organization, department, or company should be attached as an appendix.

CONTACT LISTS

One of the most important pieces of your Contingency Plan is the contact list. You'll want to include a staff contact list and contact lists for the vendors that make the equipment and software listed in your Business Impact Analysis and Hardware and Software Inventory. If your infrastructure spans two geographic locations, you'll want to include phone numbers for the staff in both locations. Many federal agencies employ contractors that are essential to their operations. Some of the contractors have been on site for years and are more familiar with the infrastructure than some of the government employees. Be sure to include contact information for essential contractors in your contact lists.

Once your Contingency Plan is written, the contact list will probably be the section you will need to update most often. Staff come and go, and even for the staff that remain the same, phone numbers change more often than you'd think. Contacts listed on a Contingency Plan should be updated at least once every 6 months. When you are about to submit a new Security Package for review, be sure that all the contact lists are up to date.

TESTING THE CONTINGENCY PLAN

Last but not least, the Contingency Plan should be tested at least once a year, and the testing date should be recorded in the Contingency Plan and the System Security Plan. Contingency Plan testing is not that high on the popularity list of security management activities—therefore, it is often overlooked. However, it's almost given that if your Contingency Plan is not tested, it will be cited as a finding in the *Security Assessment Report (Chapter 21)*.

Some organizations perform functional tests such as live failover tests where they cut over their entire infrastructure to a hot or warm standby site, and other organizations simply do a tabletop scenario where a fictional disaster is described and response activities are played out. Testing safeguards that maintain availability are excellent functional tests. When was the last time the Uninterruptable Power Supply (UPS) batteries were tested? Most UPS batteries only last about 5 years. If there is a room full of 50 batteries, it's possible that certain ones need to be replaced, but you won't know which ones until they are tested. Testing the UPS load off hours is an excellent test. To test the UPS load, you'll need to shut down all of the running applications (to protect data) and cut the power. When you cut the power, you should see if there are servers or devices that fail to maintain power. You should check the UPS display to see what it calibrates as far as remaining power time. If you need to shed some power consumption to enable the UPS to keep things running for a longer length of time, do you know which low-value items you might want to shut down to save on battery power?

Once you are on UPS power, how long will it take for your generators to turn on? Does your UPS hold power long enough for your generator to kick in? Does your generator turn on in time? You may think that testing the UPS and generators is not important, but these items fail more often than you might realize. At the end of June 2012, Amazon Web Services had a significant power outage due to failures related to the UPS and the generators.[1]

You should be able to justify why your Contingency Plan was tested in a particular fashion. *Contingency Planning Guide for Federal Information Systems, NIST SP 800-34, Revision 1* has additional guidance on how to test contingency plans. The higher the sensitivity level of your system, the more involved your Contingency Plan testing should be. For example, for a high-sensitivity system, independent assessors will expect to see detailed information on how you tested the failover of your systems to a live standby site. If you don't believe such involved Contingency Plan testing is necessary, and you categorized your system as high, you may want to revisit your reasons for selecting a high-sensitivity level—perhaps your system should really be categorized as a moderate level system.

Independent assessors look for consistency across documents. A high-sensitivity system will require highly available and redundant systems, a hot standby site, and far more detailed recovery procedures. It's not reasonable to state that the risk to your systems is so high that it warrants a FIPS 199 high categorization and then not perform detailed contingency preparations. Similarly, it makes little sense to categorize your system as a FIPS 199 low-sensitivity system and then state that highly available RAID systems and hot standbys are required for all the systems listed on your inventory.

---

[1]http://www.aws.amazon.com/message/67457/.

APPENDICES

A Contingency Plan is known for its numerous appendices. The Business Impact Analysis should always be an appendix of the Contingency Plan. Other items to include as appendices are:

- An Occupant Evacuation Plan
- Standard Operating Procedures
- Contact Lists
- Service-Level Agreements and Contracts

CONTINGENCY PLAN CHECKLIST

Use the following checklist to make sure you haven't forgotten anything.

- Has the Contingency Plan been tested?
- Does the staff that has been assigned contingency operations tasks have the authority to carry out these tasks?
- Has the staff that has been assigned tasks been given an opportunity to read the Contingency Plan and provide input and comments?
- Have all staff named in the Contingency Plan contact list been given a copy of the plan?
- Does a contact list exist and is it up to date?
- Are roles and responsibilities defined?
- Are procedures on recovering systems and major applications included?
- Is the off-site storage contact information and address listed?
- Is it clear who is authorized to retrieve media from the off-site storage site?
- Are restoration procedures from backup media described?
- Has a line of succession been indicated?
- Are requirements for temporary power (UPS or generator) described?
- Is the service provider that maintains the generators noted?
- Are necessary Service-Level Agreements (SLAs) documented?
- Has the Logistics Coordinator been given a copy of the SLAs?
- Does your Contingency Plan reference other pertinent and related documents?
- Has an alternative site been indicated?
- Is your Contingency Plan testing information that is provided consistent with the sensitivity level that you indicated?
- Are emergency phone numbers for local fire, police, and ambulance services noted?
- Does the plan contain a Record of Changes to record updates?

ADDITIONAL RESOURCES

Books that may be helpful to you in understanding Contingency Plan development are listed below:

Administrator's Guide to Disaster Planning and Recovery, Volume 2. TechRepublic, CNET Networks, 1995–2003. ISBN: 1931490651.

Barnes, James C. *A Guide to Business Continuity Planning.* John Wiley & Sons, LTD, July 2001. ISBN: 0471530158.

Myers, Kenneth N. *Manager's Guide to Contingency Planning for Disasters: Protecting Vital Facilities and Critical Operations.* Wiley, September 7, 1999. ISBN: 047135838X.

Toigo, Jon William. *Disaster Recovery Planning: Strategies for Protecting Critical Information Assets.* Prentice Hall, August 2002. ISBN: 0130462829.

Wallace, Michael and Lawrence Webber. *The Disaster Recovery Handbook: A Step-by-Step Plan to Ensure Business Continuity and Protect Vital Operations, Facilities, and Assets.* AMACOM, July 2004. ISBN: 0814472400.

Developing a Configuration Management Plan

15

ISC remains deeply apologetic that prior versions of BIND did not properly catch the configuration error that you appear to have built your business on.
—Paul Vixie, author of various RFCs

TOPICS IN THIS CHAPTER

- Establish definitions
- Describe assets controlled by the plan
- Describe the configuration management system
- Define roles and responsibilities
- Describe baselines
- Change control process
- Configuration management audit
- Configuration and change management tools
- Configuration Management Plan checklist

INTRODUCTION

Today's systems are constantly changing. With the onset of cloud computing, the speed of change is only going to increase. One of the primary reasons to track changes is that you can back out of them at some later point in time after realizing that a change has hosed your network. If everyone who had administrative access to production systems made changes all at once without consulting each other, and then something stopped working on the system, it would not be possible to immediately know whose change created the problem. Change management ensures that the whole team is consulted about upcoming changes ahead of time and that proposed changes are tested. If you've worked in information technology for a while, you're probably quite aware of the phenomena where you upgrade something in hopes of making your system better, faster, and smarter and then results in negatively impacting another part of the system, bringing it to its knees. Today's customers are not very forgiving. Configuration management enables you to plan and control the changes, so you have a more favorable outcome.

A *Configuration Management Plan* shows evidence that software changes, including code, operating system settings, and application configurations, are known and tracked. The settings and configurations that are known and tracked should include the configuration settings for the various servers, databases, network devices, and other products noted in the hardware and software inventory. The Configuration Management Plan describes how your organization does configuration management. It's a living document and should be updated if your configuration management process and procedures change.

Before starting to develop a Configuration Management Plan from scratch, find out if the system owner has one in place that they already follow. Some agencies may have one global Configuration Management Plan for the entire agency, and other agencies might develop Configuration Management Plans at the bureau or system level. The Configuration Management Plan that should be submitted with the Security Package is the plan that applies to your unique system that is undergoing authorization and assessment. If an agency-wide plan exists, you can use it for your Security Package as long as assets from your hardware and software inventory of your Security Package are named and tracked according to that plan. If you are unsure if an existing Configuration Management Plan will be acceptable, schedule a meeting with the assessment team and present them with your questions before you start developing a new plan. They should be able to give you guidance before you start working on your Configuration Management Plan as to what they consider to be acceptable or not.

ESTABLISH DEFINITIONS

When it comes to configuration management, terminology can mean different things to different people. Some organizations refer to a software build as a "release" and others refer to it as a "version." To ensure that the configuration management terminology that you use in your Configuration Management Plan will have a consistent meaning to all readers, it is a good idea to establish definitions up front and list them near the beginning of your document. Table 15.1 includes some commonly used configuration management terms. It's possible that these terms may be defined slightly differently by different agencies. What's important is that these terms mean the same thing to all the people that manage the system. If your agency already has configuration management terms defined through policies, use them and republish them in your Configuration Management Plan.

Guide for Security-Focused Configuration Management of Information Systems, NIST Special Publication 800-128 offers some definitions that you typically see in a Configuration Management Plan. Additionally, IEEE Standard 610-12-1990 offers some reputable and well-respected definitions. Table 15.1 includes a summary of the typical configuration management definitions which is the same summary information I developed when writing the Configuration Management section of "Guide to Understanding FedRAMP" (available at http://www.fedramp.gov).

Table 15.1 Common Configuration Management Terms[1]

Nomenclature	Definition
Alpha Release	The Alpha phase of the release cycle is the first phase to begin software testing. Alpha releases can potentially contain stability issues and are not made available to customers.
Beta Release	The Beta phase of the release cycle is a secondary phase to begin software testing after all features of the code are complete and after bugs found during the Alpha Release have been fixed
Baseline	(1) A specification or product that has been formally reviewed and agreed upon, that thereafter serves as the basis for further development, and that can be changed only through formal change control procedures. (2) A document or a set of such documents formally designated and fixed at a specific time during the life cycle of a configuration item. (3) Any agreement or result designated and fixed at a given time, from which changes require justification and approval (IEEE Std. 610-12-1990). A baseline is configuration identification formally designated and applicable at a specific point in the life cycle of a configuration item.
Build	An operational version of a system or component that incorporates a specified subset of the capabilities that the final product will provide (IEEE Std. 610-12-1990).
Configuration (or Change) Control Board (CCB)	A group of people responsible for evaluating and approving or disapproving proposed changes to configuration items, and for ensuring implementation of approved changes (IEEE Std. 610-12-1990).
Change Request	A request from either an internal or an external customer to make a change to a baseline configuration. Change requests can be related to either software releases or network components such as server or workstation configurations or any other network infrastructure component.
Configuration Control	An element of CM, consisting of the evaluation, coordination, approval or disapproval, and implementation of changes to configuration items after formal establishment of their configuration identification (IEEE Std. 610-12-1990).
Configuration Item	An identifiable part of a system that is a discrete target of configuration control processes. (NIST SP 800-128).
Configuration Management	A discipline applying technical and administrative direction and surveillance to identify and document the functional and physical characteristics of a configuration item, control changes to those characteristics, record and report change processing and implementation status, and verify compliance with specified requirements. (IEEE Std. 610-12-1990).

Continued

Table 15.1 Common Configuration Management Terms—cont'd

Nomenclature	Definition
Release	A software build that has been thoroughly tested and made available to customers.
Hardware Baseline	A current and comprehensive baseline inventory of all hardware (HW) (to include manufacturer, type, model, physical location, and network topology or architecture) required to support <Information System Name> operations is maintained by the Configuration Control Board (CCB) and is part of the Hardware and Software Inventory. A backup copy of the inventory is stored in a fire-rated container located or otherwise not collocated with the original.
Software Baseline	A current and comprehensive baseline inventory of all software that includes manufacturer, type, and version and installation manuals and procedures. A backup copy of the inventory is stored in a fire-rated container or otherwise not collocated with the original.
Version	Each software build is assigned a version number. The version number is used as a mechanism for differentiating one build from another. Version numbers are used regardless of whether or not a build is ultimately released.

[1]*4.15§* Guide to Understanding FedRAMP, *http://www.fedramp.gov.*

DESCRIBE ASSETS CONTROLLED BY THE PLAN

One of the first things you'll want to include in your Configuration Management Plan is a description of the hardware and software assets that the Configuration Management Plan pertains to. You can obtain this information quickly from your Hardware and Software Inventory. You should also include a brief system description about the system that the Configuration Management Plan is associated with. Using the same system description that you included in your Hardware and Software Inventory is perfectly acceptable. The Configuration Management Plan should be able to stand alone as its own document, which is why it is necessary to include this background information, even though it is somewhat redundant when considering the Security Package as a whole.

Always remember that most of the documents that you work on are not only parts of the Security Package you are developing but are working documents that the team managing the system uses on a daily, weekly, or monthly basis as well. It's quite likely that the staff that uses the Configuration Management Plan may not have access to the other documents in the Security Package which is one of the reasons that each document in the package needs to be able to stand alone and still be understood.

DESCRIBE THE CONFIGURATION MANAGEMENT SYSTEM

Most agencies, bureaus, or departments have a configuration management system. The configuration management system is the storage and retrieval mechanism for baseline configurations, documents, products, and code. Some configuration management systems might be simple databases, and others might be products designed specifically for configuration management tasks. Whatever system your agency uses, describe it, make note of who uses it, and also make note who has access to it. If a particular product or open source tool is used to perform configuration management, you will want to note the product and vendor name or the open source download location. Be sure to include the version numbers of any software that's installed on the configuration management system.

Additionally, you should describe the security controls that protect the configuration management system itself. Include discussion about the authentication mechanism, access to the system, perimeter protection (firewalls and routers), and host- or network-based intrusion detection systems that are used.

Finally, you should be sure to include information about how the configuration management system is backed up. Who is responsible for the backups? What programs are used to perform the backups? Where is backup media stored and who has access to it?

DEFINE ROLES AND RESPONSIBILITIES

One of the first items you'll need to discuss is to identify the folks who are actually performing configuration management. Describe their roles and responsibilities and list their names and contact information. Typical configuration management responsibilities are listed in Table 15.2. If you have a small agency, it is possible that some of these roles are consolidated into one role. Additionally, it is possible that the names of the roles found in Table 15.2 could vary from agency to agency.

DESCRIBE BASELINES

Discuss your configuration management process for establishing baselines. A baseline identifies and defines all the *configuration items* that make up a system at a particular moment in time. Baselining is a formal process, which occurs infrequently. The configuration management system should always have the current updated baseline available for review. There are generally three types of baselines:

- Functional Baseline
- Software Baseline
- Product Baseline

Table 15.2 Configuration Management Roles and Responsibilities

Director of Configuration Management (Director of CM)

- Develops and maintains CM plans, policies, and procedures
- Works with CM Analysts and CM Coordinators to ensure that configuration duties are understood
- Presides over Change Control Board (CCB) activities and meetings
- Designates a scribe to take notes or minutes during each CCB meeting
- Makes minutes available to all team members
- Approves or disapproves change requests discussed in the CCB meeting
- Maintains local records, databases, and libraries (repositories) to ensure compliance
- Authorizes access to the configuration management system
- Conducts configuration audits to ensure that CM activities are being performed correctly
- Reports compliance information to auditors as necessary
- Notifies CM Analysts and CM Coordinators about CM tools, CM policies, and procedures
- Leads the agency configuration management team
- Ensures that introduction of the proposed changes will not have a negative impact on current operations

Configuration Management Administrator (CM Administrator)

- Administers the configuration management system
- Receives new or updated documents and enters them into the configuration management system
- Receives all baselines and enters them into the configuration management system
- Catalogs change requests into the configuration management system
- Administers change request notifications and closes change request tickets
- Ensures that backups are performed on the configuration management system
- Ensures that an off-site backup of the configuration management exists
- Attends Change Control Board meetings
- Sends monthly report to the Director of CM

Configuration Management Analyst (CM Analyst)

- Ensures that all software is baselined
- Administers the release engineering system
- Performs release engineering activities
- Maintains source code and version control
- Assists in software integration and bug fixing
- Manages the software build process and controls the migration of software throughout the life cycle
- Maintains records, databases, and software libraries (repositories)
- Notifies developers and testers of configuration management status and policies
- Coordinates project configuration control activities
- Ensures that introduction of changes will not have a negative impact on current operations
- Maintains open communication with the CM Administrator
- Attends Change Control Board meetings
- Sends monthly report to Director of CM

Configuration Manager Coordinator (CM Coordinator)

- Develops and maintains CM plans, policies, and procedures for operating systems and applications
- Oversees generation of functional and product baselines
- Coordinates release of product components (hardware, software, interfaces, and documentation)
- Maintains records, databases, and libraries (repositories) to ensure compliance
- Maintains system integrity by performing configuration control
- Conducts training in CM tools and CM policies and procedures for project
- Ensures that introduction of changes will not have a negative impact on current operations
- Maintains open communication with the CM Administrator
- Attends Change Control Board meetings
- Sends monthly reports to Director of CM

A Functional Baseline describes the architecture and functions of the system according to orignal specifications. The Functional Baselines contains all of the documentation that describes the systems features, performance, design, and architecture characteristics. Each document should be assigned a document ID number and include a publication date and the author name(s).

A Software Baseline contains and describes all of a system's software. A Software Baseline includes the source code for each software configuration item and a software baseline document that provides a listing of the software and any other pertinent information such as developer, version, or software libraries. A Software Baseline locks in a version, build number, or release number at a particular moment in time.

A Product Baseline is the combination of the Functional Baseline and the Software Baseline. A product is not a product without documentation that explains how it works. A product could be an application that has been developed in-house or a commercial off-the-shelf application. Whether the product has been developed in-house or not, it should include installation and configuration information pertinent to the actual implementation. For a product developed in-house, the configuration management system should include the design and requirements documents. It's not necessary to include design documents for commercial off-the-shelf products since companies will likely not give that out.

If any license keys are used in the baselines, you will want to state how license keys are archived and preserved. You should also include the agency security policies about using unlicensed software. What method is used to ensure that software license keys are not installed on systems that have not paid for the keys?

CM Analysts and Coordinators should establish new baselines at the end of the design and build phases in the system development life cycle and again at the end of the test phase. All baselines should be entered into the configuration management system. New baselines should be continuously sent to the Director of Configuration Management, or the designated individual that updates the configuration management system.

CHANGE CONTROL PROCESS

The Configuration Management Plan should clearly describe the change management process. You'll need to explain how configuration changes are requested, approved, disapproved, and implemented. Sometimes, inserting a flowchart of the configuration management process is the best way to show how it works. Figure 15.2 depicts an example of a change control process flowchart. NIST SP 800-53, Revision 3 refers to this particular control as CM-3.

NIST SP 800-128, Appendix G, has some nice process flow charts related to configuration management. That document is currently published at http://www.csrc.nist.gov/publications/nistpubs/800-128/sp800-128.pdf. Reviewing these process diagrams may help your organization in developing (or improving) a sound configuration management process.

Change request procedures

Discuss the change request procedures in the Configuration Management Plan. Change requests typically go through the following phases:

- Initiation
- Review and analysis
- Approval or disapproval
- Notification that change will or will not occur (including the date for change)
- Implementation of change
- Closure of the change request

Change requests usually are initiated by filling out a paper form, a Web form, or sending in an e-mail request. You'll want to describe what the procedure is for initiating a change request. If there are particular time frames associated with the change request as it passes through steps 1 through 6, you should indicate those time frames in the plan.

Emergency change request procedures

Your agency should have an expedited change request process for emergency change requests. You'll want to find out what that process is and devote a small section to it in your Configuration Management Plan. There are often valid reasons for emergency change requests such as emergency bug fixes to resolve something that is hampering operations, or installing a patch to mitigate a security vulnerability.

Change request parameters

Each change request should have certain parameters that are required when submitting an initial change request. An example of a Change Control Request form that includes typical change request parameters is found in Figure 15.1. Figure 15.2 provides a flowchart depicting the Change Control process.

Configuration Control Board

The Configuration Control Board (CCB) is the forum where change requests should be discussed. An agency may have multiple CCBs that each act on behalf of their own business unit. In your Configuration Management Plan, you should identify the key information about the CCB that is relevant to the hardware and software assets for your particular Security Package as well as general information about how the CCB operates. Questions that you should answer in your discussion about the CCB are:

- When do CCB meetings take place?
- Who runs the CCB meetings?
- Are minutes/meeting notes taken?

Change Request Form

Select severity:
☐ Critical: considered essential to the system; security fix
☐ Very Important: will enhance performance or operations
☐ Important: beneficial to system users
☐ Non-Critical: desirable to implement as time permits

Initiator of request:
Email address of initiator:
Phone of initiator:

Type of change: (Select all the apply)
☐ Software code change
☐ Operating system configuration change
☐ Application configuration change
☐ Database configuration change
☐ Network device configuration change
☐ Firewall configuration change

Explain reason for change request:

Anticipated impact of change:

Test results and security impact analysis:

☐ Approved
☐ Disapproved (Explain why):

If approved, scheduled date of change:

Date of change request closure:

FIGURE 15.1

Example of a Change Request Form.

- Who are the members of the CCB?
- Are there CCB members from the Security Package's business owner's department?
- Is information about the CCB posted on an internal Web site that you can point to?
- Does the CCB generate a monthly report?
- Where can monthly CCB reports be found?
- Is there a group e-mail address for the CCB members?
- Is there an e-mail address for submitting change requests to the CCB?
- Is there a Web form for submitting change requests to the CCB?

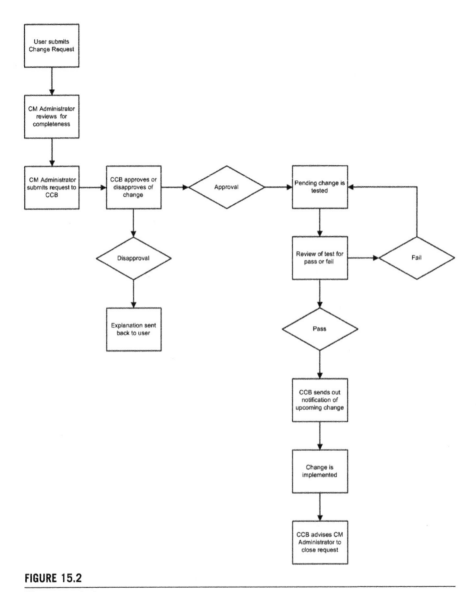

FIGURE 15.2

Change control process.

Testing and Security Impact Analysis

Before approving a change, CCBs typically require changes to be tested to see if the change works as planned or causes any unforeseen outcomes. Part of the testing should include performing a Security Impact Analysis. The purpose of a Security Impact Analysis is to determine if the change has created any new vulnerabilities in the system. The change should be analyzed for security weaknesses using whatever tool is appropriate for that particular change. If a source code change was made, performing source code analysis using a code scanner will help determine if there are memory leaks, race conditions, or deadlocks. If the change was related to a Web application, a Web application scanner should be used to look for vulnerabilities. If the change involves a change to an operating system, such as a patch, a kernel or registry modification, or a configuration setting, it makes sense to use an infrastructure scanner.

Analysis of the testing should determine if security was adversely affected. The test results should be presented to the CCB so that they can make an informed decision when determining whether to approve the change or not. The CCB will want to see evidence that the change was tested and that test results have a factual outcome. Therefore, all test results should be recorded and archived. In your Configuration Management Plan, you'll need to describe the process that your organization uses to perform testing and security impact analysis.

CONFIGURATION MANAGEMENT AUDIT

Include a section that explains how the Configuration Management Director ensures that the configuration management system archives the latest baselines. It is likely that auditing the configuration management system requires interviews and discussions with the configuration management staff. If the Configuration Management Director uses any sort of checklist to collate findings during the staff interviews, state that in the audit section. Discuss how often the audit interviews take place.

CONFIGURATION AND CHANGE MANAGEMENT TOOLS

There are numerous tools made to assist with configuration management duties and track version changes to code and documents. Some of these tools are licensable products and others are well-respected open source tools. Some products that are marketed as Business Continuity Tools offer useful configuration management features. If your agency uses particular tools or products to assist with change control and configuration management, you should name these products in your Configuration Management Plan. Popular tools that can be used to assist with configuration management include:

- CFengine
  http://www.cfengine.com/

- Chef
  http://www.opscode.com/chef/

- Concurrent Versions System (CVS), an open source tool
  http://www.cyclic.com/cyclic-pages/CVS-sheet.html

- Component Software Inc.'s CS-RCS Pro
  http://www.componentsoftware.com/csrcs/

- GIT
  http://www.git-scm.com/

- IBM's Rational Applications
  http://www-142.ibm.com/software/products/us/en/subcategory/SW750

- NetIQ's Secure Configuration Manager
  https://www.netiq.com/products/secure-configuration-manager/

- PTC Integrity (formerly MKS integrity)
  http://www.mks.com/solutions/discipline/sccm

- Puppet
  https://www.puppetlabs.com/

- SunView Software Inc.'s Change Gear CMDB
  http://www.sunviewsoftware.com/products/cmdb.aspx

- VMware vCenter Configuration Manager
  http://www.vmware.com/products/configuration-manager/overview.html

Security Content Automation Protocol (SCAP) was designed to measure security-related information. SCAP supports the use of standard reference data, such as identifiers for postcompilation software flaws and security configuration issues. SCAP can be used to maintain the security of enterprise systems by automatically verifying the installation of patches, checking system security configuration settings, and examining systems for signs of compromise. General information about the SCAP program is available from the NIST Web page http://scap.nist.gov/.

CONFIGURATION MANAGEMENT PLAN CHECKLIST

Upon completion of the Configuration Management Plan, use the following checklist to make sure you haven't forgotten anything:

- Have you described the configuration management roles and responsibilities?
- Have you described the configuration management system and tools?
- Have you described the security controls that protect the CM system?
- Is a copy of the change management request form included?
- Have you described the change control process?
- Are procedures for making emergency changes described?
- Have you described the baselines that you track?
- Have you described how license keys are archived and tracked?
- Have you described your process for establishing baselines?
- Are configuration management terms listed for reference?
- Is there a discussion about configuration management audits?

SUMMARY

A Configuration Management Plan demonstrates that your organization understands how to control change and can track all changes to your system including the settings for security controls. An effective Configuration Management Plan provides audit trails and traceability as to why change has occurred. The baselines stored in the configuration management system enable your organization to understand what the given configuration of your systems and major applications are at any given point in time. Tracking configuration changes and requests enables support staff to better troubleshoot security incidents since they will have a known good configuration for reference if the integrity of the current configuration ever comes into question.

ADDITIONAL RESOURCES

The following books and articles might help you improve your understanding of configuration management and help you to create an informative Configuration Management Plan:

Bounds, Nadine and Susan Dart. *CM Plans: The Beginning to Your CM Solutions.* Carnegie Mellon, Software Engineering Institute. http://tmcpfs.ops.fhwa.dot.gov/cfprojects/uploaded_files/cm_plans.pdf

Brad Appleton's Software Configuration Management Links. http://www.cmcrossroads.com/users/brad-appleton#Free_CM_Tools

Dreilinger, Sean. *CVS Version Control for Website Projects.* April 13, 1998. http://www.durak.org/cvswebsites/howto-cvs-websites.pdf

IEEE Standard 828-1998 for Software Configuration Management Plans. IEEE Standards Association. http://www.standards.ieee.org/findstds/standard/828-1998.html

Jonassen Hass, Anne Mette. *Configuration Management Principles and Practice.* Addison-Wesley Professional, December 30, 2002. ISBN: 0321117662.

Leon, Alexis. *Software Configuration Management Handbook, Second Edition.* Norwood, MA: Artech House Publishers. December 30, 2004. ISBN: 1580538827.

Moreira, Mario E. *Software Configuration Management Implementation Roadmap.* Hoboken, NJ: John Wiley & Sons, June 25, 2004. ISBN: 0470862645.

Preparing the System Security Plan

We spend our time searching for security and hate it when we get it.
—John Steinbeck

TOPICS IN THIS CHAPTER

- Laws, regulations, and policies
- The system description
- Security controls and requirements
- ISSO appointment letter
- System security plan checklist

INTRODUCTION

The *System Security Plan* is probably the most important document in the Security Package. If the evaluation team is pressed for time (which sometimes happens) and elects to scrutinize only one document in the entire Security Package, it is likely that the one document they will sift through with a fine-toothed comb will be the System Security Plan.

The System Security Plan sums up the system description, system boundary, architecture, and security control in one document. In the System Security Plan, you should also list pointers to the related documents that are part of the same package in your Security Plan. For example, you can say, "contingency planning is described in the *<System Name> Information System Contingency Plan, Revision 3, April 7, 2013.*" Though you don't want to rewrite the other documents in the System Security Plan, you will want to restate certain pieces of key information contained in other documents. For example, it is worth restating the sensitivity level for the system—the level that you calculated using the methodology described in Chapter 8.

Regardless of what methodology your agency uses for complying with FISMA, all systems that are general support systems or major applications must have a System Security Plan. OMB Circular A-130 §8 states:

> *Investments in the development of new or the continued operation of existing information systems, both general support systems and major applications must: Incorporate a security plan that complies with Appendix III of this Circular and in a manner that is consistent with NIST guidance on security planning....*

If you look in Appendix III[1] §A(3)(a)(2), you'll then find a list of all the elements that a System Security Plan should address including controls for general support systems, personnel security, contingency planning, technical controls, information sharing, rules of the system, training, incident response, controls for major applications, and others. Since all federal agencies (whether they are civilian agencies, intelligence agencies, or defense agencies) must abide by OMB Circular A-130, all systems that store or transmit government information must have a System Security Plan. *NIST SP 800-18, Revision 1, Guide for Developing Security Plans for Federal Information Systems* provides excellent guidance on what to include in a System Security Plan. Appendix A of SP 800-18 includes a System Security Plan template. You can find SP 800-18, Revision 1 at the following URL: http://www.csrc.nist.gov/publications/nistpubs/800-18-Rev1/sp800-18-Rev1-final.pdf.

If the agency that owns the system has a System Security Plan template already in place, you should use the agency's template for development of the System Security Plan, even if you think the template is not as good as it could be. If you believe the template could be improved, you should make notes with your recommendations on how to improve it and submit your recommendations to the department that is responsible for development of the templates. Most agencies allow the document prep team to make additions to the template, but removing sections of an existing template may elicit audit findings. If you think a section of the template does not apply to the information system you're describing, simply note the words "Not Applicable" in that section without removing the section.

LAWS, REGULATIONS, AND POLICIES

Near the beginning of your System Security Plan, you should include a list of all laws, regulations, and policies that affect the system undergoing security assessment. Your agency probably has hundreds of security policies. You don't need to republish all of them. Simply state the formal policy document name and the location where this document can be found. A formal document name for security policies would be similar to *<Agency>, Security Policies, Revision 6, October 27, 2012*. If the policy document is available on an agency intranet or wiki, include the URL. The only reason to list policies singularly is if an applicable policy is not contained in the overriding agency security policy document. (Sometimes new policies are published singularly and are then incorporated in the main agency policy document at some point in the future.)

Likely, your agency is responsible for compliance with many laws and regulations other than FISMA. List all related laws and regulations that the system must comply with alphabetically. Table 16.1 shows an example of a list of laws, regulations, and policies similar to what you may want to include in your System Security Plan.

---

[1]http://www.whitehouse.gov/omb/circulars_a130_a130appendix_iii

Table 16.1 An Example of Laws, Regulations, and Security Policy Descriptions

The system described in this System Security Plan is subject to the laws, regulations, and policies set forth by the federal government as follows:

- Clinger-Cohen Act
- Computer Security Act of 1987
- Critical Infrastructure Protection Act of 2001
- Federal Information Security Management Act (FISMA) of 2002
- Freedom of Information Act As Amended
- Government Management Reform Act (GMRA) of 1994
- Homeland Security Presidential Directive 7 (HSPD-7)
- Homeland Security Presidential Directive 12 (HSPD-12)
- OMB Circular A-130, Appendix III
- Privacy Act of 1974 as Amended

Additionally, the systems described in this Security Plan are subject to the following agency security policies:

- PIV Security Policy 1000.67, June 14, 2013
- Security Enrollment Account Policy, 1000.94, December 18, 2012
- <Agency>, Security Policies, Revision 6, October 27, 2012

THE SYSTEM DESCRIPTION

The system description section of the System Security Plan should describe, in prose, all the components of the information system or major application as defined by the authorization boundary (previously discussed in Chapter 7). For the purpose of the system description, the "system" refers to all of the components that are within the authorization boundary. Depending on how you define your information system, it could consist of anything from one computer to a large infrastructure of hundreds or thousands of computers and applications. (However, note that a system description that described only one computer within its boundary is very rare.) Each Security Package is owned by a system owner (see Chapter 4). Therefore, if major applications and general support systems have different system owners, this means that there should be different Security Packages for both. If the general support systems have the same system owner as the major applications, you can, in fact, include all these items together in one Security Package.

A system owner can choose to include as many, or as few, major applications or general support systems into a Security Package as they would like. Sometimes, deciding where to draw the line in the sand on what to include and not include in your system description takes some thought and various decisions will need to be made. Many of these decisions may have already been made when the Hardware and Software Inventory was put together. However, since you have not yet submitted your Security Package for review, you do have the liberty to go back and revise your Hardware and Software Inventory by taking servers or other components out of it and adding new ones. While writing your system description for the System Security Plan, if you notice that adjustments should be made to other documents, you have full liberty to make these changes as long as none of the documents have been submitted for evaluation. Keep in mind that if you add new servers, applications, or network devices, it could affect the sensitivity level that you originally calculated—if, for example, you add a data storage device holding highly sensitive data to a low-sensitivity system. If you find that you need to add a new device or system while in the midst of writing your System Security Plan, you will need to make sure that the addition is reflected in all your Security Package documents. If the system or device was never tested, you will need to test it and include those results in your Security Assessment Report.

In the system description, you should be sure to differentiate between general support systems and major applications. General support systems are those systems that provide the underlying infrastructure support for major applications, including file and print services.

Major applications usually get installed on top of operating systems and provide clearly defined functions. For example, some applications have server components and agent components that run on different systems. According to NIST Special Publication 800-18, Revision 1, February 2006:

> Major applications are systems that perform clearly defined functions for which there are readily identifiable security considerations and needs (e.g., an electronic funds transfer system).

If an application is not a "major application," it is referred to as a "nonmajor" application. Major applications are considered "major IT investments" which have a special meaning to the U.S. government. Major IT investments come under an agency's Capital Planning and Investment Control (CPIC) process and must be reported on Exhibit 300, the budget justification and reporting document, that is required by OMB for major IT investments. Applications that are nonmajor do not have to comply with FISMA. If you have a $29.95 software application that is being used by a handful of users, under most circumstances, there is no reason to jump through any FISMA hoops for this application.

System boundaries

In defining your system boundaries, you need to figure out where your system begins and ends. If you have a traditional IT system, defining the boundaries is much easier than if your system is a cloud system. (See Chapter 23 for information on cloud systems.) You have some flexibility in doing this, but it should all be based on logic. System boundaries are sometimes consistent with such things as:

- Windows domains
- Solaris NIS+ objects
- LDAP directory groups
- NIX netgroups
- The DMZ

- Firewalls
- Routers and switches
- VLANs
- Network segments
- Major applications
- Business mission
- Data center locations
- System ownership and management

This list should not be considered exhaustive by any means. There may very well be other devices, whether logical or physical, that can be appropriately described as system boundaries.

When describing system boundaries, keep in mind that your description should be inclusive of and should discuss the systems you described in your *Hardware and Software Inventory* (see Chapter 6). The system delineated by the boundary definition should be consistent with what comes under the purview of the system owner. You want to be careful not to take perceived ownership of another systems owner's servers and networks by going into lengthy detail about items not included in your inventory. However, it is okay to refer to systems owned by other owners for the purpose of describing your own systems. For example, you could say, "The major applications reside on network segment 21, which is bounded by Cisco firewall #2 and Checkpoint firewall #6. Both firewalls are owned by the Information Systems group and are reviewed in a separate Security Packages." If there are internal and external users that use the system, include an illustration of how they connect to the system as shown in Figure 16.1.

It can be helpful to describe your boundaries in terms of network zones (if there are in fact network zones that are known to the support staff). Network zones are segments of network infrastructure that are separated by firewalls and have different security levels associated with them. However, sometimes, different network zones are separate from each other simply to separate the administration of duties between two different business units or administrative groups. Since you should include a network topology map in your System Security Plan, it can be useful to describe the network zones on your network topology map. A simple yet effective way of describing network zones is found in Table 16.2.

System purpose (mission)

You will also want to describe the general mission of the systems in your system description. You should have a good idea of the mission at hand from having worked previously on your Business Risk Assessment. Since the evaluation team will be looking for consistency across your documents, using some of the same mission terminology that you used in your Business Risk Assessment is a good idea.

You'll want to state whether the system slated for security assessment and authorization is a general support system, major application, or both. A general support

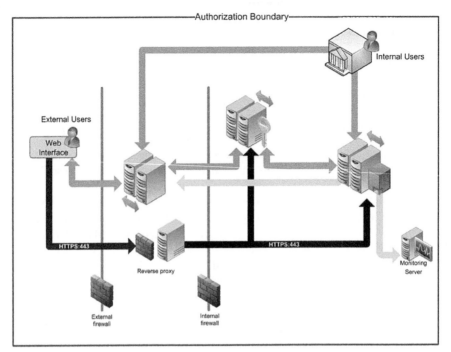

FIGURE 16.1

System and Authorization Boundary. (For color version of this figure, the reader is referred to the online version of this chapter.)

Table 16.2 A Sample Description of Network Zones

Zone Number	Zone Name	Description
0	Public zone	Open to the public. Subject to privacy regulations
1	Internal zone	Not open to the public. Protected internal network
2	High security zone	Extra secure internal network—e.g., classified network
3	Unattached zone	Not connected to other zones—e.g., a test network

system typically consists of parts of the network infrastructure used to support general operations of your business. According to *NIST Special Publication 800-18, Guide for Developing Security Plans for Information Technology Systems*:

> *A general support system is interconnected information resources under the same direct management control which shares common functionality. A general support*

system normally includes hardware, software, information, data, applications, communications, facilities, and people and provides support for a variety of users and/or applications.

For a general support system, the purpose could be to provide a platform for major applications. It also could be simply to provide a communications network for e-mail, file sharing, development, and collaboration. There may be multiple missions and if there are, you should describe all of them. In fact, most general support systems likely have multiple functions.

Major applications are most often software applications that reside on top of operating systems of general support systems. However, it is altogether possible that a major application could also consist of hardware devices. For example, a smart card system usually has both software and hardware devices. The hardware devices for a smart card system could include card readers, card issuing systems, and the cards themselves. According to *NIST Special Publication 800-18, Guide for Developing Security Plans for Information Technology Systems*:

> *A major application might comprise many individual programs and hardware, software, and telecommunications components. These components can be a single software application or a combination of hardware/software focused on supporting a specific mission-related function. A major application may also consist of multiple individual applications if all are related to a single mission function (e.g., payroll or personnel).*

Data flows

The System Security Plan should include a description, and a graphic, of how the data flow from one place to another in your system descriptions. If files are transferred either manually or automatically by a scheduler, you'll want to list the file names and state the times and under what conditions they are transferred. In Table 14.1, data sources and destinations were listed. You are going to want to describe those data sources and destinations more fully as part of the system description. In each of the examples (each row) listed in Table 16.2, you should describe in prose how the data get from its source to its destination. You may want to indicate a legend on your network topology map with numbers or letters so that you can more easily describe the data flows. An example of data flow prose used in conjunction with the fictitious network segment shown in Figure 16.2 is the following:

> *System administrators in Dallas use an automated **cron** job to distribute patches from the Dallas datacenter to the Boston datacenter via a Cisco VPN every Friday between 5 and 6pm CST so that the Boston facility can receive a copy of tested patches from the Patch Master system in Dallas.*

An example of a data flow diagram is illustrated in Figure 16.2.

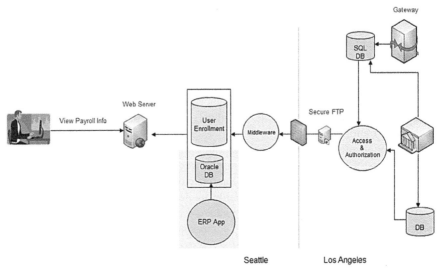

FIGURE 16.2

Example of a Data Flow Diagram. (For color version of this figure, the reader is referred to the online version of this chapter.)

Source: FISMA Center.

SECURITY CONTROLS AND REQUIREMENTS

Security controls are supposed to implement security requirements. The requirements describe the need, and the controls satisfy that need. According to *NIST SP 800-53, Revision 4 Security and Privacy Controls for Federal Information Systems and Organizations*:

> *Security controls are the safeguards/countermeasures prescribed for information systems or organizations that are designed to: (i) protect the confidentiality, integrity, and availability of information that is processed, stored, and transmitted by those systems/organizations; and (ii) satisfy a set of defined security requirements.*

In describing the security controls, you'll want to differentiate between security controls currently in place and those controls that are planned for future implementation. In FISMA compliance, you get credit for planning. If you don't have particular controls in place yet, but they will be implemented in 2 months, you should document that in your System Security Plan. Keep in mind though that if the System Security Plan says that controls have been planned, the system owner and ISSO will be on the hook for actually implementing the controls. Auditors at some point in the future will likely verify that the "planned controls" have been put into place. Therefore, if controls have not been planned, don't say that they have been.

In March 2006, the National Institute of Standards and Technology published a document titled *FIPS Publication 200, Minimum Security Requirements for*

Federal Information and Information Systems (FIPS PUB 200). NIST Special Publications are generally thought of as guidance, but the Federal Information Processing Standards (FIPS) series of publications are considered mandatory. The FIPS standards, however, point you to the Special Publications, and section 8 of FIPS PUB 200 says:

> *Federal agencies must meet the minimum security requirements as defined herein through the use of the security controls in accordance with NIST Special Publication 800-53,* Recommended Security Controls for Federal Information Systems, *as amended.*

Note that in the most current version of NIST SP 800-53, the title of that document has been slightly renamed to also include privacy controls.

Therefore, you are on the hook to use the recommended security controls in Special Publication 800-53 as they apply to your information systems. FIPS PUB 200 can be found at http://www.csrc.nist.gov/publications/fips/fips200/FIPS-200-final-march.pdf#search=%22FIPS%20200%22.

It is certainly possible that not all the guidance in Special Publication 800-53 will apply to the systems and applications listed in your Hardware and Software Inventory. Certainly you have flexibility. In fact, FIPS PUB 200 further states:

> *Organizations must meet the minimum security requirements in this standard by selecting the appropriate security controls and assurance requirements as described in NIST Special Publication 800-53,* Recommended Security Controls for Federal Information Systems.

To understand what security controls are appropriate, you need to understand your security design requirements. The system's security requirements should be documented as IT Baseline Security Requirements—often referred to in federal agencies as the BLSRs. Most agencies publish a copy of required BLSRs for their agency's systems. The security requirements for the design of the items undergoing security assessment should be based on a subset of these overriding BLSRs. It is altogether possible that the security assessment team may ask to see a copy of the security requirements for the system undergoing security assessment and authorization. You should be able to refer to a formal and separate document containing these requirements in the System Security Plan. For example, you could say:

> *This* System Security 1an *describes the security controls established to comply with the security requirements set forth in* <Agency> Information System Security Requirements, Revision 2.0, *June 10, 2013.*

It will not hurt your Security Package to attach the security requirements as an appendix to the System Security Plan.

It is altogether possible that for some legacy systems, the original security requirements cannot be located. Although that certainly is not an optimal situation, for the purpose of security assessment and authorization, you may have to

Table 16.3 Example of a Brief List of Technical Security Requirements

Security Requirements for Federal Information System, Revision 2.0

#	Technical Requirements	SP 800-53 Control ID
001	The authorizing official must approve the use of group IDs	AC-2
002	Guest and anonymous accounts are not permitted	AC-1
003	Access control shall follow the principle of least privilege	AC-6
004	Privileged account access shall follow the principle of separation of duties	AC-5
005	Accounts that have not been activated shall be removed after 60 days	AC-1
006	Privileged users (admin, root, etc.) must be recertified semiannually	CA-1
007	The information system must be protected by firewalls and Virtual Private Networks (VPNs)	SC-7
008	Sessions shall automatically terminate after 3 minutes of inactivity	AC-12
009	The information system must have built-in audit logging capabilities	AU-1
010	User interfaces must be separate from system administration interfaces	SC-2
011	All devices must be identified by their MAC and IP addresses before establishing a connection	IA-3

The NIST Special Publication (SP) 800-53 security control number abbreviation is cited in the right-hand column for further reference.

temporarily put the cart before the horse and document *ex post facto* what you believe were the intended security requirements. Documenting security requirements can be very time consuming; be sure to schedule plenty of time to create *ex post facto* security requirements. If you are trying to develop a System Security Plan at the same time, you may need to enlist another resource to help you out. Examples of security requirements are found in Tables 16.3–16.5.

For every security requirement, you should be able to map a security control to it that satisfies that requirement. If you have not yet submitted your Security Package, you can go back and make modifications to your other documents while you are developing your System Security Plan. You may also need to add in a requirement, and have the ISSO expeditiously implement another control, while the System Security Plan is still being developed. Use the self-assessment questions from Chapter 8 to help you better understand what security controls to document in the System Security Plan.

Your System Security Plan should describe the security controls in prose. Providing a list of bulleted control names is not good enough. Use words and explain how the controls work in simple and easy-to-understand English.

Table 16.4 Example of a Brief List of Operational Security Requirements

Security Requirements for Federal Information System, Revision 2.0

#	Operational Requirements	SP 800-53 Control ID
012	Incident response and reporting shall be centrally managed	IR-1
013	Accounts of terminated personnel shall be removed from the system	PS-4
014	All users must receive Security Awareness Training	AT-2
015	A copy of backup media must be stored in an off-site location	CP-6
016	An alternate processing must be identified and be ready 24 × 7 for disaster failover operations	CP-7
017	The information system must be protected from malicious code by an EAL4 antivirus product	SI-3
018	Changes to the system must be made in accordance with the agency configuration change control process	CM-3
019	The system hardware must undergo regular preventative maintenance support from an authorized vendor	MA-6
020	All removable information storage media for the information system must be labeled with external labels	MP-3
021	The information system must be housed in a facility where physical access is controlled and documented	PE-3
022	Events on the system must be monitored by a host-based intrusion detection system to detect attacks	SI-4

The NIST Special Publication (SP) 800-53 security control number abbreviation is cited in the right-hand column for further reference.

MANAGEMENT CONTROLS

Management security controls help ensure that management requirements are adhered to. By clearly describing the management controls, you should be able to convince the evaluation team that the business owner's management team understands their responsibilities, are following through with these responsibilities, and are being held accountable for them.

Risk mitigation

In the section on Management Controls, you should include a summary of how your agency or department mitigates risk. Risks are mitigated by reducing them to a level that is acceptable to the business owner. Clearly, before they can be mitigated, they need to be identified. In this section, you should, in summary fashion, briefly describe your overall risk mitigation strategy.

Risks to the system are documented by independent assessors in the Security Assessment Report. You will learn more about the *Security Assessment Report* in

Table 16.5 Example of a Brief List of Management Security Requirements

Security Requirements for Federal Information System, Revision 2.0

#	Management Requirements	SP 800-53 Control No.
023	The information system and its major applications must undergo assessment prior to being put in production	CA-1
024	A security budget for the information system must be established	SA-2
025	Statements of Work (SOW) must identify how sensitive information is handled	SA-9
026	Contracts for outsourced operations must include facility security requirements	SA-9
027	Contracts and SOWs must stipulate that contractors will protect sensitive information	SA-9
028	The information system life cycle must include decommissioning of data	SA-3
029	All documentations for the system shall be marked *Controlled Unclassified Information* (CUI)	MP-3
030	The information system must be scanned for security vulnerabilities quarterly	RA-5
040	Failure to comply with the Rules of Behavior shall be considered a security incident	PL-4
041	Private keys shall contain a minimum of 8 characters with mixed case letters, and at least one number	IA-5
042	The information system shall run only licensed operating systems and applications	SA-6

The NIST Special Publication (SP) 800-53 security control number abbreviation is cited in the right-hand column for further reference.

Chapter 21. The Security Assessment Report is put together by the evaluation team (after reviewing the entire Security Package) and it includes a summary of all the vulnerabilities. You'll want to point out that any vulnerabilities identified in the Security Assessment Report are mitigated by reducing them, accepting them, or transferring them. While the System Security Plan is in development, the Security Assessment Report does not yet exist. However, by stating the System owner's intentions on how risks noted in the Security Assessment Report will be handled in the future, it assures the evaluation team that you agree up front that any reported risks will be appropriately mitigated. You need to convince the evaluation team that all risks are, and will be, appropriately mitigated. Explaining that your risk mitigation strategy includes reducing risks found in their final Security Assessment Report makes the evaluators feel as though you are on-board with their counsel.

Additional items that you ought to mention in this section (even if you have already mentioned these items in other Security Package documents) include summary discussions about the following:

- How often you perform network- and host-based vulnerability scanning
- The fact that your system impact level is determined by an FIPS-199 process
- The fact that you recognize that OMB A-130 requires risk assessments every 3 years
- Threat sources are taken into consideration when assessing risk
- The fact that you hold external third parties (service providers) accountable for vulnerabilities

Reporting and review by management

There are multiple stipulations in FISMA that call for reporting and review by management. For example, FISMA §3543(a)(5) says:

> *The Director shall oversee agency information security policies and practices, including—reviewing at least annually, and approving or disapproving, agency information security programs required under section 3544(b)....*

Additionally, FISMA §3544(c) says:

> *Each agency shall (1) report annually to the Director, the Committee on Government Reform and Science of the House of Representatives, the Committees on Government Affairs and Commerce, Science, and Transportation of the Senate, the appropriate authorization and appropriations committees of Congress, and the Comptroller General on the adequacy of information security policies, procedures, and practices, and compliance with the requirements of this subchapter...; (2) address the adequacy and effectiveness of information security policies, procedures, and practices in plans and reports...*

This simply means that there are requirements to review your own security controls and reports, to create new reports on your findings, and to submit them to various congressional committees.

In discussing how you report and review security controls, you should summarize the process that the business owner's management team uses to review security controls. The business owner's management team needs to show evidence that they have reviewed security controls. The security assessment and authorization process itself is one way that the management team typically reviews security controls since the business owner and typically their associated managers are required to review and sign some of the documents that pertain to their role and responsibility. Therefore, in the System Security Plan, although this may seem circumlocutory, you are allowed to state that your security assessment and authorization process fulfills the reporting and review requirements.

In the reporting and review section, provide a summary list of all the documents in the Security Package that you are working on and also include the reaccreditation date for the package. If there are other documents that are not included in the Security Package that have been reviewed by the business owner's management team or ISSO and are related to security compliance, you should list those documents as well, including information on who reviewed them and when. Generally speaking, in most cases you won't want to list documents that are more than 3 years old. Other than the Security Package itself, auxiliary documents can include initial design documents, architecture documents, security standards, security policies, checklists, or even descriptive e-mail messages.

System life cycle requirements

Your discussion of system life cycle requirements first and foremost should acknowledge that your agency has system life cycle requirements. The life cycle methodology for the systems undergoing security assessment should include discussions about how the systems evolved. Before these systems were put into production, there must have been requirements, planning, procurements, and a need for them. As depicted in Figure 16.3, system life cycle requirements generally include the following phases:

- Requirements identification and analysis
- Planning and procurement

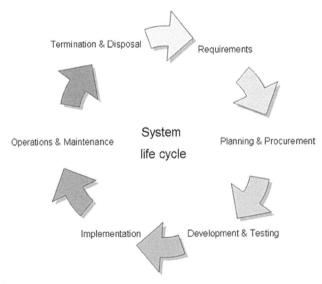

FIGURE 16.3

System life cycle process. (For color version of this figure, the reader is referred to the online version of this chapter.)

- Development and testing
- Implementation
- Operations, production, and on-going maintenance
- Terminal and disposal

It's possible that your agency has life cycle requirements and processes documented in a System Development Life Cycle (SDLC) manual or handbook. If that is the case, you can obtain much information on what to include in the life cycle requirements section from the handbook. If you are unable to find any evidence that an SDLC methodology exists, or that life cycle requirements were ever taken into consideration, you'll need to create these requirements *ex post facto*. Creating requirements *ex post facto* is never ideal, but it does show that going forward your business owner acknowledges the importance of such phases. In some cases, it may be that life cycle requirements were followed, but never documented. In the eyes of the independent security assessment team, if something is not documented, it doesn't exist. It is possible that your agency's SDLC methodology includes four or five phases, instead of six. It may also include seven phases. Don't get hung up on the number of phases since some agencies may combine a couple of phases. Use the life cycle support questions from Chapter 8 to help you make sure you have covered all the bases.

Security planning

Security planning includes controls planned for future implementation, as well as resources planned for future use. Resources include personnel, contractors, equipment, software, and budgetary allocations. If you have security controls that are in the planning process, but will not be implemented until some point in the future, you should describe those controls in this section. If you plan on hiring a security administrator or a security engineer, and have allocated budgetary funds for the next fiscal year to do that, indicate this intent. If you plan on implementing new intrusion detection systems, antivirus software, single sign-on systems, or anything that will remediate existing vulnerabilities, be sure to mention this. Security planning refers to security initiatives that will improve the security posture of your organization at some point in the future. In the world of FISMA compliance, you get credit for planning.

Documentation for managers

To provide adequate guidance on security controls, management needs to understand the controls and therefore needs documentation to read and review. Name the security documents that management reviews, comments on, and approves of. You need to list formal document names that include the revision number and the publication date. The documents described in this section should include any of the other Security Package documents, as well as any other documents related to security (e.g., security configuration guides and security architecture documents). Describe the

Table 16.6 Documentation Review and Approvals

Document Name	Review and Approval Team
Security Requirements, Version 4.0, May 1, 2013	William McKnight, ISSO Lynn Pfeiffer, Director of Application Engineering
System Security Plan, Version 3.1, July 10, 2013	William McKnight, ISSO Gregg Sokolowski, Compliance Team Lead

review and approval cycle indicating the names of the staff that signed off on the various documents. You can summarize this information in tabular form as shown in Table 16.6.

OPERATIONAL CONTROLS

Operational security controls help ensure that operational requirements are adhered to.

Personnel security

Information about personnel security should include information about background investigation. Most U.S. federal agencies require background investigations. Provide as much information as you can about the background investigation and screening process. It is very possible that your agency has a security screening branch that carries out all background investigations. The security screening branch may not make all of its processes and procedures available to everyone in the agency. If that is the case, simply state the name of the department that carries out the background investigations. Also, describe how the background investigation department can be contacted and where they are located. If there are policies that require background investigations, it is worth noting these policies.

Additionally, this section should include information on how both staff and contractors are kept safe. For example, if evacuation routes are posted in hallways, or if there are formal Emergency Response Procedures, be sure to note that in this section. In some agencies, staff (including contractors) are offered disaster preparedness training and are given disaster preparation kits that include items like flares, whistles, and food rations. Whatever measures your agency takes to ensure that their staff is safe and secure are worth stating in this section.

Physical and environmental controls and safeguards

Physical and environmental safeguards protect the facilities that host information systems. Provide descriptions that support the fact that the systems listed in the Hardware and Software Inventory are hosted in an environment that is conducive to continuous operations. This section describes the facilities and their warning systems.

Physical and environmental safeguards include such things as facilities access, emergency power, emergency lighting, fire suppression systems, fire alarms, circuit breakers, plumbing, surveillance cameras, and temperature and humidity controls. The System Security Plan should specifically describe whether uninterruptible power supplies (UPS) or generators are used, and what make and model each are. Describe the type of fire suppression system including any preventative maintenance required to test it on an annual basis. Describe emergency lighting systems and where emergency lights are located. Include information about how often emergency lights are tested.

Describe the use and positioning of any surveillance cameras. For example, specify if surveillance cameras are mounted at building entrances, server rooms, or hallways. Additionally, the type of surveillance cameras should be specified as well as whether or not active monitoring is performed using the cameras, or whether they are passive cameras that simply record events that are then stored.

Information should be given about electrical circuits, voltage requirements, circuit breakers, and wiring closets. If this information is documented in a separate facilities manual, and you list the formal name of that manual, the evaluation team will likely accept this information in lieu of reprinting it all separately in your System Security Plan.

It is necessary to describe any physical access systems to buildings and data centers. Note the location and operation of card readers. Describe the card readers' make and model numbers. Additionally, you need to describe in general terms how the card readers work. For example, do they use magnetic stripes or RFID chips? Do they require PINs? Describe the use of smart cards and badging systems. If smart cards are used, discuss a little bit about the type of cards used and the application system used to program them. The process of how an individual obtains an identification badge requires description. Provide an explanation of whether Personal Identity Verification (PIV) credentials or Personal Identity Numbers (PINs) are used. Describe the visitor registration process. For example, it should be noted who signs visitors in and if visitors require escorts while in the building.

Administration and implementation

Administration and implementation refers to the installation, configuration, and administration of your systems and applications. Create a discussion about the systems and database administrations that perform the installations and configurations. Who are these folks? What is the experience level of the systems and database administrators? Do they have any technical certifications that may help a Security Package auditor have faith in their abilities? The systems and database administrators may be part of an organization that is separate from the organization of the business owner. Describe any pertinent facts about the administration organization and management team. An example of a discussion that describes the capabilities of the administration and implementation team follows:

The enterprise resource planning systems are administered by the Information Services (IS) department, which is managed by Barbara Davidson. IS provides administrative operations and support for over 500 systems. The systems listed in the Hardware and Software Inventory, Version 2.0, February 24, 2006 *are administered by Rafael Sanchez, Tajuan McDuffie, Bruce Higgs, and Kiri Porter.*

Mr. Sanchez has been administering Solaris systems for six years and is a Sun Certified Systems Administrator. Ms. McDuffie has administered Microsoft Windows systems for five years, and recently obtained a Microsoft Certified Systems Engineer (MCSE) certification for Windows Server 2003. Mr. Higgs has been administering Oracle databases for two years, and before that, administered Microsoft SQL databases for five years. Ms. Porter specializes in Web site administration. She is knowledgeable about IBM Websphere and has written half a dozen articles on the how to secure Web-based applications. The IS administrators currently document their installation, configuration, and operations process, and these documents are available for review. All the administrators carry cell phones, and if they are not reachable, the call will automatically be transferred to the Network Operations Center (NOC), which is staffed 24/7, 365 days a year.

The objective of this particular section is to convince the evaluation team that the staff that administer the systems and applications on a day-to-day basis are competent and capable.

Preventative maintenance

Preventative maintenance refers to the maintenance required to keep equipment and hardware running. Maintenance activities include performing diagnostics on circuit boards, changing boards, performing diagnostics on memory, and BIOS and any other parts of the hardware. It's possible that certain computers at times may need a new power supply or a new fan. Who are the folks who would make this determination and perform the installation? Preventative maintenance may be done by your agency's in-house staff or it might be contracted out to a third-party organization. Whatever the case may be, document who performs preventative maintenance and whether it is performed on any sort of regular schedule. If an outside third-party performs these tasks, you'll need to include the name and contact information of the person or department responsible for managing the third-party.

A thoughtful argument can be made that preventative maintenance also includes the detection of software problems. However, I prefer to see information about the detection of software problems in the technical controls section that discusses preservation of data integrity. System diagnostics related to file system errors and file systems filling up belong in the section on Preventative Maintenance. Some systems run scheduled diagnostics on a regular schedule to check the size of the file systems to ensure that they do not fill up. If the systems in your Security Package run any regularly scheduled diagnostics on the file systems, or are regularly defragmented, be sure to indicate this.

Contingency and disaster recovery planning

The *Contingency Plan* was discussed in Chapter 14. It is not necessary to recreate all that information in the System Security Plan. However, the System Security Plan should include a brief summary, indicating that the Contingency Plan exists, providing the formal name of the Contingency Plan document and its publication date. If there are any other documents that are related to contingency planning that you would like the evaluation team to take into consideration, be sure to name those documents in this section. For example, if your Security Package describes a major application that resides on top of general support systems, it is likely that there is a separate Contingency Plan for the general support systems and such a Contingency Plan would be worth mentioning.

In addition to noting the existence of the plan and where to find it, the System Security Plan should indicate vital information on the organizational requirements surrounding the maintenance and support of the plan. The SSP should indicate who is responsible for maintaining the plan, the frequency with which it must be reviewed and updated, whether key personnel with duties in implementing the plan are trained on the plan, and what type of Contingency Plan testing is conducted.

Training and Security Awareness

We already discussed the *Security Awareness and Training Plan* in Chapter 9. However, in the System Security Plan, you should state that a Security Awareness and Training Plan exists and provide the formal document name. A Security Awareness and Training Plan is considered a type of operational security control, which is why you should make reference to it in the System Security Plan.

Additionally, the SSP should indicate key information on the organizational requirements regarding the implementation of security training, such as the levels of training employees must go through, what training records are kept, how often employees must participate in the training, and who is responsible for overseeing the program.

Incident response procedures

Your Incident Response Plan should serve as an in-depth description of your incident response process. Don't recreate that plan in the System Security Plan. However, you should provide a brief summary of the Incident Response Plan and be sure to indicate that a detailed Incident Response Plan is available, stating the formal document name, date, and version number. The Incident Response Plan is a type of operational control, which is why you need to mention it in the System Security Plan.

In addition to noting the existence of the plan and where to find it, the SSP should indicate who is responsible for maintaining the plan, the frequency with which it must be reviewed and updated, whether key personnel with duties in implementing the plan are trained on the plan, and what type of incident response testing has been conducted.

Preservation of data integrity

You need to present information that serves as evidence that data integrity is preserved. Data integrity refers to the fact that the data are pure and represents what it is supposed to represent—it hasn't been tainted or changed by either error or intentional malicious activity. Discuss antivirus software, host-based intrusion detection systems, security behavioral analysis products, file encryption, and patch management. Be sure to also discuss any customized scripts used to preserve file integrity. For example, if the information system uses scripts that check for data integrity breaches using MD5 hash functions, be sure to describe what is checked and how often. In talking about the implementation of security products that ensure data integrity, such as antivirus products, your discussion should answer the following questions:

- What is the product name and version number?
- Is there a third-party (vendor or reseller) that provides on-going product support?
- On what systems is the product implemented?
- Does it include both server and client software?
- Under what conditions do the clients interact with the server?
- Does it use agents? Where are the agents deployed?
- Is there a management console?
- Are files or databases encrypted?
- For anything that is encrypted, have you named the encryption tool and key sizes?
- Does the product rely on signatures that require updating? How often are signatures updated?
- How are updates installed (e.g., downloaded, distributed)?
- Does the product require configuration rules? If so, what are the rules?

Network and system security operations

Network and system security operations refer to the security of the network and its associated devices and monitoring systems. Unless your agency is extremely small, it likely has a Network Operations Center (NOC) and/or a Security Operations Center (SOC). Describe how your systems and network devices provide monitoring information back to the operations center. Are agents installed on host systems to monitor them? How would the NOC know if a mission critical system went down? It's possible that your agency may use any one of many different applications and tools to monitor their systems, in which case you will want to describe what application is used for monitoring, and how it works. For example, if used within your agency, you will want to describe the general implementation of the following network monitoring applications:

- BMC ProActive Net
- CA Infrastructure Management
- Ganglia
- HP Openview
- IBM Netcool
- ManageEngine
- Nagios
- NetIQ Secure Configuration Manager
- NETSCOUT nGenius Analytics for Flows
- Observium
- Solarwinds Network Configuration Manager
- Spiceworks

If your department is dependent on a separate network operations group that manages the networks on which your information systems reside, you will need to communicate with them to find out which tools they use to monitor your systems and applications. You'll want to ask them specific questions that will lead to information that you can include in your System Security Plan. It is sometimes hard to draw the line of how much you should document and how detailed you should get. You may not have time to include every last detail. However, try to include enough information so that it will be clear to the evaluation team that the business owner is well aware of who they would need to go to in order to obtain all the rest of the nitty-gritty details. For example, you could include a statement on your network monitoring system such as the following statement that includes basic information, with a pointer on where more details can be found:

> *The department of memorial flags has two networks that are monitored by the Network Management Group (NMG). NMG monitors both networks using IBM's Micromuse. The configuration and operations of NMG's Micromuse system is detailed in the* Network Management Group's Network Operations Guide, V 3.1, February 24, 2012. *This guide is maintained and updated by the Director of Information Technology, Daniel Puckett, whose contact information is listed in the phonebook on the agency intranet.*

State your firewall rule-set configuration strategy. For example, a common strategy is to deny all protocols and ports unless they are explicitly allowed. If approvals are required to allow an additional service, state what the approval process is. It's possible that the approval process may be as simple as "All approvals go through the agency Change Control Board, which is described in *Change Control Policies, Version 4.2*, August 29, 2012." If your department or agency is small, and you don't have a Change Control Board, you should state what individuals approve of the changes and include their names and qualifications (e.g., lead firewall engineer). Describe the workflow process from the initial request through the final approval and actual change. It's often helpful to include a flowchart with the description of the workflow process.

TECHNICAL CONTROLS

Technical security controls ensure that technology solutions are installed and configured correctly. It is often the case that security assessors scrutinize the technical controls more rigorously than the management or operational controls—something you'll want to keep in mind when describing these controls.

Authentication and identity verification

Identification and authorization (I&A) controls enable your information system and applications to prompt users for logon information and verify that they are who they say they are.

Discuss the user enrollment and registration procedure. An example of a user enrollment and registration process is illustrated in Figure 16.4. Your discussion should provide answers to the following questions:

• How are systems administrators informed that a new user should be added?

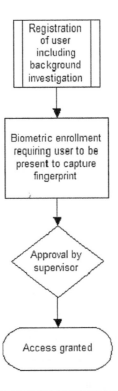

FIGURE 16.4

User registration and enrollment process.

- Before an account is established, is there either a paper form that a supervisor fills out with a signature or some sort of online registration system that requires a supervisor's approval?
- Is the enrollment process manual, automated, or semiautomated?
- Are background investigations performed before user accounts are established?
- Who decides what role and user group the user should be a part of?

You also need to describe how the identification and authorization system works. Most authentication mechanisms are based on something the user knows, something the user has, or a physical trait of the user. Examples of these three methods and their inherent risks and problems are listed in Table 16.7. Describe what is done to accommodate the potential risks or problems that may occur during usage.

Figure 16.4 diagrams the user registration and enrollment process.

If your agency uses two-factor authentication tokens that require a password and a PIN, you should describe the product that is used to provide these capabilities. Similarly, if biometric mechanisms or smart cards are used, you'll want to describe how the technical delivery of the authentication process works. For any authentication products or mechanisms that your information system uses, be sure to include information on the following:

- Product name, version number, patch level
- Vendor name and vendor contact information
- Whether there is an existing support contract through a vendor or reseller
- Strength of any encryption keys used
- Name of encryption algorithms used
- Information on digital certificates used for authentication
- Logical data flow of the authentication process
- Information on how authentication credentials are stored and protected
- Single sign-on capabilities

Table 16.7 Authentication Methods and Potential Risks

Method	Example	Potential Risks and Problems
Something user knows	Password PIN	• Can be guessed • Can be shared • Can be stolen
Something user has	Certificate Smart card Token	• Can be borrowed • Can be stolen • Can be lost
Physiological characteristic	Fingerprint Hand geometry Iris scan Retina scan Signature	• Perceived violation of privacy • False positives • False negatives

- Session time-out rules after periods of inactivity
- Strength and complexity of password rules
- Password aging requirements
- Account lockout thresholds (how many attempts allowed)
- Account removal procedures for friendly and unfriendly terminations of staff
- Procedures for handling forgotten passwords
- Usage of LDAP and Directory Services
- Kerberos policies and settings (if you use Kerberos)
- User recertification and how often unused accounts are purged
- Whether mechanisms used have an FIPS 140-2 validation certificate

Logical access controls

Logical access controls are the features of your system that enable authorized personnel access to resources. To many folks, distinguishing between logical access control and I&A is confusing. Logical access controls are those controls that either prevent or allow access to resources once a user's identity already has been established. Once a user is logged in, they should have access only to those resources required to perform their duties. Different user groups usually have access to different resources, which ensures a separation of duties. Describe how the separation of duties occurs. A good portion of this discussion should be about account management. User accounts are usually part of a role-based group. Describe the names of each role and what resources each role has access to. The resources that you will want to take into consideration include systems, directories, network shares, and files. You can summarize this information in a table similar to Table 16.8.

Discussion of anonymous and guest accounts, whether they are allowed or not, should be described. Group accounts, whether they are allowed or not, should be described. System accounts—accounts set up for the purpose of accommodating system processes and programs—may or may not be allowed. If system accounts are allowed, you'll need to give justification as to why they are allowed and what processes and programs use these accounts.

Table 16.8 Role-Based Group Accounts Mapped to Resources

Group Name	Role	Resource Access
sysadmin	Systems Administrators	Root access to all systems on .fed domain
dba	Database Administrator	DBserver1: db001, db002, db003
dev	Development Engineer	C:/user/general (read-only) D:/dev/apps (read, write, execute)
assist	Administrative Assistant	C:/user/general (read-only)

Secure configurations

Secure configurations refers to how well information systems, their applications, and databases are hardened and locked down. §3544(b)(2)(D)iii of FISMA stipulates that agencies must ensure compliance with minimally acceptable system configuration requirements, as determined by the agency.

Right out of the box, most operating systems are not as secure as they could be. Administrators typically need to turn off unneeded services and modify configuration files to tighten up the security on servers. To satisfy the FISMA requirement on secure configurations, you'll need to describe how systems are locked down. Most of the systems in place at federal agencies are based on either UNIX or a Microsoft operating system. For UNIX systems, you should discuss key configuration files that affect access or launch critical scripts. Examples of the sort of UNIX files that you should discuss include:

```
/etc/hosts.equiv
/etc/hosts.all
/.rhosts
/.netrc
/etc/services
/etc/ftpusers
/etc/syslog.conf
/etc/cron.d/cron.allow
/etc/cron.d/cron.deny
/etc/default/login
/etc/system
/etc/sulog
/etc/issue
/var/adm/loginlog
/etc/default/login
/etc/dfs/dfstab
/etc/dt/config/Xaccess
/etc/default/inetinit
/usr/local/etc/
/dev/ip
```

If you use `chmod` or `chown` commands to change file or ownership permissions to tighten security, list the names of the files that are modified and indicate their permissions. A good resource for understanding how to lock down a Sun Solaris UNIX system is the *CIS Solaris 10 Benchmark v4.0*. You can find that guide at http://www.nsa.gov/ia/_files/os/sunsol_10/CIS_Solaris_10_Benchmark_v4.pdf.

On Microsoft Windows operating systems, if you use security templates (.inf files), describe the security settings that the templates use, and if you have time, include screenshots. It's always nice to throw in a few screenshots of your security settings to show evidence that your configuration is set up the way you claim it to be. An example of a screenshot for a password aging policy setting is depicted in Figure 16.5.

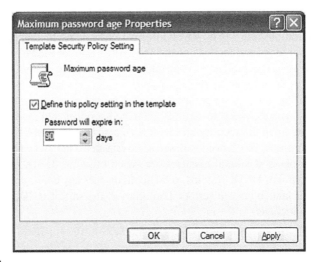

FIGURE 16.5

Screenshot that depicts password aging setting. (For color version of this figure, the reader is referred to the online version of this chapter.)

If you have existing documents that describe how operating systems are locked down, instead of reprinting everything that is listed in that guide in your System Security Plan, it should be sufficient simply to list the formal names of these secure configuration guides (e.g., *Windows 2012 Server Security Configuration and Lockdown Guide, Version 2.1, October 27, 2012* or *Solaris 10 Security Hardening Procedures, Version 7.1, January 11, 2013*). It is possible that the security assessors may ask to see any secure configuration guides that you list, so don't list any documents that you are not prepared to show.

If no security configuration guides exist that document your operating system security settings, and you have nothing to refer the evaluation team to along those lines, you are going to have more work to do. You'll have to document those settings in your System Security Plan.

The DISA Security Technical Implementation Guides (STIGs) have some excellent guidance for security configurations and they are freely available to the public at the following URL: http://iase.disa.mil/stigs/. The configurations are published in XML, but DISA publishes a STIG viewer to make reading them easier. You can also use the latest version of the Mozilla Firefox browser which has a built-in XML viewer. The Center for Internet Security (CIS) also publishes some excellent secure configuration guides here: https://benchmarks.cisecurity.org/downloads/multiform/index.cfm.

Interconnections

Interconnectivity security refers to the measures taken to secure the connection of one system to another and can be achieved through a variety of mechanisms including VPNs, firewalls, proxy servers, gateways, routers, and secure file transfer mechanisms. In discussing interconnectivity between systems, talk about how boundary protections work. Discuss how domains and networks are separated from each other and include diagrams about the trust relationships between them.

If end-to-end link encryption is used, describe how it works. Most VPNs use certificates. Note the key length and the servers that the certificates are installed on. Describe whether the VPNs are IPSec VPNs or SSL VPNs. If you are using an IPSec VPN, is it operating in transport mode or tunnel mode?

The following information should be included in your discussion about interconnections:

- What is the name of the organization that owns the remote system?
- What contracts or service level agreements govern the connection?
- What type of firewalls and proxy servers are used to safeguard the connection?
- What type of VPNs (SSL, IPSec) are used and where are the endpoints located?
- What type of routers and gateways are used and where they are deployed?
- What type of secure file transfer mechanisms are used and how they work?
- The period of idle time after which a network session is terminated
- Any PKI systems used that protect data in transit?
- Transport Layer Security (TLS) mechanisms
- Are X.509 certificates in use? What are the certificate properties?
- How critical single points of failure are eliminated (e.g., using two DNS servers)
- How session authenticity is maintained
- How man-in-the-middle attacks and unlinked session vulnerabilities are mitigated
- How TCP sequence number attacks are mitigated
- What services run across the connection and what ports are open?

Audit mechanisms

It's important to have a section of your System Security Plan dedicated to auditing. When you describe audit mechanisms, you essentially want to describe how security events are recognized, recorded, stored, and analyzed. Therefore, you should describe what is being audited, where the audit files reside, how the audit files are being protected, and how often the audit files are reviewed. When reviewing audit log files, systems administrators look for suspicious events that indicate a security violation has occurred or may occur in the future. Indicate what types of circumstances or events the systems administrators (or security engineers) look for to determine potential security violations. To obtain this information, you will likely have to talk directly to the systems administrators (or security engineers or network engineers).

Additionally, you should describe how audit log files are viewed. For example, are audit files viewed from a central Security Event Management (SEM) system or a central log server? Or do systems administrators need to log on to individual remote servers to manually read through individual system syslog files? You cannot go too far in depth in documenting audit mechanisms. This is one area that the security assessors will likely not gloss over. Examples of the types of files, events, and processes that you will want to be sure to discuss include:

- Files that store failed logon attempts of all users
- Logon records of root, admin, and privileged users
- How users are traced to actions
- Startup and shutdown of the actual audit system process (e.g., `syslogd`)
- Absolute pathnames of log files (e.g., `/var/log/secure.log`)
- Names of servers that collect log files
- How long log files are stored?
- The names and roles of the staff that read the log files
- Password auditing tools that scan for weak passwords
- Review of firewall rules for unauthorized modification
- How modification of sensitive or critical files is detected
- How audit files are protected
- How denied connections are logged
- Time stamp reliability and how it is ensured
- Who has access to log files?

You should include information on system auditing, network auditing, and firewall auditing. To investigate system auditing, find out if your agency is using host-based intrusion detection systems. Find out what events are audited for the various operating systems that are used. Microsoft operating systems are audited differently than UNIX operating systems. Windows Servers have configuration settings for Audit Policy. If your information system uses Windows, describe what the audit settings are in your section on audit.

How a UNIX system performs automated auditing depends on what version of UNIX you are using. Each type of UNIX (e.g., Solaris, Linux, OpenBSD, AIX) has audit mechanisms that are somewhat unique.

Since firewalls provide perimeter protection designed to keep unauthorized users out of the production systems that host your system, firewall auditing deserves special mention. Review your firewall rules for unauthorized modification. Who logged into the firewall last and did they log in from the console or from a remote system? Some firewalls can be administered only from the console and have remote login capabilities disabled. It is worth mentioning if the firewalls are audited directly from the console, or if administrators log into them remotely over the network. It's also possible that firewall logs are reviewed from a central management console. Whatever way your agency uses to review the firewall logs, you should describe it.

Additionally, document the review schedule of the firewall log files. If firewall logs are reviewed only on an as-needed, *ad hoc* basis, say that. Talk to the security engineers that review the firewall log files and find out what it is that they currently look for when they review these logs. Describe how suspect activity is discovered. Do the administrators have a list of suspect events that they look for or do they just scan through the log files and hope that they will notice the right thing? For example,

Table 16.9 Suspicious Events That Are Worth Auditing

Suspicious Event ID	Description
SE 1	Packets that have a source address internal to your network that originate from outside your network
SE 2	Suspicious outbound connections, e.g., outbound connections that come from a public server on your DMZ
SE 3	Repeated unsuccessful attempts to connect to a mission critical server or application
SE 4	Repeated probes to ports that are well-known hacker ports[a]
SE 5	Similar source ports used to connect to different sockets. An example of this sort of activity is shown below with three connections (now closed): TCP 128.88.41.2:1025 140.216.41.2:80 CLOSE_WAIT TCP 128.88.41.2:2180 140.216.41.2:80 CLOSE_WAIT TCP 128.88.41.2:1188 140.216.41.2:80 CLOSE_WAIT (A socket is an IP address plus a port, e.g., 206.208.163.15:80.)
SE 6	DNS requests from low number ports
SE 7	A `tcpdump` that shows numerous TCP flags set to S which could indicate a SYN flood attack

[a]Well-known hacker ports: http://www.relevanttechnologies.com/src_hacker_ports.asp.

there are certain suspect events that security administrators sometimes look for such as those listed in Table 16.9.

If your agency uses a Security Event Management system (SEM), sometimes referred to as a Security Event Information Management (SEIM) or an Intrusion Detection System (IDS), to look for aberrant network behavior, give an overview of how the system works and what events are configured to issue alarms or alerts. Intrusion detection and prevention systems also look for aberrant network behavior and anomalies. A screenshot of Sourcefire Next-Generation Intrusion Prevention System can be found in Figure 16.6. For example, if any of the following commercial products (or products similar to these) is used to generate alerts or alarms, their usage should be discussed:

- Alien Vault
- BlackStratus
- HP ArcSight
- LogRhythm
- McAfee Enterprise Security Manager
- IBM OpenService Security Log Manager
- RSA Security Analytics
- SenSage Enterprise Security Analytics
- Sourcefire Next-Generation Intrusion Prevention System

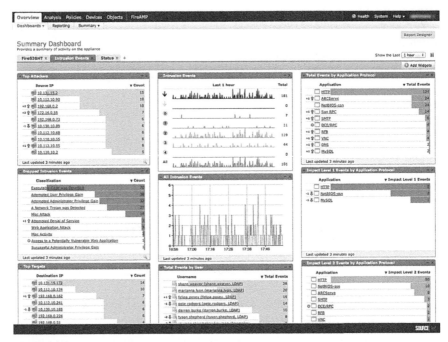

FIGURE 16.6

Sourcefire's Next-Generation Intrusion Prevention System. (For color version of this figure, the reader is referred to the online version of this chapter.)

- Splunk
- Symantec Security Information Manager
- Tibco-LogLogic
- Trustwave Security Information Event Manager
- IBM Q1Labs QRadar

If log files are reviewed only on an *ad hoc*, as-needed basis and on no particular schedule, you should truthfully document that. Don't describe an elaborate and diligent audit review process if one does not exist for the sake of trying to obtain a positive authorization on your system. If it is discovered at some later date that you documented review procedures that don't really exist, you could be accused of purposefully misleading auditors.

ISSO APPOINTMENT LETTER

The Security Plan needs to contain a copy of the signed ISSO (or ISSM) appointment letter. The ISSO appointment letter verifies to the auditors who the person is that is accountable for security of the information systems described in the Security Package and therefore the ISSO should be named in the appointment letter. The security assessors want to be able to hold someone responsible for the information contained in the Security Package and they want to be sure that they hold the right person responsible. Since the ISSO letter is usually a signed document, in most cases you will need to include a scanned copy so you can show the signature page. Figure 16.7 shows an example of an ISSO appointment letter.

Agency Name Goes Here
Memorandum

Date: September 22, 2012
To: Nancy Morrison, Information System Security Officer
From: James Smith, SAISO
Subject: ISSO Appointment Letter for the Health Information Systems (HIS)

In accordance with the Health Information Systems (HIS) entity-wide Information Technology (IT) Security Program you are being appointed as the HIS Information System Security Officer (ISSO). As the HIS ISSO, you help ensure that all IT security requirements relevant to HIS are implemented and maintained. Your specific responsibilities with regard to HIS and the IT Security Program are:

- Ensure that all requirements prescribed by the <Agency> entity-wide IT Security Program that apply to HIS are appropriately implemented.
- Complete and maintain the System Security Plan for the HIS.
- Conduct annual system self-assessments and ensure that periodic risk assessments are accomplished.
- Maintain FISMA compliance documentation on behalf of the authorizing official.
- Conduct annual re-certification of users.
- Ensure that IT security management, operational, and technical controls are incorporated through the system life-cycle.
- Provide guidance for system security acceptance tests.
- Initiate protective or corrective actions.
- Provide assistance in the completion of a waiver request, should one be required.
- Ensure the completion, maintenance, and testing of an HIS Contingency Plan.
- Develop procedures for managing accounts of HIS users.
- Enforce agency IT security policies, standards, and procedures.
- Report security incidents in accordance with <Agency> entity-wide Security Policy.
- Ensure that audit trails are reviewed periodically (e.g. weekly, monthly) and that audit records are archived for future reference.
- Evaluate known threats and vulnerabilities to ascertain if additional safeguards are needed and to brief the authorizing official accordingly.

SIGNATURE INDICATES ACCEPTANCE

> I have read the HHS ISSO appointment and fully understand the assigned duties and responsibilities.
>
> Name: Nancy Morrison   *Nancy Morrison*
>
> Date: February 24, 2013

FIGURE 16.7

Sample ISSO appointment letter.

SYSTEM SECURITY PLAN CHECKLIST

Use the following checklist to make sure you haven't forgotten anything:

- Are all the management security controls described?
- Are all the operational security controls described?
- Are all the technical security controls described?
- Is the user enrollment and registration process described?
- Have you listed the different user groups and their roles?
- Have you described your Patch Management process?
- Have you described how password aging works?
- Are the password complexity requirements described?
- Is it clear where routers, switches, firewalls, and VPNs are deployed?
- Is there a discussion about what services are allowed through the firewalls?
- Are all protection mechanisms and safeguards named?
- Are schedules documented for when audit and firewall logs are reviewed?
- Are Security Enterprise Management (SEM) systems described?
- What measures have been taken to eliminate critical points of failure?
- Have you documented the audit mechanisms that trace users to actions?
- Is information on session lockouts after periods of inactivity provided?
- Has an account termination process been explained?
- Have both friendly and unfriendly termination procedures been described?
- Is it clear what is done to harden and lockdown the operating systems?
- Is the usage of any PKI systems described?
- Is the usage of any secure file transfer mechanisms documented?
- Have you described how antivirus products protect the data?
- Are any intrusion detection systems, and how they work, described?
- Are the servers that collect log files named?
- Is it clear how long log files are retained?
- Is it clear what files are considered log files?
- Is there a discussion about intrusion detection systems?
- Has a copy of the ISSO appointment letter been included?
- Is the ISSO appointment letter signed by the ISSO?

SUMMARY

The System Security Plan is one of the most important documents in your Security Package. In the System Security Plan, you need to discuss and describe all the security controls that safeguard your information system. Management security controls stipulate the rules of the road, provide guidance to staff, and are designed to hold people (including the management team) accountable. Operational security controls stipulate what people should do on a day-to-day basis to keep the information system secure. Technical security controls include descriptions of security mechanisms that are implemented, configured, and installed.

In some cases, there may be overlap or dependent relationships between operational and technical security control. For example, it may make sense to discuss certain aspects of firewalls in both the section on operational and the one on technical controls. In the section on "Operational Controls," you may want to talk about how firewalls are administered. In the section on "Technical Controls," you want to talk about how firewalls are configured. It likely won't be disastrous if the evaluation team finds that you have discussed some operational controls in the section on Technical Controls. It's possible they may ask you to move some of the information from one section to another, but the important thing is that the information is documented somewhere and is informative.

ADDITIONAL RESOURCES

Various resources that might be useful when developing a System Security Plan include:

FIPS PUB 200 Minimal Security Requirements for Federal Information and Information Systems. Computer Security Division, Information Technology Lab. National Institute of Standards and Technology, March 2006 (http://www.csrc.nist.gov/publications/fips/fips200/FIPS-200-final-march.pdf).

Baseline Security Requirements for Network Security Zones in the Government of Canada. Communications Security Establishment, Canada. June 2007 (http://www.cse-cst.gc.ca/its-sti/publications/itsg-csti/itsg22-eng.html).

Brunette, Glen. *An Overview of Solaris 10 Operating System Security Controls*. September 25, 2007 (http://www.nsa.gov/ia/_files/os/sunsol_10/s10-cis-appendix-v1.1.pdf).

OMB Circular A-130, Revised. https://www.fismacenter.com/a130trans4.pdf.

OMB Circular A-130, Appendix III, Security of Federal Automated Information Resources. http://www.whitehouse.gov/omb/circulars_a130_a130appendix_iii.

Swanson, Marianne, Joan Hash, and Pauline Bowen. *Guide for Developing Security Plans for Federal Information Systems*. NIST Special Publication 800-18, Revision 1. National Institute of Standards and Technology, February 2006 (http://www.csrc.nist.gov/publications/nistpubs/800-18-Rev1/sp800-18-Rev1-final.pdf).

Theriault, Marlene and William Heney. *How to Write an Oracle Security Plan*. Johns Hopkins University, October 1998 (http://www.databasesecurity.com/oracle/HowToWriteAnOracleSecurityPlan.pdf).

Taylor, Laura. Understanding IPSec. *Intranet Journal*, June 13, 2002 (http://www.scribd.com/doc/77298400/IPSec-das).

Note

[1] Hacker Ports. Relevant Technologies' Security Resource Center. http://www.relevanttechnologies.com/src_hacker_ports.asp.

Performing the Business Risk Assessment

17

TOPICS IN THIS CHAPTER

- Determine the mission
- Create a mission map
- Construct risk statements
- Describe the sensitivity model
- Make an informed decision

INTRODUCTION

A *Business Risk Assessment* reviews the risks to the agency mission and determines if they are acceptable or not. If the risks are not acceptable, a determination of how to mitigate them should be described. Business risks are examined at a high level and are not concerned with the particularities of information technology. The reason that business risks are important is to give some perspective on why the information technology infrastructure exists in the first place.

First, it's worth noting that not all agencies require a Business Risk Assessment. However, the trend to include a Business Risk Assessment is growing because agencies want to understand how risks to the business are related to risks to systems. Before you begin the development of a Business Risk Assessment, make sure a Business Risk Assessment is required. Some agencies may require only a system risk assessment that focuses on the technology of the systems and applications rather than the mission. However, to be sure, a Business Risk Assessment is related to a system risk assessment. If you develop the Business Risk Assessment correctly, the *Security Assessment Report* (Chapter 21) will look like an extension of it and you will be able to see the relationship between the two. Likewise, you will also see consistencies between the Business Impact Analysis and the Business Risk Assessment.

Before you can determine the risks to your agency's mission, you need to first understand what the mission is. The process of determining the risks to the mission

201

is in part designed to force you to understand the mission. Your agency, and its different bureaus and divisions, probably has multiple missions. You need to be able to state what the primary mission functions are before you can determine the business risks—the risks to the mission.

DETERMINE THE MISSION

Business risks affect the ability for an agency to achieve its mission. You could also think of business risks as mission risks. All agencies will have different mission risks depending on the mission. Chances are your agency or bureau has multiple missions. For any particular FISMA compliance project, you should be concerned only with the missions that correlate to the particular Security Package that you are putting together. Some examples of business missions are:

- Analyze and record the annual budgetary appropriation from Congress
- Provide retirement benefits to war veterans
- Prepare the nation for natural disasters
- Process enrollment information for Medicare recipients
- Enable law enforcement officials to access information on terrorists
- Provide online access of navigational charts to mariners
- Process patent applications
- Monitor budgetary requirements for an Air Force base Child Development Center
- Provide clerical support to Probation Officers
- Track gasoline-powered vehicles deployed for work on public lands
- Analyze domestic flu infections
- Compile economic statistics
- Track administration of medications in a hospital
- Procure auxiliary generators and air compressors
- Monitor compliance of visitor rules in national parks
- Document and track evidence chain of custody

Noticing the business mission takes the information technology out of the equation so you can remember why the information technology infrastructure exists to begin with. Understanding the business mission is a process of taking a momentary step backward to look at the bigger picture. In some regards, conducting a Business Risk Assessment is a way of looking at the critical business functions from a legacy point of view and seeing things the way business processes were accomplished on paper, years ago, before computers came into existence. Sometimes we get so entrenched in the granularity of the information systems that we fail to see how all the computer infrastructure came to exist in the first place. You need to know what the essential functions are of the agency's business in order to determine what the risks are to the functions, the likelihood that the risks may occur, and their potential impact.

Questions that may help determine your agency's mission are:

- What is the largest percentage of the agency's annual budget dedicated to?
- Does your agency produce tangible assets? What are they?

- Are large financial transactions conducted by your agency?
- Is there a large central communications command center in your agency?
- Is your agency responsible for the health and safety of people?
- What do other agencies depend on your agency for?
- What vital records are being created?
- What are the key projects that are underway in the agency?
- Why was your agency originally established by the government in the first place?

Another good way of determining the agency mission is to look at the information types that exist in the Federal Enterprise Architecture (FEA). You can find these information types in the section of the FEA called Business Reference Model (BRM). The BRM begins on p. 26 of the FEA and you can find it at this URL: http://www.whitehouse.gov/sites/default/files/omb/assets/fea_docs/FEA_CRM_v23_Final_Oct_2007_Revised.pdf. Let's look at the section called Services for Citizens on p. 27 and represented in Figure 17.1. Below each dark-colored box, you'll see information types. These information types are the same information types found in NIST SP 800-60, Revision 1, Volume II. You looked at these information types previously in Chapter 8 when determining the system impact-sensitivity level. Most of these information types are representative of business missions. For example, law enforcement agencies perform the following duties as part of their mission: criminal apprehension, criminal investigation and surveillance, citizen protection, crime prevention, leadership protection, property protection, and substance control. Hopefully you are starting to understand how agency data are related to the agency mission. Instead of looking at things from the perspective of the data, we're going to now look at things from the perspective of the mission.

CREATE A MISSION MAP

Once you have determined the primary mission or tasks related to the mission, set up a mission map that shows the relationships between agency functions and the role that systems and networks play in carrying out the mission. This is one of the best ways to figure out the relationship between the agency mission and the IT infrastructure.

An example of a mission map is depicted in Figure 17.2 and notional pretend missions have been created for the purpose of this discussion. As you can see from this illustration, both the forecasting and budget process, and the time and attendance process, are dependent only on one geographic location and one network. The user enrollment process is dependent on two networks and two geographic locations. Therefore, determining the risks associated with the user enrollment process is bound to be more complex. As far as natural hazards go, the user enrollment process has to worry about both hurricanes in Houston and heavy snow in New York. The forecasting and budgetary process has fewer natural disasters to take into consideration because Washington, DC has milder weather than either Houston or New York.

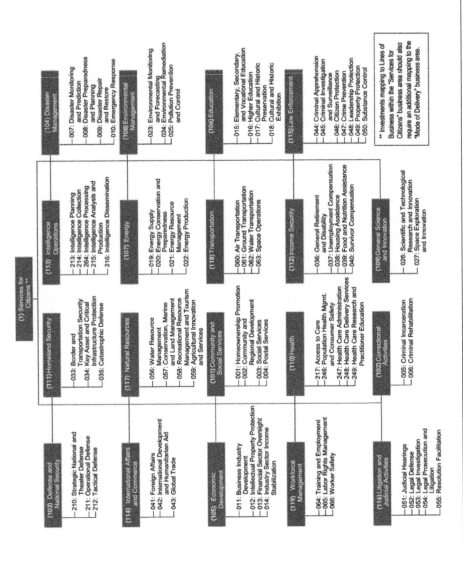

FIGURE 17.1

Information types and business missions. (For color version of this figure, the reader is referred to the online version of this chapter.)

Three different business missions

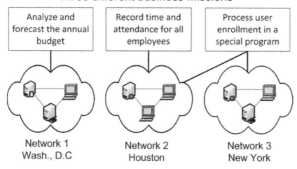

| Analyze and forecast the annual budget | Record time and attendance for all employees | Process user enrollment in a special program |

Network 1
Wash., D.C

Network 2
Houston

Network 3
New York

FIGURE 17.2

An example of a mission map.

With dependencies on two networks, you'll have to look at the risks for both locations. One risk that could be cited might be that the user enrollment process is dependent on two networks. If the Houston facility gets flooded by a hurricane and loses power, then the user enrollment process will stop working—even if the New York site remains operational. Clearly, one way to mitigate this risk would be to migrate the functionality of the user enrollment process entirely to the New York site. However, that may not be possible for all kinds of different reasons. Instead, it may be easier to build a failover system in Washington, DC that automatically picks up the user enrollment functionality provided by Houston if there is an outage in Houston. When developing a Business Risk Assessment, you have to take into consideration various different scenarios that could affect the business process. There are, of course, other risks aside from natural disasters. In taking into consideration the different scenarios, you need to construct risk statements.

CONSTRUCT RISK STATEMENTS

Risk statements are assertions that connect a possible circumstance to a forecasted impact. A common format for a risk statement is:

If <this threat circumstance occurs>, **then** <this will be the impact>.

Once risk statements have been developed, the impact can be forecasted and the potential likelihood of the threat can be determined. Risk statements state the presumed threat and the impact in the form of damage that could occur. The potential impact can then be factored with the probability of its occurrence to find out just how great the risk exposure is in actuality. Some threats will create a more severe impact to the business process than others.

When you are creating risk statements for business risks, knowing the technical details of the IT infrastructure is not really necessary. It shouldn't matter whether the firewall is a Cisco firewall or a Juniper firewall. It also shouldn't matter if the database is an Oracle or Microsoft SQL Server database. Likewise, whether the operating system is Solaris or Microsoft Windows doesn't matter. Business Risk Assessments look at things from a high level. In the Business Risk Assessment, you want to focus on business processes necessary to the organization to be able to carry out its mission(s) and the impact that the loss or degradation of one of those business processes would have. The low-level, more technical and granular risks to the information systems that support those business processes will be evaluated during security testing (Chapters 20 and 21).

Examples of risk statements for a Business Risk Assessment are:

- If the Houston facility gets flooded, then it won't be possible to enroll new users. (This is an availability threat.)
- If the Houston facility gets flooded, then it won't be possible to process time and attendance for any employees. (This is an availability threat.)
- If an unauthorized user gains access to the Washington, DC network, then the integrity and confidentiality of the annual budget could be compromised. (This is an integrity and confidentiality threat.)
- If an employee accidentally misspells a user's name, then the misspelling could be propagated to two different locations. (This is an integrity threat and most likely a relatively minor one.)
- If a disgruntled systems administrator purposefully and maliciously creates a backdoor account into the user enrollment system, it could be propagated to two different locations. (This is an integrity, confidentiality, and availability threat.)
- If a terrorist destroys the New York facility, then it won't be possible to enroll new users into the special program. (This is an availability threat.)
- If an intruder breaks into the budgeting system and changes some of the numbers in an Excel spreadsheet used for forecasting, too much, or too little money may be allocated to certain programs. (This is an integrity threat.)
- If a system administrator erroneously configures a firewall rule for the Houston firewall, then access to both user enrollment, and time and attendance, might be blocked. (This is an availability threat.)
- If a virus proliferates throughout the Houston network, both the user enrollment system, and the time and attendance system could be damaged. (This is an integrity threat, and possibly an availability threat as well.)
- If intruders break into the user enrollment system, they could steal a database of personally identifiable information. (This is a confidentiality threat.)
- If security patches are never applied to the time and attendance systems, then intruders may gain access to the attendance systems and damage them. (This is an integrity threat and possibly an availability threat as well.)

Once we know what the threats are, if we have a sensitivity model to measure their likelihood and impact, we can determine the risk exposure.

DESCRIBE THE SENSITIVITY MODEL

According to the American Heritage® Dictionary of the English Language, *risk* is the "possibility of suffering harm or loss; danger" [1]. Risk analysis can be performed in a variety of different ways. One of the goals of a FISMA compliance program is to have some consistency from one Security Package to another. Therefore, it's important to pick a risk analysis methodology, describe it, and use it as described for each Security Package you develop.

A sensitivity model takes into consideration the impact of a threat, and the likelihood of its occurrence, so that you can rank the risks according to their sensitivity for the purpose of prioritizing them. In any given organization, there is a limited amount of time and resources. If you were able to determine all of the risks to your organization, would you have enough time and resources to address each and every one? Probably not. Therefore, a goal is to describe the most obvious and likely risks and then further predict the probability of their occurrence. The objective is to think of what situational hazards and threats are most likely to occur, determine the risk exposure, and then mitigate, transfer, or accept each risk based on priority.

Your sensitivity model should consist of a process for determining the risk exposure. (We already categorized the levels of confidentiality, integrity, and availability of the data in Chapter 8, so we are not going to repeat that here.) In Business Risk Assessment, risk exposure is a value that is calculated to determine the degree of risk that the mission is exposed to. The purpose of determining the risk exposure is that you can understand which business processes and missions require additional safeguards. You'll want to mitigate the most severe risks to business missions first.

It's possible to use simple equations to determine risk exposure. You don't have to be a math genius to do this. The equations we use will multiply the likelihood of a threat by the potential impact to the organization. However, before you can set up these equations, you need to create an impact scale and a likelihood scale so you know what to multiply.

Impact scale

In qualitative risk analysis, the impact of a threat to the mission is measured in relative terms. The values that are used to measure the impact are perceived values and are not actual values. Since a threat actually has not occurred yet, it is not possible to use actual values. Table 17.1 shows an example of an impact measurement scale with five measurements. This same scale could be set up to have more, or fewer, levels of impact to fit the unique requirements of your agency or department.

The likelihood that a threat will occur is a probability expressed in relative terms. Table 17.2 lists probability levels based on likelihood of occurrence.

Table 17.1 An Example of an Impact Scale

Threat Impact	Impact Value	Description of Impact
None	0	The threat poses absolutely no risk to the mission.
Very low	20	The threat poses very little risk to the mission. Safeguards currently provide near complete protection of the mission.
Low	40	The threat poses some risk to the mission. The current safeguards provide adequate protection though it is conceivable that the mission could be impeded.
Moderate	60	The threat poses a moderate risk to the mission. The safeguards that are in place provide some protection, though it is possible for the mission to be thwarted.
High	80	The threat poses a high risk to the mission and the current safeguards provide few protections.
Severe	100	The threat may completely thwart the mission and the current safeguards provide no protection.

Table 17.2 An Example of a Likelihood Scale

Probability of Loss to Mission Expressed as a Percentage	Probability of Loss to Mission Expressed as a Decimal	Description	Likelihood
0-10	0.1	There is little to no chance that the threat could thwart the mission.	Low
10-50	0.5	There is a moderate chance that the threat could thwart the mission.	Moderate
50-100	1.0	There is a high chance that the threat could thwart the mission.	High

Calculating risk exposure

In qualitative risk analysis, risk exposure is determined by multiplying the probability of mission loss (the likelihood it will occur) by the potential severity of the impact to the agency due to that loss. If we represent probability with P, and impact severity with S, our risk exposure equation looks like this:

$$P \times S = \text{risk exposure (RE)}$$

Table 17.3 Risk Exposure Metrics	
Likelihood × Impact	**Risk Exposure**
0.1×0	0
0.1×20	2
0.1×40	4
0.1×60	6
0.1×80	8
0.1×100	10
0.5×0	0
0.5×20	10
0.5×40	20
0.5×60	30
0.5×80	40
0.5×100	50
1×0	0
1×20	20
1×40	40
1×60	60
1×80	80
1×100	100

We can also write the expression a different way to more clearly indicate that we are talking about the probability of loss (L) multiplied by the severity of the loss (L):

$$P(L) \times S(L) = R(E)$$

$P(L)$ represents the likelihood. $S(L)$ represents the impact. The probability that loss will occur is another way of referring to the likelihood. The severity of the loss is another way of referring to the impact. Therefore,

$$\text{Likelihood} \times \text{Impact} = \text{Risk exposure}$$

Now for a particular threat, we take the impact values from Table 17.1 and multiply them by the probability of loss values from Table 17.2. All the possible outcomes of multiplying the likelihood by the impact are listed in Table 17.3.

Obtaining likelihood and impact metrics

For the purpose of FISMA compliance, when putting together your risk exposure metrics, it is important to interview the support, development, and management staff to obtain their input. It is not possible to determine the impact and likelihood of a threat to a business process in a vacuum. You need to sit down with the folks that run the business. I recommend holding a Business Risk Assessment meeting and getting everyone together in a room. While it may seem unimportant to list risks that are low likelihood or low impact, the reason for doing so is so that you can record all the issues that are raised by the staff. Remember, FISMA compliance is a process for holding people accountable. When you develop the Business Risk Assessment, it's not your job to determine the likelihood and impact on your own. You should take on the role of a facilitator of the process and should use the values for impact and likelihood that the team gives you in order to determine the risk exposure.

There are many likelihood/probability metrics that can be obtained from third-party authorities. For example, earthquake probabilities can be obtained from the U.S. Geological Survey. Actuarial tables are also a good source of information. Additionally, agencies can calculate likelihood metrics based on past experiences. Through your own research, you should look for the latest likelihood information on these events:

- Likelihood that a city's electrical grid will fail
- Likelihood of earthquake happening in a particular location
- Likelihood of hurricane happening in a particular location
- Likelihood of tornado happening in a particular location
- Likelihood of major flooding in a particular location
- Likelihood of airplane flying into building
- Likelihood that supply chain could be cut off
- Likelihood that supply chain might introduce vulnerabilities in products
- Likelihood of wildfires happening in a particular location
- Likelihood of an adversary obtaining sensitive information
- Likelihood that a telecomm provider's lines will fail
- Likelihood of loss due to terrorism
- Likelihood of dangerous substance contamination

Some of these risks are more applicable to some agencies than others. For example, U.S. embassies and outposts in certain countries are very susceptible to terrorism attacks. U.S. postal workers are susceptible to dangerous substance contamination. Buildings located near airports are susceptible to having airplanes crash into them. Federal buildings in the southwest are susceptible to wildfires.

Two companies that have data models to predict losses due to terrorism are RMS (http://www.rms.com) and Air Worldwide (http://www.air-worldwide.com). There are new industry exposure databases being generated all the time that have probability statistics on a variety of potential threats.

The image in Figure 17.3 shows locations of individual properties within the foot print of the 2003 Cedar, California wildfire. This image comes from Air Worldwide's Industry Exposure Database.

Many IT professionals, in the past, have not given enough credence to the possibility of natural disasters. However, recent natural disasters such as Hurricane Katrina, which took place in the New Orleans area in August 2005, have raised the awareness of natural disasters. Agencies that don't perform Business Risk Assessments typically account for natural disasters in the Security Assessment Report (Chapter 21). However, it's often the case that a natural disaster will affect

FIGURE 17.3

Properties susceptible to wildfires in California. (For color version of this figure, the reader is referred to the online version of this chapter.)

the overall business mission. Natural disasters often threaten multiple systems and their impact can affect the entire business. Threats from natural disasters include, but are not limited to:

- Floods and heavy rains
- Earthquakes
- Fire
- Hurricanes and wind
- Snow and ice
- Lightning
- Tornados
- Volcanoes
- Tsunamis, typhoons, and tidal waves

You need to determine how likely it is that a natural disaster will occur, and estimate the impact that it will have on your operations. You can use the following URLs to do more research on natural disasters, their anticipated impact, and the likelihood that they will occur in a given area:

- Advanced National Seismic System Earthquake Maps
  http://www.ncedc.org/anss/maps/

- Federal Emergency Management Agency
  http://www.fema.gov/index.shtm

- Hazards and Vulnerability Research Institute at University of South Carolina
  http://webra.cas.sc.edu/hvri/

- NASA SEDAC Hotspots
  http://sedac.ciesin.columbia.edu/data/sets/browse?contains=hotspots

- NASA Global Change Master Directory
  http://gcmd.gsfc.nasa.gov/learn/pointers/hazards.html

- NOAA National Geophysical Data Center
  http://www.ngdc.noaa.gov/hazard/hazards.shtml

- Natural Hazards Center: All Hazards
  http://www.colorado.edu/hazards/resources/web/all.html#indices

- National Oceanic and Atmospheric Administration Central Library
  http://www.lib.noaa.gov/

Analyze the risks

Once you have determined the risk exposure, it is time to analyze the risks to prepare for making an informed decision. There are multiple reasons for analyzing risks. When a threat is exploited, otherwise competent staff are often left flustered not knowing what to do first. Analyzing risk is about anticipating the incident in order to prevent it and also to prepare for how to respond in the event it does occur. Determining business risk exposure helps you understand what risks to address first.

Even in the absence of malicious attackers, disgruntled users, and administrative errors, power outages still occur and natural disasters wreak havoc. Understanding risks, and applying safeguards to mitigate those risks, not only helps prevent loss to the mission but also helps maintain the flow of order by potentially reducing the amount of circumstances that may create disorder. You analyze risks so you can prioritize them for the purpose of managing them. Once the risk exposure is determined and ranked from high to low, the findings should be presented to the system owner. The system owner and ISSO should engage in discussions with the Business Risk Assessment team that originally assisted you in putting together the list of risks, their impact, and likelihood. Analyzing the risks means discussing the possible outcomes before making a decision on what action to take. Table 17.3 lists risk exposure metrics.

Another way of presenting the information in Table 17.3 is shown in Table 17.4.

QUANTITATIVE RISK ASSESSMENT

Once you have determined which threats create the greatest risk exposure to the business, you can then use quantitative risk assessment methods to determine how much the agency should spend to mitigate the potential threat. Quantitative risk assessment associates loss with a financial value. The goal of understanding financial loss is to give you more information in making decisions about the procurement and implementation of safeguards. Quantitative risk assessment is essential if you want to

Table 17.4 Risk Exposure Determination Table

Impact and Values	Likelihood		
	Low (0.1)	**Medium (0.5)**	**High (1.0)**
None (0)	$0 \times 0.1 = 0$	$0 \times 0.5 = 0$	$0 \times 1 = 0$
Very low (20)	$20 \times 0.1 = 2$	$20 \times 0.5 = 10$	$20 \times 1 = 20$
Low (40)	$40 \times 0.1 = 4$	$40 \times 0.5 = 20$	$40 \times 1 = 40$
Moderate (60)	$60 \times 0.1 = 6$	$60 \times 0.5 = 30$	$60 \times 1 = 60$
High (80)	$80 \times 0.1 = 8$	$80 \times 0.5 = 40$	$80 \times 1 = 80$
Severe (100)	$100 \times 0.1 = 10$	$100 \times 0.5 = 50$	$100 \times 1 = 100$

Source: Chapter 10, HIPAA Security Implementation 2.0, *SANS Press, 2004.*

perform cost-benefit analysis to figure out if implementing a particular safeguard is financially worth the cost. If the anticipated annual loss (also referred to as annual loss expectancy) is less than the annualized cost of the safeguard, then it is usually not worth it to implement the safeguard. For example, if a data center is in a city that is prone to electrical grid outages, then it might make sense to invest in more generators only if the annual loss is greater than the annualized cost of new generators (the safeguard).

(The loss caused by the electrical grid, could mean loss of data, loss of customers, or some other loss.)

Let's look at a more detailed example related to natural disasters to figure out financial loss based on quantitative risk assessment methods. If you look at Figure 17.4, you will see that in Florida alone there are different probabilities throughout the state for hurricanes with wind speeds greater than 100 knots. To calculate the risk of a hurricane occurring in Miami, Florida, you need to understand the likelihood of one occurring each year. If a hurricane occurs once every 20 years (1 of 20), then it has a 5% chance of occurring yearly since $1/20 = 0.05$, which equals 5%.

The frequency of Florida hurricanes with wind speeds greater than or equal to 100 knots is mapped in terms of the probability of occurrence during a 20-year exposure window. These probabilistic estimates, based on 1006 years of observations, illustrate that hurricanes with 100-knot winds occur more frequently in southern Florida and gradually decrease in frequency toward northern Florida [2].

The threat frequency (or likelihood) for natural disasters can be calculated by using an Annualized Rate of Occurrence (ARO). An ARO is a constant number that tells you how often a threat might occur each year. AROs can be broken down into subvalues known as Standard Annual Frequency Estimates (SAFE) and Local Annual Frequency Estimates (LAFE). The SAFE value is the number of times a specific threat is expected to occur annually in a large geographic region such as North America. The LAFE value is the number of times a specific threat can be expected to occur annually in a smaller, local geographic region such as Miami, Florida. For the purpose of FISMA compliance, it is more appropriate to use LAFE values. (If we were going to assess all the systems in North America in one Security Package, we might use SAFE values for that. Such a Security Package of course would be a Sisyphean exercise.)

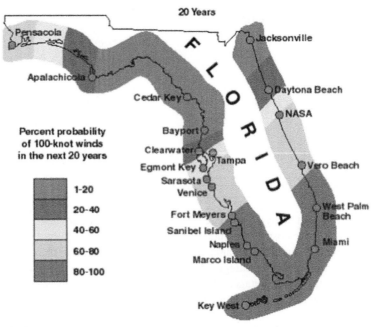

FIGURE 17.4

Probabilities of hurricanes in Florida localities. (For color version of this figure, the reader is referred to the online version of this chapter.)

Source: USGS.

ARO values (SAFE and LAFE) typically are represented as rational numbers or as a decimal value as shown in Table 17.5. (A rational number is a number that can be expressed equivalently as a fraction.)

The reduction in the value of an information system from one threat (or incident) is referred to as a Single Loss Expectancy (SLE). If one of the servers in your hardware and software inventory is valued at $100,000, and a hurricane destroys 90% of it, the value of the system has been reduced by $90,000, which is represented by the SLE equation:

$$SLE = Original Total Cost - Remaining Value$$
$$SLE\$90,000 = \$100,000 - \$10,000$$

It is possible that instead of a hurricane, a hacker might destroy 90% of the server and the same SLE formula would apply. Once you know the SLE, you can determine an Annual Loss Expectancy (ALE). ALE is a risk exposure standard that is computed by multiplying the probability of a loss from a threat (or incident) by the reduction in value of the information system [1].

> ALE is a metric that was developed by the National Bureau of Standards in 1979. In the mid-1980s, the National Bureau of Standards became part of the National Institute of Standards and Technology.

Table 17.5 Threat Values for Annualized Rates of Occurrence

ARO (LAFE) Values			
Expressed as a Percentage	**Expressed as a Decimal**	**Expressed as a Fraction**	**Frequency of Occurrence**
1	0.01	1/100	Once every 100 years
2	0.02	1/50	Once every 50 years
5	0.05	1/20	Once every 20 years
10	0.10	1/10	Once every 10 years
20	0.2	1/5	Once every 5 years
100	1	1/1	Once a year
1000	10	10/1	10 times a year
10,000	20	20/1	20 times a year

ALE values are useful to perform cost-benefit analysis so that you can figure out if spending money on a particular safeguard is worth it or not. ALE values can be determined for any type of threat whether it is a threat launched by an adversary, or a natural disaster. To determine the ALE for this same $100,000 system, use the formula:

$$ALE = LAFE \times SLE$$
$$R(E) = P(L) \times S(L)$$

The LAFE value is the probability of potential loss, or $P(L)$. The SLE, or the loss from a one-time occurrence of the incident, is the severity of the loss, $S(L)$.

If the system is located in Miami, Florida, and hurricanes have a 5% chance of occurring yearly:

$$ALE = \$0.05 \times \$90,000 = 4,500$$

Every year, the one-information system located in Miami, Florida, is being exposed to an annual loss expectancy of 4,500 from hurricanes alone. If there are 1000 systems at this facility in Miami, all with the same ALE, that would come to a whopping cumulative ALE of $4,500,000. Even if moving the facility to a different location costs $1,000,000, in this case it would be worth it since the safeguard (e.g., the move) would be far less expensive than the Annual Loss Expectancy.

An additional resource that explains quantitative risk assessment is an article titled "Security Scanning is not Risk Analysis" in the *Intranet Journal* (http://www.web. archive.org/web/20030207102906/http://www.intranetjournal.com/articles/200207/ se_07_14_02a.html).

QUALITATIVE VERSUS QUANTITATIVE RISK ASSESSMENT

When you use ALE values to determine cost-benefit analysis, you are performing quantitative risk analysis. When you use high, moderate, and low rankings that are relative to each other, you are performing qualitative risk analysis. Whether the threat is a hurricane or a hacker, you can use either method to determine risk exposure. There are advantages and disadvantages to both methods of determining risk.

Whether you use qualitative or quantitative methods to determine your risk exposure, you should state which methodology you are using and why. Your reasons for selecting one methodology over the other might be straightforward and simple. Perhaps you decided to use qualitative risk assessment because that's what your agency requires. To use quantitative risk assessment effectively, you need to know the current dollar value of an asset. If your agency does not track that kind of information, quantitative risk assessment presents many challenges. If you are able to use quantitative risk assessment, it is an indispensable tool for determining whether an expensive safeguard is worth purchasing or not.

Qualitative risk assessment has the following attributes:

- A faster process
- Emphasizes descriptions
- Findings are simple and expressed in relative terms
- Values are perceived values, not actual values
- Requires less training

Quantitative risk assessment has the following attributes:

- Very time intensive
- Yields results that are financial in nature
- Used for cost-benefit analysis
- Good for justifying the procurement of safeguards
- Requires tracking the financial value of assets

Today, most Security Packages use qualitative risk assessment methods simply because it's usually faster to perform than quantitative methods. However, as FISMA compliance programs evolve over time, it is likely that quantitative methods will gain more traction. The more expensive the safeguards are that your agency is taking into consideration, the more valuable quantitative risk assessment can be.

MAKE AN INFORMED DECISION

Once risks have been identified and analyzed, a decision can be made on what action to take. Your choices are to accept the risk, transfer the risk, or mitigate the risk. You should be able to justify your reason for whatever decision you make.

Accept the risk

If the risk exposure is extremely low, and the cost to remove such a small risk is extremely high, the best solution may be to accept the risk. Keep in mind that for the purposes of FISMA compliance, it is up to the system owner to accept the risk. The system owner usually will accept the risk or not based on the recommendation from the ISSO and the staff that prepares the Business Risk Assessment. The system owner usually always wants a recommendation on whether to accept the risk or not so be prepared to make one.

Transfer the risk

When you transfer the risk, you make another entity responsible for it. When you buy insurance, you are transferring the risk to a third party who has agreed to assume the risk for an agreed upon cost. In a federal agency, in many situations it may not be possible to buy insurance to transfer risks. However, there are other ways to transfer risk. It's possible that you may not have the appropriate personnel to support a business function. A system owner could possibly negotiate with another department to take on the responsibility of supporting the business function.

If you know something is at risk, and you know another department could manage the risk better, you might be able to transfer the risk to the other department. For example, if one of the risks to your business process is that you don't have a UNIX Systems Administrator to manage a business process that runs on a UNIX system, you may decide to transfer the management of the business process to the department that provides UNIX systems administration. The system owner will be looking for recommendations on transferring risks. A system owner is not preserving any sort of managerial territory or integrity by insisting on retaining a substantial risk that they know they cannot mitigate. A smart system owner will want to get rid of all substantial risks. A risk to a business process puts the system owner's career at risk. Imagine the outcome if an expensive security incident occurs and in the process of resolving the incident it becomes known that the system owner knew all along that a substantial risk was present, and yet did nothing about it.

Mitigate the risk

To mitigate the risk means to either remove it completely or reduce it to an acceptable level. If the risk exposure is very high, you'll want to consider mitigating the risk. You can mitigate risks by putting safeguards in place or reconfiguring existing safeguards. You can also remove the factors that contribute to the risk (e.g., move the business to a location that is not prone to hurricanes) or remove some of the dependencies of the business process. Typically, the more dependencies that a business process has, the more risks there are. When a business process is dependent on multiple systems, multiple software packages, and multiple locations, there most certainly will be multiple risks.

> Remember the following risk monikers:
>
> L = Likelihood
>
> I = Impact
>
> RE = Risk exposure
>
> Probability of loss = $P(L)$ = Likelihood
>
> Severity of loss = $S(L)$ = Impact

Multiple physical locations can go either way when it comes to risk. Two locations mean that there are two facilities to protect, which doubles the necessary safeguards. However, if the reason you have two facilities is so that one can serve as a backup site in the event of a natural disaster, you may not be mitigating risks by consolidating to one location. Every situation is unique and you should keep in mind that each business unit may have risks that are incomparable to another agency, bureau, or line of business.

For the purpose of tracking and managing your decision, you can summarize your risk statements and risk exposure metrics in a table. Table 17.6 shows a sample risk summary table.

SUMMARY

Before you take the time to implement security controls, it's important to find out where your risk exposure lies. A Business Risk Assessment examines risk from a high-level global view. By determining business risk first, you will be better able to determine system risk. During the business risk analysis process, you will come to understand your organization's business mission, and see how those functions are related to your information technology infrastructure. After determining your business risk exposure, once you come to understand which functions are prone to the greatest risk, you can more accurately focus your system risk assessment on the most highly exposed functional areas. You may not have the time and resources to perform a penetration test on all of your systems; however, you may have time to perform one on your most highly exposed functional areas.

Performing a Business Risk Assessment helps you to understand that business that you are supporting. Sometimes IT professionals lose sight of the forest and see only the trees. By understanding the business mission, and its vulnerability exposures, you can more easily justify your decisions. For example, an auditor may ask you why you decided to scan only one network domain for vulnerabilities, and not a different one. Or perhaps you scanned all your networks with one scanning tool, and then you scanned a particular high-risk network segment with two other scanning tools. An auditor may ask why you scanned only the first network with one scanner and the other network with three different scanners. Auditors are looking for you to

Table 17.6 Risk Summary Table with Decision

Risk Statement	L	I	RE	Decision
If an unauthorized user gains access to a Veteran's hospital enrollment system, then the intruder could remove patients from the system and impede treatment.	0.1	80	8	Mitigate the risk by installing a host-based intrusion detection system on the enrollment system.
If John Smith (who has cancer) dies, then we won't have anyone to administer the enrollment database.	0.5	60	30	Transfer the risk by getting the platform engineering department to provide the database support.
If the levees in New Orleans are not repaired, then large loss of life could occur during the next hurricane.	1	100	100	Mitigate the risk by allocating $10 billion to have the Army Corps of Engineers repair the levees.
If an unauthorized user gains access to an FAA system used to track cargo on passenger planes, then hazardous materials bound for Atlanta could be rerouted to Chicago.	1	80	80	Mitigate the risk by installing an additional security access control system.
If an unauthorized user gains access to a certain U.S. federal court system used for preserving evidence, then evidence and chain of custody could be altered and prosecution of a hacker could be thwarted.	0.1	60	6	Accept the risk. The evidence system is not connected to any computer networks and is a standalone system. It is locked in a security room that requires two-factor authentication for entrance. There are surveillance cameras in every corner of the room.

justify your reasons for your decisions. A Business Risk Assessment serves to help justify your decisions, and make appropriate choices on security controls.

BOOKS AND ARTICLES ON RISK ASSESSMENT

The following list includes books that have sections on risk assessment and various articles that might be useful for understanding Business Risk Assessment:

Bragg, Roberta. *CISSP Training Guide*. Que Publishing, 2002. ISBN: 078972801X.

Taylor, Laura. *Risk Analysis Tools and How They Work*. Relevant Technologies, 2002.

Taylor, Laura. *Security Scanning Is Not Risk Analysis. Intranet Journal*. Jupiter Media Corp., 2002. (http://www.web.archive.org/web/20030207102906/http://www.intranetjournal.com/articles/200207/se_07_14_02a.html).

Young, Carl. *Metrics and Methods for Security Risk Assessment*. Syngress, July 8, 2010.

References

[1] American Heritage Dictionary of the English Language, 4th ed. Boston: Houghton Mifflin. 2000. New York: Bartleby.com. 2000. http://www.bartleby.com/61/.

[2] Natural Disasters—Forecasting Economic and Life Losses. U.S. Department of the Interior. U.S. Geological Survey. http://pubs.usgs.gov/fs/natural-disasters/figures/fig7.html.

Getting Ready for Security Testing

18

Distrust and caution are the parents of security.
—**Benjamin Franklin**

TOPICS IN THIS CHAPTER

- Introduction and authorities
- Planning
- Scoping
- Assumptions and constraints
- Schedule
- Rules of Engagement
- Limitation of Liability
- End of testing

INTRODUCTION AND AUTHORITIES

FISMA requires that all system security controls undergo testing and FISMA Section 3544(a)(2) states:

> The head of each agency shall—ensure that senior agency officials provide information security for the information and information systems that support the operations and assets under their control, including through—periodically testing and evaluating information security controls and techniques to ensure that they are effectively implemented...

Section 3544 further stipulates that policies, procedures, and practices are tested and states:

> ...periodic testing and evaluation of the effectiveness of information security policies, procedures, and practices, to be performed with a frequency depending on risk, but no less than annually...

In most agencies, all of the agency systems typically fall under the purview of the same security policies. When it comes to security policies, procedures, and practices, on an overall agency level, each policy does not have to be tested repeatedly for each system. Section 3545 of FISMA states:

... testing of the effectiveness of information security policies, procedures, and practices of a representative subset of the agency's information systems...

The process of security control testing is often referred to as a *Security Test & Evaluation* and is sometimes referred to as an *ST&E*. The outcome of the ST&E is documented in a report known as the *Security Assessment Report*. A Security Assessment Report is a document that demonstrates that an agency has performed due diligence in testing security controls. I'll be talking more specifically about *Security Assessment Reports in Chapter 22*.

PLANNING

For the purpose of an annual security assessment, testing of the security controls should be planned in advance and should be performed by an independent third-party assessor. The staff that developed the system, the ISSO, the system's administrators, and network engineers should not be part of the annual independent security assessment team. However, in preparing for an annual assessment, the ISSO can preempt a lot of findings by performing periodic informal testing throughout the year which can be done by anyone on the system team. A nice thing about performing information ad hoc security testing is that if any vulnerabilities are discovered during information testing, the ISSO can work on enlisting the operations team to close the vulnerabilities without the hassle of filling out administrative paperwork. If vulnerabilities are discovered during annual formal assessments, to close out a vulnerability typically always requires additional paperwork and corrective action forms to prove that a vulnerability has in fact been closed.

Security control testing tends to give agencies a lot of trouble. It's not clear to many agencies what tests they should be doing, who should be doing them, and what the analysis of the tests should include. When planning for testing, something to keep in mind is that, in the security world, separation of duties is always important. To that end, an ST&E will certainly appear to be more ingenuous if it is performed by someone other than the people who built and run the system.

NIST SP 800-115, Technical Guide to Information Security Testing and Assessment states:

. ...engaging third parties (e.g., auditors, contractor support staff) to conduct the assessment offers an independent view and approach that internal assessors may not be able to provide.

Similarly, *NIST SP 800-39, Managing Information Security Risk* states:

Assessor independence is an important factor in: (i) preserving the impartial and unbiased nature of the assessment process; (ii) determining the credibility of the security assessment results; and (iii) ensuring that the authorizing official receives the most objective information possible in order to make an informed, risk-based, authorization decision.

It is the responsibility of the information system owner to ensure that the testing actually takes place. However, the information system owner in most cases designates this responsibility to the ISSO. The federal guidance on what to include in your testing is somewhat vague, and though this leaves lots of room for flexibility, it leaves many information system owners, ISSOs, and security assessors wondering what a good ST&E should include.

Before security testing begins, a plan for what will occur during security testing should be created. This plan should be developed by the independent assessor performing the testing. The testing plan has been traditionally referred as a Security Test & Evaluation Plan; however, there has been an increasing trend to refer to the planning document as a *Security Assessment Plan*. Going forward, I'll be referring to it as a Security Assessment Plan. You should generally follow the standard naming for the planning document that your agency uses. Regardless of what you call the planning document, it should include the following sections:

- Authorities and policies related to security control testing
- Name(s) of independent assessors and points of contact
- Organization that independent assessors are associated with
- A description of the test environment (staging or production, physical location)
- System name, acronym, and unique identifier
- IP addresses slated for testing
- Life of Web applications slated for testing
- Life of databases slated for testing
- List of user roles slated for testing
- Assumptions and constraints
- Methodology description
- System owner name, ISSO, and points of contact
- What tests will be performed using automated tools?
- What tests will be performed through manual methods?
- Schedule
- Rules of Engagement (RoE)
- Disclosures
- Limitation of Liability
- End of testing notification
- People that resulting Security Assessment Report will be sent to
- Signatures of system owner and security assessors

SCOPING

All components of the system that will be tested should be described in the Security Assessment Plan. When describing the testing environment, the locations of the data center where the servers and network devices are installed should be noted. Security assessors will need to review the physical and environmental controls for the system and that will mean that they have to travel to the data center location(s) to perform an inspection.

The security assessors should describe what IP address will be tested. If it is not possible to test all IP addresses because the system includes such an extensive number of hosts, a representative sampling of each type of host should be selected for testing. The security assessors should justify and describe in the planning document why the sampling size that they selected is appropriate. An example table for listing the IP addresses slated for testing is shown in Table 18.1.

Databases slated for testing should be clearly indicated. A template for listing databases to test is shown in Table 18.2.

Web applications slated for testing should be noted. A template for listing Web applications to test is shown in Table 18.3.

The purpose of role testing is to test the authorization privileges for each role. The assessors should access the system while logged in as different user types and attempt to perform restricted functions as unprivileged users. A template for listing the roles to test is shown in Table 18.4.

Any manual testing that will take place should be described. Manual testing could include a large variety of items such as penetration testing, testing the backup media, ensuring that the Rules of Behavior appear prior to an initial logon, or ensuring that a Captcha function is working properly. More information about manual testing is presented in Chapter 21.

Table 18.1 IP Addresses Slated for Testing

IP Address(s) or Ranges	Hostname	Software & Version	Function

Table 18.2 Template for Listing Databases to Be Tested

Database Name	Hostname	IP Address	Additional Info

Table 18.3 Template for Listing Web Applications to Be Tested

Login URL	IP Address of Login Host	Function

Table 18.4 Template for Listing Roles to Be Tested

Role Name	Test User ID	Associated Functions

ASSUMPTIONS AND CONSTRAINTS

A section on assumptions and constraints will help the ISSO and system owner understand the limitations and dependencies of the planned security assessment. Examples of the types of things that the independent assessor may want to include in this section are:

- System owner resources, including documentation and individuals with knowledge of the system and infrastructure and their contact information, will be available to the independent assessors during the time necessary to complete assessments.
- The system owner will provide login account information/credentials necessary for the independent assessors to use its testing devices to perform authenticated scans of devices and applications.
- The system owner will permit the independent assessor to connect its testing laptops to the system's networks defined within the scope of this assessment.
- The system owner will permit communication from the independent assessor's testing appliances to an internet-hosted vulnerability management service to permit the analysis of vulnerability data.
- Security controls that have been identified as "Not Applicable" (e.g., AC-18 wireless access) in the System Security Plan will be verified as such and further testing will not be performed on these security controls.
- Significant upgrades or changes to the infrastructure and components of the system undergoing testing will not be performed during the security assessment period.
- Staff from the system owner's team will be available for on-site testing if the independent assessor determines that after hours work, or weekend work, is necessary to support the security assessment.

SCHEDULE

The system owner and ISSO will want to know when the testing will occur and how long it will take. The systems and network administrators need to know when the testing will occur, otherwise, they might think that the system is under attack when you start scanning the system and its networks. It is up to the security assessors to create a testing schedule to share with the system owner and ISSO. The ISSO typically works with the security assessment team, on behalf of the system owner,

Table 18.5 Security Assessment Testing Schedule

Task Name	Start Date	Finish Date
Kick-off Meeting		
Prepare Test Plan		
Meeting to Review Test Plan		
Test Plan Update		
Review System Documentation		
Conduct Interviews of System Staff		
Perform Testing		
Vulnerability Analysis and Threat Assessment		
Risk Exposure Table Development		
Complete Draft Security Assessment Report (SAR)		
Draft SAR Delivered to ISSO		
Issue Resolution Meeting		
Complete Final Version of SAR		
Send Final Version of SAR to System Owner and ISSO		

to help facilitate the testing. Both the ISSO and security assessors need to be in agreement on the schedule. The security assessors should present the schedule to the ISSO and allow for an open dialogue as to whether the draft testing schedule is acceptable. If the testing is going to take place on a production system, the testing should occur off hours, in the evenings or weekends. If testing is going to be performed on a staging system that is a clone of the production system, then there is typically much more flexibility on when the testing can take place.

After presenting the initial schedule, the security assessment team may need to revise the schedule based on feedback from the ISSO. It is important that someone from the ISSO team is on call when the testing takes place in case any issues arise during testing. Certain tests may create an adverse impact on the system and the ISSO will want to know about this as soon as possible. The security assessors could also run into roadblocks that prevent the testing from moving forward. It's best to address these roadblocks while the testing is taking place so that they can be resolved as soon as possible. Security assessors shouldn't wait 3 days to tell the ISSO that some of the tests need to be rescheduled due to an issue that prevented testing from moving forward. Table 18.5 presents a template for scheduling testing with the various tasks noted.

RULES OF ENGAGEMENT

A Rules of Engagement (RoE) is a document designed to describe proper notifications and disclosures between the owner of tested systems and an independent assessor. In particular, an ROE includes information about targets of automated scans and

---

Table 18.6 Disclosure Statements

Security testing may include the following activities:
- Port scans and other network service interaction and queries
- Network sniffing, traffic monitoring, traffic analysis, and host discovery
- Attempted logins or other use of systems, with any account name/password
- Attempted SQL injection and other forms of input parameter testing
- Use of exploit code for leveraging discovered vulnerabilities
- Password cracking via capture and scanning of authentication databases
- Spoofing or deceiving servers regarding network traffic
- Altering running system configuration except where denial of service would result
- Adding user accounts

Security testing will not include:
- Changes to assigned user passwords
- Modification of user files or system files
- Telephone modem probes and scans (active and passive)
- Intentional viewing of staff e-mail, Internet caches, and/or personnel cookie files
- Denial of Service attacks (smurf, land, SYN flood, etc.)
- Exploits that will introduce new weaknesses to the system
- Intentional introduction of malicious code (viruses, Trojans, worms, etc.)

IP address origination information of automated scans (and other testing tools). Together with the information provided in preceding sections of this document, this document shall serve as a Rules of Engagement once signed. The RoE should include any necessary disclosures such as the IP address(es) where scans will originate from. The purpose of identifying the IP address from where scanning originates from is that when assessors are performing scans, the system and network administrators will understand that the rapid and high-volume network traffic coming from the scanner (and the IP address associated with the scanner) is part of the testing and is not an attack.

The RoE should include a section on disclosures with some general statements about what will and will not take place during the security testing as shown in Table 18.6.

LIMITATION OF LIABILITY

A Limitation of Liability statement enables the independent assessor to reduce or limit the costs of any damage that could occur as a result of the testing. It's possible that the security assessor's insurance company requires such a statement. Even if the assessor's insurance company requires such a statement, the system owner will still have to agree to it before signing the RoE. An example of a Limitation of Liability statement is shown in Table 18.7.

The RoE should include signature lines and should be signed by the system owner, the ISSO, and the independent assessor team lead.

Table 18.7 Limitation of Liability Statement

<Independent Assessor>, and its stated partners, shall not be held liable to <System Owner> for any and all liabilities, claims, or damages arising out of or relating to the security vulnerability testing portion of this Agreement, howsoever caused and regardless of the legal theory asserted, including breach of contract or warranty, tort, strict liability, statutory liability, or otherwise.

<System Owner> acknowledges that there are limitations inherent in the methodologies implemented, and the assessment of security and vulnerability relating to information technology is an uncertain process based on past experiences, currently available information, and the anticipation of reasonable threats at the time of the analysis. There is no assurance that an analysis of this nature will identify all vulnerabilities or propose exhaustive and operationally viable recommendations to mitigate all exposure.

END OF TESTING

The Security Assessment Plan should indicate who will be notified when the security testing has officially ended. The system owner or ISSO will want to let the system administrators and network support staff know when the testing has been completed so that they understand when test scans will no longer create additional network traffic. Testing has the potential to cause intrusion detection systems to generate alerts, and once testing ends, the network administrators will know that any alerts generated by intrusion detection systems could be due to an actual intrusion.

SUMMARY

Testing the security controls on an information system requires some thought and planning. The scope of the testing should be described prior to testing and should be reviewed by the system owner, the ISSO team, and the security assessors before testing commences. Everyone needs to be on the same page as far as what will and what won't be tested. Communications should occur between the ISSO and independent assessors every step of the way, and the different communications activities should be noted in the schedule.

ADDITIONAL RESOURCES

This section provides you with a list of books and articles to refer to for more information and techniques on security testing:

Doar, Matthews B. *Practical Development Environments*. O'Reilly Media, September 2005. ISBN: 0596007965.
Faircloth, Jeremy. *Penetration Tester's Open Source Toolkit*, 3rd Edition. Syngress Publishing, July 2011. ISBN: 978-1-59749-627-8.

Graff, Mark G. and Kenneth van Wyk. *Secure Coding: Principles and Practices*. O'Reilly Media, June 2003. ISBN: 0596002424.

Hoagland, Greg and Gary McGraw. *Exploiting Software: How to Break Code*. Addison-Wesley, 2004. ISBN: 02017865958.

Hope, Paco and Ben Walther. *Web Security Testing Cookbook*. O'Reilly Media Inc., October, 2008. ISBN: 978-0-596-51483-9.

Howard, Michael and David LeBlanc. *Writing Secure Code*. Microsoft Press, December 2002. ISBN: 0735617228.

Jackson, Chris. *Network Security Auditing*. Cisco Press, June 2010. ISBN: 978-1-58705-352-8.

Joint Task Force. *NIST SP 800-39, Managing Information Security Risk*. National Institute of Standards and Technology, March 2011.

Scarfone, Karen, Murugiah Souppaya, Amanda Cody, and Angela Orebaugh. *NIST SP 800-155, Technical Guide to Information Security Testing and Assessment*. National Institute of Standards and Technology, September 2008.

Splaine, Steve. *Testing Web Security*. Wiley, 2002. ISBN: 0471232815.

Viega, John and Matt Messier. *Secure Programming Cookbook*. O'Reilly Media, July 2003. ISBN: 0596003943.

Weiss, Martin and Michael G. Solomon. *Auditing IT Infrastructures for Compliance*. Jones & Bartlett Learning, November 14, 2011. ISBN: 978-0-7637-9181-0.

Whittaker, J., H.H. Thompson, and H. Thompson. *How to Break Software Security*. Addison-Wesley, May 2003 ISBN: 0321194330.

Submitting the Security Package

If I see an ending, I can work backward.
—**Arthur Miller**

TOPICS IN THIS CHAPTER

- Structure of documents
- Who puts the package together?
- Markings and format
- Signature pages
- A word about "Not Applicable" information
- Submission and revision
- Defending the Security Package
- Checklist

INTRODUCTION

Ostensibly, like most published works, you could forever add more details to a Security Package and continue adding more details until the additional details eventually begin to detract from the intended focus. Part of understanding the package preparation process is knowing when to draw the line in the sand and proclaim that all the documents are finished. Once you have put together your first Security Package, you will soon come to the realization that you could have gone on forever documenting picayune details to no end. In most cases, how far you should go will be determined by a date on the calendar. As of this writing, FISMA compliance on all federal information systems has to be done every 3 years. If the last security assessment for a system resulted in a formal authorization on July 24, 2013, then the next authorization for that system must be completed by July 24, 2016—that means that an authorization letter granting an Authority to Operate must be in hand by 3-year calendar date regardless of whether you started the project 6 days ago or 6 months ago.

STRUCTURE OF DOCUMENTS

I have already described the different documents required for a FISMA compliant Security Package. In addition to what I have already suggested you include, each of your documents should have the following sections:

- Introduction
- Purpose
- Scope and applicability
- References, requirements, and authorities
- Record of Changes

A Record of Changes should be inserted near the beginning of each document. The Record of Changes is a history of changes made to the document over time, and it should include information about the section numbers that have been updated, the date that the change occurred, who made the change, and a brief summary of the changes. It is better to reference a change by section number, rather than page number, because page numbers change as you add more content. Section numbers can change if you add (or remove) sections, but that usually doesn't happen as often as a change to page numbers. A sample Record of Changes is shown in Table 19.1.

WHO PUTS THE PACKAGE TOGETHER?

The ISSO should collect the documents from the document preparation team and submit the documents securely to the assessment team. Usually a draft package is put together for review before a final package is put together. In some agencies, the document preparation team puts the draft package together and in other agencies, the assessment team puts the package together after the documents have been submitted to them. As far as putting the package together goes, the preparation team should always defer to the assessment team's guidance. If you're not sure who should put the package together, ask the assessment team.

Table 19.1 Example of a Record of Changes

Section #	Change Comment	Date of Change	Name
2.5	Changed the release of from 3.2 to 3.3 to reflect a software upgrade	4/7/13	Glenn Jones
5.2	Added in discussion about new single sign-on server	6/10/13	Ellen Frank
9.7	Updated the network diagram to reflect the new single sign-on server	6/10/13	Ellen Frank

MARKINGS AND FORMAT

The cover page of each document should have a statement about who is authorized to read the documents and should also indicate the document classification level. A typical document classification warning that would be suitable for the cover page might read as follows:

> The <Agency Name> **Controlled Unclassified Information** contained herein is the sole, proprietary, and exclusive property of <Agency Name> and may only be used by individuals with a need to know. All information contained herein is privileged whether such information is in written, graphic, electronic, or physical form. Those granted limited use to the information must hold these materials and information in strict confidence. Access to and use of this information by any other entity or individual is strictly prohibited.

The data classification should be marked on every page. For example, if all the data are considered Controlled Unclassified Information, every single page of the Security Package should have **Controlled Unclassified Information** marked on it either at the header or at the footer.

SIGNATURE PAGES

Certain documents inside the Security Package have to be signed by the ISSO, the system owner, and members of the system owner's management team. In most cases, agencies require the *System Security Plan* and the *Information System Contingency Plan* to be signed. Your agency may require signatures from specific individuals for the different documents. If you're not sure, ask someone in the assessment team if there are particular signature requirements. If there are not predefined signature requirements, usually the ISSO and business owner decide who should review and sign the documents before they are submitted.

Some agencies don't require signatures on the individual documents though it is certainly more difficult to hold anyone accountable for the contents of the document, and the information security of the systems, without signatures. Agencies that don't require signatures should move toward requiring them in the future.

It's sometimes the case that in large agencies, obtaining signatures can be very time consuming because the documents have to be routed manually from person to person. Once documents have been signed, you need to scan in the signature pages to obtain an image file to paste into the signature page. Agencies can expedite the signing process by using digital signatures or electronic signatures in SMART documents. SMART[1] documents are based on Extensible Markup Language (XML) and can be integrated with digital signature technologies to create

---

[1]SMART = Securable, Manageable, Archivable, Retrievable, Transferable.

tamper-evident seals. Using XML offers the ability to generate new and updated documents much more expeditiously.

Digital signature technologies and electronic signing pads exist that make signing a Microsoft Word or .pdf file as easy as signing with a pen. Using digital signature products, it is easy to route the document in need of signature from one signatory to another. Signing documents electronically generates a time-stamped history of the review and approval process. Not all agencies use digital signature technologies today, and for those that don't, it would certainly create efficiencies if such signing technologies were used.

The following vendors offer easy-to-use digital signature solutions:

- Arx (http://www.arx.com/)
- CIC (http://www.cic.com)
- DocuSign (http://www.docusign.com)
- Topaz Systems Inc. (http://www.topazsystems.com)
- Adobe (http://www.adobe.com)

Any digital signature solution you put into place for document signing should be thoroughly tested to make sure that signatures are encrypted using FIPS 140-2 compliant algorithms.

A WORD ABOUT "NOT APPLICABLE" INFORMATION

When you don't include a particular section in a Security Package document, even if it is not applicable to your system, the auditors may come to the conclusion that you forgot it. Including a section and then proclaiming it "not applicable" shows that you haven't forgotten to include a particular section. Any item in a document that is not applicable to your information system or major application undergoing an assessment should be marked as such. Not forgetting to mark particular sections as not applicable will stave off a lot of questions from the security assessment team.

SUBMISSION AND REVISION

Submit the Security Package according to guidance from the assessment team. They may want you to e-mail them documents, or upload them into an online library or database. If an e-mail solution is used, and the assessment team is at a remote location, be sure that you don't e-mail the documents out over the Internet without encrypting them. Some agencies use secure portals and they often want the ISSOs to upload the Security Package documents to a secure portal. Today, fewer agencies and assessment teams require a paper copy of the Security Package. However, if a paper copy is requested by the assessment team, the ISSO should put all of the documents in a 3-ring binder, putting a CD/DVD that contains the documents in the binder pocket.

Establish a dialogue with the assessment team so that you can accommodate their preference for package submission. One thing you'll need to find out is how much time the assessment team requires to review the documents. Be sure to submit them early enough so that you can have an authorization letter in hand by your required deadline. Most assessment teams need approximately 6 weeks to review documents and perform independent testing. Submitting the documents a week before an authorization letter is needed is entirely unreasonable.

Even on a stable group of systems that have had few changes, each time you submit a new Security Package you are opening up yourself to new audit findings. The assessment team could be an entirely new team that is more stringent on package evaluations than the former team. New requirements may have been put into place by your agency since the last time the general support systems were reviewed. Not all assessors do things the same way, but they all have the upper hand in whether to be extremely picky or more flexible in interpreting requirements.

DEFENDING THE SECURITY PACKAGE

After submitting the Security Package, the assessment team will start reviewing it. The process for evaluating the Security Package is discussed in Chapter 21. Most likely the assessment team will have questions about various items. They may e-mail questions to the ISSO or ask the preparation team and ISSO to participate in meetings for the purpose of getting questions answered.

The team that prepares the Security Package should prepare themselves to defend the package. During the assessment process, the assessment team may have checklists that they fill out while questions are being answered. It's possible that the assessment team could be in a hurry, and due to this, they may not even read all sections of all documents in your Security Package that you diligently took the time to write. They may ask questions about items that are clearly answered in the Security Package documents. They may even mark down on their checklists certain items as "findings" simply because they did not spend enough time to look for the information in the various documents. If you believe certain items marked with "findings" should not be marked as such, and that the information pertaining to that item is included in the documents, advise the assessment team what section of what document to look in and explain to them why you feel the "finding" should be removed.

Unquestionably, every item that the assessment team marks as a finding should be adequately researched by the preparation team. Assessment teams can make mistakes—they are human. The assessment team should give you adequate time to research and comment on their findings. You should look at all draft findings and verify them to ensure you can reproduce them. If your package has some findings, that doesn't mean that the system will not receive an authorization. It is nearly impossible to receive a *Security Assessment Report* that has no findings in it. If the noted findings in the Security Assessment Report are justifiable, you won't win any points with the assessors by arguing about these citations. Accept the findings and be glad the assessors found vulnerabilities before a hacker found them. It's very important to address any findings professionally and politely.

Findings are not necessarily a reflection on the folks who put the Security Package together. After all, the document preparation team is simply reporting on the state of the system. The state of the security controls is the result of a large team of people who worked together—the design and architecture team, the developers, the administrators, and the management team. If certain controls are not in place, it is likely not the fault of the documentation preparation team. The preparation teams have responsibilities to document the security that actually exists and they cannot be expected to invent good security controls that don't exist through creative writing.

If the assessment team does not request to schedule time with the preparation team and ISSO to review the Security Package, it is worth taking the initiative to suggest a meeting to discuss any issues that may arise. It is in the best interest of the assessment team to make time to discuss any issues that they have with the system owner of the documents. It's not really acceptable for the assessment team to mark down findings and not give the ISSO and document preparation team a chance to comment on the issue at hand. Some agencies refer to the discussion between the document preparers and the assessment team as Comment Resolution sessions.

If the document preparation team that prepares the Security Package does their work diligently and in good faith, it will be second nature to defend any questions posed by the auditors. True leaders are not afraid of the inspection process that a Security Package goes through. Don't hedge the truth—answer all questions honestly. If you don't know the answer to a question, simply acknowledge that and advise the assessment that you will be happy to get back to them.

CHECKLIST

Use the following checklist to make sure that you don't forget anything during the submission process:

- Have you ensured that all documents that require signatures have been signed?
- Are all documents included in the Security Package?
- Have you spoken to the assessment team to obtain specific submission guidance?
- Have you set up a Comment Resolution session to discuss issues?
- Have you researched anything marked as a finding to see if the assessment team made a mistake?

SUMMARY

Once you have submitted the Security Package, you have achieved a major milestone. The package itself is an incredibly valuable suite of documents. Without it, the risks to the systems, networks, and applications would be much harder to identify, and without these documents, the security controls might be completely unknown. The Security Package is indicative of a security baseline that is far more substantial than one that a simple network scan report can give you. There is much more to assessing security than performing a network scan or penetration test.

ADDITIONAL RESOURCES

The following resources provide information about XML digital signatures that offer improved signing methods for C&A documents:

Downen, Mike and Shawn Farkas. *Exchange Data More Securely with XML Signatures and Encryption*. Microsoft Corporation, November 2004 (http://www.msdn.microsoft.com/en-us/magazine/cc185723.aspx).

Donald Eastlake, Joseph Reagle, and David Solo. *RFC 3275, XML-Signature Syntax and Processing*. Internet Engineering Task Force, March 2002.

Geuer-Pollmann, Christian. Confidentiality of XML documents by Pool Encryption. University of Seigen, 2004. (http://www.ub.uni-siegen.de/pub/diss/fb12/2004/geuer/geuer.pdf).

Sanin, Aleksey, Igor Zlatkovic, Tej Arora, Wouter Ketting, and Dmitry Belyavsky. *XML Digital Signature*. XMLSec Library (http://www.aleksey.com/xmlsec/xmldsig.html).

Simon, Ed, Paul Madsen, and Carlisle Adams. *An Introduction to XML Digital Signatures*. O'Reilly XML.com, August 8, 2001 (http://www.xml.com/pub/a/2001/08/08/xmldsig.html).

Smallwood, Robert F. and Barclay T. Blair. *Safeguarding Critical E-Documents: Implementing a Program for Securing Confidential Information Assets*. John Wiley & Sons, July 31, 2012.

Sokolowski, Rachael. *SMART Document Version 1.1 Quick Reference Card*. Magnolia Technologies, LLC (http://www.magnoliatech.com/SMARTDoc_QuickRef11.pdf).

Independent Assessor Audit Guide

20

To give no trust is to get no trust.
—Lao-Tzu (sixth century B.C.)

TOPICS IN THIS CHAPTER

- Testing against the system's security control baseline
- How does confidentiality, integrity, and availability fit in?
- Manual and automated testing
- Security testing tools
- Checklists for compliance
- Evaluations by an OIG
- Evaluations by the GAO

INTRODUCTION

Once a Security Package is complete and the test plan has been approved, the ISSO submits the documents in the package to the independent security assessors. The security assessment team begins reviewing the package documents and then proceeds with security testing. The person or team of people who evaluate the Security Package should not be the same people who prepared it. Something that the OIG and GAO will be looking for are instances of the fox guarding the hen house. There needs to be a separation of duties between the folks who prepare the documents and the folks who evaluate them and test the security controls.

Determining vulnerabilities during testing is key to keeping information systems secure. There are different levels of granularity that should be applied when looking for vulnerabilities. The higher the system sensitivity level, the more comprehensive and more involved the testing process should be for determining vulnerabilities.

TEST AGAINST THE SYSTEM'S SECURITY CONTROL BASELINE

Whether you're testing controls for a civilian agency, an intelligence agency, the Department of Defense (DoD), or a private sector company that has a contract with the government, there will be a security control baseline that you'll need to test against. For civilian agencies, that security control baseline will be based on NIST

800-53, Revision 4. For DoD agencies, that baseline will be based on the DIACAP security controls which are listed in DoD Instruction 8500.2 (the DoD will be transitioning from 8500.2 to CNSSI 1253 in the near future as mentioned previously). Intelligence agencies will be using CNSSI 1253 in most cases. Go back and review Chapter 3 for more information on these different security control sets. By the time the system is ready for testing, the agency would have already created a security control baseline based on one of these control sets. It's a good idea for the security assessment team to have the guidance documents from the appropriate security control set available for reference during testing.

For systems that use controls from NIST SP 800-53, a document known as *SP 800-53A, Revision 1, Guide for Assessing the Security Controls in Federal Information Systems and Organizations*, is available for security assessors to use to guide them through the testing process. If the assessment team is testing a DIACAP or intelligence system, the assessment team may still find SP 800-53A useful, even though the security control identifiers will be different from the security control identifiers that the system uses. SP 800-53A, Revision 1, is available at the following URL: http://www.csrc.nist.gov/publications/nistpubs/800-53A-rev1/sp800-53A-rev1-final.pdf. SP 800-53A helps security assessors understand how to conduct security testing and contains assessment procedures for all of the NIST SP 800-53, Appendix F, security controls.

HOW DOES CONFIDENTIALITY, INTEGRITY, AND AVAILABILITY FIT IN?

When considering security testing, keep in mind that the system owner is trying to obtain an authorization for an information technology implementation, not a product. That said, system implementations typically use many commercial off-the-shelf products. Figuring out where to draw the line in the sand on where a product ends and where an implementation begins is part of the challenge. If the system uses commercial off-the-shelf products, presumably due diligence was already done in selecting products. System owners are not trying to justify the purchase of the products—that should have already occurred during the acquisition process. System owners are hoping to show that products were correctly installed and configured, and integrated with the network so that the risk exposure of the system is low enough to warrant an Authorization to Operate.

Refreshing your memory from Chapter 3, security controls are based on safeguarding confidentiality, integrity, and availability. Therefore, tests should be designed to determine if confidentiality, integrity, and availability are preserved by the security controls that are in place. The security controls that safeguard confidentiality, integrity, and availability are management controls, technical controls, or operational controls. However, in the most recent version of NIST SP 800-53, NIST has elected not to differentiate between management, operational, and technical controls since some controls might fall into several of these categories.

Confidentiality tests

Confidentiality tests determine if unauthorized disclosure is possible. When you perform confidentiality tests, you are trying to determine if data are disclosed to people that they are not intended for. Before you can perform confidentiality testing, you have to understand a bit about confidentiality risks and vulnerabilities. Some of the ways that confidentiality can be lost are:

- Data traveling in plaintext over communications lines (vulnerable to sniffing)
- Weak passwords compromised (using password crackers)
- Papers left on printers (can be read by unauthorized individuals)
- Inadvertently publishing sensitive information on publicly accessible Web sites
- Shoulder surfing
- Unauthorized intruders
- System authorizations and permissions incorrectly configured (allowing unauthorized roles to view data)

Confidentiality tests look to ensure that authentication and encryption mechanisms work according to the security requirements. Proper authentication helps ensure that only the authorized individuals can use the system and view the data. It's important to ensure that authentication and encryption mechanisms are not only implemented, but that they have safeguards built around the controls themselves from being sabotaged.

If it appears that "shoulder surfing" is a risk, then security assessors should report that on the Security Assessment Report so that the system owner and ISSO can work on correcting it. If you have reason to believe social engineering (tricking a user into revealing sensitive information to unauthorized individuals) is a risk, security assessors may want to recommend addressing social engineering during annual security training.

If password files exist, you may want to perform a test to ensure that the passwords are properly encrypted using a salted hash to prevent discovery using a brute-force dictionary attack. Security assessors may also want to verify that the permissions on the password files are set correctly and are not writeable to the world. Last, passwords should always be created using a salted hash and the salt should never be reused. A short list of tools for testing the security of passwords appears later in the section on "Security testing tools."

If VPNs are a part of the system that is being tested, the assessors will need to devise some tests to ensure that VPNs have been properly configured and cannot be penetrated by unauthorized users. Assessors should describe in the test report whether the VPNs in use by the system are secure remote access VPNs (used by remote users) or end-to-end VPNs that encrypt all traffic that goes between designated sites. VPNs can be configured to pass packets in *tunnel mode*, *transport mode*, or both. Which modes does your security policy require? Assessors should make sure that VPNs are configured in accordance with that system's security policy.

Confidentiality problems that you'll want to check for include:

- Passwords that do not comply with the security policy
- Authentication mechanisms that are not properly configured
- Use of encryption algorithms that do not comply with the security policy
- Correct configurations of encryption products (VPNs, PKI, etc.)
- Implementations that do not produce logging capabilities (to review who has viewed data).

Integrity tests

Integrity tests answer the question, "Is the data adequately protected to prevent unauthorized modification?" A goal of any information technology implementation is to preserve the integrity of the data. You need good data and you need to determine if it is possible for someone to inadvertently, or purposefully, generate bad data. For example, buffer-overflow attacks overwrite the data in memory, essentially changing it. Testing the integrity of the implementation allows you to determine if secure coding principles were adhered to and if all the right patches are in place.

Coding gaffes that should be reviewed that could affect data integrity are:

- Buffer-overflow vulnerabilities
- Extraneous lines of code
- Race conditions
- Temporary files writeable by the world
- Hard-coded passwords

There are many good source code scanners that can look for coding vulnerabilities. A short list of leading code scanners can be found in the section on "Security testing tools."

Integrity can also be compromised by privilege escalation attacks which occur when authorizations on files and directories and databases are not correctly configured. An ordinary user should not have the same permissions as a systems administrator. However, if read, write, and execute parameters are not properly configured, it may be possible for an ordinary user write to files that they should not have permission to write to, thereby changing information to something different than what it is supposed to be.

If unauthorized intruders are able to gain access to the system, that can jeopardize integrity since unauthorized intruders can modify, remove, or delete anything that they get access to. Scanners are often the best way to discover vulnerabilities that could be exploited by unauthorized intruders. A list of scanners that can be useful to security assessors is found in the section on "Security testing tools."

Availability tests

Availability tests ensure that availability is preserved. Tests for availability should verify that there are safeguards in place that prevent the system, or any of its components, from becoming unavailable. The types of security tests that safeguard availability are:

- Testing of the configuration management system
- Testing of the Contingency Plan
- Testing of backups
- Testing of fault-tolerant disk arrays (striping, mirroring, and duplexing)
- Testing of load balancers
- Testing of high-availability mission critical systems (e.g., firewalls, DNS servers)

MANUAL AND AUTOMATED TESTING

Tests can be manual or automated, or a combination of both, as long as they get the job done. Either way, the security assessors need to document how the tests are conducted. If the security assessors use a software test management package, the test management package, and how it works, should be described in the Security Assessment Report. Examples of manual testing procedures are listed in Table 20.1. MT-1 stands for "Manual Test 1."

Penetration testing, where security assessors simulate attacks from hackers, is an excellent way to discover vulnerabilities. Traditionally, penetration testing was always performed manually. However, certain intrusive scanners now have the ability to not just discover vulnerabilities—they can go to the next step and exploit them. A list of penetration testing scanners can be found in the next section. Any penetration testing that is performed manually should be added to the manual testing table.

SECURITY TESTING TOOLS

There are a multitude of security testing tools that can be used to automate certain security tests. Since every system is different, not every type of testing tool is applicable to every system. In the Security Assessment Report, security assessors will need to describe what was tested, and how, so it's important to take notes when using any testing tools so that the details can be recalled. Some security testing tools produce automated reports, but some may don't. Some of the details that security testers may want to discuss in the Security Assessment Report include how the tool was configured prior to performing the tests. Some security testing tools worth considering are found in the sections that follow.

Algorithm testing

The biggest problem with encryption algorithms is that about 25% of the time encryption algorithms are not implemented correctly in security products. As a result of this problem, there are now laws and standards that specify how encryption algorithms need to be implemented.

If an information system implementation includes encryption products, it is a federal law that the encryption products be FIPS 140-2[2] compliant (unless they have been

Table 20.1 Examples of Manual Testing Procedures

ID	Test	Procedure	Test Results
MT-1	Verify that Event Viewer is running and that security events are being generated and are available for review	(1) Set security properties to filter all 5 event types. (2) Generate a security event in each category and verify that Event Viewer creates a record to reflect the appropriate event.	
MT-2	Verify that passwords use at least eight characters with both letters and numbers	(1) Logon as initial user (2) Try to change password to new password that has less than 8 characters (3) Try to change password to new password that has 8 characters but does not use numbers (4) Try to change password to new password that has 8 characters but does not use letters (5) Ensure that password field will accept an 8-character password with letters and numbers	
MT-3	Verify that the system requires user to change the initial password at first logon	(1) Logon as initial user (2) Check to see if system instructs user to change their password (3) Don't change the initial password and see if logon is possible (4) Change the initial password and ensure that user can logon	
MT-4	Verify that Rules of Behavior are displayed before initial logon and before being prompted for password	(1) Logon as initial user (2) Look for Rules of Behavior (3) Ensure that you can view them before you are prompted for your password (4) Ensure that there is an acceptance box that can be checked and that it is working properly (5) Ensure that initial password is not accepted if user does not check box to agree to Rules of Behavior	

Table 20.1 Examples of Manual Testing Procedures—cont'd

ID	Test	Procedure	Test Results
MT-5	Verify that you can restore a file from the backup media	(1) Obtain backup media from 1 week ago, 1 month ago, 3 months ago (2) Attempt to restore the admin (or root) password file from each of the three archives (3) Verify that the password file accepts the known admin (or root) password (4) Restore the password file (or shadow file)	
MT-6	Verify that the only port open on the messaging server is TCP port 25	(1) Scan the messaging server with a port scanner (2) Verify that the only port found open is TCP port 25	
MT-7	Verify that no modems are connected to network.49	(1) Scan network.49 with a modem scanner (2) Verify that no modems are discovered	
MT-8	Determine is manually forcing the browser to different URLs enables user to access data that they should not be able to access	Login as customer and try to gain access to the Network Administrator and Database Administrator privileges and authorizations by navigating to different views and manually forcing the browser to various URLs	
MT-9	Verify if OCSP is validating X.509 certificates	Use Firefox to perform OCSP testing	
MT-10	Verify if system is vulnerable to SQL injection attacks	Perform manual SQL injection attacks using fake names and 0 OR '1' = '1' statements	

approved and validated for classified use). Originally passed as FIPS 140-1 in 1995, FIPS 140-2 is a Federal Information Processing Standard (FIPS) that was instituted as a result of the Information Technology Reform Act of 1996 (Public Law 104-106) and the Computer Security Act of 1987 (Public Law 100-235). FIPS 140-2 was published in May of 2001 and now supersedes FIPS 140-1. Encryption products are not supposed to be procured and implemented in federal systems unless they have been officially certified and validated through the Cryptographic Module Validation Program (CMVP).

Through the CMVP program, Cryptographic Module Testing (CMT) labs use a tool called the Cryptographic Algorithm Validation System (CAVS) that can only be obtained from NIST and is used exclusively for testing encryption products. CAVS generates correct algorithm vectors that CMT labs use to ensure that encryption algorithms are correctly implemented. If an encryption product has compliant algorithms, the CMT lab validates the findings and submits the results to the CMVP program for review and acceptance.

All encryption products implemented on government systems are supposed to be FIPS 140-2 compliant. Security assessors can check this by finding out if a valid FIPS 140-2 certificate exists for the product on the CMVP Web site. FIPS 140-2 certificates are considered public information and you can see all of them for every product ever validated from the following URL: http://www.csrc.nist.gov/groups/STM/cmvp/validation.html.

Products that are not FIPS 140-2 compliant are not supposed to be implemented on government systems; however, in practice, this doesn't always hold true. Encryption products that are not FIPS 140-2 compliant can often be found on government networks. Keep in mind that FIPS 140-2 only requires that algorithms are correctly implemented in the product. It will not tell you if the encryption product has been correctly installed and configured.

Code and memory analyzers

If the system being tested uses code that is custom written and is not associated with any commercial off-the-shelf product, it is a good idea to scan your source code for coding gaffes and vulnerabilities. Code and memory analyzers can help you uncover source code vulnerabilities and memory leaks. The following code and memory analyzers can help security assessors uncover vulnerabilities that the system owner will want to know about:

- Rational Purify by IBM (http://www.ibm.com)
- TotalView by RogueWave (http://www.roguewave.com/products/totalview.aspx)
- CodeSonar by Grammatech (http://www.grammatech.com)
- Memory Analyzer (MAT) by Eclipse (http://www.eclipse.org)
- HP Fortity Static Code Analyzer (http://www.hp.com)
- Sentinel Source by Whitehat (http://www.whitehat.com)
- Dynamic Leak Check by DMS (http://www.dynamic-memory.com)
- Jtest: Java Testing, Static Analysis, Code Review by Parasoft (http://www.parasoft.com)

INFRASTRUCTURE SCANNERS

The tools today that scan for system, network, and application vulnerabilities are very advanced. These tools are indispensable for security risk assessments. Most of the leading vulnerability assessment scanners have teams of security engineers that are populating the scanner engine on a daily basis with new signatures, similar to the way antivirus engines can be loaded with new antivirus signatures daily.

Once properly configured and set up, infrastructure scanners can run unattended and automatically look for well-known security vulnerabilities. Infrastructure scans can be performed by logging in to a credentialed account or without logging in at all. A credentialed scan typically returns fewer false positives and outputs more information. However, a noncredentialed scan will give the system owner a view of the network and hosts the way that a hacker might see it. There are advantages and disadvantages to both types of scans.

Care must be taken when configuring scanners taking into consideration whether the system being tested is a production system or a staging system. Scanners can perform either intrusive or nonintrusive scans. An intrusive scanner finds vulnerabilities and then tries to exploit them. A nonintrusive scanner simply reports vulnerabilities without trying to exploit them. Scanners can be configured to scan a single IP address, a range of IP addresses, a domain, a database, or a Web site. High-end scanners have the ability to generate a network map. Popular infrastructure scanners include the following:

- GFiLANguard (http://www.gfi.com)
- IP360 by nCircle (http://www.ncircle.com)
- Nexpose by Rapid7 (http://www.rapid7.com)
- Nessus by Tenable Network Security (http://www.tenable.com)
- QualysGuard by Qualys (http://www.qualys.com)
- Retina by Beyond Trust (http://www.beyondtrust.com)

Before performing scanning, it is very important to obtain permission in writing from the agency, bureau, or department that owns the systems being scanned. An agreement should be established on specifically what will be scanned, and when the scanning will occur. Whether the person performing the scanning is an agency employee or a consultant, it is important for security assessors to obtain a signature on the agreement in order to be protected from liabilities. Without a signed Rules of Engagement, the assessment team could be accused of being an unauthorized intruder or a malicious insider.

Penetration testing scanners

After performing basic scanning, security assessors typically perform penetration testing in attempt to exploit vulnerabilities. Penetration testing can be performed using manual methods or automated tools. Scanners that are able to exploit vulnerabilities are known as penetration testing scanners. Note that penetration testing scanners could damage a system or cause it to reboot. It is the security assessor's responsibility to inform system owners and ISSOs if they plan on using an intrusive scanner. There should be no assumption that because assessors have permission to conduct scanning they have permission to conduct penetration testing and use intrusive scanners. Using penetration testing tools without permission can be considered an attack on the systems.

Popular tools that are specifically designed to conduct automated penetration testing include the following:

- Metasploit by Rapid7 (http://www.rapid7.com)
- Core Impact by Core Security (http://www.coresecurity.com)
- CANVAS by Immunity (http://www.immunityinc.com)
- Kali Linux (http://www.kali.org)

By no means is this list inclusive of all the available penetration testing tool sets. Penetration Testing is an extension of scanning. Remember before performing any scanning or any testing, it is very important to obtain permission in writing from the agency, bureau, or department that owns the systems. An agreement should be established on specifically what will be scanned, and when the scanning will occur. Whether the assessor performing scanning and/or penetration testing is an agency employee or a consultant, it is important to obtain a signed Rules of Engagement so that the assessor is not accused of being an unauthorized intruder or a malicious insider.

Port scanners

A subcategory to infrastructure scanning is port scanning. Port scanners simply scan for open ports. The reason to use a port scanner is to find out if the open ports are consistent with what is being reported in the System Security Plan. It is a security risk to have more ports open than necessary. Often hackers scan for open ports to see which open ports they may want to exploit. Once hackers find an open port, they often use particular hacker programs that are uniquely coded to exploit a particular port. When doing a port scan, you'll want to scan both the TCP and UDP ports. Many network scanners also scan for open ports.

By a long shot, the most popular port scanner is an open source tool called nmap. However, there are some commercial port scanners available as well. Various port scanners that you may find useful include:

- Atelier AWRC Pro (http://www.atelierweb.com/)
- Fport by Mcafee (http://www.mcafee.com)
- Nmap (http://www.nmap.org)
- Port Scanner ActiveX Control by Magneto Software (http://www.magnetosoft.com)

Application scanners

Some scanners specialize in scanning applications. Instead of looking for operating system vulnerabilities, their goal is to uncover vulnerabilities in Web sites and Web-based applications. Scanners that typically find the most vulnerabilities in Web applications must run as credentialed scans, logging in to the Web application with a userID and password. Popular Web application scanners include the following:

- Acunetix WVS by Acunetix (http://www.acunetix.com)
- AppScan by IBM (http://www.ibm.com)
- Burp Suite by Portswigger (http://www.portswigger.net)
- WebInspect by HP (http://www.hp.com)
- Lumension Scan by Lumension (http://www.lumension.com)
- Nikto by Cirt.net (http://www.cirt.net)
- Samurai by InGuardians (http://www.samurai.inguardians.com/)
- Zed Attack Proxy, an open source tool (http://www.owasp.org)
- An excellent resource for testing applications is the OWASP testing guide which can be found here: (https://www.owasp.org/index.php/OWASP_Testing_Guide_v4_Table_of_Contents)

Port listeners

Probably, the most popular port listener available is netcat, and since it is open source, it is free to use. You can obtain netcat from http://www.netcat.sourceforge.net/download.php.

A good test of your firewall is to run netcat on one of your mission critical servers that is protected by the firewall. Have netcat listen on a port that is supposedly being blocked by the firewall and see if an attacking machine can connect to this port—if it can, the firewall is being circumvented. You can also use netcat to see if the port banner can be grabbed for the purpose of finding out the version number of the operating system that is running.

Websnarf is a port listener written in perl that is made just for Web sites. You can use this tool to find out local and remote IP addresses that are trying to connect through port 80. If your firewall is blocking port 80, then no one should ever be able to connect through port 80. If websnarf logs any connections to port 80, then someone is getting around the firewall. You can obtain websnarf from the following URL: http://www.unixwiz.net/tools/websnarf.html.

Modem scanners

Modem scanners have historically been referred to as "war dialing" tools. The purpose of modem scanners is to find out if there are any modems (or fax machines) that are connected to systems in violation of your security policy. Modems are not used nearly as much as they were 10 or 20 years ago; however, fax machines are still prevalent and fax machine connections to systems and networks could be vulnerable to interceptions. It's possible for fax machines to transmit over satellite or microwave links. Through commercial fax interception devices, it is possible to intercept satellite or microwave links.[1] One particular commercial fax interception device can decode up to 150 simultaneous fax transmissions from a 6000 phone line satellite link.[2] A fax transmission could be intercepted even by accident due to the route a fax travels through the common carrier networks.[2] The following product offers the ability to find modems and fax machines that could create security vulnerabilities:

• Phonesweep by Niksun (http://www.niksun.com/product.php?id=17)

Wireless network scanners

Wireless network scanners are sometimes referred to as "war-driving" tools or wireless protocol analyzers. These tools are good for detecting open wireless networks in your facility. If you have a policy that prohibits wireless networks, you may want to walk around the facility with a wireless network scanner to see if you detect any unauthorized WiFi networks. Popular wireless network scanners are available at the following URLs:

• WiFiScanner, an open source tool (http://www.wifiscanner.sourceforge.net)
• CommView for WiFi by Tamosoft (http://www.tamos.com)
• OmniPeek by WildPackets (http://www.wildpackets.com)
• iStumbler for Max OSX wireless network discovery (http://www.istumbler.net/)
• WifiInfoView by NirSoft Freeware (http://www.nirsoft.net)
• WIFi Locator by TCPEeye (http://www.tcpmonitor.altervista.org)
• WiFi Scanner (for Mac OS X) by WLANBook (http://www.wlanbook.com)
• WiFi Channel Scanner by Wifichannelscanner (http://www.wifichannelscanner.com)

Wireless intrusion detection systems

Wireless intruders can be detected through various host-based intrusion detection systems available at the following URLs:

• AirSnare by Digital Matrix (http://www.home.comcast.net/~jay.deboer/airsnare/)
• AirMagnet WiFi Analyzer PRO by Fluke Networks (http://www.flukenetworks.com)
• Kismet, an open source tool (http://www.kismetwireless.net/)

Wireless key recovery

Wireless key recovery tools are basically wireless key crackers. Although they can be used to recover lost keys, they are more often used to find out if the wireless keys that are being used are easy to crack. Wireless networks often are secured by the

---

[1]Patel, Yogesh, Laura Taylor, Richard Graubart, and Emily Hawthorn. *IRS FAX Filing Strategy, Considerations and Legal Ramifications*. MITRE Corporation, July, 2001.
[2]Ibid. Patel, Taylor, Graubart, Hawthorn.

Wireless Equivalent Privacy (WEP), which isn't that secure; however, it's certainly better than no security at all. Wireless networks are better off using WPA2. If any wireless networks are using WEP, security assessors will want to report that as a vulnerability. Using these popular open source tools, security assessors can determine how secure any wireless devices are:

- Aircrack-ng, an open source tool (http://www.aircrack-ng.org/doku.php)
- Elcomsoft Wireless Security Auditor by Elcomsoft (http://www.elcomsoft.com)
- WEPWedgie (http://www.sourceforge.net/projects/wepwedgie/)
- WirelessKeyView by NirSoft Freeware (http://www.nirsoft.net)

It's possible that the system does not include any wireless networks. And if that is the case, there is nothing to test as far as wireless goes. It's still worth a look around to see if a cavalier user plugged in a wireless router in contradiction with the security policy.

Password auditing tools

Password auditing tools, sometimes referred to as *password crackers*, can be used to help you find out if your users are complying with the password security policy. Most commercial password auditing tools are marketed as "password recovery tools." You can run the password file through leading password crackers to find out if users are choosing easy-to-guess passwords that use words that are commonly found in dictionaries. Password auditing tools that can help you determine weak passwords include:

- Hash Suite by Hash Suite http://hashsuite.openwall.net/
- Password Recovery Bundle by Elcomsoft (http://www.elcomsoft.com)
- John the Ripper by the Openwall Project (http://www.openwall.com/john/)
- Revelation by Snadboy (http://revelation.en.lo4d.com/)
- Password Recovery Toolkit by AccessData (http://www.accessdata.com)

Database scanners

Database scanners help you discover vulnerabilities in leading databases. Many application scanners include the capability for testing of databases; however, they typically don't perform as well as scanners that are designed just for scanning databases. Popular database vulnerability discovery tools include:

- AppDetectivePro by Application Security, Inc. (http://www.appsecinc.com)
- McAfee Security Scanner for Databases by McAfee (http://www.mcafee.com)
- Scuba by Imperva (http://www.imperva.com)

One of the best guides for understanding how to lock down databases is the *Department of Defense Database Security Technical Implementation Guide* for databases available at: http://iase.disa.mil/stigs/app_security/database/general.html.

> Scanning, penetration testing, and security testing can be considered "hacking" which is illegal. So please make sure you have written permission before conducting any scanning or testing.

Testing biometrics

If the system is using biometric devices, the False Acceptance Rates (FAR), the False Reject Rates (FRR), and the Cross-over Error Rates (CER) should be tested. A biometric device is more accurate and reliable as the CER goes down and you will want to establish acceptable thresholds in your test plan. Other metrics to take into consideration for biometrics include the Failure to Enroll (FTE) rate and the Failure to Acquire (FTA) rate. FTE denotes the amount of people who are not able to use the system due to some sort of incompatibility and FTA denotes the number of users who are not able to render an acceptable enrollment image to use the device.

SECURING BIOMETRIC DEVICES

The following list explains the various rates that should be tested whenever you use biometric devices.

- FAR = the percent of unauthorized users incorrectly matched to a valid user's biometric
- FRR = the percent of incorrectly rejected valid users
- CER = the error rate at which FAR equals FRR
- FTA = the failure to acquire rate
- FTE = the failure to enroll rate

Test management packages

Test management software organizes your testing initiatives. These types of software packages are not required for FISMA compliance, but security assessors may find that they help manage the testing program. Test management packages help you create a controlled test environment, automate tests, and create test script scenarios. Popular test management packages include:

- QA Complete by SMARTBEAR (http://www.smartbear.com)
- Silk Central by Borland (http://www.borland.com)
- TestTrack Pro by Seapine (http://www.seapine.com)
- Zephyr by Zephyr (http://www.getzephyr.com)

Test management packages are especially useful for tracking life-cycle changes in an application or implementation that stands to be around for a long time and will evolve over the years.

Checklists for compliance

Almost all independent security assessors have compliance checklists that they use. The checklists will be different based on the FISMA compliance methodology that is used (Chapter 3). If you're evaluating a Security Package for the first time, you'll want to either develop your own checklists or find out if the agency using the system has some that have already been developed that they are able to make available. Like the documents in the Security Package, the compliance checklists usually evolve over time, and it is certainly acceptable to update them and refine them as the evaluation team gains more experience.

The compliance checklists should include checks for management controls, operational controls, and technical controls. Each control should have a policy number, a security standard, a security control ID, a citation from FISMA, or some other reference that can be referred to as the source of the requirement. Examples of compliance checklists are found in Tables 20.2–20.4. Note that the examples are not exhaustive, and there may be more compliance checks that are not included in these checklists that security assessors should take into consideration. The reference to "system" in the compliance checklist refers to all of the components together that are listed in your Security Package. So if your Hardware and Software Inventory consists of multiple servers and other devices, a check for compliance means all of them.

It is possible that some of compliance checks will not apply to certain systems and major applications, and those checks should be marked N/A (not applicable) when evaluating a package for compliance. For example, if a system does not use encryption keys, there is no need to check to see if encryption keys are FIPS 140-2 compliant.

Some evaluation teams use Yes/No on their compliance checklists and others use Pass/Fail. NIST prescribes the use of "Satisfied" or "Other Than Satisfied" for indicating the results of security tests. It is altogether possible that a security control can be partially implemented, though that would be considered "Other than Satisfied" if you're using the NIST prescribed terminology.

Security assessors should have the Security Package document alongside them when filling out the compliance checklists. Additionally, security assessors will want to have any reports generated from automated testing tools and any notes that they took while performing testing. Be sure to take the time to look through all the information when making decisions. With soft copies of the package documents, it is easy to search through the document to find relevant information. For any audit check that is questionable—you can't decide whether it is satisfied or not—indicate this in some way and meet with the ISSO and the preparation team to obtain clarification. It is okay to ask for more information and more documentation from the ISSO. However, any ancillary documentation given to you by the ISSO or prep team should be documentation that already exists. If you need to speak with systems administrators, database administrators, or security engineers to obtain a better understanding of anything, it is certainly acceptable to ask the ISSO to set up such a meeting.

Compliance checklist for management controls

Table 20.2 Examples of Compliance Checks for Management Controls

ID No.	Description of Audit Check on Operations	Yes, No, N/A	Comments	Source of Requirement
M-1	During the initiation phase of the system development life cycle, were security requirements established?			
M-2	Do the initial security requirements appear to be adequate?			
M-3	Are the implemented security controls consistent with the system FIPS 199 impact level?			
M-4	Was a data classification scheme taken into consideration when determining confidentiality levels?			
M-5	Was confidentiality and impact of loss of confidentiality taken into consideration when determining the confidentiality characterization?			
M-6	Was integrity and impact of loss of integrity taken into consideration when determining the integrity characterization?			
M-7	Was availability and impact of loss of availability taken into consideration when determining the availability characterization?			
M-8	Was mission criticality taken into consideration when determining the FIPS 199 characterization?			
M-9	Are the FIPS 199 information types correct?			
M-10	Did the information owner sign an explanatory memo supporting the selection of the FIPS 199 impact level?			

M-11	Was the explanatory memo to support the selection of the FIPS 199 impact level signed by the Authorizing Official?
M-12	Is the depth and granularity of the compliance documents commensurate with the established FIPS 199 impact level?
M-13	Is security testing performed every three years or whenever there is a significant change in configurations or functionality?
M-14	Does the *Security Assessment Report* adequately determine the risk exposure posed by vulnerabilities?
M-15	Was a *Business Risk Assessment* performed?
M-16	Does the *Business Risk Assessment* include a mission map?
M-17	Does the *Business Risk Assessment* adequately describe the business mission(s)?
M-18	Does the *Business Risk Assessment* include risk statements ("If . . .then.")?
M-19	Does the *Business Risk Assessment* include a risk summary table with decisions?
M-20	Are adequate system life-cycle requirements defined and considered in the *System Security Plan*?
M-21	Are security controls for future implementation described in the *System Security Plan*?
M-22	Are the security documents that are reviewed by management listed in the *System Security Plan*?
M-23	Is the *System Security Plan* reviewed and updated at least once annually to address minor changes?

Continued

Table 20.2 Examples of Compliance Checks for Management Controls—cont'd

ID No.	Description of Audit Check on Operations	Yes, No, N/A	Comments	Source of Requirement
M-24	Do *Rules of Behavior* exist for the users that describes responsibilities and expected behavior with regard to usage of the system(s)?			
M-25	Do users have to agree (either online or by written signature) to the *Rules of Behavior* before they are granted access?			
M-26	Are users informed that they will be held accountable for failure to comply with the *Rules of Behavior*?			
M-27	Are users aware that disciplinary action could occur as a result of failure to comply with the *Rules of Behavior*?			
M-28	Has a *Privacy Impact Assessment* been conducted?			
M-28	Have the privacy laws, regulations, and policies that the agency is required to abide by cited in the *Privacy Impact Assessment*?			
M-29	Has all Personally Identifiable Information (PII) that is taken into consideration described in the *Privacy Impact Assessment*?			
M-30	Have applications that collect PII been identified in the *Privacy Impact Assessment*?			
M-31	Is unnecessary PII collected?			
M-32	Does the *Privacy Impact Assessment* adequately describe what users (and their roles) will have access to PII?			
M-34	Does the *Privacy Impact Assessment* describe why PII is collected?			
M-35	Have persistent tracking technologies been adequately identified in the *Privacy Impact Assessment*?			

M-36	Have risks to PII been identified?
M-37	Do the risks to PII that have been identified appear to be credible?
M-38	Have privacy threats, safeguards, and assets been identified in the *Privacy Impact Assessment*?
M-39	Has the purpose of the systems/applications been described in the *Privacy Impact Assessment*?
M-40	Has the privacy policy been posted publicly where users can read it?
M-41	Does the publicly accessible privacy policy disclose for how long PII will be retained/stored?
M-42	Is a process for the proper decommissioning of PII included in the *Privacy Impact Assessment*?
M-43	Have risks listed on POA&M items from prior assessments been mitigated?
M-44	Does all documentation in the Security Package have appropriate markings on each page indicating the disclosure sensitive level of the documents?
M-45	Were all security controls tested?
M-46	Do documented security tests have a unique test ID number?
M-47	Is a copy of a signed ISSO appointment letter included in the System Security Plan?
M-48	Are all pages of all Security Package documents dated?
M-49	Do all pages of all documents have sensitivity markings listed in the header or footer?
M-50	Is all documentation restricted to those individuals having a need to know?

Compliance checklist for operational controls

Table 20.3 Examples of Compliance Checks for Operational Controls

ID No.	Description of Audit Check on Operations	Yes, No, N/A	Comments	Source of Requirement
O-1	Has a *Business Impact Assessment* been conducted?			
O-2	Does the *Business Impact Assessment* include estimated recovery times?			
O-3	Does the *Business Impact Assessment* include relative recovery priorities?			
O-4	Does the *Business Impact Assessment* include recovery escalation thresholds?			
O-5	Does the *Business Impact Assessment* include asset tracking numbers?			
O-6	Does the *Business Impact Assessment* include primary points of contact (phone and e-mail)?			
O-7	Does the *Business Impact Assessment* include secondary points of contact (phone and e-mail)?			
O-8	Does the *Business Impact Assessment* include hardware make and model numbers?			
O-9	Are locations of systems (address, building, room) listed in the *Business Impact Assessment*?			
O-10	Do the assets listed on the *Business Impact Assessment* include hostnames and IP addresses?			
O-11	Are system/asset roles listed on the Business *Impact Assessment*?			
O-12	Has a *Contingency Plan* been developed?			
O-13	Has the *Contingency Plan* been adequately tested?			

O-14	Are roles and responsibilities defined in the *Contingency Plan*?
O-15	Are staff members (or contactors) associated with all roles and responsibilities designated in the *Contingency Plan*?
O-16	Is contact information listed for all staff members named in the *Contingency Plan*?
O-17	Do contact lists in the *Contingency Plan* include a primary and secondary phone number, as well as e-mail address, for each staff member?
O-18	Does the staff that have been assigned contingency roles and responsibilities have the authority to carry out these tasks?
O-19	Are procedures for recovering server components (operating systems and applications) included in the *Contingency Plan*?
O-20	Is information about where to obtain a configuration guide for hardening the systems (e.g., securing the operating system) included in the *Contingency Plan*?
O-21	Are the procedures for recovering systems adequate?
O-22	Are adequate application recovery procedures included in the *Contingency Plan*?
O-23	Are adequate connectivity recovery procedures included in the *Contingency Plan*?
O-24	Are adequate key recovery procedures described in the *Contingency Plan*?
O-25	Is the off-site storage facility for backup media indicated (with contact information and address) in the *Contingency Plan*?
O-26	Are requirements (e.g., facility access cards, PINs) for accessing the off-site storage facility noted in the *Contingency Plan*?

Continued

Table 20.3 Examples of Compliance Checks for Operational Controls—cont'd

ID No.	Description of Audit Check on Operations	Yes, No, N/A	Comments	Source of Requirement
O-27	Does the *Contingency Plan* designate who is authorized to retrieve media from the off-site storage location?			
O-28	Does the *Contingency Plan* include adequate procedures for how to restore systems from backup media?			
O-29	Are emergency phone numbers for local fire, police, and ambulance services noted in the *Contingency Plan*?			
O-30	Is notification and activation criteria described in the *Contingency Plan*?			
O-31	Is the notification and activation criteria adequate?			
O-32	Has a line of succession been indicated in the *Contingency Plan*?			
O-33	Are levels of disruption defined in the *Contingency Plan*?			
O-34	Are all Service Level Agreements (SLAs) documented in the *Contingency Plan*?			
O-35	Has the logistics coordinator as named in the *Contingency Plan* been given a copy of the SLAs?			
O-36	Are requirements for temporary power described in the *Contingency Plan*?			
O-37	Are power recovery procedures described in the *Contingency Plan*?			
O-38	Are the power recovery procedures adequate?			
O-39	Is an *Occupant Evacuation Plan* included in the *Contingency Plan* appendices?			
O-40	Are *Standard Operating Procedures* included in the *Contingency Plan* appendices?			
O-41	Has a *Configuration Management Plan* been developed?			

O-42	Are baselines defined in the *Configuration Management Plan*?
O-43	Have adequate baselines been established in the *Configuration Management Plan*?
O-44	Are roles and responsibilities defined in the *Configuration Management Plan*?
O-45	Has the change management process been adequately described in the *Configuration Management Plan*?
O-46	Is a copy of the Change Management Form depicted in the *Configuration Management Plan*?
O-47	Are adequate parameters indicated on the Change Management Form?
O-48	Are emergency change management procedures documented in the *Configuration Management Plan*?
O-49	Are the emergency change management procedures adequate?
O-50	Are configuration management terms defined in the *Configuration Management Plan*?
O-52	Do all documents archived in the configuration management system have a unique ID number?
O-53	Are appropriate background investigations performed on staff before access is given to systems and applications?
O-53	Are appropriate background investigations performed on contractors before they are granted access to systems and applications?
O-54	Do user roles and responsibilities adhere to the principle of separation of duties?
O-57	Is the principle of least privilege followed when granting access to systems and applications?

Continued

Table 20.3 Examples of Compliance Checks for Operational Controls—cont'd

ID No.	Description of Audit Check on Operations	Yes, No, N/A	Comments	Source of Requirement
O-55	When an unfriendly termination occurs, is access from systems and applications revoked immediately?			
O-56	When a friendly termination occurs, is access from systems and applications revoked within 1 day?			
O-57	Are critical points of failure noted in the *System Security Plan*?			
O-58	Are safeguards in place to mitigate the risk posed by critical points of failure?			
O-59	Is there a user provisioning process used for requesting, issuing, and closing user accounts?			
O-60	Is the humidity and temperature of the data center where the servers are housed controlled?			
O-61	Does the data center have an alarm system that alerts appropriate personnel if the temperature and humidity exceeds acceptable levels?			
O-62	Is a fire suppression system installed in the data center where the systems are housed?			
O-63	Does the data center where the systems are housed have an alarm system that alerts appropriate personnel in the event of a fire?			
O-64	Are the systems described in the *Hardware and Software Inventory* backed up on a regular schedule?			
O-65	Is a copy of the system backup schedule included in the *System Security Plan*?			
O-66	Are the tools used to perform the backups adequately described in the *System Security Plan*?			

O-67	Are full backups performed at the minimum of once weekly with incremental backups performed nightly?
O-68	Does an *Incident Response Plan* exist?
O-69	Does the *Incident Response Plan* include adequate information on roles and responsibilities?
O-70	Does the *Incident Response Plan* include a current list of key personnel that fill the roles and responsibilities?
O-71	Does the *Incident Response Plan* include a diagram and description of the escalation framework?
O-72	Does the *Incident Response Plan* include an adequate description of incident types?
O-73	Does the *Incident Response Plan* include information on how to contact the agency CSIRC?
O-74	Does the *Incident Response Plan* include an informative section on security forensics?
O-75	Does the *Incident Response Plan* include incident handling guidelines?
O-76	Does the *Incident Response Plan* include adequate information in incident severity levels?
O-77	Does the *Incident Response Plan* include a copy of the *Security Incident Reporting Form*?
O-78	Are members of both the CSIRT and CSIRC teams included in the *Incident Response Plan*?
O-79	Does the *Incident Response Plan* include information on how to report a security incident?
O-80	Are safeguards in place to ensure that only authorized individuals can access systems to perform maintenance tasks?
O-81	Are systems backed up before maintenance tasks are performed?

Continued

Table 20.3 Examples of Compliance Checks for Operational Controls—cont'd

ID No.	Description of Audit Check on Operations	Yes, No, N/A	Comments	Source of Requirement
O-82	Is a log kept (that includes date and time) of who performs maintenance tasks on which systems?			
O-83	Is there an NOC or SOC that monitors the system $24 \times 7 \times 365$?			
O-84	Is the staff in the NOC or SOC competent?			
O-85	Is access to the NOC or SOC controlled?			

Compliance checklist for technical controls

Table 20.4 Examples of Compliance Checks for Technical Controls

ID No.	Description of Audit Check on Technical Controls	Yes, No, N/A	Comments	Source of Requirement
T-1	Does a *System Security Plan* exist?			
T-2	Does the *System Security Plan* accurately describe the systems that it applies to?			
T-3	Does the *System Security Plan* include an adequate description of the system boundaries?			
T-4	Are the procedures for authenticating users (passwords, tokens, biometrics, smart cards, etc.) fully explained in the *System Security Plan*?			
T-5	Does each user have a unique user ID?			
T-6	Are all user IDs associated with a person?			
T-7	Do all user IDs identify a user to the system, and verify their identity, before the user is allowed to perform any actions on the system?			

T-8	Are all users assigned to groups based on access requirements that comply with the principle of least privilege?
T-9	Is the display of passwords suppressed on the monitor when users enter their passwords into the system?
T-10	Are passwords for new users distributed securely?
T-11	Are users informed not to share their passwords with others?
T-12	Are users forced by the system to change their password upon initial activation of their account?
T-13	Do passwords meet the agency password complexity rules?
T-14	Do user passwords expire every 90 days?
T-15	Do root, admin, all system administration, and all privileged account passwords expire every 30 days?
T-16	Have all guest and anonymous accounts been removed?
T-17	Does the system provide a mechanism that notifies the user when a password change is required?
T-18	Are all passwords stored encrypted and not displayed in clear text anywhere on the system?
T-19	Is it certain that passwords are not hard-coded into scripts, software, or applications?
T-20	Are password auditing tools used to scan for weak passwords?
T-21	When weak passwords are found are the users with weak passwords required to change their password?
T-22	Is there a secure process to assist users who have forgotten their passwords?
T-23	Are all requests for account creation approved by the user's supervisor prior to giving the user access?

Continued

Table 20.4 Examples of Compliance Checks for Technical Controls—cont'd

ID No.	Description of Audit Check on Technical Controls	Yes, No, N/A	Comments	Source of Requirement
T-24	Are nonactivated accounts removed from the system after 60 days?			
T-25	Are systems configured to lock an account/user ID after three consecutive failed logon attempts?			
T-26	Is it possible to trace all system actions to user IDs?			
T-27	Are all logon attempts recorded in an audit log?			
T-28	Does the system/applications have audit logging capabilities?			
T-29	Is the absolute pathname of all log files used by the system documented in the *System Security Plan*?			
T-30	Are login records of root, admin, and privileged users recorded in audit logs?			
T-31	Are the processes (e.g., syslogd) that control auditing noted and adequately discussed in the *System Security Plan*?			
T-32	Does information recorded in audit logs include a date and timestamp?			
T-33	Are all denied connections to servers logged?			
T-34	Are audit logs protected so that read access is limited to only those individuals who are authorized to review audit data?			
T-35	Are safeguards in place to prevent unauthorized alteration of audit logs?			
T-36	Are security audit logs reviewed on regular schedule?			
T-37	Does the system disconnect a user's session after 30 minutes of inactivity?			
T-38	Is access to security configuration settings restricted to systems administrators?			

T-39	Is an approved logon banner displayed warning unauthorized users of the consequences of unauthorized access?
T-40	Does the system prevent concurrent user logins except where operationally required?
T-41	Do inbound services provide strong authentication using one-time passwords, session passwords, change and response protocols, two-factor authentication, digital signatures, or encryption?
T-42	Do all software encryption products have a FIPS 140-2 validation certificate to ensure compliance with correct algorithm implementation?
T-43	Are all encryption keys securely stored?
T-44	Does the *System Security Plan* clearly describe where encryption is used and what is encrypted?
T-45	Are scripts that are resident on the system secured such that they prevent users from obtaining command level access to the system?
T-46	Are scripts that are resident on the system secured such that they prevent users from passing a command string to a server through a script?
T-47	Is perimeter security (firewalls, routers, switches) adequately described in the *System Security Plan*?
T-48	Are there safeguards in place to protect the firewall rules file from unauthorized modification?
T-49	Are there safeguards in place to protect router ACLs from unauthorized modification?
T-50	Are firewall logs reviewed on a regular schedule and is the schedule included in the *System Security Plan*?

Continued

Table 20.4 Examples of Compliance Checks for Technical Controls—cont'd

ID No.	Description of Audit Check on Technical Controls	Yes, No, N/A	Comments	Source of Requirement
T-51	Does the *System Security Plan* make it clear who reviews the firewall logs?			
T-52	Does the *System Security Plan* include information on what open ports and services are required by the system?			
T-53	Does the *System Security Plan* include a topological network map of all the items listed in the *Hardware and Software Inventory*?			
T-54	Are PKI systems adequately described in the *System Security Plan*?			
T-55	Are any VPNs used by the system adequately described in the *System Security Plan*?			
T-56	Are all Transport Layer Security (TLS) mechanisms discussed in the *System Security Plan*?			
T-57	Does the *System Security Plan* make it clear where (on what systems) X.509 certificates are installed?			
T-58	Do all digital certificates use support at the minimum 128 bit encryption?			
T-59	Is the usage of any wireless networks discussed in the *System Security Plan*?			
T-60	Are all wireless network access points noted in the *System Security Plan*?			
T-61	Are all wireless networks adequately secured?			
T-62	Are any secure file transfer methods that are used adequately discussed in the *System Security Plan*?			
T-63	Do all file transfer log the start of transfer time, end of transfer time, what was transferred, and whether the transfer was successful or not?			

T-64	Is the system protected from malware (e.g., viruses, Trojans, worms) by reputable antivirus software?
T-65	Are antivirus signatures updated regularly?
T-66	Does the *System Security Plan* discuss how modification of sensitive or critical files is detected?
T-67	Is the usage of host-based intrusion detection systems adequately discussed in the *System Security Plan*?
T-68	Is the usage of network based intrusion detection systems adequately discussed in the *System Security Plan*?
T-69	Have all intrusion detection systems been tested?
T-70	Is information on how the intrusion detection system(s) are configured and setup adequately documented?
T-71	Are the systems adequately monitored for suspicious activity?
T-72	Does the *System Security Plan* describe how man-in-the-middle attacks and unlinked session vulnerabilities are mitigated?
T-73	Does the *System Security Plan* adequately describe how session authenticity is maintained?
T-74	Does the *System Security Plan* adequately describe how threats to mobile code (ActiveX, JavaScript, JAVA) are mitigated?
T-75	Does the *System Security Plan* explain how security patches are tested before they are deployed to production systems?
T-76	Are security patches applied promptly?
T-77	Do all remote access capabilities provide strong identification and authentication and protect sensitive information in transit?

Continued

Table 20.4 Examples of Compliance Checks for Technical Controls—cont'd

ID No.	Description of Audit Check on Technical Controls	Yes, No, N/A	Comments	Source of Requirement
T-78	Are friendly and unfriendly termination procedures adequately described in the *System Security Plan*?			
T-79	Does the system automatically establish encrypted channels (HTTPS, SSL, etc. ...) for the transmission of sensitive information?			
T-80	Are systems checked for the "SANS Top 20" vulnerabilities on a monthly basis?			
T-82	Is all media sanitized and properly decommissioned before it is disposed of?			
T-82	Are record retention requirements met prior to the disposal and decommissioning of media?			
T-83	Are security events monitored by the enterprise *Security Information Management (SIM)* system?			
T-84	Are the security events the SIM monitors adequately described in the *System Security Plan*?			
T-85	Is the ISSO informed of significant security events?			

EVALUATIONS BY INSPECTOR GENERALS

Refreshing your memory from Chapter 4, each agency has an Office of Inspector General (OIG) that ensures that the agency is complying with all laws. Many agencies usually receive little notice that the OIG is going to be paying a visit. The objective of the OIG is to assess the information security program for compliance with FISMA and generate a report that documents the results of that evaluation. In accordance with the principles of the Freedom of Information Act (5 U. S.C. 552, as amended by Public Law 104-231), OIG reports are available to the general public.

OIG teams from different agencies will not necessarily assess the information security program in the same way. The reports generated by different OIG teams will not necessarily have the same format and include all the same information. OIG reports from different agencies usually often different looks and formats. An example of an OIG reports are found at the following URLs:

- U.S. Securities and Exchange Commission, 2012 FISMA Executive Summary Report
  http://www.sec-oig.gov/Reports/AuditsInspections/2013/512.pdf
- U.S. Department of Interior, Office of Inspector General Audit Report
  http://www.oig.dot.gov/sites/dot/files/DOT%20OIG%20FISMA%20Report.pdf
- U.S. Veterans Administration, FISMA Assessment for Fiscal Year 2011
  http://www.va.gov/oig/pubs/VAOIG-11-00320-138.pdf
- U.S. Health and Human Services, Information Security Program Evaluations For FY 2004
  http://www.oig.hhs.gov/oas/reports/cms/180502600.pdf

The inspectors could ask to see just about any type of document related to the information security program. They may ask for a *FISMA Program Handbook*, and they may ask to see 10 randomly selected Security Packages. It's almost impossible to prepare for what they may ask for. The best thing to do is to accommodate them as best as possible and give them everything that they ask to see. They will likely not ask to logon to systems and ISSOs are not obligated to give them a userID and password to allow them to logon.

One of the best things your agency can do to prepare for a visit from the OIG is to read the OIG report for your agency that was issued the previous year. Look through to see what it is that they asked to review, and what their recommendations were for your agency. They will likely want to know if any action was taken on their prior recommendations.

EVALUATIONS BY THE GOVERNMENT ACCOUNTABILITY OFFICE

Evaluations and assessments are made by the GAO to verify if the OIG is reporting information correctly. Similar to OIG evaluations, the GAO inspectors could ask to see just about any type of document related to the information security program. Aside from evaluating each agency's FISMA compliance program, the GAO will be collecting information to assemble for an annual report to Congress.

The 2011 GAO report can be found at http://www.gao.gov/new.items/d12137.pdf.

The 2010 Report to Congress on the Implementation of the Federal Information Security Management Act of 2002 can be found at http://www.whitehouse.gov/sites/default/files/omb/assets/egov_docs/FY10_FISMA.pdf.

If you go to http://www.gao.gov and put "FISMA" in the search box you can find several GAO reports on FISMA as shown in Figure 20.1.

FIGURE 20.1

GAO Web site with FISMA reports. (For color version of this figure, the reader is referred to the online version of this chapter.)

All GAO inspectors are different, and different inspectors may ask for different items to review. Some GAO inspectors are contractors and come from companies that are well versed in computer security and some GAO inspectors are government employees. I have seen GAO inspectors ask for items as specific as those listed in Table 20.5. The GAO inspectors may record the date they ask for specific items and the date the items are received. It is best to give them what they want as quickly as possible.

Table 20.5 Real Examples of Items That GAO Inspectors Have Asked For

Listing of the names of security reports generated by the system and the name(s) of the individual(s) responsible for reviewing those reports

Printout of `find/ -user root -perm 4000 -exec ls -l {} \`

Printout of `find / -user root -perm 2000 -exec ls -l {} \`

Printout of the contents of `.rhosts` file

Printout of the contents of `/etc/security/audit/events` file

Printout of `host.equiv` file

Memorandum of agreements with business partners

Copy of AIX security configuration procedures

A system-generated list of all users, and user profiles, with access to the system

Printout of file access rights (using `ls -l /etc/passwd`)

The GAO inspectors will likely not give the agency much notice before showing up. Every effort should be made to accommodate their requests as expeditiously as possible. The agency should warn ISSOs as soon as they know that GAO inspectors will be arriving so that the ISSOs can make themselves available to answer any questions.

SUMMARY

Evaluating a Security Package is a big undertaking. Many evaluation teams don't leave enough time for reading through the information-rich Security Package documents that were so thoughtfully prepared. The evaluation team should treat the preparation team and ISSO with professionalism and respect and avoid having the evaluation process degenerate into a squabbling affair. The evaluation team, through its recommendations, has an opportunity to make a difference by pointing out vulnerabilities that may have been missed by the preparation team and ISSO. Though most Security Packages always have some findings, that doesn't mean that the package and systems are not worthy of accreditation. Recommendations on whether to accredit a group of systems (or not) should be made very thoughtfully, with justifications behind every recommendation.

During this chapter, we discussed a lot of different tools, techniques, and areas of coverage with regard to security testing and evaluation. The list of tools in this chapter should not be construed as the only tools that are good for security testing. Independent assessors should practice using any automated tools before they run them on client systems.

Developing the Security Assessment Report

21

It always seems impossible until it is done.
—Nelson Mandela

TOPICS IN THIS CHAPTER

- Analysis of test results
- Risk assessment methodology
- Present the risks
- Checklist
- Make decisions
- Certification
- Authority to Operate
- Interim Authority to Operate

INTRODUCTION

The *Security Assessment Report* is the document written by independent assessors after they have finished performing security testing on the system. This report focuses on risks to the system and its networks, applications, and facilities. The same risk exposure principles that you learned in Chapter 17 apply also to systems, networks, and applications. Security Assessment Reports for FISMA compliance are based on qualitative methods. The system owner and ISSO depend on the Security Assessment Report to understand where the system is vulnerable.

Aside from vulnerabilities, the Security Assessment Report should include a list of recommended corrective actions. Each vulnerability cited should have a recommendation for corrective action. According to *NIST Special Publication 800-37, Revision 1, Guide for Applying the Risk Management Framework to Federal Information Systems*:

> The assessment report includes information from the assessor necessary to determine the effectiveness of the security controls employed within or inherited by the information system based upon the assessor's findings.

NIST SP 800-37, Revision 1, can be found at the following URL: http://www.csrc.nist.gov/publications/nistpubs/800-37-rev1/sp800-37-rev1-final.pdf.

ANALYSIS OF TEST RESULTS

Results from the security tests should be considered factual information. Security assessors should set aside time to analyze the test results and draw conclusions. The analysis should include a statement on whether the objectives of the tests adequately tested the security controls. If there were certain controls that were not possible to test, the security assessors should indicate that in the Security Assessment Report. The Security Assessment Report should describe the tests that were performed and the outcome of those tests.

Security assessors need to take into consideration the test results from both automated tools and test results from interviews and examination of artifacts. The security of a system has many dependencies related to policies, processes, procedures, and practices. Something to consider is that even if an organization's policies and procedures are flawed, the staff might still follow good practices because they are highly competent staff. Possible scenarios that should yield audit findings are:

- Policies and procedures are good but are not followed.
- Policies and procedures are missing or inadequate but are followed.
- Policies and procedures are missing or inadequate, are not followed, and practices are deficient.
- Policies and procedures are missing or inadequate, but good practices are followed.

Almost all security testing includes perform scans of various parts of the system, and therefore, more security assessors will need to assess scan results. Typically, scanning tools use qualitative rankings and automatically classify risks as high, medium, or low. Figure 21.1 shows an example of how the popular scanner QualysGuard depicts vulnerabilities.

Security assessors should take caution with using reported scanner severity levels. In some cases, scanners report false positives. In reports automatically generated by scanning tools, vulnerability severity levels may show up that are not entirely warranted. For example, if a scanner ranks a vulnerability as high, but it has been found on a server that has a relatively low importance to the business mission, there may be little justification to rank the vulnerability as "high" in your Security Assessment Report. If necessary, the reported severity level should be adjusted to a different risk level to more accurately depict the true severity. Figure 21.2 shows that a vulnerability was found on an application server with a severity rating of 5 out of 5—according to the scanner.

If this server has been purged of all data and is about to be decommissioned and is used only to store the online cafeteria menu, then it probably isn't as significant of a vulnerability as it appears to be. Therefore, once security assessors have a vulnerability assessment report in hand from an automated scanner, they should go through it and review each reported vulnerability, and then make a decision on whether the severity of the vulnerabilities should be adjusted or not. The more important

▲	5	Microsoft SQL Server Multiple Vulnerabilities	
▲	5	Microsoft Windows ASN.1 Library Integer Handling Vulnerability (MS04-007)	
▲	5	Multiple Microsoft Windows Vulnerabilities (MS04-011)	
▲	5	MS-SQL 8.0 UDP Slammer Worm Buffer Overflow Vulnerability	port 1434/udp
▲	4	Microsoft SQL Server 2000 Latest Patch Not Installed	port 1433/tcp
▲	4	Microsoft SQL Server Query Method Enables Cached Administrator Connection to be Reused	port 1433/tcp
▲	4	Microsoft IIS Malformed HTR Request Buffer Overflow Vulnerability	port 80/tcp
▲	4	Microsoft IIS HTR ISAPI Extension Heap Overflow Vulnerability	port 80/tcp
▲	4	Microsoft IIS Administrative Pages Cross-Site Scripting Vulnerability	port 80/tcp
▲	4	Windows TCP/IP Remote Code Execution and Denial of Service Vulnerabilities (MS05-019)	
▲	3	Microsoft SQL Server Patch Not Installed (MS00-092)	port 1433/tcp
▲	3	Microsoft SQL Server Cumulative Patch Not Installed (MS02-034)	port 1433/tcp
▲	3	Microsoft IIS HTTP Redirect Cross Site Scripting Vulnerability	port 80/tcp
▲	3	Microsoft IIS Help File Search Cross Site Scripting Vulnerability	port 80/tcp
▲	3	Microsoft IIS ISAPI Filter Access Violation Denial of Service Vulnerability	port 80/tcp
▲	3	Microsoft IIS HTTP Error Page Cross Site Scripting Vulnerability	port 80/tcp
▲	3	Service Pack 4 Not Installed on Windows 2000	
▲	2	Microsoft SQL Server Text Format Functions Contain Unchecked Buffer	port 1433/tcp
▲	2	Microsoft SQL Server 2000 Cumulative Patch Not Installed (MS02-043)	port 1433/tcp
▲	2	WebDAV HTTP Method 'PROPFIND' Enabled	port 80/tcp
▲	2	Web Server HTTP Trace/Track Method Support Cross-Site Tracing Vulnerability	port 80/tcp
▲	2	Account Brute Force Possible Through IIS NTLM Authentication Scheme	port 80/tcp
▲	2	NetBIOS Name Accessible	
▲	2	TCP Sequence Number Approximation Based Denial of Service	
▲	2	ICMP Based TCP Reset Vulnerability	

FIGURE 21.1

Screenshot from the QualysGuard Security Scanner. (For color version of this figure, the reader is referred to the online version of this chapter.)

▆▆▆▆▆	5	JBoss Application Server Web Console and JMX Management Console Authentication Bypass Vulnerability	port 8080/tcp

FIGURE 21.2

Vulnerability ranking from a leading scanner. (For color version of this figure, the reader is referred to the online version of this chapter.)

the system is to the agency, the greater the impact of is if the system is compromised. Security assessors may decide that many of the vulnerabilities should retain the same risk classification reported by your scanner, and that other vulnerabilities should have their reported severity rating lowered or increased. In summary, security assessors should create a summary list of all the vulnerabilities reported from scanners, adjust the vulnerabilities, and then create a final list of vulnerabilities with final severity level adjustments.

RISK ASSESSMENT METHODOLOGY

Independent assessors should dedicate a section of the Security Assessment Report to explaining their risk assessment methodology. Vulnerabilities work in concert with threats to create risk. Part of the analysis that the security assessors must do is to determine what threats have the potential to exploit the vulnerabilities that have been discovered. Additionally, security assessors need to determine the likelihood that a threat will exploit the vulnerability and the impact to the system if the vulnerability was in fact exploited. The security assessors will also need to determine the severity level of the vulnerabilities discovered during testing.

When you use relative concepts to determine risk exposure, you are using qualitative risk analysis. Relative classification systems compare one component with another, allowing you to rank a classification as high, medium, or low. (In FISMA reports, the terminology "moderate" is used instead of "medium" for discussing risks.) It's useful to rank risk exposures caused by vulnerabilities so you can more easily make decisions on what to do about them and how to prioritize them.

Once the vulnerabilities have been clearly established, security assessors need to determine the likelihood that the vulnerability will be exploited, and the impact of the loss that would occur if the exploit actually occurred. Similar to *business risk assessment* (Chapter 17), risk exposure is determined by multiplying the severity of the loss by the likelihood. As a reminder:

Likelihood × Impact = Risk Exposure

In order to determine the likelihood that a vulnerability will be exploited, the threats need to be considered. For FISMA compliance purposes, the threats to take into consideration are:

- Threats initiated by people
- Threats initiated by computers (or other network devices)
- Threats from natural disasters

If natural disasters are accounted for in a Business Risk Assessment, it may not be necessary to account for them in a Security Assessment Report. However, natural disasters should always be considered in a Security Assessment Report if a Business Risk Assessment has not been performed. People who intentionally initiate threats are considered *adversaries*. Whether or not adversaries have the capability, knowledge, and motivation to initiate threats are important factors for consideration.

A vulnerability by itself does not equate to a security incident. Without a threat to exploit the vulnerability, the existence of the vulnerability in and of itself does not equate to a loss. Determining the likelihood factor means that threats first have to be identified and then a prediction that the threat will manifest itself needs to be made. Today, models for determining the likelihood of cyber threats are not well developed. Scientists from Oak Ridge National Laboratories suggest that the consideration of *threat signatures* and *threat observables* can be used to assist in determining threat likelihood.[1] Threat signatures show indication that a threat can be detected and are used in antivirus products, intrusion detection systems, and scanners. Threat observables show indication that threats have been attempted. Event logs that reveal reconnaissance probes would be considered as threat observables. Many threat observables for the same vulnerability indicate that an adversary has strong motivation, capability, and knowledge to initiate a threat. Security Information Event Management (SIEM) applications take threat observables from different devices and pull them all together into a correlation engine to provide real-time threat analysis. SIEMs can determine attack frequency and the number of targets attacked.

If a vulnerability was discovered by a scanner or an intrusion detection system, then a signature for the threat clearly exists. Security assessors typically will not have much time to comb through event logs to look for threat observables, and even if an agency has an SIEM that they are willing to allow the assessors to observe, assessors will have limited time to review what could be thousands of observables. So, there are challenges in determining the likelihood characteristics of threats for a Security Assessment Report.

What can security assessors do to get relevant information quickly on the likelihood that a threat will manifest itself? First, it is important to realize that the science of threat analysis is not black and white—gray areas are the norm. It's possible that two different highly skilled security assessors may come up with different qualitative ratings for threat likelihood metrics. Until threat theory becomes more mature, security assessors need to use their own judgment on the qualitative rating for likelihood. However, there are places that security assessors can go to obtain information to make this job easier. The organizations (and their URLs) listed in Table 21.1 have well-respected research on vulnerabilities that may enable security assessors to

---

[1]http://cda.ornl.gov/publications/Publication%2015531_Beaver_072009.pdf.

Table 21.1 Sources of Threat and Vulnerability Information

Organization	URL	Description
FIRST	http://www.first.org/cvss	**Common Vulnerability Scoring System (CVSS)** standard calculates vulnerability severity scores by taking into consideration Exploitability Metrics, Impact Metrics, General Modifiers, Impact Subscore Modifiers, and Temporal Score Metrics. Essentially, the CVSS standard consists of various metrics associated with Impact and Likelihood
SEI Carnegie Mellon	http://www.kb.cert.org/vuls/	Vulnerability notes database
OWASP	https://www.owasp.org/index.php/Category:OWASP_Top_Ten_Project	**OWASP Top 10** represents a broad consensus about what the most critical Web application security flaws are
MITRE	http://www.cve.mitre.org/	**CVE** is a dictionary of publicly known information security vulnerabilities and exposures
MITRE	http://capec.mitre.org/data/slices/2000.html	**CAPEC 2000** methods of attack database
MITRE, DHS, NIST	http://web.nvd.nist.gov/view/vuln/search	**National Vulnerability Database**
WASC	http://projects.webappsec.org/w/page/13246978/Threat%20Classification	**WASC Threat Classification V2.0**
WASC	http://projects.webappsec.org/w/page/13246995/Web-Hacking-Incident-Database	**Web Hacking Incident Database**

accelerate their analysis process. The Web Application Security Consortium publishes outcomes of attack methods as illustrated in Figure 21.3. To get the latest data for the Top Attack Methods visit URL http://projects.webappsec.org/w/page/13246995/Web-Hacking-Incident-Database#nbspTopAttackMethodsAllEntries.

It is easy to understand how a hackers or cyber criminals can intentionally threaten systems. However, threats can be caused by unintentional human errors as well. An untrained firewall engineer could pose a threat to your systems and networks by accidentally configuring a firewall rule to open a port instead of closing it. The number of ways that your own staff can unintentionally create threats to your systems is infinite, which is one of the reasons that such a large number of checks, balances, and accountability features are built into systems (e.g., separate accounts,

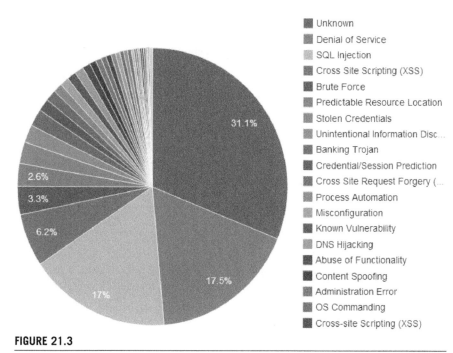

Legend:
- Unknown
- Denial of Service
- SQL Injection
- Cross Site Scripting (XSS)
- Brute Force
- Predictable Resource Location
- Stolen Credentials
- Unintentional Information Disc...
- Banking Trojan
- Credential/Session Prediction
- Cross Site Request Forgery (...
- Process Automation
- Misconfiguration
- Known Vulnerability
- DNS Hijacking
- Abuse of Functionality
- Content Spoofing
- Administration Error
- OS Commanding
- Cross-site Scripting (XSS)

FIGURE 21.3

Top attack methods. (For color version of this figure, the reader is referred to the online version of this chapter.)

logging capabilities, separation of roles and responsibilities). Therefore, lack of required training should always be considered an audit finding.

Sometimes, devices themselves can create threats and even security incidents. Years ago, I worked at a networking company where there were certain models of Hewlett Packard printers that on various occasions sprayed the networks with enough broadcast packets to create a denial-of-service attack to the other systems on the network. We thought someone was attacking the network until we put a protocol analyzer on some of the network segments and traced the broadcast storm back to printers that had buggy software in them (Table 21.2).

In summary, during the development of the Security Assessment Report, security assessors will:

- Analyze test results and research vulnerabilities and threats
- Adjust risk ratings from security testing tools
- Determine the system's vulnerabilities
- Determine the likelihood that the vulnerabilities will be exploited
- Determine the impact that an exploit of a vulnerability would create
- Determine final risk exposure
- Present your risks in an easy-to-understand table
- Include a recommendation for corrective action for each vulnerability reported

Table 21.2 Qualitative Risk Exposure Table

Impact	Likelihood				
	Very Low	**Low**	**Moderate**	**High**	**Very High**
Very high	Low	Moderate	High	Very high	Very high
High	Low	Low	Moderate	High	High
Moderate	Very low	Low	Moderate	Moderate	Moderate
Low	Very low	Low	Low	Low	Low
Very low	Very low	Very low	Very low	Very low	Very low

This table is consistent with Table I-2 in the NIST SP 800-30, Revision 1, Guide for Conducting Risk Assessments, *September 2012.*

PRESENT THE RISKS

In order to make decisions on risks, you need to present the risks in an easy-to-follow table. For a qualitative risk assessment, create columns for the following fields:

- ID number
- Vulnerability name
- Description
- Source of discovery
- Likelihood
- Impact
- Risk exposure
- Recommendation

The ID number should reference the security control that is affected by the vulnerability. Before developing a Security Assessment Report, independent assessors should find out if the agency they are developing the report for has a report template that they want the assessors to use. Table 21.3 shows an example of an easy-to-follow format to present your risks. There is an excellent Security Assessment Report template on the FedRAMP Web site. Though this template was designed for FedRAMP's security assessment of cloud systems, it can for the most part be used for any type of system. The FedRAMP Web site can be found at the following URL: http://www.fedramp.gov.

CHECKLIST

Upon completion of the Security Assessment Report, security assessors should use the following checklist to make sure that they haven't forgotten to include something in the Security Assessment Report:

- Do the test results appear to be accurate?
- Have members of the test team been described?

Table 21.3 Risks to Systems and Recommendations

ID No.	Name	Vulnerability Description	Source of Discovery	Likelihood	Impact	Risk Exposure	Recommendation
1	SSH Vuln on host erp02	Due to a buffer overflow vulnerabilities and design flaws in SSH1, an attacker could gain root shell access to erp02 on the network 5.	Infrastructure scanner report	Moderate	High	Moderate	Mitigate the risk by disabling SSH1. Since we now use Connect:Direct for security file transfers, nobody uses SSH1 anymore anyway.
2	Blind SQL injection on host serverJ6	It is possible to view, modify or delete database entries and tables by manipulating input parameters.	Application scanner report	High	High	High	The system should use a stored procedure *in lieu* of a dynamically built SQL query string. Use input validation controls on all fields in Web forms.
3	Administration of user provisioning database	There is no database administrator's guide. If our database administrator becomes ill or ends his employment, it will be difficult to understand how to administer the database.	Interviews with staff and examination of documents	Moderate	Moderate	Moderate	Mitigate the risk by developing a database administration guide that includes information on how to perform all database administration functions. Include information on database configuration in the guide.
4	No separation of duties	One of the users at Office 2 has admin access to all systems in Office 2.	Review of /etc/passwd file	Low	Low	Low	Accept the risk. Office 2 is a small office with only two users. It doesn't make sense to hire a systems administrator for two people.

- Were the tests conducted in a controlled setting or on a production system?
- Were the tests conducted according to the test plan?
- Are the tests indicative of the security requirements?
- Do all tests have a unique ID number?
- Are test dates included?
- Is the use of all security testing tools documented?
- Is the risk assessment methodology explained?
- Are the risks presented in an easy-to-follow table?
- Are known vulnerabilities adequately described?
- Does each reported vulnerability have a threat or threats associated with it?
- Is the impact of exploitation of vulnerabilities taken into consideration?
- Is the likelihood of exploitation of vulnerabilities taken into consideration?
- If vulnerabilities were discovered, are recommendations made to correct the security weakness?

MAKE DECISIONS

With the Security Assessment Report in hand, the system owner and ISSO are armed with all the right information to formulate decisions. One of the objectives of the decisions will be to balance risk exposure with the cost of implementing safeguards. The cost of safeguards should not only include the up-front cost of procuring the safeguard but also the yearly maintenance costs of implementing it. For example, a set of firewalls may cost $30,000 to purchase and install, but it also requires the hiring of a full-time firewall engineer to administer the firewall. Be sure to consider the firewall engineers salary or hourly costs in labor rates as well as in the cost of a product.

Mitigating risks means reducing them to acceptable levels, which of course is different than mitigating risks at all costs. Most information technology risks can be reduced. Sometimes a high-risk item can be reduced by simply checking a box in a GUI to turn on a particular security feature. Other times, reducing a risk can be complex, very involved, and very expensive.

Since there is usually a price to pay for mitigating risks, the price is something that perceptive IT managers will want to take into consideration. Sometimes that price might be only an hour of a systems administrator's time. Other times it could be hundreds of hours of many systems administrators' time, or it may mean purchasing an enterprise product that costs several million dollars. When it comes to reducing risks, one of the first questions your business owner and ISSO should be asking is, "What will it cost?" ISSOs and system owners can perform a quantitative cost-benefit analysis to determine how much to spend on any given safeguard (see Chapter 17).

Consistent with the options in Chapter 17, the system owner's options are to accept the risk, transfer the risk, or mitigate the risk. Generally speaking, high-risk items that don't cost much should always be mitigated. Moderate-risk items that don't cost much should also be mitigated. Low-risk items may not be worth reducing at all, particularly if it costs a lot to do so. On federal agency systems, high-risk vulnerabilities are required to be mitigated within 30 days. Moderate-risk vulnerabilities require mitigation within 90 days. Low-risk vulnerabilities typically require mitigation as time permits.

CERTIFICATION

As of NIST SP 800-37, Revision 1, agencies are no longer required to use certification agents or certifying officials. That said, in reality, many still do. If your agency still uses certifying officials, that official will need to review the Security Assessment Report and make a recommendation to the authorizing official by way of a certification letter. If your agency no longer uses certifying officials, the independent assessors should include a final comprehensive recommendation based on the results of the testing and their professional opinion. An example of a certification letter can be found in Figure 21.4. If a certifying official is not used, the Security Assessment Report should be delivered directly to the authorizing official.

Agency Name Goes Here
Memorandum

Date: August 16, 2013
To: Samuel Thomas, authorizing official
From: Melinda Blake, Certifying Official
Subject: Certification Statement for Dallas Datacenter General Support Systems

A security review of the Dallas Datacenter and General Support Systems has been conducted in accordance with the provisions of the <Agency Name> certification and accreditation program. Certification is the comprehensive testing and evaluation of the technical and non-technical security controls, features, risks, and safeguards used in support of the accreditation process. Certification establishes the extent to which a particular IT design and implementation meetsa specified set of security requirements. The Dallas Datacenter and General Support Systems were evaluated for compliance, and meet those federal and <Agency Name> requirements with residual risk remaining as described in the Certification and Accreditation Package developed by Generic Government Contractor dated July 27, 2013.

Based on the residual risk identified in the Certification and Accreditation Package, I recommend that an authorization be issued for the Dallas Datacenter General Support Systems for a period of no longer than three years of when a significant change occurs to these systems. The issues on which you plan to take corrective action should be incorporated into a Plan of Actions and Milestones (POA&M), and attached to your authorization letter.

Samuel Thomas, authorizing official

       < signature >

Cc: Daniel Bramah, Director of IT, Dallas Datacenter
     William Carroll, ISSO

FIGURE 21.4

Sample certification letter.

AUTHORITY TO OPERATE

After receiving a copy of the recommendation on whether a Security Package should be accredited or not, the authorizing official writes a letter, known as an Authority to Operate (ATO), and addresses it to the business owner and ISSO that authorizes the operations of the systems. The ATO is usually not longer than two pages and will likely mention that there is an expectation that any POA&M items will be adequately reconciled. A sample authorization letter is illustrated in Figure 21.5.

Agency Name Goes Here
Memorandum

Date: April 7, 2013
To: Charles Smith, Chief Information Officer
From: Samuel Thomas, authorizing official
Subject: Authority to Operate Dallas Datacenter

In accordance with the provisions of <Agency Name> Information Technology Security Policy 4.1 on security assessment and authorization, I hereby grant full authorization to the Dallas Datacenter General Support Systems. This authorization is based on my review of the information provided by 1) the Dallas Datacenter General Support Systems Security Package prepared by *Generic Security Contractor* dated February 24, 2013 and 2) the *Security Assessment Report* developed by *Generic Security Contractor*on March 15, 2013.

This authorization is my formal declaration that the Dallas Datacenter General Support System security controls have been properly implemented and is at a satisfactory level of security, commensurate with the known risks, at present. As a result of the assessment effort, vulnerabilities that were identified are listed in the Dallas Datacenter General Support Systems Plan of Actions and Milestones (POA&M). The POA&M has been established to track the removal these vulnerabilities which the Director of IT, Dallas Datacenter will implement by the scheduled completion dates identified in the POA&M.

I accept the residual risk from these vulnerabilities in view of the fact that the Dallas Datacenter General Support Systems process low sensitive and unclassified data.

This authorization is valid for three years from the date of this letter. The Dallas Datacenter General Support Systems will be re-assessed and re-authorized earlier if modifications are implemented that result in significant changes to the system security controls.

Acknowledgement _____
<Signature of Charles Smith, CIO>

Cc: Daniel Bramah, Director of IT, Dallas Datacenter
    William Carroll, ISSO

FIGURE 21.5

Sample authorization letter.

INTERIM AUTHORITY TO OPERATE

If the Security Package does not pass muster with the security assessment team, but it appears that it is on the right track and has the potential to remediate missing information within a short time period, the business owner may be awarded an Interim Authority to Operate (IATO). All IATOs are awarded with an expiration date assigned to it; most expire after 6 months. The criteria used for being awarded an IATO vary from agency to agency. Although an IATO is certainly not as desirable as an ATO, it does mean you can continue operating your systems up until the expiration date. Something worth noting is that the OMB does not recognize IATOs, so for annual FISMA reporting purposes IATOs are not reportable.

SUMMARY

The fundamental concepts for a Security Assessment Report should be similar to the concepts used to develop your Business Risk Assessment. However, the vulnerabilities that are discussed will likely be more technical and more specific. Security assessors need to include enough information about the vulnerability so that the ISSO can understand where what the weakness is. Additionally, security assessors need to make a recommendation on how to resolve each reported vulnerability. System owners and ISSOs should be provided enough information in the Security Assessment Report so that they could easily duplicate the finding. If security assessors don't list any vulnerabilities and claim the system, major application, and networks don't have any, the system owner and ISSO will likely come to the conclusion that the assessment team didn't know what they were doing. There are always some vulnerabilities. Don't forget to take into consideration natural disasters—particularly, if a Business Risk Assessment was not performed and the agency has offices and systems in areas that have a history of weather-related disasters.

ADDITIONAL RESOURCES

Additional resources that may help improve your understanding of system risk assessments are listed here:

Beaver, Justin, Ryan A. Kerekes, and Jim N. Treadwell. *An Information Fusion Framework for Threat Assessment*. Oak Ridge National Laboratory, July 2009.
Bidgoli, Hossein. *Handbook of Information Security, Volume 3, Threats, Vulnerabilities, Prevention, Detection, and Management*. Wiley, January 2006. ISBN: 0471648329.
Gregg, Michael and David Kim. *Inside Network Security Assessment*. Sams, November 18, 2005.

Jones, Andy and Debi Ashenden. *Risk Management for Computer Security*. Butterworth-Heinemann, March 15, 2005. ISBN: 0750677953.

Landoll, Douglas J. CRC. *The Security Risk Assessment Handbook*. December 12, 2005. ISBN: 0849329981.

Long, Johnny, Chris Hurley, Mark Wolfgang, and Mike Petruzzi. *Penetration Tester's Open Source Toolkit*. Rockland, MA: Syngress Publishing, December 1, 2005. ISBN: 1597490210.

Long, Johnny and Ed Skoudis. *Google Hacking for Penetration Testers*. Rockland, MA: Syngress Publishing, 2005. ISBN: 1931836361.

McCumber, John. *Assessing and Managing Security Risk in IT Systems*. Auerbach, June 15, 2004. ISBN: 0849322324.

McNab, Chris. *Network Security Assessment*. O'Reilly, March 1, 2004. ISBN: 059600611X.

Rogers, Russ, Ed Fuller, Greg Miles, Matthew Hoagberg, Travis Schack, Ted Dykstra, and Bryan Cunningham. *Network Security Evaluation*. Rockland, MA: Syngress Publishing, August 2005. ISBN: 1597490350.

Talabis, Mark and Jason Martin. *Information Security Risk Assessment Toolkit*. Syngress Publishing, October 17, 2012.

Addressing FISMA Findings

22

I don't believe in failure. It is not failure if you enjoyed the process.
—Oprah Winfrey

TOPICS IN THIS CHAPTER

- POA&Ms
- Development and approval
- POA&M elements
- A word to the wise
- Checklist

INTRODUCTION

Understanding how to resolve the reported vulnerabilities is the final step in the FISMA compliance process. When you read the Security Assessment Report, don't panic if you see findings. Security Assessment Reports are supposed to contain findings. It's still possible for your system to get authorized, even if the system has findings—as long as the findings are not too severe. In fact, most systems that get authorized do have findings.

POA&MS

Whether you receive a full Authority to Operate (ATO), or an Interim Authority to Operate (IATO), you will be required to correct weaknesses related to your security controls. If you are awarded an IATO, there will likely be far more weaknesses that you'll need to correct than if you were awarded an ATO. The weaknesses noted in the Security Assessment Report need to be identified and described in a document known as the Plan of Action & Milestones (POA&M). The POA&M represents the ISSO's to-do list and typically needs to be approved by the evaluation team that evaluated the system before they send in the recommendation for authorization.

The objective of the POA&M is to have all the vulnerabilities and below-standard security controls identified and listed in one consolidated document. The POA&M is the final output of the FISMA compliance process. When OIG and GAO come in to perform agency audits, it's possible that they may review POA&Ms to determine if vulnerabilities are being mitigated as scheduled.

DEVELOPMENT AND APPROVAL

Typically, the POA&M is created by the ISSO and managed by the ISSO on behalf of the system owner. The ISSO may delegate this task to a staff member or a contractor. Once your POA&M is complete, it needs to be approved. The ISSO should submit the POA&M to the security assessment team who will review it before sending it on to the authorizing official.

Sometimes some of the mitigation activities will be nothing more than updating software or installing the latest patches at little to no cost to the organization. Other mitigation activities could cost thousands of dollars and need upper level management approval for the funds. The ISSO and system owner need to make sure that the authorizing official has seen and approved the POA&M—that way, when the system owner requests the money to complete the tasks, there should be no problems getting the funding. Typically, the authorizing official will issue an Authority to Operate contingent on the fact that the vulnerabilities on the POA&M will be corrected.

POA&M ELEMENTS

OMB Memo M-04-25, *FY 2004 Reporting Instructions for the Federal Information Security Management.*

Act offers detailed agency guidance on what information to include in POA&Ms. That OMB Memo is available for review here: http://www.whitehouse.gov/sites/default/files/omb/memoranda/fy04/m04-25.pdf. According to this OMB Memo:

> *The heading of each POA&M must include the unique project identifier from the exhibits 300 and 53, where applicable.... .*

Further, in that OMB Memo, a footnote states:

> *OMB Circular A-11 requires that agencies develop and submit to OMB capital asset plans (exhibit 300) for major acquisition projects. For information technology projects, plans for major systems must be reported to OMB on an exhibit 300 and 53. The agency assigns a unique identifier to each system and applies it to both exhibits.*

The above statement illustrates the fact that POA&Ms are used by system owners and ISSOs to justify security funding for the system. System owners and ISSOs that are aware of security vulnerabilities need to be sure that to include all vulnerabilities in the system POA&M if they expect to obtain additional funding to resolve the security weakness.

A POA&M is typically put together in spreadsheet format and includes information about the cited weakness or vulnerability, milestones, and cost as shown in Table 22.1. You should make sure that the following information is included in each POA&M item:

- **ID No**. A unique number used by the organization to track mitigation activities.
- **Weakness** Include a description of the weakness identified by the annual program review, OIG, or GAO audit.
- **Severity** High, Moderate, or Low.
- **POC** Include contact information for the office and/or organization that the agency will hold responsible for resolving the weakness.
- **Resources Required** List the estimated funding and resources required to resolve the weakness. Include the anticipated source of funding (e.g., within the department or as a part of a crosscutting security infrastructure program). Include whether a reallocation of base resources or a request for new funding is anticipated. This column should also identify other nonfunding obstacles and challenges to resolving the weakness (e.g., lack of personnel or expertise, development of new system to replace insecure legacy system, etc.). To determine resource costs for employees, use the latest agency average salary and benefit hourly rate, then multiply the rate by the number of hours. Remember, this is just an estimate.
- **Projected Completion Date** Identify the date for resolving the weakness. Typically, the projected completion date cannot be changed. If a weakness is resolved before or after the projected completion date, you should show the actual completion date in the status column.
- **Milestones with Actual Completion Dates** Identify specific requirements to correct the weakness and include actual completion dates.
- **Source of Discovery** State how the weakness was discovered (e.g., penetration testing, OIG audit). If the weakness that is identified is reportable to the OIG, include the specific language and/or law from the pertinent audit report.
- **Status—Ongoing or Completed** Completed should be used only when a weakness has been fully resolved and the corrective action has been validated. For cancelled milestones, update the Status column to say Completed with the date and give a brief explanation in the Comments column.
- **Comments** Include a Comments column to record additional status.

Some agencies require even more information than what is listed above to be included in POA&Ms. The US Department of Health & Human Services has a very detailed and comprehensive POA&M management process that can be reviewed at the following URL: http://www.hhs.gov/ocio/policy/standard_2012-0001_001s.html.

A WORD TO THE WISE

Now, the Security Package is complete. It has been delivered and reviewed by the security assessors, and you have an Authority to Operate in hand from the authorizing official. Good job to everybody involved! It was a long hard road, and the job is

Table 22.1 Shows an Example of a POA&M

ID No.	Weakness	Severity	Point of Contact	Resources Required	Projected Completion Date	Milestones with Completion Dates	Identified in C&A Evaluation or Other Review?	Status
1	No IDS system installed in the environment	Moderate	Timothy Toms 111-222-3333	2 techs/ 80 hours System costs $10,000.00 Total cost: $26,000	December 15, 2012	Procure Servers October 15, 2012 Procure Software October 15, 2012 Build out system November 15, 2012 Test system December 10, 2012	Identified by security assessors annual testing	On-going
2	Windows 2012 Servers do not have the latest patches	Moderate	Harold Barns 111-333-2222	1 techs/ 80 hours cost $8000.00	October 15, 2013	Download all patches August 30, 2013 Test patches September 10, 2013	Identified by scanner during annual security assessment	On-going
3	No *Configuration Management Plan* for system	Low	Alice Jackson 222-111-3333	2 techs/ 80 hours System costs $16,000	December 1, 2013	Develop *Configuration Management Plan*	Identified by security assessment team during annual security assessment	On-going
4	Settings on Telnet port 25 on numerous servers are not sufficiently restrictive to prevent e-mail masquerading	High	James Wilson 111-222-3333	Not applicable	September 15, 2013	Completed September 15, 2013	Identified by security assessors when performing penetration testing	Transferred to ISSO in department G73

done... or is it? Unfortunately, it's often the case that once an Authority to Operate has been obtained, the organization puts the Security Package on a shelf and forgets about the POA&M. The next year when the security assessment team comes around to obtain updates for FISMA reporting, it can create a big worriment to find out the status of the mitigation activities. In some cases, the mitigation activities may have never even been started and there may be no way to complete them before the end of the reporting period. Such scenarios defeat the purpose of the entire FISMA compliance process.

If an agency does not ensure that system owners and ISSOs mitigate vulnerabilities in POA&Ms as required, they may get cited in an Office of Inspector General report. An example of what such a citing might look like is this citation from an Office of Inspector General report from April 6, 2013 for the Veteran's Administration:

> *VA has not implemented processes to fully account for security-related costs within its Capital Planning and Investment Control budget process. As a result, the assessment team was unable to trace Plan of Action and Milestone (POA&M) remediation costs to corresponding Exhibit 300s for certain mission critical systems.*[1]

The point of performing a security assessment is to identify vulnerabilities in your system and mitigate those vulnerabilities to improve the security posture. Don't waste all the hard work and effort that you and your colleagues put into the compliance process by not tracking and following up on the mitigation activities. If you track, follow up on, and validate that the mitigation activities are being completed, the next year, reporting will be an easy task. You'll know the status of the activities, your systems will be more secure, and your work will have made a difference.

CHECKLIST

Use the following checklist to make sure that you don't forget anything when developing your POA&M:

- Are all system weaknesses identified and listed?
- Does each system weakness have at least one corresponding milestone?
- Does the mitigation strategy information include a scheduled completion date?
- Does each milestone have a projected completion date?
- Does the mitigation strategy information include a Point of Contact?
- Are changes to milestones identified and listed?
- Does the weakness identified include a source (e.g., penetration test)?
- Is the status of the identified weakness indicated?
- Does the mitigation strategy information include the required financial resources?

---

[1]http://www.va.gov/oig/pubs/VAOIG-11-00320-138.pdf.

SUMMARY

The findings that result from the evaluation of the system and the Security Package should be turned into action items. ISSOs use a Plan of Action & Milestones (POA&M) document to summarize and track the action items. In subsequent audits, security assessors, OIG, and GAO may investigate to find out if corrective actions were applied to all security weaknesses. Addressing the findings that result from the compliance process is key to getting the value out of all the time and resources that were put into the security documents and the assessment process. Following through on POA&M action items is imperative to improving the secure posture of your systems.

FedRAMP: FISMA for the Cloud

23

I've looked at clouds from both sides now
From up and down, and still somehow
It's cloud illusions I recall,
I really don't know clouds at all.
—Joni Mitchell

TOPICS IN THIS CHAPTER

- What is cloud computing?
- Looking at virtual machines another way
- Sharding
- Content Delivery Networks
- FedRAMP security assessments
- The great value of FedRAMP

INTRODUCTION

The Federal Risk and Authorization Management Program (FedRAMP) is a government-wide initiative to apply FISMA to cloud computing. FedRAMP provides a standardized approach to security assessment, authorization, and continuous monitoring for cloud computing services. When a managed service provider sells services to a government agency, the service provider has to undergo a security assessment and obtain an Authorization to Operate from the agency. With traditional FISMA, if a service provider sells the same service to a second agency, the service provider has to have its platform assessed and authorized a second time by the second agency. Security assessments are expensive, and it is costly to perform a full assessment on the same system twice (within a short timeframe) for the purpose of signing up another customer—illustrated in Figure 23.1.

FedRAMP centralizes and standardizes security assessments of cloud systems across the U.S. government so that a system can be assessed once and used by many agencies as illustrated in Figure 23.2.

Before I explain further how the FedRAMP process works, it's important to understand some basics about cloud computing—FedRAMP applies only to cloud systems (at least as of this writing).

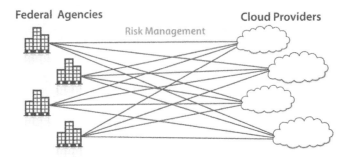

FIGURE 23.1

Cloud security assessments prior to FedRAMP. (For color version of this figure, the reader is referred to the online version of this chapter.)

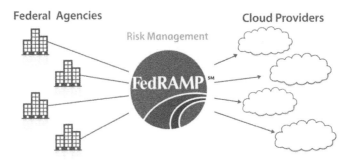

FIGURE 23.2

Cloud security assessments the FedRAMP way. (For color version of this figure, the reader is referred to the online version of this chapter.)

WHAT IS CLOUD COMPUTING?

Not everyone agrees on what cloud computing is and isn't. Even among knowledgeable information technology experts, there are differences of opinion. In *Special Publication 800-145*, *The NIST Definition of Cloud Computing*, the National Institute of Standards and Technology has defined five characteristics of a cloud system:

- On-demand self-service
- Broad network access
- Resource pooling
- Rapid elasticity
- Measured service

If you read SP 800-145, you'll find a definition to accompany each of these bullets. You can read these definitions yourself by reviewing SP 800-145 which can be found at the following URL http://www.csrc.nist.gov/publications/nistpubs/800-145/SP800-145.pdf.

Sometimes, managed service providers (system owners) and federal customers do not always agree on whether a system is a cloud system or not. The FedRAMP office does not make decisions on whether a particular system is or isn't cloud system. It is up to the agency using the system, in collaboration with the service provider, to decide if the system is a cloud system or not. Both parties should review the NIST definition and work together to come to an agreement. Even though the FedRAMP office does not make decisions for agencies or system owners on whether or not a system is a cloud system FedRAMP subject matter experts may be able to offer thoughtful insight to enable agencies and system owners to make this decision for themselves. You can contact the FedRAMP office by writing to info@fedramp.gov.

The most common techniques used to create a cloud are:

- Virtualization
- Sharding
- Content caching
- Other proprietary methods

A virtual machine (sometimes referred to as a virtual host) is the most typical method of creating a cloud system. The use of virtual machines has exploded in the past 5 years. However, virtual machines are not new. IBM began using virtual machines and virtualization techniques in the 1960s. Jim Rymarczyk is the person most often attributed to being the original pioneer of virtual machines while working for IBM in Cambridge, Massachusetts. As an internal research project, Rymarczyk developed a virtualization prototype that was akin to a time-sharing system where each user had their own dedicated virtual memory space. Later, in 1974, Popek and Goldberg published an ACM landmark white paper on virtual machines where they described virtual machines as "an efficient, isolated duplicate of the real machine." A virtual machine is essentially a host computer encapsulated within another host computer, giving the user the illusion that they are interfacing with a traditional host.

Today, cloud service providers offering Infrastructure as a Service (IaaS) provide self-service control panels where users can select what type of computer they want to build from a software interface. Through dropdown menus, radio buttons, and check boxes, users can select what type of operating system they want, how much storage they want, how much memory they want, how many virtual interfaces, virtual firewalls, and various other application plug-ins. After selecting the system they want to build, the user presses the Go button and the system builds itself. Once built, users can install applications, databases, Web services, and anything else that one typically install on a traditional system.

LOOKING AT VIRTUAL MACHINES ANOTHER WAY

Here is another way of looking at how a virtual machine works. Imagine that you need a computer to use but you don't have one. Your friend says that he has a computer that can create other computers out of nothing, and that he will create a computer for you to use, but it will live inside his computer. It will work so well, and look so realistic, that you won't know it's living inside his computer. Let's call your friend's computer the Universe Host. Let's call your computer (the computer that is inside your friend's computer) a *virtual host*.

When you use your new virtual host computer, you can't see the Universe Host...it is invisible to you. You start developing applications, creating projects, and processing numbers on your computer. Before long, you realize that you need more space and you want more processing power. You see a button on the user interface that says "push this button for more space and more power." You push the button, and storage space grows as you use more, and shrinks as you delete data, similar to how an accordion works. While you are happily computing, your friend uses the Universe Host to create more virtual hosts for other people to use. You can't see these other virtual hosts (or the people using them) and they can't see your computer (or you). Before long, the Universe Host has created 1,000 virtual hosts, for 1,000 different users. None of the users can see the other 999 other systems (or the other system owners). The Universe Host is protecting all 1,000 virtual hosts, preventing the owner of one virtual host from seeing all of the other virtual hosts.

As your virtual host needs more space and power, it is able to give you more space and power, by rearranging magic puzzle pieces that hold data. The magic puzzle pieces are being rearranged so that all 1,000 hosts always have as much space as they need, but never more than they need. Whenever a virtual host computer deletes data, the magic puzzle pieces rearrange themselves and shrink the storage space (remember the accordion) giving it to another virtual host that is at the moment expanding and needs more space. The Universe Host, and its 1,000 virtual hosts, is a cloud system.

SHARDING

Another technique used to create cloud systems is database *sharding*. Database sharding refers to replicating a database across other databases in chunks of data called shards. The data in all of the shards put together represent the original complete database. Sharding solves various capacity challenges such as data exceeding the storage capacity of a single database. If everything is in the same database node, user requests for data can significantly degrade network performance; however, with sharding that doesn't happen. Job requests pull data from different shards and reassemble the shards at the application layer seamlessly, unbeknownst to the user. Figure 23.3 shows an example of sharding architecture.

CONTENT DELIVERY NETWORKS

Another cloud technique involves the use of content delivery networks where the system replicates content across a vast and expansive network of replication servers. Content delivery techniques are typically proprietary and unique to the service

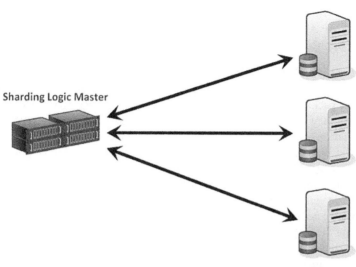

FIGURE 23.3

Sharding logic master and shards. (For color version of this figure, the reader is referred to the online version of this chapter.)

provider that provides this service. The primary purpose of Content Delivery Networks (CDN) is to replicate data and cache it on servers in other geographic areas for the purpose of speeding up the delivery of the data to the customer/user. CDN servers are typically disbursed throughout the world and deliver data to the customer/user from the server that is closest to the customer/users geographic location. By caching data on servers close to users, network latency is taken out of the picture and users are able to retrieve data at much higher speeds. Leading CDNs include Akamai, Microsoft Windows Azure, and Amazon Cloud Front.

FedRAMP SECURITY INDEPENDENT ASSESSORS

FedRAMP third-party-independent security assessors are known as 3PAOs. In order to become a 3PAO, a company has to fill out an application which requires certain competencies related to FISMA. Additionally, the company must show conformance with ISO 17020 and the existence of a Quality Management System in use at their company. There is information on how to apply to become a FedRAMP-accredited 3PAO on the FedRAMP Web site at http://www.fedramp.gov.

FedRAMP SECURITY ASSESSMENTS

There are three different methods that Cloud Service Providers (CSPs) can use to have their Security Package put into the FedRAMP secure repository for agency prospects to review for potential use. The three categories are known as:

- JAB Provisional Authorization
- FedRAMP Agency ATO
- CSP Supplied

CSPs can elect to have their system assessed for FedRAMP compliance by going through an agency or the FedRAMP PMO. CSPs that go through the PMO will have their entire package reviewed by FedRAMP's Joint Advisory Board (JAB) which is made up of the CIOs from the Department of Defense (DoD), the General Services Administration (GSA), and the Department of Homeland Security (DHS). The JAB reviews the 3PAOs Security Assessment Report and all of the other Security Package documents and then makes a risk-based decision on whether to grant a FedRAMP Provisional Authorization. Reviews by the JAB are very comprehensive. All CSP systems that get reviewed by the JAB must have their system assessed by a FedRAMP accredited 3PAO. An illustration of the JAB review process and estimated time the review takes is found in Figure 23.4.

CSPs can also have their system reviewed by a federal agency. The process and requirements are exactly the same except that the independent assessor does not necessarily have to be an accredited 3PAO—it can be any competent-independent assessor of the agency's choosing. When going through an agency, only one entity is reviewing the entire Security Package, so the process is generally quicker.

If a CSP believes that its system meets FedRAMP requirements, it can hire any FedRAMP accredited 3PAO to assess its system. The CSP can then submit the Security Package and the resulting POA&M to the FedRAMP PMO for inclusion in FedRAMP's secure repository. The FedRAMP PMO reviews the packages for completeness and conformance with FedRAMP requirements to agencies to review. Until an agency authorizes the package, the CSP-supplied package will be designated as Unauthorized.

THE GREAT VALUE OF FedRAMP

FedRAMP enables federal agencies to build and use systems without having to go through the expensive endeavor of buying hardware or building datacenters. Agencies will reap the greatest savings the higher up the stack they go in purchasing services. Software as a Service (SaaS) inherits more security controls than lower layered clouds. SaaS users inherit security controls from lower layers and also inherit the assessments performed on lower layers. Security assessments are expensive, and the fewer controls an agency has to assess, the lower the cost of using the service.

Costs aside, cloud systems enable users to launch new systems faster and get new services up and running faster. Cloud customers typically only pay for compute cycles while they are actually processing data. Storage is paid for only while data is being housed on the cloud system. For agencies that are creating alternate sites for contingency planning and disaster recovery, cloud systems are optimal because they can replicate servers, but agencies only pay for storage until the contingency plan is activated.

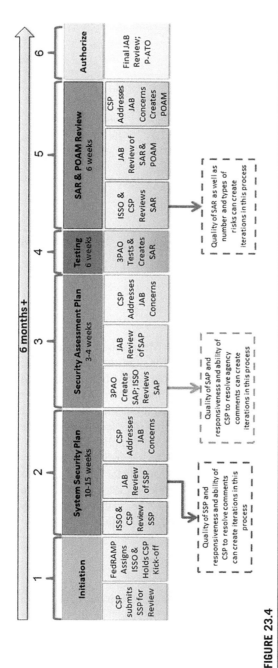

FIGURE 23.4

The FedRAMP security assessment process. (For color version of this figure, the reader is referred to the online version of this chapter.)

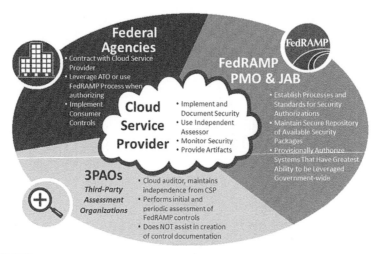

FIGURE 23.5

FedRAMP organization. (For color version of this figure, the reader is referred to the online version of this chapter.)

FedRAMP ORGANIZATION

FedRAMP is managed through a Program Management Office (PMO) that acts as a central hub and communications vehicle for all of the FedRAMP activities as illustrated in Figure 23.5. The PMO has a staff of FedRAMP ISSOs that review JAB Security Packages before the package gets submitted to the JAB for approval. The PMO also has a development team that develops all of the FedRAMP Security Package templates and guidance. The FedRAMP development team continuously puts out new and updated guidance information and templates that are available on the FedRAMP Web site. The PMO maintains a security repository for the storage of FedRAMP Security Packages which are available for federal departments and agencies to review prior to signing up for services. Last, the PMO manages the 3PAO program in conjunction with an expert review board that assists the PMO in ensuring that 3PAOs are competent and meet the 17,020 requirements.

SUMMARY

FedRAMP is a program that standardizes the security assessments of cloud service providers. It is managed through a central PMO and it enables a system to be assessed once and then used by multiple agencies. If cloud service providers want to do business with the federal government, their system must comply with FedRAMP. The Office of Management and Budget (OMB) has mandated that all government cloud must comply with FedRAMP by June 6, 2014. FedRAMP baseline security requirements, templates, and guidance are available on the FedRAMP Web site at http://www.fedramp.gov.

RESOURCES

Terry L. Borden, James. P. Hennessy and James. W. Rymarczyk. *Multiple Operating Systems on One Processor Complex*, IBM Systems Journal, Volume 26, No. 1, 1989.

Brodkin, John. *With Long History of Virtualization Behind It, IBM Looks to the Future. Network World*, April 30, 2009.

Hay, Chris and Brian Prince. *Azure in Action*. Manning Publications, October 15, 2010.

Gerald J. Popek and Robert P. Goldberg. *Formal Requirements For Virtualizable Third-Generation Architectures*. Communications of the ACM, Volume 17, No. 7, 1974, 412-421.

Wilder, Bill. *Cloud Architecture Patterns*. O'Reilly Media, September 28, 2012.

Vaquero, Luis, Juan Cáceres, and Juan Hierro. *Open Source Cloud Computing Systems*. IGI Global, January 31, 2012.

FISMA

TITLE III—INFORMATION SECURITY
SEC. 301. INFORMATION SECURITY

(a) SHORT TITLE.—This title may be cited as the "Federal Information Security Management Act of 2002."

(b) INFORMATION SECURITY.—

(1) IN GENERAL.—Chapter 35 of title 44, United States Code, is amended by adding at the end the following new subchapter:

"SUBCHAPTER III—INFORMATION SECURITY

"§ 3541. Purposes

"The purposes of this subchapter are to—

"(1) provide a comprehensive framework for ensuring the effectiveness of information security controls over information resources that support Federal operations and assets;

"(2) recognize the highly networked nature of the current Federal computing environment and provide effective government-wide management and oversight of the related information security risks, including coordination of information security efforts throughout the civilian, national security, and law enforcement communities;

"(3) provide for development and maintenance of minimum controls required to protect Federal information and information systems;

"(4) provide a mechanism for improved oversight of Federal agency information security programs;

"(5) acknowledge that commercially developed information security products offer advanced, dynamic, robust, and effective information security solutions, reflecting market solutions for the protection of critical information infrastructures important to the national defense and economic security of the nation that are designed, built, and operated by the private sector; and

"(6) recognize that the selection of specific technical hardware and software information security solutions should be left to individual agencies from among commercially developed products.

"§ 3542. Definitions

"(a) IN GENERAL.—Except as provided under subsection (b), the definitions under section 3502 shall apply to this subchapter.

"(b) ADDITIONAL DEFINITIONS.—As used in this subchapter:

"(1) The term 'information security' means protecting information and information systems from unauthorized access, use, disclosure, disruption, modification, or destruction in order to provide—

"(A) Integrity, which means guarding against improper information modification or destruction, and includes ensuring information nonrepudiation and authenticity;

"(B) Confidentiality, which means preserving authorized restrictions on access and disclosure, including means for protecting personal privacy and proprietary information; and

"(C) Availability, which means ensuring timely and reliable access to and use of information.

"(2)(A) The term 'national security system' means any information system (including any telecommunications system) used or operated by an agency or by a contractor of an agency, or other organization on behalf of an agency—

"(i) the function, operation, or use of which—

"(I) involves intelligence activities;

"(II) involves cryptologic activities related to national security;

"(III) involves command and control of military forces;

"(IV) involves equipment that is an integral part of a weapon or weapons system; or

"(V) subject to subparagraph (B), is critical to the direct fulfillment of military or intelligence missions; or

"(ii) is protected at all times by procedures established for information that have been specifically authorized under criteria established by an Executive order or an Act of

Congress to be kept classified in the interest of national defense or foreign policy.

"(B) Subparagraph (A)(i)(V) does not include a system that is to be used for routine administrative and business applications (including payroll, finance, logistics, and personnel management applications).

"(3) The term 'information technology' has the meaning given that term in section 11101 of title 40.

"§ 3543. Authority and functions of the Director

"(a) IN GENERAL.—The Director shall oversee agency information security policies and practices, including—

"(1) developing and overseeing the implementation of policies, principles, standards, and guidelines on information security, including through ensuring timely agency adoption of and compliance with standards promulgated under section 11331 of title 40;

"(2) requiring agencies, consistent with the standards promulgated under such section 11331 and the requirements of this subchapter, to identify and provide information security protections commensurate with the risk and magnitude of the harm resulting from the unauthorized access, use, disclosure, disruption, modification, or destruction of—

"(A) information collected or maintained by or on behalf of an agency; or

"(B) information systems used or operated by an agency or by a contractor of an agency or other organization on behalf of an agency;

"(3) coordinating the development of standards and guidelines under section 20 of the National Institute of Standards and Technology Act (15 U.S.C. 278g-3) with agencies and offices operating or exercising control of national security systems (including the National Security Agency) to assure, to the maximum extent feasible, that such standards and guidelines are complementary with standards and guidelines developed for national security systems;

"(4) overseeing agency compliance with the requirements of this subchapter, including through any authorized action under section 11303 of title 40, to enforce accountability for compliance with such requirements;

"(5) reviewing at least annually, and approving or disapproving, agency information security programs required under section 3544(b);

"(6) coordinating information security policies and procedures with related information resources management policies and procedures;

"(7) overseeing the operation of the Federal information security incident center required under section 3546; and

"(8) reporting to Congress no later than March 1 of each year on agency compliance with the requirements of this subchapter, including—

"(A) a summary of the findings of evaluations required by section 3545;

"(B) an assessment of the development, promulgation, and adoption of, and compliance with, standards developed under section 20 of the National Institute of Standards and Technology Act (15 U.S.C. 278g-3) and promulgated under section 11331 of title 40;

"(C) significant deficiencies in agency information security practices;

"(D) planned remedial action to address such deficiencies; and

"(E) a summary of, and the views of the Director on, the report prepared by the National Institute of Standards and Technology under section 20(d)(10) of the National Institute of Standards and Technology Act (15 U.S.C. 278g-3).

"(b) NATIONAL SECURITY SYSTEMS.—Except for the authorities described in paragraphs (4) and (8) of subsection (a), the authorities of the Director under this section shall not apply to national security systems.

"(c) DEPARTMENT OF DEFENSE AND CENTRAL INTELLIGENCE

AGENCY SYSTEMS.—(1) The authorities of the Director described in paragraphs (1) and (2) of subsection (a) shall be delegated to the Secretary of Defense in the case of systems described in paragraph (2) and to the Director of Central Intelligence in the case of systems described in paragraph (3).

"(2) The systems described in this paragraph are systems that are operated by the Department of Defense, a contractor of the Department of Defense, or another entity on behalf of the Department of Defense that processes any information the unauthorized access, use, disclosure, disruption, modification, or destruction of which would have a debilitating impact on the mission of the Department of Defense.

"(3) The systems described in this paragraph are systems that are operated by the Central Intelligence Agency, a contractor of the Central Intelligence Agency, or another entity on behalf of the Central Intelligence Agency that processes any information the unauthorized access, use, disclosure, disruption, modification, or destruction of which would have a debilitating impact on the mission of the Central Intelligence Agency.

"§ 3544. Federal agency responsibilities

"(a) IN GENERAL.—The head of each agency shall—

"(1) be responsible for—

"(A) providing information security protections commensurate with the risk and magnitude of the harm resulting from unauthorized access, use, disclosure, disruption, modification, or destruction of—

"(i) information collected or maintained by or on behalf of the agency; and

"(ii) information systems used or operated by an agency or by a contractor of an agency or other organization on behalf of an agency;

"(B) complying with the requirements of this subchapter and related policies, procedures, standards, and guidelines, including—

"(i) information security standards promulgated under section 11331 of title 40; and

"(ii) information security standards and guidelines for national security systems issued in accordance with law and as directed by the President; and

"(C) ensuring that information security management processes are integrated with agency strategic and operational planning processes;

"(2) ensure that senior agency officials provide information security for the information and information systems that support the operations and assets under their control, including

through—

"(A) assessing the risk and magnitude of the harm that could result from the unauthorized access, use, disclosure, disruption, modification, or destruction of such information or information systems;

"(B) determining the levels of information security appropriate to protect such information and information systems in accordance with standards promulgated under section 11331 of title 40, for information security classifications and related requirements;

"(C) implementing policies and procedures to cost-effectively reduce risks to an acceptable level; and

"(D) periodically testing and evaluating information security controls and techniques to ensure that they are effectively implemented;

"(3) delegate to the agency Chief Information Officer established under section 3506 (or comparable official in an agency not covered by such section) the authority to ensure compliance with the requirements imposed on the agency under this subchapter, including—

"(A) designating a senior agency information security officer who shall—

"(i) carry out the Chief Information Officer's responsibilities under this section;

"(ii) possess professional qualifications, including training and experience, required to administer the functions described under this section;

"(iii) have information security duties as that official's primary duty; and

"(iv) head an office with the mission and resources to assist in ensuring agency compliance with this section;

"(B) developing and maintaining an agency-wide information security program as required by subsection

(b);

"(C) developing and maintaining information security policies, procedures, and control techniques to address all applicable requirements, including those issued under section 3543 of this title, and section 11331 of title 40;

"(D) training and overseeing personnel with significant responsibilities for information security with respect to such responsibilities; and

"(E) assisting senior agency officials concerning their responsibilities under paragraph (2);

"(4) ensure that the agency has trained personnel sufficient to assist the agency in complying with the requirements of this subchapter and related policies, procedures, standards, and guidelines; and

"(5) ensure that the agency Chief Information Officer, in coordination with other senior agency officials, reports annually to the agency head on the effectiveness of the agency information security program, including progress of remedial actions.

"(b) AGENCY PROGRAM.—Each agency shall develop, document, and implement an agency-wide information security program, approved by the Director under section 3543(a)(5), to provide information security for the information and information systems that support the operations and assets of the agency, including those provided or managed by another agency, contractor, or other source, that includes—

"(1) periodic assessments of the risk and magnitude of the harm that could result from the unauthorized access, use, disclosure, disruption, modification, or destruction of information and information systems that support the operations and assets of the agency;

"(2) policies and procedures that—

"(A) are based on the risk assessments required by paragraph (1);

"(B) cost-effectively reduce information security risks to an acceptable level;

"(C) ensure that information security is addressed throughout the life cycle of each agency information system; and

"(D) ensure compliance with—

"(i) the requirements of this subchapter;

"(ii) policies and procedures as may be prescribed by the Director, and information security standards promulgated under section 11331 of title 40;

"(iii) minimally acceptable system configuration requirements, as determined by the agency; and

"(iv) any other applicable requirements, including standards and guidelines for national security systems issued in accordance with law and as directed by the President;

"(3) subordinate plans for providing adequate information security for networks, facilities, and systems or groups of information systems, as appropriate;

"(4) security awareness training to inform personnel, including contractors and other users of information systems that support the operations and assets of the agency, of—

"(A) information security risks associated with their activities; and

"(B) their responsibilities in complying with agency policies and procedures designed to reduce these risks; "(5) periodic testing and evaluation of the effectiveness of information security policies, procedures, and practices, to be performed with a frequency depending on risk, but no less than annually, of which such testing—

"(A) shall include testing of management, operational, and technical controls of every information system identified in the inventory required under section 3505(c); and

"(B) may include testing relied on in a evaluation under section 3545;

"(6) a process for planning, implementing, evaluating, and documenting remedial action to address any deficiencies in the information security policies, procedures, and practices of the agency;

"(7) procedures for detecting, reporting, and responding to security incidents, consistent with standards and guidelines issued pursuant to section 3546(b), including—

"(A) mitigating risks associated with such incidents before substantial damage is done;

"(B) notifying and consulting with the Federal information security incident center referred to in section 3546; and

"(C) notifying and consulting with, as appropriate—

"(i) law enforcement agencies and relevant Offices of Inspector General;

"(ii) an office designated by the President for any incident involving a national security system; and

"(iii) any other agency or office, in accordance with law or as directed by the President; and

"(8) plans and procedures to ensure continuity of operations for information systems that support the operations and assets of the agency.

"(c) AGENCY REPORTING.—Each agency shall—

"(1) report annually to the Director, the Committees on Government Reform and Science of the House of Representatives, the Committees on Governmental

Affairs and Commerce, Science, and Transportation of the Senate, the appropriate authorization and appropriations committees of Congress, and the Comptroller General on the adequacy and effectiveness of information security policies, procedures, and practices, and compliance with the requirements of this subchapter, including compliance with each requirement of subsection (b);

"(2) address the adequacy and effectiveness of information security policies, procedures, and practices in plans and reports relating to—

"(A) annual agency budgets;

"(B) information resources management under subchapter 1 of this chapter;

"(C) information technology management under subtitle III of title 40;

"(D) program performance under sections 1105 and 1115 through 1119 of title 31, and sections 2801 and 2805 of title 39;

"(E) financial management under chapter 9 of title 31, and the Chief Financial Officers Act of 1990 (31 U.S.C. 501 note; Public Law 101-576) (and the amendments made by that Act);

"(F) financial management systems under the Federal Financial Management Improvement Act (31 U.S.C. 3512 note); and

"(G) internal accounting and administrative controls under section 3512 of title 31, (known as the 'Federal Managers Financial Integrity Act'); and

"(3) report any significant deficiency in a policy, procedure, or practice identified under paragraph (1) or (2)—

"(A) as a material weakness in reporting under section 3512 of title 31; and

"(B) if relating to financial management systems, as an instance of a lack of substantial compliance under the Federal Financial Management Improvement Act (31 U.S.C. 3512 note).

"(d) PERFORMANCE PLAN.—(1) In addition to the requirements of subsection (c), each agency, in consultation with the Director, shall include as part of the performance plan required under section 1115 of title 31 a description of—

"(A) the time periods, and

"(B) the resources, including budget, staffing, and training, that are necessary to implement the program required under subsection (b).

"(2) The description under paragraph (1) shall be based on the risk assessments required under subsection (b)(2)(1).

"(e) PUBLIC NOTICE AND COMMENT.—Each agency shall provide the public with timely notice and opportunities for comment on proposed information security policies and procedures to the extent that such policies and procedures affect communication with the public.

"§ 3545. Annual independent evaluation

"(a) IN GENERAL.—(1) Each year each agency shall have performed an independent evaluation of the information security program and practices of that agency to determine the effectiveness of such program and practices.

"(2) Each evaluation under this section shall include—

"(A) testing of the effectiveness of information security policies, procedures, and practices of a representative subset of the agency's information systems;

"(B) an assessment (made on the basis of the results of the testing) of compliance with—

"(i) the requirements of this subchapter; and

"(ii) related information security policies, procedures, standards, and guidelines; and

"(C) separate presentations, as appropriate, regarding information security relating to national security systems.

"(b) INDEPENDENT AUDITOR.—Subject to subsection (c)—

"(1) for each agency with an Inspector General appointed under the Inspector General Act of 1978, the annual evaluation required by this section shall be performed by the Inspector General or by an independent external auditor, as determined by the Inspector General of the agency; and

"(2) for each agency to which paragraph (1) does not apply, the head of the agency shall engage an independent external auditor to perform the evaluation.

"(c) NATIONAL SECURITY SYSTEMS.—For each agency operating or exercising control of a national security system, that portion of the evaluation required by this section directly relating to a national security system shall be performed—

"(1) only by an entity designated by the agency head; and

"(2) in such a manner as to ensure appropriate protection for information associated with any information security vulnerability in such system commensurate with the risk and in accordance with all applicable laws.

"(d) EXISTING EVALUATIONS.—The evaluation required by this section may be based in whole or in part on an audit, evaluation, or report relating to programs or practices of the applicable agency.

"(e) AGENCY REPORTING.—(1) Each year, not later than such date established by the Director, the head of each agency shall submit to the Director the results of the evaluation required under this section.

"(2) To the extent an evaluation required under this section directly relates to a national security system, the evaluation results submitted to the Director shall contain only a summary and assessment of that portion of the evaluation directly relating to a national security system.

"(f) PROTECTION OF INFORMATION.—Agencies and evaluators shall take appropriate steps to ensure the protection of information which, if disclosed, may adversely affect information security. Such protections shall be commensurate with the risk and comply with all applicable laws and regulations.

"(g) OMB REPORTS TO CONGRESS.—(1) The Director shall summarize the results of the evaluations conducted under this section in the report to Congress required under section 3543(a)(8).

"(2) The Director's report to Congress under this subsection shall summarize information regarding information security relating to national security systems in such a manner as to ensure appropriate protection for information associated with any information security vulnerability in such system commensurate with the risk and in accordance with all applicable laws.

"(3) Evaluations and any other descriptions of information systems under the authority and control of the Director of Central Intelligence or of National Foreign Intelligence Programs systems under the authority and control of the Secretary of Defense shall be made available to Congress only through the appropriate oversight committees of Congress, in accordance with applicable laws.

"(h) COMPTROLLER GENERAL.—The Comptroller General shall periodically evaluate and report to Congress on—

"(1) the adequacy and effectiveness of agency information security policies and practices; and

"(2) implementation of the requirements of this subchapter.

"§ 3546. Federal information security incident center

"(a) IN GENERAL.—The Director shall ensure the operation of a central Federal information security incident center to—

"(1) provide timely technical assistance to operators of agency information systems regarding security incidents, including guidance on detecting and handling information security incidents;

"(2) compile and analyze information about incidents that threaten information security;

"(3) inform operators of agency information systems about current and potential information security threats, and vulnerabilities; and

"(4) consult with the National Institute of Standards and Technology, agencies or offices operating or exercising control of national security systems (including the National Security Agency), and such other agencies or offices in accordance with law and as directed by the President regarding information security incidents and related matters.

"(b) NATIONAL SECURITY SYSTEMS.—Each agency operating or exercising control of a national security system shall share information about information security incidents, threats, and vulnerabilities with the Federal information security incident center to the extent consistent with standards and guidelines for national security systems, issued in accordance with law and as directed by the President.

"§ 3547. National security systems

"The head of each agency operating or exercising control of a national security system shall be responsible for ensuring that the agency—

"(1) provides information security protections commensurate with the risk and magnitude of the harm resulting from the unauthorized access, use, disclosure, disruption, modification, or destruction of the information contained in such system;

"(2) implements information security policies and practices as required by standards and guidelines for national security systems, issued in accordance with law and as directed by the President; and

"(3) complies with the requirements of this subchapter.

"§ 3548. Authorization of appropriations

"There are authorized to be appropriated to carry out the provisions of this subchapter such sums as may be necessary for each of fiscal years 2003 through 2007.

"§ 3549. Effect on existing law

"Nothing in this subchapter, section 11331 of title 40, or section 20 of the National Standards and Technology Act (15 U.S.C. 278g-3) may be construed as affecting the authority of the President, the Office of Management and Budget or the Director thereof, the National Institute of Standards and Technology, or the head of any agency, with respect to the authorized use or disclosure of information, including with regard to the protection of personal privacy under section 552a of title 5, the disclosure of information under section 552 of title 5, the management and disposition of records under chapters 29, 31, or 33 of title 44, the management of information resources under subchapter I of chapter 35 of this title, or the disclosure of information to the Congress or the Comptroller General of the United States. While this subchapter is in effect, subchapter II of this chapter shall not apply."

(2) CLERICAL AMENDMENT.—The table of sections at the beginning of such chapter 35 is amended by adding at the end the following:

"SUBCHAPTER III—INFORMATION SECURITY
"Sec.

"3541. Purposes.
"3542. Definitions.
"3543. Authority and functions of the Director.
"3544. Federal agency responsibilities.
"3545. Annual independent evaluation.
"3546. Federal information security incident center.
"3547. National security systems.
"3548. Authorization of appropriations.
"3549. Effect on existing law."
(c) INFORMATION SECURITY RESPONSIBILITIES OF CERTAIN AGENCIES.

—

NATIONAL SECURITY RESPONSIBILITIES.—(A) Nothing in this Act (including any amendment made by this Act) shall supersede any authority of the Secretary of Defense, the Director of Central Intelligence, or other agency head, as authorized by law and as directed by the President, with regard to the operation, control, or management of national security systems, as defined by section 3542(b)(2) of title 44, United States Code.
(B) Section 2224 of title 10, United States Code, is amended—
in subsection (b), by striking "(b) OBJECTIVES AND MINIMUM REQUIREMENTS.—(1)" and inserting "(b) OBJECTIVES OF THE PROGRAM.—";

in subsection (b), by striking paragraph (2); and

in subsection (c), in the matter preceding paragraph

(1), by inserting ", including through compliance with subchapter III of chapter 35 of title 44" after "infrastructure."

ATOMIC ENERGY ACT OF 1954.—Nothing in this Act shall supersede any requirement made by or under the Atomic Energy Act of 1954 (42 U.S.C. 2011 et seq.). Restricted data or formerly restricted data shall be handled, protected, classified, downgraded, and declassified in conformity with the Atomic Energy Act of 1954 (42 U.S.C. 2011 et seq.).

SEC. 302. MANAGEMENT OF INFORMATION TECHNOLOGY

IN GENERAL.—Section 11331 of title 40, United States Code, is amended to read as follows:

"§ 11331. Responsibilities for Federal information systems standards

"(a) STANDARDS AND GUIDELINES.—

"(1) AUTHORITY TO PRESCRIBE.—Except as provided under paragraph (2), the Secretary of Commerce shall, on the basis of standards and guidelines developed by the National Institute of Standards and Technology pursuant to paragraphs (2) and (3) of section 20(a) of the National Institute of Standards and Technology Act (15 U.S.C. 278g-3(a)), prescribe standards and guidelines pertaining to Federal information systems.

"(2) NATIONAL SECURITY SYSTEMS.—Standards and guidelines for national security systems (as defined under this section) shall be developed, prescribed, enforced, and overseen as otherwise authorized by law and as directed by the President.

"(b) MANDATORY REQUIREMENTS.—

"(1) AUTHORITY TO MAKE MANDATORY.—Except as provided under paragraph (2), the Secretary shall make standards prescribed under subsection (a)(1) compulsory and binding to the extent determined necessary by the Secretary to improve the efficiency of operation or security of Federal information systems.

"(2) REQUIRED MANDATORY STANDARDS.—(A) Standards prescribed under subsection (a)(1) shall include information security standards that—

"(i) provide minimum information security requirements as determined under section 20(b) of the National Institute of Standards and Technology Act (15 U.S.C. 278g-3(b)); and

"(ii) are otherwise necessary to improve the security of Federal information and information systems.

"(B) Information security standards described in subparagraph

(A) shall be compulsory and binding.

"(c) AUTHORITY TO DISAPPROVE OR MODIFY.—The President may disapprove or modify the standards and guidelines referred to in subsection (a)(1) if the President determines such action to be in the public interest.

The President's authority to disapprove or modify such standards and guidelines may not be delegated. Notice of such disapproval or modification shall be published promptly in the Federal Register. Upon receiving notice of such disapproval or modification, the Secretary of Commerce shall immediately rescind or modify such standards or guidelines as directed by the President.

"(d) EXERCISE OF AUTHORITY.—To ensure fiscal and policy consistency, the Secretary shall exercise the authority conferred by this section subject to direction by the President and in coordination with the Director of the Office of Management and Budget.

"(e) APPLICATION OF MORE STRINGENT STANDARDS.—The head of an executive agency may employ standards for the cost-effective information security for information systems within or under the supervision of that agency that are more stringent than the standards the Secretary prescribes under this section if the more stringent standards—

"(1) contain at least the applicable standards made compulsory and binding by the Secretary; and

"(2) are otherwise consistent with policies and guidelines issued under section 3543 of title 44.

"(f) DECISIONS ON PROMULGATION OF STANDARDS.—The decision by the Secretary regarding the promulgation of any standard under this section shall occur not later than 6 months after the submission of the proposed standard to the Secretary by the National Institute of Standards and Technology, as provided under section 20 of the National Institute of Standards and Technology Act (15 U.S.C. 278g-3).

"(g) DEFINITIONS.—In this section:

"(1) FEDERAL INFORMATION SYSTEM.—The term 'Federal information system' means an information system used or operated by an executive agency, by a contractor of an executive agency, or by another organization on behalf of an executive agency.

"(2) INFORMATION SECURITY.—The term 'information security' has the meaning given that term in section 3542(b)(1) of title 44.

"(3) NATIONAL SECURITY SYSTEM.—The term 'national security system' has the meaning given that term in section 3542(b)(2) of title 44."

(b) CLERICAL AMENDMENT.—The item relating to section 11331 in the table of sections at the beginning of chapter 113 of such title is amended to read as follows:

"11331. Responsibilities for Federal information systems standards."

SEC. 303. NATIONAL INSTITUTE OF STANDARDS AND TECHNOLOGY

Section 20 of the National Institute of Standards and Technology Act (15 U.S.C. 278g-3) is amended by striking the text and inserting the following:

"(a) IN GENERAL.—The Institute shall—

"(1) have the mission of developing standards, guidelines, and associated methods and techniques for information systems;

"(2) develop standards and guidelines, including minimum requirements, for information systems used or operated by an agency or by a contractor of an agency or other organization on behalf of an agency, other than national security systems (as defined in section 3542(b)(2) of title 44, United States Code); and
"(3) develop standards and guidelines, including minimum requirements, for providing adequate information security for all agency operations and assets, but such standards and guidelines shall not apply to national security systems.
"(b) MINIMUM REQUIREMENTS FOR STANDARDS AND GUIDELINES.

—The standards and guidelines required by subsection (a) shall include, at a minimum—

"(1)(A) standards to be used by all agencies to categorize all information and information systems collected or maintained by or on behalf of each agency based on the objectives of providing appropriate levels of information security according to a range of risk levels;
"(B) guidelines recommending the types of information and information systems to be included in each such category; and
"(C) minimum information security requirements for information and information systems in each such category;
"(2) a definition of and guidelines concerning detection and handling of information security incidents; and
"(3) guidelines developed in conjunction with the Department of Defense, including the National Security Agency, for identifying an information system as a national security system consistent with applicable requirements for national security systems, issued in accordance with law and as directed by the President.
"(c) DEVELOPMENT OF STANDARDS AND GUIDELINES.—In developing standards and guidelines required by subsections (a) and
(b), the Institute shall—
"(1) consult with other agencies and offices and the private sector (including the Director of the Office of Management and Budget, the Departments of Defense and Energy, the National Security Agency, the General Accounting Office, and the Secretary of Homeland Security) to assure—
"(A) use of appropriate information security policies, procedures, and techniques, in order to improve information security and avoid unnecessary and costly duplication of effort; and
"(B) that such standards and guidelines are complementary with standards and guidelines employed for the protection of national security systems and information contained in such systems;
"(2) provide the public with an opportunity to comment on proposed standards and guidelines;
"(3) submit to the Secretary of Commerce for promulgation under section 11331 of title 40, United States Code—
"(A) standards, as required under subsection (b)(1)(A), no later than 12 months after the date of the enactment of this section; and

"(B) minimum information security requirements for each category, as required under subsection (b)(1)(C), no later than 36 months after the date of the enactment of this section;

"(4) issue guidelines as required under subsection (b)(1)(B), no later than 18 months after the date of the enactment of this section;

"(5) to the maximum extent practicable, ensure that such standards and guidelines do not require the use or procurement of specific products, including any specific hardware or software;

"(6) to the maximum extent practicable, ensure that such standards and guidelines provide for sufficient flexibility to permit alternative solutions to provide equivalent levels of protection for identified information security risks; and

"(7) to the maximum extent practicable, use flexible, performance-based standards and guidelines that permit the use of off-the-shelf commercially developed information security products.

"(d) INFORMATION SECURITY FUNCTIONS.—The Institute shall—

"(1) submit standards developed pursuant to subsection

(a), along with recommendations as to the extent to which these should be made compulsory and binding, to the Secretary of Commerce for promulgation under section 11331 of title

40, United States Code;

"(2) provide technical assistance to agencies, upon request, regarding—

"(A) compliance with the standards and guidelines developed under subsection (a);

"(B) detecting and handling information security incidents; and

"(C) information security policies, procedures, and practices;

"(3) conduct research, as needed, to determine the nature and extent of information security vulnerabilities and techniques for providing cost-effective information security;

"(4) develop and periodically revise performance indicators and measures for agency information security policies and practices;

"(5) evaluate private sector information security policies and practices and commercially available information technologies to assess potential application by agencies to strengthen information security;

"(6) assist the private sector, upon request, in using and applying the results of activities under this section;

"(7) evaluate security policies and practices developed for national security systems to assess potential application by agencies to strengthen information security;

"(8) periodically assess the effectiveness of standards and guidelines developed under this section and undertake revisions as appropriate;

"(9) solicit and consider the recommendations of the Information Security and Privacy Advisory Board, established by section 21, regarding standards and

guidelines developed under subsection (a) and submit such recommendations to the Secretary of Commerce with such standards submitted to the Secretary; and
"(10) prepare an annual public report on activities undertaken in the previous year, and planned for the coming year, to carry out responsibilities under this section.
"(e) DEFINITIONS.—As used in this section—
"(1) the term 'agency' has the same meaning as provided in section 3502(1) of title 44, United States Code;
"(2) the term 'information security' has the same meaning as provided in section 3542(b)(1) of such title;
"(3) the term 'information system' has the same meaning as provided in section 3502(8) of such title;
"(4) the term 'information technology' has the same meaning as provided in section 11101 of title 40, United States Code; and
"(5) the term 'national security system' has the same meaning as provided in section 3542(b)(2) of title 44, United States Code.
"(f) AUTHORIZATION OF APPROPRIATIONS.—There are authorized to be appropriated to the Secretary of Commerce $20,000,000 for each of fiscal years 2003, 2004, 2005, 2006, and 2007 to enable the National Institute of Standards and Technology to carry out the provisions of this section."

SEC. 304. INFORMATION SECURITY AND PRIVACY ADVISORY BOARD

Section 21 of the National Institute of Standards and Technology
      Act (15 U.S.C. 278g-4), is amended—

in subsection (a), by striking "Computer System Security and Privacy Advisory Board" and inserting "Information Security and Privacy Advisory Board";
in subsection (a)(1), by striking "computer or telecommunications" and inserting "information technology";
in subsection (a)(2)—
by striking "computer or telecommunications technology" and inserting "information technology"; and
by striking "computer or telecommunications equipment" and inserting "information technology";
in subsection (a)(3)—
by striking "computer systems" and inserting "information system"; and
by striking "computer systems security" and inserting "information security";
in subsection (b)(1) by striking "computer systems security" and inserting "information security";
in subsection (b) by striking paragraph (2) and inserting the following:
"(2) to advise the Institute, the Secretary of Commerce, and the Director of the Office of Management and Budget on information security and privacy issues

pertaining to Federal Government information systems, including through review of proposed standards and guidelines developed under section 20; and";

in subsection (b)(3) by inserting "annually" after "report";

by inserting after subsection (e) the following new subsection: "(f) The Board shall hold meetings at such locations and at such time and place as determined by a majority of the Board";

by redesignating subsections (f) and (g) as subsections (g) and (h), respectively; and

by striking subsection (h), as redesignated by paragraph (9), and inserting the following: "(h) As used in this section, the terms 'information system' and 'information technology' have the meanings given in section 20."

SEC. 305. TECHNICAL AND CONFORMING AMENDMENTS

COMPUTER SECURITY ACT.—Section 11332 of title 40, United States Code, and the item relating to that section in the table of sections for chapter 113 of such title, are repealed.

FLOYD D. SPENCE NATIONAL DEFENSE AUTHORIZATION ACT FOR FISCAL YEAR 2001.—The Floyd D. Spence National Defense Authorization Act for Fiscal Year 2001 (Public Law 106-398) is amended by striking section 1062 (44 U.S.C. 3531 note).

PAPERWORK REDUCTION ACT.—(1) Section 3504(g) of title 44, United States Code, is amended—

by adding "and" at the end of paragraph (1);

in paragraph (2)—

by striking "sections 11331 and 11332(b) and (c) of title 40" and inserting "section 11331 of title 40 and subchapter II of this chapter"; and

by striking "; and" and inserting a period; and

by striking paragraph (3).

(2) Section 3505 of such title is amended by adding at the end—

"(c) INVENTORY OF MAJOR INFORMATION SYSTEMS.—(1) The head of each agency shall develop and maintain an inventory of major information systems (including major national security systems) operated by or under the control of such agency.

"(2) The identification of information systems in an inventory under this subsection shall include an identification of the interfaces between each such system and all other systems or networks, including those not operated by or under the control of the agency.

"(3) Such inventory shall be—

"(A) updated at least annually;

"(B) made available to the Comptroller General; and

"(C) used to support information resources management, including—

"(i) preparation and maintenance of the inventory of information resources under section 3506(b)(4);

"(ii) information technology planning, budgeting, acquisition, and management under section 3506(h), subtitle III of title 40, and related laws and guidance;

"(iii) monitoring, testing, and evaluation of information security controls under subchapter II;

"(iv) preparation of the index of major information systems required under section 552(g) of title 5, United States Code; and

"(v) preparation of information system inventories required for records management under chapters 21, 29, 31, and 33.

"(4) The Director shall issue guidance for and oversee the implementation of the requirements of this subsection."

(3) Section 3506(g) of such title is amended—

by adding "and" at the end of paragraph (1);

(B) in paragraph (2)—

by striking "section 11332 of title 40" and inserting "subchapter II of this chapter"; and

by striking "; and" and inserting a period; and

by striking paragraph (3).

OMB Circular A-130
Appendix III

B

SECURITY OF FEDERAL AUTOMATED INFORMATION RESOURCES

A Requirements

1 Purpose

This appendix establishes a minimum set of controls to be included in Federal automated information security programs, assigns Federal agency responsibilities for the security of automated information, and links agency automated information security programs and agency management control systems established in accordance with OMB Circular No. A-123. This appendix revises procedures formerly contained in Appendix III to OMB Circular No. A-130 (50 FR 52730; December 24, 1985) and incorporates requirements of the Computer Security Act of 1987 (P.L. 100-235) and responsibilities assigned in applicable national security directives.

2 Definitions

The term:

a. "Adequate security" means security commensurate with the risk and magnitude of the harm resulting from the loss, misuse, or unauthorized access to or modification of information. This includes assuring that systems and applications used by the agency operate effectively and provide appropriate Confidentiality, Integrity, and Availability, through the use of cost-effective management, personnel, operational, and technical controls.

b. "Application" means the use of information resources (information and information technology) to satisfy a specific set of user requirements.

c. "General support system" or "system" means an interconnected set of information resources under the same direct management control which shares common functionality. A system normally includes hardware, software, information, data, applications, communications, and people. A system can be, for example, a local area network (LAN) including smart terminals that supports a branch office, an agency-wide backbone, a communications network, a departmental data processing center including its operating system and utilities, a tactical radio network, or a shared information processing service organization (IPSO).

d. "Major application" means an application that requires special attention to security due to the risk and magnitude of the harm resulting from the loss, misuse, or unauthorized access to or modification of the information in the application. Note: All Federal applications require some level of protection. Certain applications, because of the information in them, however, require special management oversight and should be treated as major. Adequate security for other applications should be provided by security of the systems in which they operate.

3 Automated information security programs

Agencies shall implement and maintain a program to assure that adequate security is provided for all agency information collected, processed, transmitted, stored, or disseminated in general support systems and major applications.

Each agency's program shall implement policies, standards, and procedures which are consistent with government-wide policies, standards, and procedures issued by the Office of Management and Budget, the Department of Commerce, the General Services Administration and the Office of Personnel Management (OPM). Different or more stringent requirements for securing national security information should be incorporated into agency programs as required by appropriate national security directives. At a minimum, agency programs shall include the following controls in their general support systems and major applications:

a. Controls for general support systems
  (1) Assign Responsibility for Security. Assign responsibility for security in each system to an individual knowledgeable in the information technology used in the system and in providing security for such technology.
  (2) System Security Plan. Plan for adequate security of each general support system as part of the organization's information resources management (IRM) planning process. The security plan shall be consistent with guidance issued by the National Institute of Standards and Technology (NIST). Independent advice and comment on the security plan shall be solicited prior to the plan's implementation. A summary of the security plans shall be incorporated into the strategic IRM plan required by the Paperwork Reduction Act (44 U.S.C. Chapter 35) and Section 8(b) of this circular. Security plans shall include:
  (a) Rules of the System. Establish a set of rules of behavior concerning use of, security in, and the acceptable level of risk for, the system. The rules shall be based on the needs of the various users of the system. The security required by the rules shall be only as stringent as necessary to provide adequate security for information in the system. Such rules shall clearly delineate responsibilities and expected behavior of all individuals with access to the system. They shall also include appropriate limits on interconnections to other systems and shall define service

provision and restoration priorities. Finally, they shall be clear about the consequences of behavior not consistent with the rules.

(b) Training. Ensure that all individuals are appropriately trained in how to fulfill their security responsibilities before allowing them access to the system. Such training shall assure that employees are versed in the rules of the system, be consistent with guidance issued by NIST and OPM, and apprise them about available assistance and technical security products and techniques. Behavior consistent with the rules of the system and periodic refresher training shall be required for continued access to the system.

(c) Personnel Controls. Screen individuals who are authorized to bypass significant technical and operational security controls of the system commensurate with the risk and magnitude of harm they could cause. Such screening shall occur prior to an individual being authorized to bypass controls and periodically thereafter.

(d) Incident Response Capability. Ensure that there is a capability to provide help to users when a security incident occurs in the system and to share information concerning common vulnerabilities and threats. This capability shall share information with other organizations, consistent with NIST coordination, and should assist the agency in pursuing appropriate legal action, consistent with Department of Justice guidance.

(e) Continuity of Support. Establish and periodically test the capability to continue providing service within a system based upon the needs and priorities of the participants of the system.

(f) Technical Security. Ensure that cost-effective security products and techniques are appropriately used within the system.

(g) System Interconnection. Obtain written management authorization, based upon the acceptance of risk to the system, prior to connecting with other systems. Where connection is authorized, controls shall be established which are consistent with the rules of the system and in accordance with guidance from NIST.

(3) Review of Security Controls. Review the security controls in each system when significant modifications are made to the system, but at least every 3 years. The scope and frequency of the review should be commensurate with the acceptable level of risk for the system. Depending on the potential risk and magnitude of harm that could occur, consider identifying a deficiency pursuant to OMB Circular No. A-123, "Management Accountability and Control" and the Federal Managers' Financial Integrity Act (FMFIA), if there is no assignment of security responsibility, no security plan, or no authorization to process for a system.

(4) Authorize Processing. Ensure that a management official authorizes in writing the use of each general support system based on implementation of its security plan before beginning or significantly changing processing in the system. Use of the system shall be reauthorized at least every 3 years.

b. Controls for Major Applications.

(1) Assign Responsibility for Security. Assign responsibility for security of each major application to a management official knowledgeable in the nature of the information and process supported by the application and in the management, personnel, operational, and technical controls used to protect it. This official shall assure that effective security products and techniques are appropriately used in the application and shall be contacted when a security incident occurs concerning the application.

(2) Application Security Plan. Plan for the adequate security of each major application, taking into account the security of all systems in which the application will operate. The plan shall be consistent with guidance issued by NIST. Advice and comment on the plan shall be solicited from the official responsible for security in the primary system in which the application will operate prior to the plan's implementation. A summary of the security plans shall be incorporated into the strategic IRM plan required by the Paperwork Reduction Act. Application security plans shall include:

(a) Application Rules. Establish a set of rules concerning use of and behavior within the application. The rules shall be as stringent as necessary to provide adequate security for the application and the information in it. Such rules shall clearly delineate responsibilities and expected behavior of all individuals with access to the application. In addition, the rules shall be clear about the consequences of behavior not consistent with the rules.

(b) Specialized Training. Before allowing individuals access to the application, ensure that all individuals receive specialized training focused on their responsibilities and the application rules. This may be in addition to the training required for access to a system. Such training may vary from a notification at the time of access (e.g., for members of the public using an information retrieval application) to formal training (e.g., for an employee that works with a high-risk application).

(c) Personnel Security. Incorporate controls such as separation of duties, least privilege and individual accountability into the application and application rules as appropriate. In cases where such controls cannot adequately protect the application or information in it, screen individuals commensurate with the risk and magnitude of the harm they could cause. Such screening shall be done prior to the individuals' being authorized to access the application and periodically thereafter.

(d) Contingency Planning. Establish and periodically test the capability to perform the agency function supported by the application in the event of failure of its automated support.

(e) Technical Controls. Ensure that appropriate security controls are specified, designed into, tested, and accepted in the application in accordance with appropriate guidance issued by NIST.

(f) Information Sharing. Ensure that information shared from the application is protected appropriately, comparable to the protection provided when information is within the application.

(g) Public Access Controls. Where an agency's application promotes or permits public access, additional security controls shall be added to protect the Integrity of the application and the confidence the public has in the application. Such controls shall include segregating information made directly accessible to the public from official agency records.

(3) Review of Application Controls. Perform an independent review or audit of the security controls in each application at least every 3 years. Consider identifying a deficiency pursuant to OMB Circular No. A-123, "Management Accountability and Control" and the Federal Managers' Financial Integrity Act if there is no assignment of responsibility for security, no security plan, or no authorization to process for the application.

(4) Authorize Processing. Ensure that a management official authorizes in writing use of the application by confirming that its security plan as implemented adequately secures the application. Results of the most recent review or audit of controls shall be a factor in management authorizations. The application must be authorized prior to operating and reauthorized at least every 3 years thereafter. Management authorization implies accepting the risk of each system used by the application.

4 *Assignment of responsibilities*

a. Department of Commerce. The Secretary of Commerce shall:

(1) Develop and issue appropriate standards and guidance for the security of sensitive information in Federal computer systems.

(2) Review and update guidelines for training in computer security awareness and accepted computer security practice, with assistance from OPM.

(3) Provide agencies guidance for security planning to assist in their development of application and system security plans.

(4) Provide guidance and assistance, as appropriate, to agencies concerning cost-effective controls when interconnecting with other systems.

(5) Coordinate agency incident response activities to promote sharing of incident response information and related vulnerabilities.

(6) Evaluate new information technologies to assess their security vulnerabilities, with technical assistance from the Department of Defense, and apprise Federal agencies of such vulnerabilities as soon as they are known.

b. Department of Defense. The Secretary of Defense shall:

(1) Provide appropriate technical advice and assistance (including work products) to the Department of Commerce.

(2) Assist the Department of Commerce in evaluating the vulnerabilities of emerging information technologies.

c. Department of Justice. The Attorney General shall:

(1) Provide appropriate guidance to agencies on legal remedies regarding security incidents and ways to report and work with law enforcement concerning such incidents.

(2) Pursue appropriate legal actions when security incidents occur.

d. General Services Administration. The Administrator of General Services shall:

(1) Provide guidance to agencies on addressing security considerations when acquiring automated data processing equipment (as defined in section 111(a)(2) of the Federal Property and Administrative Services Act of 1949, as amended).

(2) Facilitate the development of contract vehicles for agencies to use in the acquisition of cost-effective security products and services (e.g., backup services).

(3) Provide appropriate security services to meet the needs of Federal agencies to the extent that such services are cost-effective.

e. Office of Personnel Management. The Director of the Office of Personnel Management shall:

(1) Assure that its regulations concerning computer security training for Federal civilian employees are effective.

(2) Assist the Department of Commerce in updating and maintaining guidelines for training in computer security awareness and accepted computer security practice.

f. Security Policy Board. The Security Policy Board shall coordinate the activities of the Federal government regarding the security of information technology that processes classified information in accordance with applicable national security directives;

5 Correction of deficiencies and reports

a. Correction of Deficiencies. Agencies shall correct deficiencies which are identified through the reviews of security for systems and major applications described above.

b. Reports on Deficiencies. In accordance with OMB Circular No. A-123, "Management Accountability and Control," if a deficiency in controls is judged by the agency head to be material when weighed against other agency deficiencies, it shall be included in the annual FMFIA report. Less significant deficiencies shall be reported and progress on corrective actions tracked at the appropriate agency level.

c. Summaries of Security Plans. Agencies shall include a summary of their system security plans and major application plans in the strategic plan required by the Paperwork Reduction Act (44 U.S.C. 3506).

B Descriptive information

The following descriptive language is explanatory. It is included to assist in understanding the requirements of this appendix.

This appendix reorients the Federal computer security program to better respond to a rapidly changing technological environment. It establishes government-wide responsibilities for Federal computer security and requires Federal agencies to adopt a minimum set of management controls. These management controls are directed at individual information technology users in order to reflect the distributed nature of today's technology.

For security to be most effective, the controls must be part of day-to-day operations. This is best accomplished by planning for security not as a separate activity, but as an integral part of overall planning.

"Adequate security" is defined as "security commensurate with the risk and magnitude of harm resulting from the loss, misuse, or unauthorized access to or modification of information." This definition explicitly emphasizes the risk-based policy for cost-effective security established by the Computer Security Act.

This appendix no longer requires the preparation of formal risk analyses. In the past, substantial resources have been expended doing complex analyses of specific risks to systems, with limited tangible benefit in terms of improved security for the systems. Rather than continue to try to precisely measure risk, security efforts are better served by generally assessing risks and taking actions to manage them. While formal risk analyses need not be performed, the need to determine adequate security will require that a risk-based approach be used. This risk assessment approach should include a consideration of the major factors in risk management: the value of the system or application, threats, vulnerabilities, and the effectiveness of current or proposed safeguards. Additional guidance on effective risk assessment is available in "An Introduction to Computer Security: The NIST Handbook" (March 16, 1995).

Discussion of the Appendix's Major Provisions. The following discussion is provided to aid reviewers in understanding the changes in emphasis in this appendix.

Automated Information Security Programs. Agencies are required to establish controls to assure adequate security for all information processed, transmitted, or stored in Federal automated information systems. This appendix emphasizes management controls affecting individual users of information technology. Technical and operational controls support management controls. To be effective, all must interrelate. For example, authentication of individual users is an important management control, for which password protection is a technical control. However, password protection will only be effective if a strong technology is employed and it is managed to assure that it is used correctly.

Four controls are set forth: assigning responsibility for security, security planning, periodic review of security controls, and management authorization. This appendix requires that these management controls be applied in two areas of management responsibility: one for general support systems and the other for major applications.

The terms "general support system" and "major application" were used in OMB Bulletins Nos. 88-16 and 90-08. A general support system is "an interconnected set of information resources under the same direct management control which shares common functionality." Such a system can be, for example, a local area network

(LAN) including smart terminals that support a branch office, an agency-wide backbone, a communications network, a departmental data processing enter including its operating system and utilities, a tactical radio network, or a shared information processing service organization. Normally, the purpose of a general support system is to provide processing or communications support.

A major application is a use of information and information technology to satisfy a specific set of user requirements that require special management attention to security due to the risk and magnitude of harm resulting from the loss, misuse, or unauthorized access to or modification of the information in the application. All applications require some level of security, and adequate security for most of them should be provided by security of the general support systems in which they operate. However, certain applications, because of the nature of the information in them, require special management oversight and should be treated as major. Agencies are expected to exercise management judgment in determining which of their applications are major.

The focus of OMB Bulletins Nos. 88-16 and 90-08 was on identifying and securing both general support systems and applications which contained sensitive information. This appendix requires the establishment of security controls in all general support systems, under the presumption that all contain some sensitive information, and focuses extra security controls on a limited number of particularly high-risk or major applications.

a. General Support Systems. The following controls are required in all general support systems:
   (1) Assign Responsibility for Security. For each system, an individual should be a focal point for assuring there is adequate security within the system, including ways to prevent, detect, and recover from security problems. That responsibility should be assigned in writing to an individual trained in the technology used in the system and in providing security for such technology, including the management of security controls such as user identification and authentication.
   (2) Security Plan. The Computer Security Act requires that security plans be developed for all Federal computer systems that contain sensitive information. Given the expansion of distributed processing since passage of the Act, the presumption in this appendix is that all general support systems contain some sensitive information which requires protection to assure its Integrity, Availability, or Confidentiality, and therefore all systems require security plans.

   Previous guidance on security planning was contained in OMB Bulletin No. 90-08. This appendix supersedes OMB Bulletin 90-08 and expands the coverage of security plans from Bulletin 90-08 to include rules of individual behavior as well as technical security. Consistent with OMB Bulletin 90-08, the appendix directs NIST to update and expand security planning guidance and issue it as a Federal Information Processing

Standard (FIPS). In the interim, agencies should continue to use the Appendix of OMB Bulletin No. 90-08 as guidance for the technical portion of their security plans.

Thise appendix continues the requirement that independent advice and comment on the security plan for each system be sought. The intent of this requirement is to improve the plans, foster communication between managers of different systems, and promote the sharing of security expertise.

This appendix also continues the requirement from the Computer Security Act that summaries of security plans be included in agency strategic information resources management plans. OMB will provide additional guidance about the contents of those strategic plans, pursuant to the Paperwork Reduction Act of 1995.

The following specific security controls should be included in the security plan for a general support system:

(a) Rules. An important new requirement for security plans is the establishment of a set of rules of behavior for individual users of each general support system. These rules should clearly delineate responsibilities of and expectations for all individuals with access to the system. They should be consistent with system-specific policy as described in "An Introduction to Computer Security: The NIST Handbook" (March 16, 1995). In addition, they should state the consequences of noncompliance. The rules should be in writing and will form the basis for security awareness and training.

The development of rules for a system must take into consideration the needs of all parties who use the system. Rules should be as stringent as necessary to provide adequate security. Therefore, the acceptable level of risk for the system must be established and should form the basis for determining the rules.

Rules should cover such matters as work at home, dial-in access, connection to the Internet, use of copyrighted works, unofficial use of government equipment, the assignment and limitation of system privileges, and individual accountability. Often rules should reflect technical security controls in the system. For example, rules regarding password use should be consistent with technical password features in the system. Rules may be enforced through administrative sanctions specifically related to the system (e.g., loss of system privileges) or through more general sanctions as are imposed for violating other rules of conduct. In addition, the rules should specifically address restoration of service as a concern of all users of the system.

(b) Training. The Computer Security Act requires Federal agencies to provide for the mandatory periodic training in computer security awareness and accepted computer security practice of all employees who are involved with the management, use or operation of a Federal computer system within or under the supervision of the Federal agency.

This includes contractors as well as employees of the agency. Access provided to members of the public should be constrained by controls in the applications through which access is allowed, and training should be within the context of those controls. This appendix enforces such mandatory training by requiring its completion prior to granting access to the system. Each new user of a general support system in some sense introduces a risk to all other users. Therefore, each user should be versed in acceptable behavior—the rules of the system—before being allowed to use the system. Training should also inform the individual how to get help in the event of difficulty with using or security of the system.

Training should be tailored to what a user needs to know to use the system securely, given the nature of that use. Training may be presented in stages, for example, as more access is granted. In some cases, the training should be in the form of classroom instruction. In other cases, interactive computer sessions or well-written and understandable brochures may be sufficient, depending on the risk and magnitude of harm.

Over time, attention to security tends to dissipate. In addition, changes to a system may necessitate a change in the rules or user procedures. Therefore, individuals should periodically have refresher training to assure that they continue to understand and abide by the applicable rules.

To assist agencies, this appendix requires NIST, with assistance from the Office of Personnel Management (OPM), to update its existing guidance. It also proposes that OPM assures that its rules for computer security training for Federal civilian employees are effective.

(c) Personnel Controls. It has long been recognized that the greatest harm has come from authorized individuals engaged in improper activities, whether intentional or accidental. In every general support system, a number of technical, operational, and management controls are used to prevent and detect harm. Such controls include individual accountability, "least privilege," and separation of duties.

Individual accountability consists of holding someone responsible for his or her actions. In a general support system, accountability is normally accomplished by identifying and authenticating users of the system and subsequently tracing actions on the system to the user who initiated them. This may be done, for example, by looking for patterns of behavior by users.

Least privilege is the practice of restricting a user's access (to data files, to processing capability, or to peripherals) or type of access (read, write, execute, delete) to the minimum necessary to perform his or her job.

Separation of duties is the practice of dividing the steps in a critical function among different individuals. For example, one system programmer can create a critical piece of operating system code, while another authorizes its implementation. Such a control keeps a single individual from subverting a critical process.

Nevertheless, in some instances, individuals may be given the ability to bypass some significant technical and operational controls in order to perform system administration and maintenance functions (e.g., LAN administrators or systems programmers). Screening such individuals in positions of trust will supplement technical, operational, and management controls, particularly where the risk and magnitude of harm is high.

(d) Incident Response Capability. Security incidents, whether caused by viruses, hackers, or software bugs, are becoming more common. When faced with a security incident, an agency should be able to respond in a manner that both protects its own information and helps to protect the information of others who might be affected by the incident. To address this concern, agencies should establish formal incident response mechanisms. Awareness and training for individuals with access to the system should include how to use the system's incident response capability.

To be fully effective, incident handling must also include sharing information concerning common vulnerabilities and threats with those in other systems and other agencies. This appendix directs agencies to effectuate such sharing, and tasks NIST to coordinate those agency activities government wide.

This appendix also directs the Department of Justice to provide appropriate guidance on pursuing legal remedies in the case of serious incidents.

(e) Continuity of Support. Inevitably, there will be service interruptions. Agency plans should assure that there is an ability to recover and provide service sufficient to meet the minimal needs of users of the system. Manual procedures are generally NOT a viable backup option. When automated support is not available, many functions of the organization will effectively cease. Therefore, it is important to take cost-effective steps to manage any disruption of service.

Decisions on the level of service needed at any particular time and on priorities in service restoration should be made in consultation with the users of the system and incorporated in the system rules. Experience has shown that recovery plans that are periodically tested are substantially more viable than those that are not. Moreover, untested plans may actually create a false sense of security.

(f) Technical Security. Agencies should assure that each system appropriately uses effective security products and techniques, consistent with standards and guidance from NIST. Often such techniques will correspond with system rules of behavior, such as in the proper use of password protection.

This appendix directs NIST to continue to issue computer security guidance to assist agencies in planning for and using technical security products and techniques. Until such guidance is issued, however, the planning guidance included in OMB Bulletin 90-08 can assist in determining techniques for effective security in a system and in addressing technical controls in the security plan.

    (g) System Interconnection. In order for a community to effectively manage risk, it must control access to and from other systems. The degree of such control should be established in the rules of the system and all participants should be made aware of any limitations on outside access. Technical controls to accomplish this should be put in place in accordance with guidance issued by NIST.

        There are varying degrees of how connected a system is. For example, some systems will choose to isolate themselves, others will restrict access such as allowing only e-mail connections or remote access only with sophisticated authentication, and still others will be fully open. The management decision to interconnect should be based on the Availability and use of technical and nontechnical safeguards and consistent with the acceptable level of risk defined in the system rules.

(3) Review of Security Controls. The security of a system will degrade over time, as the technology evolves and as people and procedures change. Reviews should assure that management, operational, personnel, and technical controls are functioning effectively. Security controls may be reviewed by an independent audit or a self-review. The type and rigor of review or audit should be commensurate with the acceptable level of risk that is established in the rules for the system and the likelihood of learning useful information to improve security. Technical tools such as virus scanners, vulnerability assessment products (which look for known security problems, configuration errors, and the installation of the latest patches), and penetration testing can assist in the on-going review of different facets of systems. However, these tools are no substitute for a formal management review at least every 3 years. Indeed, for some high-risk systems with rapidly changing technology, 3 years will be too long.

        Depending upon the risk and magnitude of harm that could result, weaknesses identified during the review of security controls should be reported as deficiencies in accordance with OMB Circular No. A-123, "Management Accountability and Control" and the Federal Managers' Financial Integrity Act. In particular, if a basic management control such as assignment of responsibility, a workable security plan, or management authorization are missing, then consideration should be given to identifying a deficiency.

(4) Authorize Processing. The authorization of a system to process information, granted by a management official, provides an important quality control (some agencies refer to this authorization as accreditation). By authorizing processing in a system, a manager accepts the risk associated with it. Authorization is not a decision that should be made by the security staff.

        Both the security official and the authorizing management official have security responsibilities. In general, the security official is closer to the day-to-day operation of the system and will direct or perform security tasks. The authorizing official will normally have general responsibility for the organization supported by the system.

Management authorization should be based on an assessment of management, operational, and technical controls. Since the security plan establishes the security controls, it should form the basis for the authorization, supplemented by more specific studies as needed. In addition, the periodic review of controls should also contribute to future authorizations. Some agencies perform "certification reviews" of their systems periodically. These formal technical evaluations lead to a management accreditation, or "authorization to process." Such certifications (such as those using the methodology in FIPS Pub 102 "Guideline for Computer Security Certification and Accreditation") can provide useful information to assist management in authorizing a system, particularly when combined with a review of the broad behavioral controls envisioned in the security plan required by this appendix.

Re-authorization should occur prior to a significant change in processing, but at least every 3 years. It should be done more often where there is a high risk and potential magnitude of harm.

b. Controls in Major Applications. Certain applications require special management attention due to the risk and magnitude of harm that could occur. For such applications, the controls of the support system(s) in which they operate are likely to be insufficient. Therefore, additional controls specific to the application are required. Since the function of applications is the direct manipulation and use of information, controls for securing applications should emphasize protection of information and the way it is manipulated.

(1) Assign Responsibility for Security. By definition, major applications are high risk and require special management attention. Major applications usually support a single agency function and often are supported by more than one general support system. It is important, therefore, that an individual be assigned responsibility in writing to assure that the particular application has adequate security. To be effective, this individual should be knowledgeable in the information and process supported by the application and in the management, personnel, operational, and technical controls used to protect the application.

(2) Application Security Plans. Security for each major application should be addressed by a security plan specific to the application. The plan should include controls specific to protecting information and should be developed from the application manager's perspective. To assist in assuring its viability, the plan should be provided to the manager of the primary support system which the application uses for advice and comment. This recognizes the critical dependence of the security of major applications on the underlying support systems they use. Summaries of application security plans should be included in strategic information resource management plans in accordance with this Circular.

(a) Application Rules. Rules of behavior should be established which delineate the responsibilities and expected behavior of all individuals with access to the application. The rules should state the consequences of inconsistent behavior. Often the rules will be associated with technical controls implemented in the application. Such rules should include, for example, limitations on changing data, searching databases, or divulging information.

(b) Specialized Training. Training is required for all individuals given access to the application, including members of the public. It should vary depending on the type of access allowed and the risk that access represents to the security of the application and information in it. This training will be in addition to that required for access to a support system.

(c) Personnel Security. For most major applications, management controls such as individual accountability requirements, separation of duties enforced by access controls, or limitations on the processing privileges of individuals, are generally more cost-effective personnel security controls than background screening. Such controls should be implemented as both technical controls and as application rules. For example, technical controls to ensure individual accountability, such as looking for patterns of user behavior, are most effective if users are aware that there is such a technical control. If adequate audit or access controls (through both technical and non-technical methods) cannot be established, then it may be cost-effective to screen personnel, commensurate with the risk and magnitude of harm they could cause. The change in emphasis on screening in this appendix should not affect background screening deemed necessary because of other duties that an individual may perform.

(d) Contingency Planning. Normally the Federal mission supported by a major application is critically dependent on the application. Manual processing is generally NOT a viable backup option. Managers should plan for how they will perform their mission and/or recover from the loss of existing application support, whether the loss is due to the inability of the application to function or a general support system failure. Experience has demonstrated that testing a contingency plan significantly improves its viability. Indeed, untested plans or plans not tested for a long period of time may create a false sense of ability to recover in a timely manner.

(e) Technical Controls. Technical security controls, for example tests to filter invalid entries, should be built into each application. Often these controls will correspond with the rules of behavior for the application. Under the previous appendix, application security was focused on the process by which sensitive, custom applications were developed. While that process is not addressed in detail in this appendix, it remains an effective method for assuring that security controls are built into applications. Additionally, the technical security controls defined in OMB Bulletin No. 90-08 will continue, until that guidance is replaced by NIST's security planning guidance.

(f) Information Sharing. Assure that information which is shared with Federal organizations, State and local governments, and the private sector is appropriately protected comparable to the protection provided when the information is within the application. Controls on the information may stay the same or vary when the information is shared with another entity. For example, the primary user of the information may require a high level of Availability while the secondary user does not, and can therefore relax some of the controls designed to maintain the Availability of the information. At the same time, however, the information shared may require a level of Confidentiality that should be extended to the secondary user. This normally requires notification and agreement to protect the information prior to its being shared.

(g) Public Access Controls. Permitting public access to a Federal application is an important method of improving information exchange with the public. At the same time, it introduces risks to the Federal application. To mitigate these risks, additional controls should be in place as appropriate. These controls are in addition to controls such as "firewalls" that are put in place for security of the general support system.

In general, it is more difficult to apply conventional controls to public access systems, because many of the users of the system may not be subject to individual accountability policies. In addition, public access systems may be a target for mischief because of their higher visibility and published access methods.

Official records need to be protected against loss or alteration. Official records in electronic form are particularly susceptible since they can be relatively easy to change or destroy. Therefore, official records should be segregated from information made directly accessible to the public. There are different ways to segregate records. Some agencies and organizations are creating dedicated information dissemination systems (such as bulletin boards or World Wide Web servers) to support this function. These systems can be on the outside of secure gateways which protect internal agency records from outside access.

In order to secure applications that allow direct public access, conventional techniques such as least privilege (limiting the processing capability as well as access to data) and Integrity assurances (such as checking for viruses, clearly labeling the age of data, or periodically spot checking data) should also be used. Additional guidance on securing public access systems is available from NIST Computer Systems Laboratory Bulletin "Security Issues in Public Access Systems" (May, 1993).

(3) Review of Application Controls. At least every 3 years, an independent review or audit of the security controls for each major application should be

performed. Because of the higher risk involved in major applications, the review or audit should be independent of the manager responsible for the application. Such reviews should verify that responsibility for the security of the application has been assigned, that a viable security plan for the application is in place, and that a manager has authorized the processing of the application. A deficiency in any of these controls should be considered a deficiency pursuant to the Federal Manager's Financial Integrity Act and OMB Circular No. A-123, "Management Accountability and Control."

The review envisioned here is different from the system test and certification process required in this appendix. That process, however, remains useful for assuring that technical security features are built into custom-developed software applications. While the controls in that process are not specifically called for in this appendix, they remain in Bulletin No. 90-08, and are recommended in appropriate circumstances as technical controls.

(4) Authorize Processing. A major application should be authorized by the management official responsible for the function supported by the application at least every 3 years, but more often where the risk and magnitude of harm is high. The intent of this requirement is to assure that the senior official whose mission will be adversely affected by security weaknesses in the application periodically assesses and accepts the risk of operating the application. The authorization should be based on the application security plan and any review(s) performed on the application. It should also take into account the risks from the general support systems used by the application.

4 Assignment of responsibilities

This appendix assigns government-wide responsibilities to agencies that are consistent with their missions and the Computer Security Act.

a. Department of Commerce. The Department of Commerce, through NIST, is assigned the following responsibilities consistent with the Computer Security Act.
   (1) Develop and issue security standards and guidance.
   (2) Review and update, with assistance from OPM, the guidelines for security training issued in 1988 pursuant to the Computer Security Act to assure they are effective.
   (3) Replace and update the technical planning guidance in this appendix to OMB Bulletin 90-08. This should include guidance on effective risk-based security absent a formal risk analysis.
   (4) Provide agencies with guidance and assistance concerning effective controls for systems when interconnecting with other systems, including the Internet. Such guidance on, for example, so-called firewalls is becoming widely available and is critical to agencies as they consider how to interconnect their communications capabilities.

(5) Coordinate agency incident response activities. Coordination of agency incident response activities should address both threats and vulnerabilities as well as improve the ability of the Federal government for rapid and effective cooperation in response to serious security breaches.

(6) Assess security vulnerabilities in new information technologies and apprise Federal agencies of such vulnerabilities. The intent of this new requirement is to help agencies understand the security implications of technology before they purchase and field it. In the past, there have been too many instances where agencies have acquired and implemented technology, then found out about vulnerabilities in the technology, and had to retrofit security measures. This activity is intended to help avoid such difficulties in the future.

b. Department of Defense. The Department, through the National Security Agency, should provide technical advice and assistance to NIST, including work products such as technical security guidelines, which NIST can draw upon for developing standards and guidelines for protecting sensitive information in Federal computers.

Also, the Department, through the National Security Agency, should assist NIST in evaluating vulnerabilities in emerging technologies. Such vulnerabilities may present a risk to national security information as well as to unclassified information.

c. Department of Justice. The Department of Justice should provide appropriate guidance to Federal agencies on legal remedies available to them when serious security incidents occur. Such guidance should include ways to report incidents and cooperate with law enforcement.

In addition, the Department should pursue appropriate legal actions on behalf of the Federal government when serious security incidents occur.

d. General Services Administration. The General Services Administration should provide agencies guidance for addressing security considerations when acquiring information technology products or services. This continues the current requirement.

In addition, where cost-effective to do so, GSA should establish government-wide contract vehicles for agencies to use to acquire certain security services. Such vehicles already exist for providing system backup support and conducting security analyses.

GSA should also provide appropriate security services to assist Federal agencies to the extent that provision of such services is cost effective. This includes providing, in conjunction with the Department of Defense and the Department of Commerce, appropriate services which support Federal use of the National Information Infrastructure (e.g., use of digital signature technology).

e. Office of Personnel Management. In accordance with the Computer Security Act, OPM should review its regulations concerning computer security training and assure that they are effective.

In addition, OPM should assist the Department of Commerce in the review and update of its computer security awareness and training guidelines.

OPM worked closely with NIST in developing the current guidelines and should work with NIST in revising those guidelines.

f. Security Policy Board. The Security Policy Board is assigned responsibility for national security policy coordination in accordance with the appropriate Presidential directive. This includes policy for the security of information technology used to process classified information.

Circular A-130 and this appendix do not apply to information technology that supports certain critical national security missions, as defined in 44 U.S.C. 3502(9) and 10 U.S.C. 2315. Policy and procedural requirements for the security of national security systems (telecommunications and information systems that contain classified information or that support those critical national security missions (44 U.S.C. 3502(9) and 10 U.S.C. 2315)) are assigned to the Department of Defense pursuant to Presidential directive. The Circular clarifies that information classified for national security purposes should also be handled in accordance with appropriate national security directives. Where classified information is required to be protected by more stringent security requirements, those requirements should be followed rather than the requirements of this appendix.

5 Reports

This appendix requires agencies to provide two reports to OMB:

The first is a requirement that agencies report security deficiencies and material weaknesses within their FMFIA reporting mechanisms as defined by OMB Circular No. A-123, "Management Accountability and Control," and take corrective actions in accordance with that directive.

The second, defined by the Computer Security Act, requires that a summary of agency security plans be included in the information resources management plan required by the Paperwork Reduction Act.

FIPS 199

C

FIPS PUB 199
 FEDERAL INFORMATION PROCESSING STANDARDS PUBLICATION
 Standards for Security Categorization of Federal Information and Informa-
tion Systems
 Computer Security Division
 Information Technology Laboratory
 National Institute of Standards and Technology
 Gaithersburg, MD 20899-8900
 February 2004

U.S. DEPARTMENT OF COMMERCE
Donald L. Evans, Secretary
TECHNOLOGY ADMINISTRATION
Phillip J. Bond, Under Secretary for Technology
NATIONAL INSTITUTE OF STANDARDS AND TECHNOLOGY
Arden L. Bement, Jr., Director

FOREWORD

The Federal Information Processing Standards Publication Series of the National Institute of Standards and Technology (NIST) is the official series of publications relating to standards and guidelines adopted and promulgated under the provisions of Section 5131 of the Information Technology Management Reform Act of 1996 (Public Law 104-106) and the Federal Information Security Management Act of 2002 (Public Law 107-347). These mandates have given the Secretary of Commerce and NIST important responsibilities for improving the utilization and management of computer and related telecommunications systems in the federal government. The NIST, through its Information Technology Laboratory, provides leadership, technical guidance, and coordination of government efforts in the development of standards and guidelines in these areas.

Comments concerning Federal Information Processing Standards Publications are welcomed and should be addressed to the Director, Information Technology Laboratory, National Institute of Standards and Technology, 100 Bureau Drive, Stop 8900, Gaithersburg, MD 20899-8900.

—SUSAN ZEVIN, ACTING DIRECTOR
INFORMATION TECHNOLOGY LABORATORY ii

AUTHORITY

Federal Information Processing Standards Publications (FIPS PUBS) are issued by the National Institute of Standards and Technology (NIST) after approval by the Secretary of Commerce pursuant to Section 5131 of the Information Technology Management Reform Act of 1996 (Public Law 104-106) and the Federal Information Security Management Act of 2002 (Public Law 107-347).

TABLE OF CONTENTS

1 PURPOSE

The E-Government Act of 2002 (Public Law 107-347), passed by the one hundred and seventh Congress and signed into law by the President in December 2002, recognized the importance of information security to the economic and national security interests of the United States. Title III of the E-Government Act, entitled the Federal Information Security Management Act of 2002 (FISMA), tasked NIST with responsibilities for standards and guidelines, including the development of:

- Standards to be used by all federal agencies to categorize all information and information systems collected or maintained by or on behalf of each agency based on the objectives of providing appropriate levels of information security according to a range of risk levels;
- Guidelines recommending the types of information and information systems to be included in each category; and

- Minimum information security requirements (i.e., management, operational, and technical controls), for information and information systems in each such category.

FIPS Publication 199 addresses the first task cited—to develop standards for categorizing information and information systems. Security categorization standards for information and information systems provide a common framework and understanding for expressing security that, for the federal government, promotes: (i) effective management and oversight of information security programs, including the coordination of information security efforts throughout the civilian, national security, emergency preparedness, homeland security, and law enforcement communities; and (ii) consistent reporting to the Office of Management and Budget (OMB) and Congress on the adequacy and effectiveness of information security policies, procedures, and practices. Subsequent NIST standards and guidelines will address the second and third tasks cited.

2 APPLICABILITY

These standards shall apply to: (i) all information within the federal government other than that information that has been determined pursuant to Executive Order 12958, as amended by Executive Order 13292, or any predecessor order, or by the Atomic Energy Act of 1954, as amended, to require protection against unauthorized disclosure and is marked to indicate its classified status; and (ii) all federal information systems other than those information systems designated as national security systems as defined in 44 United States Code Section 3542(b)(2). Agency officials shall use the security categorizations described in FIPS Publication 199 whenever there is a federal requirement to provide such a categorization of information or information systems. Additional security designators may be developed and used at agency discretion. State, local, and tribal governments as well as private sector organizations comprising the critical infrastructure of the United States may consider the use of these standards as appropriate. These standards are effective upon approval by the Secretary of Commerce.

3 CATEGORIZATION OF INFORMATION AND INFORMATION SYSTEMS

This publication establishes security categories for both information[1] and information systems. The security categories are based on the potential impact on an organization should certain events occur which jeopardize the information and

---

[1]Information is categorized according to its *information type*. An information type is a specific category of information (e.g., privacy, medical, proprietary, financial, investigative, contractor sensitive, security management) defined by an organization or, in some instances, by a specific law, Executive Order, directive, policy, or regulation.

information systems needed by the organization to accomplish its assigned mission, protect its assets, fulfill its legal responsibilities, maintain its day-to-day functions, and protect individuals. Security categories are to be used in conjunction with vulnerability and threat information in assessing the risk to an organization.

Security objectives

The FISMA defines three security objectives for information and information systems:

CONFIDENTIALITY

"Preserving authorized restrictions on information access and disclosure, including means for protecting personal privacy and proprietary information..." [44 U.S.C., Sec. 3542] A loss of *Confidentiality* is the unauthorized disclosure of information.

INTEGRITY

"Guarding against improper information modification or destruction, and includes ensuring information non-repudiation and authenticity..." [44 U.S.C., Sec. 3542] A loss of *Integrity* is the unauthorized modification or destruction of information.

AVAILABILITY

"Ensuring timely and reliable access to and use of information..." [44 U.S.C., SEC. 3542] A loss of *Availability* is the disruption of access to or use of information or an information system.

Potential impact on organizations and individuals

FIPS Publication 199 defines three levels of *potential impact* on organizations or individuals should there be a breach of security (i.e., a loss of Confidentiality, Integrity, or Availability). The application of these definitions must take place within the context of each organization and the overall national interest.

The *potential impact* is **LOW** if—

– The loss of Confidentiality, Integrity, or Availability could be expected to have a **limited** adverse effect on organizational operations, organizational assets, or individuals.[2]

AMPLIFICATION: A limited adverse effect means that, for example, the loss of Confidentiality, Integrity, or Availability might: (i) cause a degradation in mission capability to an extent and duration that the organization is able to perform its primary functions, but the effectiveness of the functions is noticeably reduced; (ii) result

---

[2]Adverse effects on individuals may include, but are not limited to, loss of the privacy to which individuals are entitled under law.

in minor damage to organizational assets; (iii) result in minor financial loss; or (iv) result in minor harm to individuals.

The *potential impact* is **MODERATE** if—

– The loss of Confidentiality, Integrity, or Availability could be expected to have a **serious** adverse effect on organizational operations, organizational assets, or individuals.

AMPLIFICATION: A serious adverse effect means that, for example, the loss of Confidentiality, Integrity, or Availability might: (i) cause a significant degradation in mission capability to an extent and duration that the organization is able to perform its primary functions, but the effectiveness of the functions is significantly reduced; (ii) result in significant damage to organizational assets; (iii) result in significant financial loss; or (iv) result in significant harm to individuals that does not involve loss of life or serious life threatening injuries.

The *potential impact* is **HIGH** if—

– The loss of Confidentiality, Integrity, or Availability could be expected to have a **severe or catastrophic** adverse effect on organizational operations, organizational assets, or individuals.

AMPLIFICATION: A severe or catastrophic adverse effect means that, for example, the loss of Confidentiality, Integrity, or Availability might: (i) cause a severe degradation in or loss of mission capability to an extent and duration that the organization is not able to perform one or more of its primary functions; (ii) result in major damage to organizational assets; (iii) result in major financial loss; or (iv) result in severe or catastrophic harm to individuals involving loss of life or serious life threatening injuries.

Security categorization applied to information types

The security category of an information type can be associated with both user information and system information[3] and can be applicable to information in either electronic or nonelectronic form. It can also be used as input in considering the appropriate security category of an information system (see description of security categories for information systems below). Establishing an appropriate security category of an information type essentially requires determining the *potential impact* for each security objective associated with the particular information type.

---

[3]System information (e.g., network routing tables, password files, and cryptographic key management information) must be protected at a level commensurate with the most critical or sensitive user information being processed, stored, or transmitted by the information system to ensure Confidentiality, Integrity, and Availability.

The generalized format for expressing the security category, SC, of an information type is:

SC information type = {(**Confidentiality**, *impact*), (**Integrity**, *impact*),

(**Availability**, *impact*)},

where the acceptable values for potential impact are LOW, MODERATE, HIGH, or NOT APPLICABLE[4].

EXAMPLE 1: An organization managing *public information* on its Web server determines that there is no potential impact from a loss of Confidentiality (i.e., Confidentiality requirements are not applicable), a moderate potential impact from a loss of Integrity, and a moderate potential impact from a loss of Availability. The resulting security category, SC, of this information type is expressed as:

SC public information = {(**Confidentiality**, NA), (**Integrity**, MODERATE),

(**Availability**, MODERATE)}.

EXAMPLE 2: A law enforcement organization managing extremely sensitive *investigative information* determines that the potential impact from a loss of Confidentiality is high, the potential impact from a loss of Integrity is moderate, and the potential impact from a loss of Availability is moderate. The resulting security category, SC, of this information type is expressed as:

SC investigative information = {(**Confidentiality**, HIGH),

(**Integrity**, MODERATE), (**Availability**, MODERATE)}.

EXAMPLE 3: A financial organization managing routine *administrative information* (not privacy-related information) determines that the potential impact from a loss of Confidentiality is low, the potential impact from a loss of Integrity is low, and the potential impact from a loss of Availability is low. The resulting security category, SC, of this information type is expressed as:

SC administrative information = {(**Confidentiality**, LOW),

(**Integrity**, LOW), (**Availability**, LOW)}.

Security categorization applied to information systems

Determining the security category of an information system requires slightly more analysis and must consider the security categories of all information types resident on the information system. For an information system, the potential impact values assigned to the respective security objectives (Confidentiality, Integrity, Availability) shall be the highest values (i.e., high water mark) from among those security

---

[4]The potential impact value of *not applicable* only applies to the security objective of Confidentiality.

categories that have been determined for each type of information resident on the information system.[5]

The generalized format for expressing the security category, SC, of an information system is:

$$\text{SC information system} = \{(\textbf{Confidentiality}, \textit{impact}),$$

$$(\textbf{Integrity}, \textit{impact}), (\textbf{Availability}, \textit{impact})\},$$

where the acceptable values for potential impact are LOW, MODERATE, or HIGH.

Note that the value of *not applicable* cannot be assigned to any security objective in the context of establishing a security category for an information system. This is in recognition that there is a low minimum potential impact (i.e., low water mark) on the loss of Confidentiality, Integrity, and Availability for an information system due to the fundamental requirement to protect the system-level processing functions and information critical to the operation of the information system.

EXAMPLE 4: An information system used for large acquisitions in a contracting organization contains both sensitive, presolicitation phase contract information and routine administrative information. The management within the contracting organization determines that: (i) for the sensitive contract information, the potential impact from a loss of Confidentiality is moderate, the potential impact from a loss of Integrity is moderate, and the potential impact from a loss of Availability is low; and (ii) for the routine administrative information (nonprivacy-related information), the potential impact from a loss of Confidentiality is low, the potential impact from a loss of Integrity is low, and the potential impact from a loss of Availability is low. The resulting security categories, SC, of these information types are expressed as:

$$\text{SC contract information} = \{(\textbf{Confidentiality}, \text{MODERATE}),$$

$$(\textbf{Integrity}, \text{MODERATE}), (\textbf{Availability}, \text{LOW})\},$$

and

$$\text{SC administrative information} = \{(\textbf{Confidentiality}, \text{LOW}),$$

$$(\textbf{Integrity}, \text{LOW}), (\textbf{Availability}, \text{LOW})\}.$$

The resulting security category of the information system is expressed as:

---

[5]It is recognized that information systems are composed of both programs and information. Programs in execution within an information system (i.e., system processes) facilitate the processing, storage, and transmission of information and are necessary for the organization to conduct its essential mission-related functions and operations. These system processing functions also require protection and could be subject to security categorization as well. However, in the interest of simplification, it is assumed that the security categorization of all information types associated with the information system provides an appropriate *worst case* potential impact for the overall information system—thereby obviating the need to consider the system processes in the security categorization of the information system.

$$\text{SC acquisition system} = \{(\textbf{Confidentiality}, \text{MODERATE}),$$
$$(\textbf{Integrity}, \text{MODERATE}), (\textbf{Availability}, \text{LOW})\},$$

representing the high water mark or maximum potential impact values for each security objective from the information types resident on the acquisition system.

EXAMPLE 5: A power plant contains a SCADA (supervisory control and data acquisition) system controlling the distribution of electric power for a large military installation. The SCADA system contains both real-time sensor data and routine administrative information. The management at the power plant determines that: (i) for the sensor data being acquired by the SCADA system, there is no potential impact from a loss of Confidentiality, a high potential impact from a loss of Integrity, and a high potential impact from a loss of Availability; and (ii) for the administrative information being processed by the system, there is a low potential impact from a loss of Confidentiality, a low potential impact from a loss of Integrity, and a low potential impact from a loss of Availability. The resulting security categories, SC, of these information types are expressed as:

$$\text{SC sensor data} = \{(\textbf{Confidentiality}, \text{NA}), (\textbf{Integrity}, \text{HIGH}),$$
$$(\textbf{Availability}, \text{HIGH})\},$$

and

$$\text{SC administrative information} = \{(\textbf{Confidentiality}, \text{LOW}), (\textbf{Integrity}, \text{LOW}),$$
$$(\textbf{Availability}, \text{LOW})\}.$$

The resulting security category of the information system is initially expressed as:

$$\text{SC SCADA system} = \{(\textbf{Confidentiality}, \text{LOW}), (\textbf{Integrity}, \text{HIGH}),$$
$$(\textbf{Availability}, \text{HIGH})\},$$

representing the high water mark or maximum potential impact values for each security objective from the information types resident on the SCADA system. The management at the power plant chooses to increase the potential impact from a loss of Confidentiality from low to moderate reflecting a more realistic view of the potential impact on the information system should there be a security breach due to the unauthorized disclosure of system-level information or processing functions. The final security category of the information system is expressed as:

$$\text{SC SCADA system} = \{(\textbf{Confidentiality}, \text{MODERATE}), (\textbf{Integrity}, \text{HIGH}),$$
$$(\textbf{Availability}, \text{HIGH})\}.$$

Table C.1 summarizes the potential impact definitions for each security objective—Confidentiality, Integrity, and Availability.

Table C.1 Potential Impact Definitions for Security Objectives

Security Objective	Potential Impact		
	Low	Moderate	High
Confidentiality			
Preserving authorized restrictions on information access and disclosure, including means for protecting personal privacy and proprietary information. [44 U.S.C., SEC 3542]	The unauthorized disclosure of information could be expected to have a **limited** adverse effect on organizational assets or individuals.	The unauthorized disclosure of information could be expected to have a **serious** adverse affect on organizational operations, organizational assets, or individuals.	The unauthorized disclosure of information could be expected to have a **severe or catastrophic** adverse effect on organizational operations, organizational assets, or individuals.
Integrity			
Guarding against improper information modification or destruction, and includes erasing information nonrepudiation and authenticity. [44 U.S.C., SEC 3542]	The unauthorized modification or destruction of information could be expected to have a **limited** adverse effect on organizational operations, organizational assets, or individuals.	The unauthorized modification or destruction of information could be expected to have a **serious** adverse effect on organizational operations, organizational assets, or individuals.	The unauthorized modification or destruction of information could be expected to have a **severe or catastrophic** adverse effect on organizational operations, organizational assets, or individuals.
Availability			
Ensuring timely and reliable access to and use of information. [44 U.S.C., SEC 3542]	The disruption of access to or use of information or an information system could be expected to have a **limited** adverse effect on organizational operations, organizational assets, or individuals.	The disruption of access to or use of information or an information system could be expected to have a **serious** adverse effect on organizational assets or individuals.	The disruption of access to or use of information or an information system could be expected to have a **severe or catastrophic** adverse effect on organizational operations, organizational assets, or individuals.

APPENDIX A **TERMS AND DEFINITIONS**

AVAILABILITY: Ensuring timely and reliable access to and use of information. [44 U.S.C., SEC. 3542]

CONFIDENTIALITY: Preserving authorized restrictions on information access and disclosure, including means for protecting personal privacy and proprietary information. [44 U.S.C., SEC. 3542]

EXECUTIVE AGENCY: An executive department specified in 5 U.S.C., SEC. 101; a military department specified in 5 U.S.C., SEC. 102; an independent establishment as defined in 5 U.S.C., SEC. 104(1); and a wholly owned Government corporation fully subject to the provisions of 31 U.S.C., CHAPTER 91. [41 U.S.C., SEC. 403]

FEDERAL INFORMATION SYSTEM: An information system used or operated by an executive agency, by a contractor of an executive agency, or by another organization on behalf of an executive agency. [40 U.S.C., SEC. 11331]

INFORMATION: An instance of an information type.

INFORMATION RESOURCES: Information and related resources, such as personnel, equipment, funds, and information technology. [44 U.S.C., SEC. 3502]

INFORMATION SECURITY: The protection of information and information systems from unauthorized access, use, disclosure, disruption, modification, or destruction in order to provide Confidentiality, Integrity, and Availability. [44 U.S.C., SEC. 3542]

INFORMATION SYSTEM: A discrete set of information resources organized for the collection, processing, maintenance, use, sharing, dissemination, or disposition of information. [44 U.S.C., SEC. 3502]

INFORMATION TECHNOLOGY: Any equipment or interconnected system or subsystem of equipment that is used in the automatic acquisition, storage, manipulation, management, movement, control, display, switching, interchange, transmission, or reception of data or information by the executive agency. For purposes of the preceding sentence, equipment is used by an executive agency if the equipment is used by the executive agency directly or is used by a contractor under a contract with the executive agency which: (i) requires the use of such equipment; or (ii) requires the use, to a significant extent, of such equipment in the performance of a service or the furnishing of a product. The term information technology includes computers, ancillary equipment, software, firmware and similar procedures, services (including support services), and related resources. [40 U.S.C., SEC. 1401]

INFORMATION TYPE: A specific category of information (e.g., privacy, medical, proprietary, financial, investigative, contractor sensitive, security management), defined by an organization, or in some instances, by a specific law, Executive Order, directive, policy, or regulation.

INTEGRITY: Guarding against improper information modification or destruction, and includes ensuring information nonrepudiation and authenticity. [44 U.S.C., SEC. 3542]

NATIONAL SECURITY SYSTEM: Any information system (including any telecommunications system) used or operated by an agency or by a contractor of an agency, or other organization on behalf of an agency—(i) the function, operation, or use of which involves intelligence activities; involves cryptologic activities related to national security; involves command and control of military forces; involves equipment that is an integral part of a weapon or weapons system; or is critical to the direct fulfillment of military or intelligence missions (excluding a system that is to be used for routine administrative and business applications, for example, payroll, finance, logistics, and personnel management applications); or (ii) is protected at all times by procedures established for information that have been specifically authorized under criteria established by an Executive Order or an Act of Congress to be kept classified in the interest of national defense or foreign policy. [44 U.S.C., SEC. 3542]

SECURITY CATEGORY: The characterization of information or an information system based on an assessment of the potential impact that a loss of Confidentiality, Integrity, or Availability of such information or information system would have on organizational operations, organizational assets, or individuals.

SECURITY CONTROLS: The management, operational, and technical controls (i.e., safeguards or countermeasures) prescribed for an information system to protect the Confidentiality, Integrity, and Availability of the system and its information.

SECURITY OBJECTIVE: Confidentiality, Integrity, or Availability.

APPENDIX B **REFERENCES**

[1] Privacy Act of 1974 (Public Law 93-579), September 1975.

[2] Paperwork Reduction Act of 1995 (Public Law 104-13), May 1995.

[3] OMB Circular A-130, Transmittal Memorandum #4, *Management of Federal Information Resources*, November 2000.

[4] Information Technology Management Reform Act of 1996 (Public Law 104-106), August 1996.

[5] Federal Information Security Management Act of 2002 (Public Law 107-347), December 2002.

Index

Note: Page numbers followed by *f* indicate figures, *t* indicate tables, and *b* indicate boxes.